Other Worlds Here

Critical Insurgencies

A Book Series of the Critical Ethnic Studies Association

Series Editors: Jodi A. Byrd and Michelle M. Wright

Critical Insurgencies features activists and scholars, as well as artists and other media makers, who forge new theoretical and political practices that unsettle the nation-state, neoliberalism, carcerality, settler colonialism, Western hegemony, legacies of slavery, colonial racial formations, gender binaries, and ableism, and challenge all forms of oppression and state violence through generative future imaginings.

About CESA The Critical Ethnic Studies Association organizes projects and programs that engage ethnic studies while reimagining its futures. Grounded in multiple activist formations within and outside institutional spaces, CESA aims to develop an approach to intellectual and political projects animated by the spirit of decolonial, antiracist, antisexist, and other global liberationist movements. These movements enabled the creation of ethnic studies and continue to inform its political and intellectual projects.

www.criticalethnicstudies.org

Other Worlds Here

Honoring Native Women's Writing in Contemporary Anarchist Movements

Theresa Warburton

Northwestern University Press
Evanston, Illinois

Northwestern University Press
www.nupress.northwestern.edu

An earlier version of chapter 3 appeared as "Coming to Terms: Rethinking Popular Approaches to Anarchism and Feminism," in *Perspectives on Anarchist Theory* 29 (May 2016) and is reprinted by permission from the Institute for Anarchist Studies.

Selections from Janet Rogers's *Totem Poles and Railroads* appear courtesy of copyright © Janet Rogers and is preprinted by permission from Arbeiter Ring Publishing.

Selections from Heid Erdrich, *National Monuments* (2008), republished by permission of Michigan State University Press; permission conveyed through Copyright Clearance Center.

Printed in the United States of America

10 9 8 7 6 5 4 3 2 1

Library of Congress Cataloging-in-Publication Data

Names: Warburton, Theresa, author.
Title: Other worlds here : honoring Native women's writing in contemporary anarchist movements / Theresa Warburton.
Other titles: Critical insurgencies.
Description: Evanston, Illinois : Northwestern University Press, 2021. | Series: Critical insurgencies | Includes bibliographical references and index.
Identifiers: LCCN 2020050536 | ISBN 9780810143456 (paperback) | ISBN 9780810143463 (cloth) | ISBN 9780810143470 (ebook)
Subjects: LCSH: American literature—Indian authors—History and criticism. | American literature—Women authors—History and criticism. | Anarchism in literature. | Anarchism—North America—History—20th century. | Anarchism—North America—History—21st century.
Classification: LCC PS153.I52 W365 2021 | DDC 810.9/928708997—dc23
LC record available at https://lccn.loc.gov/2020050536

For Dorothy Taddia, whom I miss dearly

CONTENTS

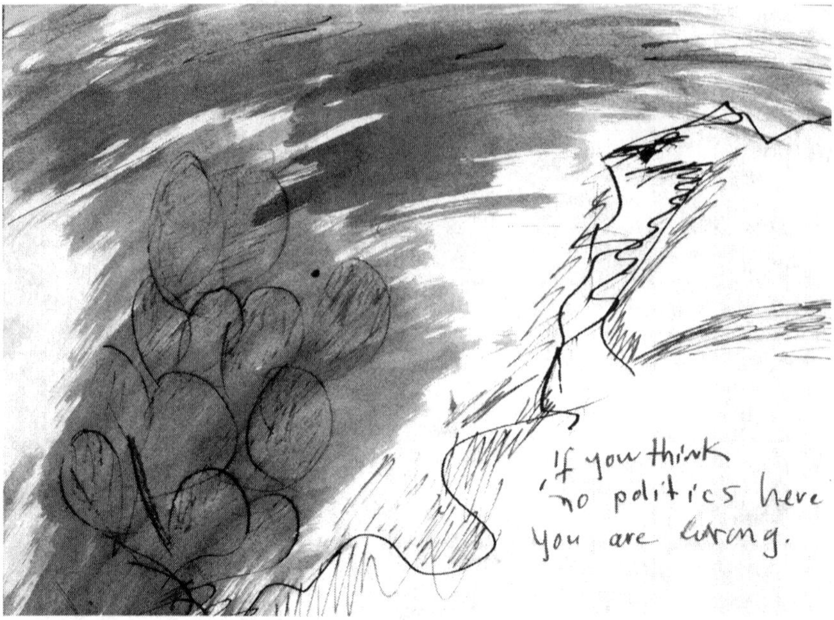

Fig. 1. Leslie Marmon Silko (Laguna Pueblo). *Untitled*. Watercolor and pen on paper. © 1975 by Leslie Marmon Silko, reproduced by permission from the Wylie Agency LLC.

INTRODUCTION

Like a Moth to a Flame

In October 2013, officers of the Royal Canadian Mounted Police (RCMP) moved into Elsipogtog First Nation territory to enforce an injunction against a blockade on Highway 11 on behalf of the Texas-based energy company Southwestern Natural Resources. Members of Elsipogtog First Nation, a Mi'kmaq community in New Brunswick, and their allies had been blocking equipment being used to map the area for hydraulic fracturing, or fracking, since May. Though the blockade had been in place for almost five months, the arrival of the RCMP escalated the situation, leading to over forty arrests. The images of burning RCMP vehicles circulated across independent media sites and spread quickly through social media.[1] Anarchist news sites picked up coverage of the protests, often expressing a sense of hope. For instance, in their article "Goodbye to the Future," the anarchist collective Out of the Woods insisted:

> the new utopian movement . . . will not be Eurocentric. It will incorporate that which is vibrant right now, the indigenous awakening which dwarfs the struggles in Europe. Idle No More in North America . . . [has] shown a nascent potency which only blossoms when the government sends in cops or troops. Real hope is revealed in the light from burning cop cars outside Elsipogtog.[2]

This excitement, especially at the sight of burning RCMP vehicles, proliferated across anarchist posts on social media. For many, this signaled a moment of radical uprising that should be celebrated across North America, not least because it evoked a sense that state power was burning in effigy. Left-leaning media continued to circulate and consume these images, bringing what was happening at Elsipogtog into a broader radical consciousness.

When I went into Onondaga scholar Theresa McCarthy's office for a meeting the afternoon after these images began circulating, she too was glued to the computer watching coverage of the standoff at Elsipogtog. But there was no exclamation of hope at the sight of burning RCMP cars. Instead, we talked about how afraid she was for what would happen to the community, what the judicial system would do to the protestors, and what would be left once the fires died out. Having spent years writing about similar events she had witnessed in her community at Six Nations of Grand River as they fought for land claims at Caledonia, McCarthy spoke with me about how these images reiterated the complicated interplay between violence against Native communities and increased public attention.[3]

Nishnaabeg writer and activist Leanne Betasamosake Simpson echoed these sentiments in her reflection on Elsipogtog, in which she worried that the proliferation of these images contributed to an ongoing cycle in which people saw images of Native communities only in crisis, perpetually linking their struggles for self-determination with "hunting rifles, a basket full of bullets, and the burning police cars."[4] In particular, she worried that these images contributed to prominent misunderstandings across the politics spectrum of movements fighting for Native self-determination, since both liberal celebrations of a movement they associated with environmentalism and conservative condemnations of a movement they associated with violence ignored the central issues of land reclamation and self-determination.

Following from Athabascan scholar Dian Million's assertion that the affective registers of colonialism remain an understudied element of settlement's persistence in the age of liberal multiculturalism, *Other Worlds Here* arises from the affective dissonance between these responses, not only to Elsipogtog but also to Native uprisings more generally.[5] For me, the juxtaposition of anarchist excitement and Native trepidation at the sight of the burning RCMP cars at Elsipogtog signals a fundamental divergence in how these events are apprehended by two groups that some might assume have an inherently parallel orientation.

For instance, the heightened unease with which McCarthy and Simpson approach the attack on Elsipogtog is not bound to respect for the RCMP or allegiance to the state. Much to the contrary, they know firsthand from their work in Native communities how the state suppresses Native self-determination and continues the violence through which settlement is structured. As is evident in the anarchist schadenfreude at the sight of burning RCMP vehicles, a rejection of the state is also foundational to that milieu. So, despite this seemingly parallel orientation to the settler state, why is the affective dissonance in response to Elsipogtog so pronounced? And how might this dissonance signal a more ingrained issue that permeates anarchist approaches to settlement in North America? Or, posed a different way, what do we make of the fact that anarchists are drawn to the burning of RCMP cars like moths to a flame when they aren't the ones getting burned?

In *Other Worlds Here*, I argue that this dissonance is an effect of the persistence of the structure of settlement within what David Graeber and Andrej Grubačić have called "the new anarchism."[6] Rather than being an inheritance of hegemonic models of political, social, and economic ordering, I suggest that the new model of anarchist activism that developed in the late twentieth and early twenty-first centuries, which I refer to as New Anarchism throughout, remade the structure of settlement within anarchist logics. The result is the persistence of what I call "settler anarchism," or a model of anarchist politics that reifies the structure of settlement within its own political philosophy.

I begin my exploration of the structure of settler anarchism with Elsipogtog not because this is a singular moment but because it is part of a broader history of dissonance between anarchist and Native responses to the violent exertion of the settler state in Native communities. As both McCarthy and Simpson noted, Elsipogtog was a dispiritingly common event in the history of Native dispossession across North America, resonating throughout Native communities. This is true also of anarchist invocations of other violent state responses to Native uprisings. For instance, we can see this dissonance in anarchist treatments of the blockade at Kanehsatà:ke in 1990, often referred to as the "Oka Crisis," as well.[7] I take a moment here to offer a comparative look at anarchist invocations of both events not only because the parallels are telling but also because these events form the temporal bookends of the time period with which *Other Worlds Here* is concerned. In this, we can trace the development of settler anarchism as a distinct part of the resurgence of anarchism across North America in the late twentieth and early twenty-first centuries.

In summer 1990, twenty-three years before the conflict at Elsipogtog, the Canadian state deployed the police, as well as the Canadian Armed Forces (CAF), to Kanehsatà:ke, a community west of Montreal, as part of a crackdown on protestors who had set up blockades along state highways. Though often articulated as a conflict about the construction of a golf course, the blockades at Kanehsatà:ke were part of a 270-year-long conflict between Kanien'kehá:ka (Mohawk) communities and the municipality of Oka, as well as the broader Canadian state.[8] When the Canadian and provincial governments sent in troops with military-grade artillery to confront the protesters, some of whom were armed with hunting rifles, the conflict escalated, leading to an armed siege that lasted seventy-eight days. As Kanien'kehá:ka scholar Audra Simpson has pointed out, what happened at Kanehsatà:ke was an "act of 'domestic warfare'" and the spectacularized images that came out of it continue to inform public discussions of Native movements.[9] The parallels to Elsipogtog are palpable, with even the former Elsipogtog chief Susan Levi-Peters commenting, "I think it's very important to bring in peacekeepers. We don't want another Oka."[10]

Though anarchist interest in Kanehsatà:ke is limited, reflecting a broader lack of engagement with both Native histories and the history of settlement, its appearance in anarchist materials mirrors many of the same issues to which I gestured above. For instance, it is described as a conflict over a golf course rather than a resistance to settler occupation of Native territory, paralleling the portrayal of Elsipogtog as a conflict over fracking. But what is perhaps even more compelling here is the circulation of images from Kanehsatà:ke and their parallel in the image of the burning RCMP vehicles at Elsipogtog. One place that I encountered a mention of Kanehsatà:ke was in a reproduction of the most lasting image from the siege in the widely circulated 2012 pamphlet "Who Is Oakland?: Anti-Oppression Activism, the Politics of Safety, and State Co-optation," published by a group called Croatan during the height of the Occupy Movement. Co-opting the name of a Native community on the coast of what is currently North Carolina, a community that is sometimes connected to the Lost Colony of Roanoke, the statement invokes indigeneity as the specter of contemporary radical resistance.[11]

In this pamphlet, an image from Kanehsatà:ke is reproduced as a visual aid, along with images of Black activist Pam Echols punching a police officer during 1968 open housing demonstrations in Milwaukee, Tunisian street vendor Mohamed Bouazizi whose suicide is often said to have sparked the Arab Spring, and an image of a "young Chilean feminist" holding a sign that reads (in Spanish) "Without god, without law, without husband: free, beautiful, and crazy."[12] Capturing a tense showdown between CAF infantryman Patrick Cloutier and Anishnaabe activist Brad Larocque, this defining image of Kanehsatà:ke has had a long life among the Canadian public, some of whom see Cloutier's calm face as a mark of heroism in the face of a violent opponent, whereas others see validation for the claim that the Canadian state is, at its core, a military occupation of Native communities.[13]

Anarchists appear to take neither interpretation, instead invoking both the image and the conflict at Kanehsatà:ke as an example of the possibilities of armed struggle. The photograph is reproduced in "Who Is Oakland?" untethered from a discussion of the events at Kanehsatà:ke, which is mentioned only as support for the claim that "the belief that communities of color in the US to [*sic*] represent coherent bounded internal colonies or 'nations' working for self-determination has been stretched to the breaking point by class divisions within these communities."[14] Following a criticism of how "indigenous traditions" are used to "justify caste or caste-like social divisions," the protestors at Kanehsatà:ke are mentioned only as "the Mohawk people in the Municipality of Oka" in a list of groups for whom "21st century decolonization in the US would be unrecognizable to the individuals who have fought for liberation under the banner of anticolonial struggle in the past."[15]

Of course, the work of Native scholars and activists, including Theresa McCarthy, Leanne Simpson, and Audra Simpson, makes clear that what happened at Kanehsatà:ke is intensely recognizable as part of anticolonial struggles across North America. In this, this anarchist invocation of Kanehsatà:ke in the era of Occupy Wall Street, and the subsequent anarchist engagement with Elsipogtog, contains within it a microcosm of the questions of *Other Worlds Here*. Namely, how do anarchist movements conspire with the normative investments of settler states (including their racial, gendered, and imperial structures) against our assumed antistate position?[16]

Throughout *Other Worlds Here*, I aim for self-reflexive critique of the movements in which I participate. As a white non-Native scholar who was raised exclusively within the borders claimed by the United States, I am imbricated within the very critiques that I present throughout. I name this not as a form of absolution, but as an acknowledgment of my responsibility to more clearly identify the grounding for some of the core terms that I engage herein: most importantly "anarchist," "settler," "Native," and "North America." Though I hope that, in the course of your reading, you'll find that this work complicates the use of these terms, I do want to take a moment to be clear about my use of them.

My use of the term "anarchist" refers to both a political philosophy and a group of scholars, activists, and organizations that espouse it. I use this term to refer to a sector of the political left with explicit commitments to anticapitalism, antistatism, and horizontal methods of political organizing. And, what is more, I will use the terms "we" and "our" to refer to these moments to signal my own continued investment in them. Throughout *Other Worlds Here*, I speak almost exclusively about anarchists in a place I refer to as "North America." Since this project is concerned with the reproduction of settlement within anarchist spaces, I have chosen to use "North America" rather than "Turtle Island" to refer to my geographic scope, since to use the latter felt a disingenuous adoption of Native nomenclature given the critique at the heart of this book.

Although there are many discussions about how and when to use the variety of terms available to refer to the Indigenous peoples of North America, I've chosen to rely almost exclusively on the term "Native," following Tonawanda Seneca scholar Mishuana Goeman. As she argues in her book *Mark My Words: Native Women Mapping Our Nations*, "I use 'Native' when referring to those indigenous to North America and 'Indigenous' to refer to indigenous peoples on a global scale."[17] Therefore, it is only in the last section when I turn to questions of transnationalism that I use the term *Indigenous* instead of *Native*, since I am no longer referring to the place from which I am writing.

Relatedly, my use of the term *settler* throughout is indelibly connected to whiteness. Though I discuss more in-depth in chapter 5 the troubled relationship that anarchists in North America have had to reckoning with the whiteness of the milieu, I have no qualms about using settler as a term that refers largely to white non-Native people living in this place though throughout I try to emphasize the normalization of whiteness as a structure rather than focus on the racial status of individuals. Given the substantial and significant scholarship that has given us better language to refer to the multiple relationships that immigrants, refugees, and descendants of enslaved people have to the structure of the US and Canadian settler states, I feel the need to be especially clear about which communities and configurations at which my critique is aimed.[18]

In these ways and using these terms, I seek to move beyond the recognition that settler *attitudes* persist in anarchist spaces so that I may shift to a focus that explores how settlement endures as a *structural* issue within anarchist political work.[19] And then, to explore how to develop new approaches to anarchist political movement that confront it. In these flashpoints of anarchist engagement with images of Native struggles against the state, I locate the three main interventions that support my argument about how the structure of settlement is reified within contemporary anarchist movements using anarchist logics: first, that contemporary anarchists in North America have not reckoned with the specific histories of settlement that live with the land on which we organize; second, that subsequently our analyses are unable to account for the gendered dynamics of settlement and the concomitant exaction of colonial violence *as* gendered violence; and third, that attempts to advance a transnational narrative of anarchist resistance remain steeped in a territorial ordering of US empire that subsumes Native nationhood into the fabric of US sovereignty.

For instance, in the "Who Is Oakland?" pamphlet, the invocation of images from Kanehsatà:ke rather than, say, the six-month occupation of Alcatraz Island by members of the American Indian Movement (AIM) is curious, considering that many of the lasting images from that standoff speak to the core themes articulated in the pamphlet itself, including the militarization of police and the consequences for communities of color. The visual of "Indian Land" spray-painted over the sign of the federal penitentiary at Alcatraz that reads "United States property" starkly engages the related histories of imprisonment and settlement in the Bay Area—a local history that is absent from the discussion offered by the Croatan collective.

In terms of the approaches to gender, the invocation of both the image of the burning RCMP vehicles at Elsipogtog and the standoff between Cloutier and Larocque overwrite the fundamentally gendered dynamics of those conflicts, not only supplanting the central role of women in their execution but also ignoring the gendered process threaded through settlement.[20] Lastly, the attempt to connect these movements to global resistance through their characterization as grounded in environmentalist and antipolice motivations ignores the centrality of land reclamation and self-determination to these struggles. In *Other Worlds Here*, I engage these processes on a broader scale to explore how they operate across the development of New Anarchism in North America over the past thirty years.

Why Anarchism?

My focus on New Anarchism stems from the recognition that it forms what Richard J. F. Day has called the "anarchist undercurrent" of social movements in North America in the late twentieth and early twenty-first centuries.[21] Day identifies this resurgence in the centering of what he calls an "affinity for affinity" or "for non-universalizing, non-hierarchical, non-coercive relationships based on mutual aid and shared ethical commitments" in social movement organizing at the turn of the twenty-first century.[22] And though Andrew Cornell has done an excellent job of tracing the presence of anarchist movements in the United States throughout the twentieth century, Day's identification of resurgent interest in anarchism represents its rise to prominence in radical politics that hadn't been seen since the heyday of early twentieth-century anarchism rooted in immigrant labor movements.[23] Reckoning with the shapes of these historical ebbs and flows is one of the undercurrents, to use Day's term, of *Other Worlds Here*.

In some ways, then, the term *anarchism* in the context with which both Day and I are concerned ends up being shorthand for a range of connected radical antiauthoritarian social movements, which Chris Dixon has described as a "tendency composed of activists, organizers, fighters, and dreamers who . . . are forging a shared politics through struggle." For him, this tendency is coalesced around a series of related commitments:

> We believe in the power of people to fight for justice and dignity, and to shape history in the process. We oppose all forms of domination, exploitation, and oppression, and we maintain a critical stance towards the state. We carry a rich democratic vision of everyone being able to directly participate in the decisions that affect them in their relationships, homes, communities, workplaces, schools, and elsewhere . . . We ground ourselves in the day-to-day work of building mass movements capable of fundamentally transforming the world. We see the importance of developing organizations and institutions to advance our movements, and we favor organizing approaches that involve building collective power to challenge ruling institutions.[24]

I reproduce Dixon's description at length because it gives a sense of the scope of the movements that I engage herein, whose diffuse character has both strengthened the tendency by imbuing it with the ability to adapt while also making it difficult to talk about in a cohesive way. Though he suggests that there are a variety of terms that participants in this tendency use to define ourselves, I choose to use "anarchist" and "anarchism" throughout this text for a few reasons.

First of all, I wanted a cohesive nomenclature through which to refer to the movements that I discuss, not to flatten them but to emphasize what they share. This terminological move helps to emphasize the scope of my project as one that asks how New Anarchism engages with other forms of social movement rather than being rooted in more insulated discussions about anarchist political philosophy. Secondly, I choose "anarchism" because it centralizes both the antistatist and anticapitalist dimensions of contemporary social movements, highlighting a distinction from both Marxist and liberal modes. The emphasis on antistate politics is particularly important here, since this is the node through which people often assume an inherent coherence between New Anarchist and Native movements. Lastly, I want to signal both a connection to and divergence from classical anarchism to more carefully situate the temporal and spatial specificity of New Anarchism.

As scholars like Day, Graeber, and Todd May have pointed out, one way we can understand the resurgence in anarchist politics in the late twentieth and early twenty-first centuries is as a response to the 1991 dissolution of the Soviet Union. As May has argued, "The collapse of communism in Eastern Europe . . . has reshaped the terrain so that the foundation of existence upon which was built much of the vision of what could be has also collapsed. This is the meaning of the slogan that Marxism is dead."[25] For Day, this collapse forged the path for both the dramatic rise of neoliberalism, which grew in the vacuum left by the Soviet Union to "increase its reach even further," and the concurrent rise in an anarchist politics that took aim at the institutions that promulgated neoliberalism on a global scale, including the World Bank (WB), World Trade Organization (WTO), and the International Monetary Fund (IMF).[26]

Throughout the 1990s, protests against the policies of these institutions (and the countries in the Global North in whose interests such policies were imposed on countries in the Global South) marked the emergence of a new form of social movement across the world. Events like the interruption of the fiftieth celebration of the IMF and the WB in Madrid in 1994; the Carnival Against Capital coinciding with the meeting of the G8 and against the third ministerial conference of the WTO in Seattle in 1999; protests against the meetings of the WB and IMF in Washington, DC, in 2000; protests against the Summit of the Americas in Quebec City and the meeting of the G8 in Genoa in 2001; and protests against the Free Trade Area of the Americas (FTAA) negotiations in Miami in 2003, signaled the arrival of a new era of global resistance to neoliberalism that has been referred to by numerous names, including the "anti-globalization," "alter-globalization" and "global justice" movement.[27]

This resurgence of anarchism as a primary mode of social movement after the collapse of the Soviet Union and the rise of neoliberalism in the late twentieth century was particularly influential in North America. Fresh from the backlash in the 1980s against the advances of the radical struggles of the 1960s and 1970s, this resurgence in radical social movement in the 1990s evidenced a renewed tradition of leftist uprising.[28] Owing in part to the success of large-scale protests, especially the 1999 protests against the WTO in Seattle, this era of social movement became defined both by anarchist commitments to antistatism and anticapitalism and to anarchist tactics of direct action and affinity-based organizing. In this way, this resurgence marked the emergence of a new form of anarchism in North America. This new movement maintained an emphatic commitment to antistate and anticapitalist politics, as earlier generations of North American anarchists had done, yet moved away from the foundations of syndicalism and transatlantic immigration through which many of those mid-nineteenth and early twentieth-century movements had been defined. Incorporating the legacies of radical social movements in North America, this New Anarchism extended beyond the foci of earlier anarchist organizing to usher in a new paradigm of social struggle.

In *Other Worlds Here*, I demonstrate how this development of New Anarchism in North America has neglected the analysis of the foundational structure of the US and Canadian nation-states—that of settlement. I argue that this lacuna has resulted in the remaking of the structure of settlement as a characteristic of New Anarchism, signaling a paradoxical anarchist investment in the particular method of statecraft through which the United States and Canada are constituted. Proving this anarchist investment in settler structure is not an argument about the dangers of its exclusion, but how it is taken up as a matter of radicalism in its most literal sense of returning to the root.

As Chickasaw scholar Jodi Byrd has argued, "there must be the possibility of the originary in the new world, and that is located within the historical experiences of new world colonizations, genocides, and violences."[29] To assert a resistance to neoliberalism from the North American context, even on a global scale, without accounting for the structure of settlement is to ignore the fundamental structure of the US and Canadian settler states and, thus, to ignore the specific character that antistatism must take in this place. Byrd reminds us that "there is a long line of continuity between the past and the present that has not been disrupted despite the fact that the stories we tell may or may not acknowledge that continuity."[30] Therefore, whether or not anarchists articulate clearly the rootedness of neoliberalism in the settler character of the US and Canadian states, that continuity remains. However, without such an acknowledgement, New Anarchism becomes swept away in the flow of that continuity as well.

By focusing on this inherent contradiction between an affirmed commitment to antistatism and a lack of engagement with the actual structure of the US and Canadian settler states, I disrupt the assumption that New Anarchism and Native movements are inherently linked through a shared orientation against the state. However, this is not an attempt to assert a fatal flaw in the logic of New Anarchism. In fact, my extensive engagement with New Anarchism indicates an implicit commitment to the ability of the milieu to respond to its exigent issues and, in this way, solidifies it as a salient model for organizing in the contemporary moment.

As Graeber has observed, one of the qualities that makes anarchism a more fertile method of political organizing than other radical strands is precisely how this emphasis on *method* enables a transformative, rather than rigid, praxis: "One need only to compare the historical schools of Marxism, and anarchism . . . to see we are dealing with fundamentally different things. Marxist schools have founders. Just as Marxism sprang from the mind of Marx, so we have Leninists, Maoists, Trotskyites, Gramscians, Althusserians . . . Schools of anarchism, in contrast, emerge from some kind of organizational principle or form of practice: Anarcho-Syndicalists and Anarcho-Communists, Insurrectionists and Platformists, Cooperativists, Individualists, and so on."[31]

Thus, though anarchist political philosophy does maintain guiding principles, most especially antistatism and anticapitalism, this orientation emphasizes the focus in the milieu on, in Dixon's words, the fact that anarchists "try to build the world we would like to see through the ways in which we struggle."[32] This focus on the *method* of political engagement eschews the dominance of what Nick Montgomery and carla bergman have called "rigid radicalism," or the inability to shift one's radical commitments based on thoughtful intervention from similarly aligned groups.[33] In this way, my project of critique here is not one that seeks to destabilize the potential of New Anarchism as a form of radical politics in the contemporary moment but, rather, attempts to hold it accountable to its own politics, which are lauded for their ability to adapt strategies of resistance to the exertion of a dynamic structure of global postmodern power. In this sense, this is not an exercise in the politics of purity, which Alexis Shotwell has pointed out is a fundamentally conservative tactic often employed in an attempt to discredit leftist movements as hypocritical.[34]

As Shotwell argues, to commit to a politics grounded in purity is to base our attempts at ethical life on the assumption of a pure past to which we can return. Because of this, "all there is, while things perpetually fall apart, is the possibility of acting from where we are . . . There is not a preracial state we could access, erasing histories of slavery, forced labor on railroads, colonialism, genocide, and their concomitant responsibilities and requirements."[35] This project, then, attempts to engage those responsibilities that Shotwell invokes to imagine alternative formations of New Anarchist politics that might account for the structure of settlement within New Anarchism. As longtime anarchist activist Cindy Milstein has argued, one of the hallmarks of anarchist politics is that "the 'end' of anarchism is not a final destination . . . ends for anarchists are instead the constellation of ethics, tested time and again, that offer greater amounts of lived freedom, even as people continue to fill out what freedom looks like in practice."[36]

To this end, I do not understand my analysis as simply a negative critique. Though I am committed to elucidating how the structure of settlement is reproduced in anarchist spaces using anarchist logics, I also want to understand how anarchists might better attend to the promises, relations, and protocols that live with the land on which we organize. And, what is more, my critique is fundamentally rooted in my belief that anarchism contains within its structure the possibility for such a transformation.

Therefore, I balance my critique with a commitment to believing that New Anarchism can be transformed through a more careful engagement with the interventions that Native women's literatures provide. My argument, then, is not that there in an "unbridgeable chasm," to use Murray Bookchin's term, between New Anarchism and Native movements. Instead, I agree that there are fundamental connections to be considered here. However, contemporary anarchists have too often invoked these fundamental connections in an attempt to merely absorb the interventions of Native scholars, activists, and writers under the cover of New Anarchism rather than considering how such contributions might require a difficult process of reckoning with how settlement has permeated radical spaces.

What I propose here is a reordering of this relationship, one that works to honor the myriad networks of relation, to use Abenaki scholar Lisa Brooks's term, that have long lived with the land and its people and continue to do in the contemporary moment.[37] In general, the phrase "other worlds here" signals a reframing of the popular anarchist adage "another world is possible" by asking: what other worlds live here already and how might we better participate in enabling their flourishing? Anarchists often speak about "prefigurative politics," which Milstein describes as a praxis that "aligns one's values to one's practice and practices the new society before it is fully in place."[38] What I question here is the orientation of this praxis around the concept of the "new society."

As Alix Olson has pointed out, this singular focus on imagining new futures is easily taken as part of the project of settlement, as in the US government's project of inviting citizens to imagine what (American) life on Mars might look like.[39] Rather than focus only on the possibilities of prefiguring new societies, this project insists that not only are other worlds possible but that there are other worlds *here*—other worlds that live with the land and for which we already have models for relation outside those espoused by a capitalist settler model. Thus, my aim in using the qualifier "other" is not meant to participate in a structure that alienates such worlds from "here," rendering them extraterrestrial to the places to which they are related. Instead, this word signals the broader project I undertake of signaling to contemporary anarchists that our visions of the "other worlds" to which we are purportedly oriented are not only possible, but are already here. Below, I explain more in-depth this vision of "other worlds here" as both a transformative political model provided by Native women's literatures and as the framing for this project. Before doing so, however, I discuss some of the already existing approaches to anarchism and Native politics.

Anarch@indigenism

Since mine is not the first study to consider the relationship between anarchist and Native movements, I turn here to describing briefly some of the previous approaches and how my work both builds on and diverges from them. Perhaps one of the places that discussions of Native nations and movements is most prevalent is in the literature on green anarchism, typified by the work of Derrick Jensen. A foundational thinker in the rise of green anarchism, Jensen remains a controversial figure in the world of New Anarchist politics. He and his organization Deep Green Resistance (DGR), remain one of the few self-proclaimed anarchist organizations that take as foundational the question of Native land and its repatriation to Native nations. However, this commitment is bound up in two related issues that position the work in conflict with the core commitments of *Other Worlds Here*: in the first place, their commitment to Native peoples and Native lands seems to stem exclusively from an understanding of such groups as indelibly connected to nature.[40] The anticivilization ideology through which Jensen and DGR have built their supposed commitment to Native peoples traffics in colonial tropes of such communities both as tied to a time before civilization and as the guides who may be able to lead settlers back.

The second issue that leads me to discount the relevance of both Jensen's and DGR's work more broadly is the transphobia within the organization. Both Jensen and cofounder Lierre Keith have long been committed to a transexclusionary radical feminism that has led other radical environmentalists, including one of DGR's confounders, to publicly distance themselves from the organization.[41] This antagonism toward trans individuals, but also to the conceptual contributions of trans theory, is foundational rather than ancillary to their anticivilization ideology and thus to the particular ways that they integrate a politics of Native land repatriation. As prominent DGR speaker Rachel Ivey has noted, antitrans gender politics "is the core of DGR."[42] In her conversations with activists confronting her about the centrality of transphobia to DGR's political philosophy, cofounder Keith has articulated DGR's approach by invoking indigeneity:

> Try this on . . . I am really Native American. How do I know? I've always felt a special connection to animals, and started building tee pees in the backyard as soon as I was old enough. I insisted on wearing moccasins to school even though the other kids made fun of me and my parents punished me for it. I read everything I could on Native people, started going to pow wows and sweat lodges as soon as I was old enough, and I knew that was the real me. And if you bio-Indians don't accept us trans-Indians, then you are just as genocidal and oppressive as the Europeans. Gender is no different. It is a class condition created by a brutal arrangement of power.[43]

* * *

Though Keith is being tongue-in-cheek in her description of indigeneity, her synonymizing it with gender indicates a lack of understanding of indigeneity and a willingness to flatten complicated conversations about Native authenticity to forward a transphobic politics. Indeed, gender and indigeneity are related yet distinct for a number of different reasons, least of all that the latter is indelibly tied to place. Because of both the rendering of Native nations as relevant only inasmuch as they are connected to the environment and the appropriation of Native discussions about authenticity to forward a transphobic party line, the approach of DGR to anarchist and Native politics is an untenable place from which to begin exploring new relationships between anarchist and Native movements in good faith.

DGR's approach is, thankfully, not the only way that people have begun to conceptualize the connections between New Anarchism and Native movements. Many Native scholars have recognized the connections between anarchist and Native political philosophies, the latter of which is sometimes referred to as "indigenism." Perhaps the most exciting example of another approach has been the development of "anarcho-indigenism," which has been recently stylized as "anarch@ indigenism" to indicate the integration of feminist sensibilities. First proposed by Kanien'kehá:ka scholar Taiaiake Alfred, the term *anarcho-indigenism* has been taken up across a variety of scholarly and activist venues, indicating a burgeoning interest in the question of how anarchist and Native political philosophies might be connected. For Alfred, the term *anarcho-indigenism* can capture the spirit of the ethical framework he develops in *Wasasé: Indigenous Pathways of Action and Freedom* in terms that more clearly relate to contemporary political terminology and movements.

He argues that the "two elements" of anarchism and indigenism come together since the latter evokes "cultural and spiritual rootedness in this land and the Onkwehonwe [indigenous] struggle for justice and freedom," while the former triangulates this ethic within "the political philosophy and movement that is fundamentally anti-institutional, radically democratic, and committed to taking action to force change."[44] Alfred even notes specifically the connections to New Anarchism by noting the affinity between "anarchists and Onkwehonwe in the anti-globalization movement."[45] Much as I do in this introduction, he sees this as temporally connected to the standoff at Kanehsatà:ke, where he argues we can see that "the logic of contending with state power is inescapable."[46]

Other Native scholars have built on the concept of anarcho-indigenism to think about its use in transforming prominent approaches to self-determination. For instance, Cherokee scholar Joshua B. Nelson has built on Alfred's concept, as well as Jacqueline Lasky's feminist modification "anarch@indigenism," to develop an approach to Cherokee literary production that eschews tropes that depend on the mutual exclusivity of progressivism and traditionalism in Cherokee political philosophy. Instead, his study evidences what he calls an "indigenous anarchism," or an approach to Cherokee literature and culture that "embraces paradox and pluralism as it simultaneously adapts to new circumstances and conserves inherited values and practices."

As he notes, recognizing these patterns in Indigenous practices creates an affinity with anarchist political philosophy, since anarchism is also invested in "pluralism, local independence, decentralization, consensus, noncoercion, and dissent from nation, state, and hierarchy."[47] Nelson's "indigenous anarchism" forms an important mechanism for his critical intervention into reconceptualizing how the Cherokee Nation can work to assert its sovereignty without ascribing to the state form. Though I remain unsure of the distinctions between a nation and a nation-state in Nelson's analysis, his "indigenous anarchism" represents an important intervention into the conversation that I am engaging throughout in *Other Worlds Here* in that it confirms the interest in anarchism among Native scholars thinking through the political realities of contemporary Native nations.

This interest in taking up not only the term *anarch@indigenism* but also the more general question of what relationship we might articulate between anarchism and indigenism characterizes a significant portion of the work with which *Other Worlds Here* intersects. For instance, in a special issue of *Affinities: Theory, Culture, Action*, titled "Working Across Difference for Post-Imperial Futures: Intersections Between Anarchism, Indigenism, and Feminism," editors Glen Coulthard (Yellowknives Dene), Jacqueline Lasky, Adam Lewis, and Vanessa Watts (Mohawk and Anishnaabe) bring together articles that explore the connections between anarchism, feminism, and indigenism; Indigenous feminism and the nation-state; anarch@-Zapatismo; urban indigeneity and international relationships; and Hawaiian nationhood within activist spaces.[48] In addition, Richard Day has written on Native political theory within the context of liberal multiculturalism and the rise of New Anarchism.[49] His work has laid the foundation for work by anarchist activists like Stephen Arthur, who seek to engage the question of anarcho-indigenism to assert Native political and cultural forms as examples of existing instantiations of anarchist politics.[50] Following Alfred, this body of work aims to explore the possible parallels between anarchist and Native praxis, thought, and history.

Activists and scholars like Adam Barker, carla bergman, Craig Fortier, Adam Lewis, and Nick Montgomery have offered other critical approaches to these questions by exploring how non-Native activists might work to build more accountable relationships with Native nations. For instance, Barker's work has explored settler identity in Canada and its impact on the possibilities of effective organizing between Native and non-Native communities.[51] Similarly, Fortier's recent book *Unsettling the Commons* builds on interviews with antiauthoritarian activists to engage the tension of using the "commons" as a framework for activism on stolen land, while Lewis's work suggests a turn to Indigenous political theory as a way to center land in social movements.[52] Such work illuminates the limitations of contemporary anarchist movements and tries to theorize strategies for attending to the structure of settlement. This resonates with contemporary work on the affective dimensions of anarchism, including Montgomery and bergman's articulation of "joyful militancy," one component of which is an attempt to understand how "Indigenous resurgence implicates us, as settlers, in complicated ways . . . [and] compels us to learn, together, how to support Indigenous resurgence and resist settler colonial violence."[53]

This ongoing work explores both the possible connections between anarchist and Native movements and how to better build these connections by being attentive to the dynamics of settlement in movement spaces. The interplay between these approaches evidences what Maia Ramnath has termed a "decolonizing anarchism" in her study of antiauthoritarian currents in liberation movements in India, an approach that seeks to decolonize anarchism itself while also locating the presence of anarchist movements focused on decolonization.[54] And though both approaches have been influential to my thinking, the analysis in *Other Worlds Here* extends from within a slippage that I identify between them.

Namely, if there is a correlation between the ethical commitments of anarchist and Native movements and ample discussion about how to develop an activist praxis that addresses settlement, why is there not a more concerted engagement with the question of *how* settlement has become normalized, or *settled*, in such movement spaces? In practice, the presumption of a natural affinity between anarchist and Native political movements obfuscates the problems that underlie the need for the restructuring of the relationships between Native and non-Native activists. In order to address this lacuna, *Other Worlds Here* explores the connection between anarchism and settlement, rather than anarchist and Native movements. It is my contention that by centering the question of settler anarchism (a term I develop in-depth in chapter 1) rather than anarch@indigenism, we might come to a better understanding of what precisely it is that needs to be restructured.

For this reason, I speak throughout the book of anarchist and Native communities as separate, though this is not always the case on the ground. Indeed, there are many Native activists and scholars who are longstanding and influential participants in the anarchist milieu, like J. Kēhaulani Kauanui (Kanaka Maoli), Gord Hill (Kwakwaka'wakw), Waziyatawin (Dakota), and Klee Benally (Diné). Therefore, throughout *Other Worlds Here*, I speak of these as separate spaces as a rhetorical strategy that emphasizes the fact that, despite the interventions of Native and Indigenous activists and scholars, New Anarchism has not radically transformed its approach to center settlement as a foundational part of capitalism and the state. In addition, much of the previous work has emanated from the Canadian context, leaving the US context drastically undertheorized within the conversation. For this reason, I focus most extensively on the US context throughout while including work that transcends the colonial border as well. In what follows, I argue that the obfuscation of settlement in New Anarchism, particularly in the US context, signals not only the persistence of a hegemonic structure within the milieu but also a tacit investment in that structure as a crux of New Anarchist politics.

Why Native Women's Literatures?

Then, what is to be done? Though I invoke this question with a small sense of mischief, its reminiscence of Lenin's famed 1901 pamphlet orients my use of Native women's literatures as an intervention in the question of how radical consciousness is developed, on what scale, and by what interlocutors. I have no interest here in evaluating the connections or dissimilarities of Leninist vanguardism and New Anarchism. Not only have other anarchist writers done so already, but this is also the type of intra-anarchist debate from which *Other Worlds Here* attempts to turn away to, instead, frame our politics by better honoring the networks of relation that live with the land on which we organize.[55] Rather,

I am interested in arguing for a new approach to the anarchist study of literature as an important part of radical social movement. In doing so, I seek to also make interventions into the study of Native women's literatures not only as a significant body of work within the broader field but also as a particularly rich example of how literary production provides both methodological and theoretical interventions that are attuned to some of the most pressing contemporary political and social issues.

In the current scholarship, the apprehension of literature as part of New Anarchism remains relatively underdeveloped. Few scholars and activists emphasize the impact of literary interventions in the post-1999 era, despite the fact that, as Jeffrey Shantz has argued, "in anarchist movements the literary imagination plays a rich part."[56] For instance, Allan Antliff's work on anarchism and art remains unparalleled in its exploration of anarchism as a definitive texture of modernism in the United States, and he has extended this into a broader exploration of anarchism and art history from the Paris Commune to the fall of the Berlin Wall.[57] This echoes earlier work such as André Breton's writing on surrealism and anarchism in the early twentieth century, as well as Herbert Read's *Poetry and Anarchism* (1938).[58] Shelley Streeby has offered an account of the "cultures of sentiment and sensation" in anarchist literature, media, and culture following the Haymarket Affair in 1886, which she traces into the early twentieth century to demonstrate the development of global connections between radical struggles.[59] The richness of these inquiries has not been matched in anarchist interest in contemporary literature, though there is some work that takes up this challenge.

Jesse Cohn's work has extended the temporal boundaries of previous engagements to establish what he calls an "anarchist resistance culture," which he describes as the "main body of the cultural production to emerge from the anarchist movements of the nineteenth and twentieth centuries," a period he bookends with the Revolutions of 1848 and the Occupy Movement in 2011.[60] A growing body of work on a small number of contemporary anarchist authors like Alan Moore and Ursula K. LeGuin has also contributed to a richening of a contemporary focus in anarchist literary studies, complemented by less author-focused work by anarchist thinkers like Sandra Jeppesen, Lewis Call, Dani Spinosa, and Margaret Killjoy.[61]

In each of these cases, we get a better sense of the genealogy of contemporary anarchist literature, as well as reflections on the importance of this literature to social movement. But, this thought-provoking work in anarchist literary studies has yet to enjoy more widespread consideration within the milieu, evidenced by the few contemporary collections of anarchist scholarship that contain any writing on literature and the fact that monographs published on these topics remain woefully outnumbered by those focused on more philosophical or sociological accounts of anarchism.

Another important limitation to these approaches leads me to turn to Native women's literatures as the source of methodological and theoretical interventions able to address the structure of settler anarchism. While the scholarship on anarchist literature moves through historical and literary analysis across a variety of locations, it remains resolutely focused on the study of *anarchist* literature, meaning both works by anarchist writers and works that offer representations of anarchism.[62] There is little consideration of literary work that might not be considered anarchist, leading to an insularity that limits engagement with other bodies of work that might provide necessary interventions into some of the far-reaching core questions on which anarchist studies of literature (and anarchist movements more broadly) are focused, including the very nature of freedom, struggle, and power. Reflecting the broader lack of engagement with Native and Indigenous Studies, the consideration of Native literatures remains absent within both anarchist scholarship and anarchist movement ephemera. This absence is particularly relevant beyond the mere recognition of exclusion because it overlooks the close-knit relationship between Native literatures and Native movements.

Other Worlds Here, then, looks to Native literatures not as an ethnographic appraisal of the state of Native persons, nations, or movements but rather as works that, as Brooks has pointed out, may "often resemble a map" rather than a strictly narrative-based endeavor.[63] This focus on mapping not only emphasizes spatialization as a foundational feature of Native literatures but also centers the relationship between place and systems of relation with each other and with the land. As Goeman has argued, this type of mapping is rooted in an understanding of "land as a storied site of human interaction."[64] Understanding Native literatures in this way emphasizes the connection between land and story, since, according to Goeman, "land is not only given meaning through consensus of claiming territory, but also through narrative practices."[65] This understanding of Native literatures is at the root of Cherokee author Daniel Heath Justice's assertion that Native literatures *matter*, both in the sense that they are significant contributions and that they maintain material worlds. As he argues, Native and Indigenous literatures are of "vital significance . . . to healthy decolonization efforts and just expressions of community resurgence," since "politics without art moves quickly toward efficient dehumanization and intellectual myopia."[66]

I focus on Native women's literatures in particular because of how central this approach to storytelling *as* methodology has been within that body of work. As Nez Perce and Tejana scholar Inés Hernández-Avila writes in her introduction to "Indigenous Women," a 2002 special issue of *Frontiers: A Journal of Women Studies*:

> How do indigenous women writers and artists manifest, critically and creatively, their awareness of this unending war? How do they acknowledge and pay tribute to their own and others' expressions of indigenous ways of knowing, including principles of humanity and relationship to all that lives? . . . They "tell story." Conscious of the power of language(s) . . . they/we tell story. Conscious of the way language(s) mediate, conscious of how narratives are created, how and where and why they emerge, whose interests are served, which stories become official (for some), which ones are ignored (by some), which ones could help humanity and the relations of the earth, they/we tell story.[67]

The creative and critical manifestation of interpretive models is imperative to the practices of storytelling from which Native women's literatures emerge. Along with Hernández-Avila, foundational writers including Leslie Marmon Silko (Laguna Pueblo), Beth Brant (Tyendinega Mohawk), Paula Gunn Allen (Laguna Pueblo), Joy Harjo (Muscogee), Rayna Green (Cherokee), and Gloria Bird (Spokane) have all pointed to the way that such literary practices insist on the connection between storytelling, revitalization, and nation building.[68] As Silko has observed, this marks a pivotal contribution of "Native American cultures to the English language."[69] Through *Other Worlds Here*, I argue that this must also be understood as a pivotal contribution of Native literatures to anarchist movements. My invocation of Native women's literatures signals an approach to the anarchist study of literature that understands it as a form of theorization capable of providing effective methodologies for attending to the limits of New Anarchism as it has thus far been conceived. Evidenced in my use of the term *honoring* in the subtitle to this book, my engagement with Native women's literatures is bound to this focus on how anarchist politics must learn to read and then honor the material and relational maps provided by such texts, especially those that illuminate the relationship between settlement, gender, and imperialism.

My exploration of Native women's literatures also seeks to intervene in the field of Native and Indigenous literatures by contributing to the growing scholarly work on Native women's writing. As Diné poet Laura Tohe notes in her introduction to the collection *Sister Nations: Native Women Writing on Community*, "the scarcity of books that have collected Native American women's writing—what amounts to one major publication a decade for the past three" makes clear that the richness of Native women's writing is not reflected in the critical scholarship, despite the prominence of Native women's writing in the history of Native literatures.[70] Recent work by scholars like Goeman, Molly McGlennen (Anishnaabe), Dory Nason (Anishnaabe/Chicana), and Deborah Miranda (Ohlone-Costanoan Esselen/Chumash) have provided nuanced, innovative, and exciting scholarship that reflects the groundbreaking work that Native women writers once have and still continue to produce. However, both the volume and reception of this work remains overshadowed by the broader arc of scholarship focused on writing by Native men.[71] By taking up Native women's literatures as a particularly fruitful space through which necessary political methodologies have been theorized, I hope to contribute to this body of scholarship not by assigning some inherent character to the field but by elevating some particularly notable contributions of a diverse body of literature.

I use this method of analysis, of exploring the role that the methodological interventions of Native women's literatures can play in contemporary social movement, to emphasize the dual connotations of Heath Justice's important assertion that Indigenous literatures matter. *Other Worlds Here* takes up this insistence by arguing not only that Native women's literatures are important but also that they function in the world in material ways. In this sense, my argument is that we not only recognize more fully the *existence* of Native women's literatures in the world but also acknowledge their important role in *shaping* the world through the mapping of structures of relation. Like Goeman, I believe that Native women's literatures present ways of thinking through "the contradictions that arise from the paradoxes . . . that colonialism presents and that Native people experience on a daily basis."[72] Though I suspect that this form of analysis would be useful across an array of temporal scopes, here I have chosen to engage with contemporary works to mirror the era of New Anarchism under analysis.

Other Worlds Here

I now return to the concept of "other worlds here" that frames this project, which emerges from a desire to center a place-based method of engagement in our anarchist inquiries. This arises not from an intellectual longing but from a concerted effort to honor my relationship to place in general, as well as the specific places in which I've taken on this work. And, then, to encourage other non-Native anarchists to do the same. As Goeman reminds us, "We do not act upon a stagnant landscape, but instead are part of it. Place is created in the process of remembering and telling stories and the ability for the receiver to understand the meanings of place."[73] Therefore, my framing of "other worlds here" is rooted in the stories I was told while living in the places where this project took shape and in my desire to practice responsibility to those stories as a white settler living on Native land.

I first began this project on Haudenosaunee territory in Buffalo, New York. While there, I learned about the Two Row Wampum, a seventeenth-century treaty between the Haudenosaunee and Dutch settlers, which was part of a series of agreements that, according to McCarthy, "established the political parameters of mutual recognition of sovereignty and the relationships of coexistence with European settlers on the basis of peace and friendship."[74] As McCarthy and Brooks, among others, have pointed out, this treaty is not an ephemeral story or a moralistic fable. Rather, as Brooks notes, "wampum symbolized permanence. When an agreement, an alliance, or an event was put in wampum, a transformation in Native space was solidified."[75] In this, the Two Row is at once a story, a map, an agreement, and a system of relation. It is one that, as McCarthy noted above, recognizes the sovereignty of the signatory nations but also, as Tuscarora writer Alicia Elliott has noted, governs the interpersonal networks of relation that constitute those nations. Speaking to her non-Native partner, Elliott writes: "Because of you, I understand how the Two Row Wampum can be more than just a treaty between two nations of people; it can be a lived treaty between two individuals, between us . . . These boundaries don't have to be bruises."[76]

I continued working on this project once I moved to Lummi territory in Bellingham, Washington. Outside the Whatcom County Courthouse stands the Centennial Pole, a totem pole carved by Lummi Carver Joe Hillaire for the 1952 centennial celebration of Bellingham's founding. As Lummi artist, teacher, conservator, author, and storyteller Pauline

Hillaire describes it, the Centennial Pole "explains in great pictorial detail the historic culture of the Lummi people and commemorates the first meeting of white settlers and Lummi leaders in 1852." In her essay on the Centennial Pole, Pauline Hillaire offers a reading of the pole as both a text and a story. She begins at the base, where there is a wide canoe, which "carries two Indians and two white men. Only the Indians in the canoe are using paddles, which represent their generosity and the trust they received."[77] Much like the Two Row Wampum codifies an agreement based on the mutual recognition and respect necessary to live with the land and its people, the Centennial Pole similarly asks those of us living in Bellingham to consider how we might live in a way that honors the generosity and trust that both Hillaires articulate, one that sees us all in a canoe together but one in which only the Lummi have paddles.

I finished this project in Narragansett and Wampanoag territories in Providence, Rhode Island, which proved to be a particularly salient place to consider the project of *Other Worlds Here* because of its centrality to the narrative of the United States itself. As I wrote this, I sat less than a mile from the site of Roger Williams's landing after his expulsion from the Massachusetts Bay Colony and only about fifty miles from Plymouth, the site that is often mistaken for the initial landing place of the Pilgrims. I lived in a place shaped immeasurably by one of the most popular stories of Native and non-Native relations: the story of the first Thanksgiving. In its popular narrativization, the story of Thanksgiving is meant to justify a claim to land on the part of settlers: that local Wampanoag people showed generosity to settlers as a signal of their welcome. This narrative overwrites the histories of violent settlement that characterized such meetings both in the seventeenth century and into the contemporary moment. Yet, in her essay reflecting on Thanksgiving, Narragansett elder Dawn Dove offers a reading of the story of Thanksgiving that reframes it within the scope of texts like the Two Row Wampum and the Centennial Pole that I described above.

According to Dove, employing the story of the first Thanksgiving as a metonym for the broader practice of generosity between Native and non-Native peoples ignores the fact that "Thanksgiving is ceremony," one that like the Two Row and the Centennial Pole establishes relationships not only between people but also with the land. Drawing together traditional Narragansett stories with those from her own life, Dove writes that "as we give thanks each day for the gift of life and the gift of beauty that surrounds us we understand that the Creator is with us. This Place is sacred."[78] Tying the story to both practice and place, Dove insists that "in order to understand Thanksgiving, one must understand the sacredness of the gift."[79] Invoking the gift, Dove highlights the same generosity that McCarthy, Elliott, and Hillaire emphasize in their discussions of the Two Row and the Centennial Pole. These are the worlds that live with these places, worlds that have been shaped through stories that lay out quite clearly methods of building reciprocal relationships with the land and its people.

These stories form the basis of *Other Worlds Here* as both a project and as the political method that I attempt to establish in its writing. As people living in and with these places, we are party to these agreements and have a responsibility to honor them. They are not unchanging or unadaptable, but to enter into those conversations we must first recognize that these other worlds are here. As part of her watercolor painting of a sparse Southwest landscape that acts as the epigraph to this book, Laguna Pueblo writer Leslie Marmon Silko writes, "if you think 'no politics here'—you are wrong." *Other Worlds Here* draws on the worlds and works of Native women's literatures to demonstrate that anarchists can no longer depend on a politics that looks at this place and assumes that there are no politics here; that such politics must be created to envision a world without the state and without capitalism.

In invoking the term *other worlds here*, I also aim to draw a connection between stories such as these and other ways that Native scholars have written about how Native nations have worked to ensure their self-determination. In this way, I want to emphasize that my project is not one that theorizes a new way of understanding place, but rather signals a broader term that can be used to understand the relationship between myriad significant ways of understanding how Native nations insist on the political, social, and economic significance of the worlds that live here. For instance, some of ways that such worlds have been described elsewhere are Glen Coulthard's "grounded normativity," Audra Simpson's "nested sovereignty," Kevin Brunyeel's "the third space of sovereignty," and Shiri Pasternack's "grounded authority."[80] Similarly, Lower Brule Sioux scholar and activist Nick Estes's rooting of his study of the history of Indigenous resistance in the phrase "our history is the future" and Leanne Betasamosake Simpson's embedding of hers in the phrase "as we have always done" also represent significant examples of this orientation toward the existence of worlds that live with the land and its people here.[81]

Structure

The structure of *Other Worlds Here* aims to put these theoretical interventions into material practice. This is mirrored in my approaches to both methodology and content. In this first place, I do not wish to replicate the assumption that there is an uncomplicated parallelism between anarchism and Native sovereignty movements. Second, I want to emphasize that the burden of responsibility for honoring these worlds, both for me as a non-Native scholar and for the communities of non-Native anarchists of and with whom I speak, lies with us. To this end, *Other Worlds Here* is divided into three parts, each consisting of two chapters. Each part offers distinct chapters focusing first on a critical analysis of how the structure of settlement has become built into contemporary anarchist movements and second on the interventions in Native women's literatures that anarchists can draw on to learn how to better respond to the responsibilities of these worlds and the relations therein.

This structure realizes my first goal of refusing parallelism between anarchism and Native women's literatures by eschewing the type of integration that many contemporary anarchist approaches seek. Instead of simply amalgamating my critical analyses of contemporary anarchist movements and my readings of Native women's literatures, I separate these discussions spatially while drawing connections between them rhetorically to signal both an unease with claims to kinship and a belief in the possibility that such networks of relation can still be established. The structure realizes my second goal of emphasizing responsibility on the part of non-Native anarchists by foregrounding the work of internal critique in the first chapter of each section to establish the necessary practice for responsible engagement with Native texts that occur in the second chapters of each part. In creating distinct parts, I also use this structure to invite the reader, at the end of each of the three sections, to continuing asking the question at the core of *Other Worlds Here*: in each of these issues, how can we better answer the responsibilities to place and to each other that are mapped in Native women's literatures? I also hope that readers might find it easier to share the component parts with others, since each offers a relatively stand-alone analysis that nonetheless remains connected to the broader project.

In part 1—"Settler Anarchism"—I establish the contours of the settler structure through which New Anarchism has been constituted. The first chapter explores the narration of the 1999 protests against the

WTO in Seattle, often referred to as at the "Battle in Seattle," as a New Anarchist origin story to demonstrate its rootedness in a settler structure. Juxtaposing the ubiquity of the 1999 Battle in Seattle in anarchist texts where it is invoked as a natal moment of struggle with the concomitant absence of a consideration of the 1856 Battle of Seattle, this chapter traces the recurring narration of the emergence of New Anarchism to more carefully excavate US anarchist claims to place. I locate in the omnipresence of the 1999 Battle in Seattle and the absence of the 1856 Battle of Seattle a lack of consideration of the relationship between settlement and neoliberalism, as well as the importance of the Pacific Northwest to this historical liaison. In the second chapter, I turn to memoirs by Chumash and Ohlone/Costanoan-Esselen writer Deborah Miranda and Cowlitz writer Elissa Washuta to show how both have turned to form-conscious creative nonfiction to create new methods of commemoration capable of reckoning with the palimpsestic histories that contain rather than resolve the multiple contradictions of settlement. Emphasizing how Miranda and Washuta draw together personal, tribal, and settler histories while providing expectant orientations toward the future, I demonstrate how they draw on the material presence of worlds living with the land to structure their engagement with both the present and the future.

In part 2, "Relocating Gendered Violence," I extend this analysis of settler anarchism to explore how this structure limits anarchist approaches to feminism, gender, and sexuality, restricting the ability of New Anarchism to address pressing issues, including sexual violence in radical communities and the epidemic of missing and murdered Indigenous women, girls, queer, and two-spirit people across North America. Using a statement from the Black Rose Anarchist Federation to ground my inquiry, I describe how New Anarchist approaches fall within a limited taxonomy that is hindered by its dependence on the assumption of an inherent rejection of gendered violence in anarchist spaces and thought. Tracing these taxonomies through contemporary writings on anarchism, feminism, gender, and sexuality, I demonstrate how this assumed inherent rejection depends on colonial approaches to the question of land, associating Native peoples with the environment while approaching the body as an individual entity separate from land or community. In the next chapter, I explore how poets Heid E. Erdrich (Ojibwe) and Janet Rogers (Mohawk/Tuscarora) critically engage with American literary monuments, including canonical American authors and the symbolization of Native women in national mythology, to foreground the material foundation of land within a rendering of the gendered dimensions of settlement. I argue that through this literary approach, Erdrich and Rogers materialize what Leanne Betasamosake Simpson has called "decolonial love" to conceptualize abundant methods of resistance.

In part 3, "The Limits of New Anarchist Transnationalism," I address the limits of New Anarchist approaches to transnationalism. Tracing anarchist attempts to develop a global approach to both capitalism and anarchist history, I demonstrate how New Anarchists have reified the claims to Native land on which the US state depends and have invested in an approach to global indigeneity that overwrites Native sovereignty with that of the US state. I juxtapose the anarchist fixation on the 1994 Zapatista uprising in Southern Mexico with the nonappearance of pivotal moments of Native resistance in the US and Canada in anarchist literature to demonstrate how anarchist approaches to global politics obscure the presence of Native nations. I extend this analysis to highlight the obfuscation of the history of US empire in the development of anarchist transnationalism, focusing especially on the lack of attention to the Pacific as a theater of US imperialism. In the final chapter, I offer a rereading of Leslie Marmon Silko's *Ceremony* as a transpacific novel that decenters US claims to sovereignty made via empire by reading Silko's trans-Indigenous methodology as one that locates Native nations as the core components of global comparative analysis. Drawing on original archival research to bring together a discussion of Silko's experience writing *Ceremony* while living on the Pacific coast in Southeast Alaska with transpacific readings of pivotal scenes, this chapter insists on an engagement with Native texts as important methodological interventions rather than windows into an ethnographic analysis of Native characters, authors, and communities.

Other Worlds Here ends with a discussion of Tlingit visual artist Alison Bremner, whose work demonstrates, much more succinctly than I could, the myriad ways that Native nations have mapped other worlds here, insisting on these maps as records of relational models that illuminate the difference between approaches grounded in the adage "another world is possible" and those incumbent within the mantra of "other worlds here."

Part 1

Settler Anarchism

CHAPTER 1

Battles of and in Seattle

Settler Anarchism in North America

The 1999 Seattle WTO shut down and resistance has become an icon—a story that gives other things meaning. What people think happened in Seattle shapes what they believe about protest, direct action, social change movements; about corporate globalization and capitalism; and about police, the state, and repression. Stories shape consciousness. Consciousness shapes the future.

—David Solnit, "The Battle of the Story of the Battle of Seattle"

In November 1999, upward of forty thousand protestors emerged on the streets of Seattle to protest the Third Ministerial Conference of the World Trade Organization, effectively shutting down the planned trade negotiations and throwing Seattle to the forefront of international conversations about globalization and resistance. The Battle in Seattle, as the protests came to be called, captured the imagination of radical activists across the world and swiftly incited scorn from proponents of neoliberalism. These protests mark an important inroad to discussing New Anarchism since, according to Alexander Cockburn and Jeffrey St. Clair, they marked "the flowering of a new radical movement in America and across the world, rambunctious, anarchic, internationalist, well informed and in some ways more imaginative and supple than kindred eruptions in recent decades."[1]

This description resonates in many contemporary texts on anarchism, both in terms of the qualities it ascribes to New Anarchism as a "new radical movement in America" and its invocation of the 1999 protests as a generative moment in reigniting interest in anarchism at the turn of the century. For many anarchist texts (including mine), this event remains the requisite introductory initiation with which any discussion of New Anarchism in the United States must begin. For my purposes, it also represents a significant parable through which to explore not only the content but also the structure of New Anarchist politics and the approach to US settler colonialism therein.

As Clare Hemmings has argued, the stories we tell about social movements are constitutive of how those movements are shaped since they produce and mobilize what she calls a "political grammar" of social movement.[2] Exploring the political grammar of these stories, for Hemmings, can help to identify ways that we are "inaugurated by rather than inaugurating" some of the assumed certainties proliferated through constant retellings of foundational stories.[3] Though Hemmings is particularly interested in the circulation of stories about Western feminist theories within feminist movements, I draw a connection here to the relationship between stories and settlement by building on Coll Thrush's concept of "place-stories," a term that describes "the conjunction between sites of history and the accounts we make of them."[4] By paying attention to both the political grammar and the place-stories incumbent within the story of the 1999 Battle in Seattle, I make clear the work that this story does in inaugurating us into a distinctly settler structure of anarchist movement.

Despite the proliferation of analyses, recountings, and invocations of the 1999 Battle in Seattle, I find Cockburn and St. Clair's description a particularly apt one with which to begin because it emphasizes several important ways that contemporary anarchists describe our movements to directly confront some of the most prevalent misrepresentations of them. For instance, Cockburn and St. Clair's description emphasizes that anarchist movements depend on creative, direct action rather than a formulaic reliance on legislative and state-sanctioned methods of political engagement (rambunctious); that they depend on diffuse structures of horizontal power (anarchic); that they are populated by people who are aware of and engaged in intellectual debate and inquiry (well informed); and that they are aimed at developing rich and inventive solutions to struggle (imaginative and supple).

Using the 1999 Battle in Seattle as a microcosm through which to ascribe these qualities to New Anarchist movements serves an important purpose, especially as anarchist movements are continually maligned with false representations that depict us as leftist fascists obsessed with destroying property, fomenting violent unrest, and policing the activities, identities, and language of others. Though some of this critique is levied as part of more minute intra-anarchist debate, the need to clearly articulate the methods, strategies, and political commitments of anarchist organizing and philosophy both during and since the 1999 Battle in Seattle remains an important part of confronting the still-prevalent caricatures of anarchist movements.

The plethora of texts dedicated to the 1999 Battle in Seattle attest to the centrality of this moment to New Anarchism. Along with Cockburn and St. Clair's *5 Days That Shook the World*, a number of other titles provide dynamic and thorough accounts of the 1999 Battle in Seattle and its aftermath including *The Battle of the Story of the Battle in Seattle*, edited by David and Rebecca Solnit; *The Battle in Seattle: The Story Behind and Beyond the WTO Demonstrations by* Janet Thomas; and *The Battle of Seattle: The New Challenge to Capitalist Globalization*, edited by Eddie Yuen, Daniel Burton Rose, and George Katsificas. What is more, this interest in the 1999 protests has extended beyond the relatively obscure world of anarchist politics and into more mainstream venues, including representations of the protests in popular fiction like Robert Newman's *The Fountain at the Center of the World*, Ruth Ozeki's *All Over Creation*, and Sunil Yapa's *Your Heart Is a Muscle the Size of a Fist*, as well as a film based on a fictionalized account called *Battle in Seattle* starring Charlize Theron. All these texts, some better than others, offer reflections on the planning, execution, and aftermath of the 1999 Battle in Seattle.

I am not interested here in either rehashing, rewriting, or evaluating these accounts. The fact that these narratives both align and diverge signals the rich, diverse perspectives that have emerged since the 1999 Battle in Seattle, while also highlighting the value that anarchists place on reckoning with the dynamic, sometimes shambolic examples of our politics in practice. In this way, I am quite happy to allow these texts to continue informing our understanding of what happened leading up to and during the protests. What I am interested in, instead, is the mythology surrounding the Battle in Seattle, particularly as a generative moment of New Anarchism. If, as David Solnit argues in the epigraph, the 1999 Battle in Seattle is an icon, a "story that gives other things meaning," what meanings does it give and to whom?

In particular, I am concerned with the emergence of what I call "settler anarchism" or a form of anarchism that aligns itself with the settler colonial project both structurally and philosophically. I use this term to both acknowledge and push beyond the argument that settlement is merely inherited in anarchist spaces, bleeding through into radical politics from the dominant social and political structures. In this way, the term *settler anarchism* helps me to illuminate not only the operation of settlement within anarchist spaces but also how settlement comes to be expressed in distinctly anarchist terms. My interest here is in exploring the prevalence of what I call "settler amenability," building on Hemmings's notion of amenability within the context of feminist stories. For her, we must "pay attention to the *amenability* of our own stories, narrative constructs, and grammatical forms to discursive uses . . . we might otherwise wish to disentangle ourselves from."[5] In my use of the term with the modifier "settler," I signal how the political grammar of this particular anarchist story has made New Anarchism *amenable* to the settler project, contra the assumption that anarchist movements are inherently aligned with those for Native self-determination.

In what follows, I use the narrative of the 1999 Battle in Seattle as a generative moment to trace the way New Anarchism emerged within a political grammar amenable to the structure of settlement. I locate this amenability in three specific characteristics that define the mythology surrounding the 1999 Battle in Seattle in its constant retelling: a lack of context, both historical and place based; an omission of the complicated relationships between Native and non-Native activists in Washington State at the time; and an attempt to assert an inherent parallel relationship between anarchists and Native communities.

Battle Myths

The mythology surrounding the 1999 Battle in Seattle continues to color its invocation in discussions of New Anarchism. Perhaps most overtly, anarchists continue to work against the mythology perpetuated during and in the aftermath about violence, disorganization, and naiveté. As Janet Thomas observes, "The discrepancy between being in the experience and then seeing it portrayed in the press was like cuddling up with your teddy bear and waking up with a crocodile in your bed. It was a bad dream. A repetitive bad dream. Over and over and over, the rest of the world was exposed to the same loop of burning trash cans, black-masked marauders, and broken windowpanes."[6]

According to Uri Gordon, this focus on "the use of nonlethal violence during protests," including "scenes of property destruction and confrontations with police on the streets, in particular during demonstrations against summits of government leaders and international economic organisations" is a characteristic that distinguishes New Anarchism from anarchist movements of the late nineteenth and early twentieth centuries, when violence was discussed largely in terms of "mass armed insurrection or assassinations of heads of state and capitalist bosses."[7] For Gordon, this is intrinsically tied to the type of mass mobilizations epitomized by the 1999 Battle in Seattle that he, along with others, refers to as one of the "coming out parties" of New Anarchism.[8] This depiction of the protests as "violent" continues to shape the mythology of the 1999 Battle in Seattle, whether in their invocation in news coverage on May Day protests in Seattle in 2012 or as an attempt, as David Solnit argues, to "criminalize protest since Seattle and . . . [to create] a climate of less civil rights and a greater acceptance of violence against protest."[9]

Even more than fifteen years on, organizers and activists are still forced to reckon with the imposed legacy of so-called violent protest as a marker of New Anarchism. Because of this, what happened at the 1999 Battle in Seattle continues to form the basis of popular understanding of New Anarchism, for better or (usually) for worse. Contemporary anarchists are constantly forced to reckon with the legacies of misconception left in the wake of what, by and large, is considered a successful instance of public mass mobilization. The echoes of journalist Thomas Friedman's famous editorial "Senseless in Seattle," in which he depicts anti-WTO activists and organizers as naive agitators who know nothing about global trade, still resonate widely, despite recognition from both public intellectuals like Naomi Klein as well as participating delegates that protestors were well-informed and knowledgeable on the issues at stake.[10]

But there are also myths about the 1999 Battle in Seattle that circulate *within* the anarchist milieu, tied to similar narratives about the rise of New Anarchism in less sympathetic venues. Core organizers like Chris Dixon and David Solnit have noted the frustration of dealing with the "unfortunate and distorted mythology" that what happened in Seattle was both something new or something spontaneous.[11] Positioning the 1999 Battle in Seattle in this way obfuscates the relationship between the anti-WTO protests and other global events like the mass protests in over forty cities worldwide as part of Carnival Against Capital on June 18 that same year, the emergence of the Zapatistas in the early 1990s, and the prolific global protests against Structural Adjustment Programs (SAPs) throughout the late 1980s and into the 2000s.[12] What is more, organizers like Solnit worry that the positioning of the

1999 Battle in Seattle as a spontaneous uprising "overlooks the massive amounts of grassroots organizing, mobilizing, education, alliance building, media work, and the creation of a unifying strategic framework."[13]

Though organizers like Dixon and Solnit are adamant about recognizing the fact that Seattle didn't happen in a vacuum, the particularity of the moment is also intrinsic to its legacy—taking place over five days in late November and early December, the 1999 Battle in Seattle occurred literally on the cusp of the twenty-first century. It is in the overlap between these two points, the desire to emphasize the histories of which the protests were a part while also articulating them as an incomparable expression of the fever of an auspicious historical turn, from which my location of New Anarchism's settler form emerges. Reflecting on the necessity of understanding the genealogy of the mass mobilizations in Seattle, Dixon observes that "if we understand neoliberalism as a continuation of colonization and capitalism, our rebellion in Seattle was connected to a history of Indigenous resistance that is over 500 years old."[14] In the years since the 1999 Battle in Seattle, this "if" remains an uncertain question.

In what follows, I explore this unresolved "if" to prove how the narrative about the 1999 Battle in Seattle that circulates in stories about the rise of New Anarchism replicates the structure of settlement. I do this in a number of ways, building on the consistencies that I've traced throughout this introduction by foregrounding some of the absences that have become definitive of the story's retelling. I begin by discussing how the extremely limited engagement with the 1856 Battle of Seattle alongside the ubiquitous retelling of the 1999 Battle demonstrates a disassociation of the underpinning issues of the 1999 Battle, especially neoliberalism and the concomitant globalization of corporate capitalism, from the history of settlement in the region. Then, I trace the effects of this disassociation by showing how this tendency has precluded a more thorough representation of the context in which the 1999 protests happened, focusing especially on the conflicts over Native sovereignty and treaty rights that grasped Washington State at the time due to the Makah whaling controversy. I end by turning to the rise of the Occupy Movement in 2011 to demonstrate how significantly this eschewal of a place-based foundation for radical politics has impacted the structure of New Anarchist movements in the contemporary moment.

In the most general sense, this chapter explores what happens when a prominent story of radical nativity is told and retold without a commitment to place. By taking up the memorialization of the 1999 Battle in Seattle, especially what has been consistently omitted in its retelling, I show how New Anarchist movements that continue to use this version of this story as a moment of nascent rupture invoke an approach to anarchist social movement that is both incompatible and incommensurable with the type of land-based ethic that is, in Goeman's words, "uniquely pivotal to tribal identity and survivance."[15]

The Land You Are Standing on Was Once Free

According to Coll Thrush, the 1856 Battle of Seattle remains "enshrined in local mythology as the ur-travail of early Seattle." For him, the commemoration of this battle throughout the late nineteenth and early twentieth centuries marked "a violent inverse of the Chief Seattle Speech," in which it narrates a history where "blameless white pioneers earn honor and success by surviving threats from nature, Indians, or a corrupt government" and thus functions as a justification for settlement.[16] In the Seattle region, this battle is commemorated and memorialized in many ways: for example, by the placement of a plaque in 1916 that now sits in City Hall Park and that was memorialized again with a rededication ceremony by the Daughters of the American Revolution in 2016 or in the naming of Decatur High School in Federal Way after the USS *Decatur*, which came to the aid of settlers during the 1856 Battle. This narration of the 1856 Battle of Seattle continues to live with the land in these monuments and these public memorials constantly reiterating a particular narrative about relationships between settlers and Native communities that continues to inform the structure of relations into the current moment.

Despite the relative prominence of this story in the history of the settlement of Seattle, as well as Washington Territory more broadly, an engagement with the 1856 Battle of Seattle is absent from the pervasive recitation of the 1999 protests within New Anarchist movements. This is true even as writers and activists since the protests have usurped the term *Battle in Seattle* without any reference to this earlier event. In this sense, my concern with the omission of the 1856 Battle from New Anarchist texts that routinely invoke the story of the 1999 Battle as a generative moment is relatively straightforward. That is, this omission signals an attempt to consistently erase the specific history of settlement in Seattle by obfuscating this easily discernable connection between the two events. Because of this, the question of how these two events might be related, and the concomitant discussion of the relationship between settlement in the nineteenth century and neoliberalism at the turn of the twenty-first, is precluded. To bring this conversation to the fore, I move away from attempting to catalogue this absence in the New Anarchist invocation of the 1999 Battle in Seattle and, instead, offer an in-depth analysis of the one instance of anarchist engagement with the 1856 Battle of Seattle that I could find.

The article "1856: The Battle of Seattle" appeared as an installment of "Forgotten History" in the twentieth issue of the short-lived Seattle anarchist newspaper *Tides of Flame*, published in early June 2012 toward the end of its run. With twenty-five issues published from July 2011 to December 2012, *Tides of Flame* was relatively well known among alternative and radical communities in Seattle, even gaining interest from the still-popular alternative weekly *The Stranger*.[17] The editorial board described the periodical as "part of an ongoing project of anarchist analysis and practice within the Puget Sound area" and noted that "we strive to live lives of joy, freedom, rebellion, and for this, we are criminals."[18] The story of the 1856 Battle of Seattle as it is presented in *Tides of Flame* replicates the kind of commemoration described by Thrush and evidenced in the popular local commemoration.

The short, two-page article begins: "The land you are standing on was once free. Before the foreign ideas of property and law were forcefully imported from Europe into the Puget Sound, they belonged to no one and everyone."[19] It continues by telling the story of the 1856 Battle of Seattle, shaping the narrative as one in which several Native leaders, including Chief Seattle, sold out their people, "agreeing to relocate their people to reservations and abandon their traditional way of life in exchange for money and fishing rights," while the lone Nisqually leader Chief Leschi led "the first rebellion against the authoritarian order we still live under here in Seattle."[20] It ends by lamenting the history that follows ("terrible, filled with sorrow and betrayal") and urges readers to recognize that though "none of us will ever get to experience what life in this region was like before colonization . . . it is within our ability to create a world that is free from property."[21] Contained within this place-story, to use Thrush's term, are numerous narrative choices that do the work of maintaining settlement through anarchist logics.

For instance, this retelling of the story of the 1856 Battle of Seattle replicates popular misconceptions of treaty making, some of which harken back to the arguments made by both right-wing politicians and environmentalists during numerous fights for treaty rights in the region, including the Makah whaling controversy to which I return at length below. Much as it ignores the fact that Native signatories did not exchange anything for fishing rights but rather reserved their previously held rights in the signing of the treaties, this articulation of treaties as instances in which a few treaty signers "unfortunately" signed their people's lives and traditions away for compensation ignores the complicated history of treaties for Native peoples. As Ojibwe scholar Scott Richard Lyons has argued, the x-marks by which most Native signatories signed treaties are a "sign of consent in a context of coercion." In this way, x-marks are "the agreement one makes when there seems to be little choice in the matter."[22] This is an important point, especially when considering the signatories to the treaties to which the article from *Tides of Flame* alludes, who were told by territorial governor Isaac Stevens to either sign or see their people "walk knee deep in blood."[23] Of course, as Lyons points out, this doesn't mean that Native signatories weren't exercising any agency. He observes "to the extent that little choice isn't the quite same thing as no choice, [the x-mark] signifies Indian agency" and, in this way, "signifies the political realities of the treaty era."[24]

These political realities are flattened in the narration of the account of the 1856 Battle of Seattle in *Tides of Flame*, which not only replicates the notion that Native leaders acquiesced to the exigencies of violent settlement but does so from a distinctly anarchist rationale. That is, the writers do not only associate the signing of the treaties with consent to settler governance but also assert that Native leaders sold their people out for money and property—two prominent anarchist targets. In this way, the fiction of easy acquiescence to the ferocity of settlement by Native peoples is embodied in a distinctly anarchist philosophy that rejects the acquisition of property and of capital. This works alongside their use of Nisqually leader Chief Leschi as someone who led a rebellion against "the authoritarian order we still live under here in Seattle" to create a genealogy through which contemporary anarchists can claim Leschi as their ancestor in the struggles which define New Anarchism.

In doing so, they paint anarchists, rather than contemporary Nisqually people like prominent fishing rights activist Billy Frank Jr., as the inheritors of a tradition of resistance established by Leschi.[25] Similarly, rather than use images from contemporary Nisqually events commemorating Leschi in particular or resilience of Coast Salish peoples more generally, they use historical images to lament Native peoples' ensnarement in the past. They use a black and white photograph alongside the article, representing "THE NISQUALLY" through a depiction of two women dressed in woven cedar clothing, beside a canoe, sitting on the banks of water. This dependence on historical photos of Nisqually people is curious at best, since many Nisqually still live in what is now Washington State (many on the Nisqually reservation) and have dozens of photos available of Nisqually people with canoes and cedar hats. Most notably, there was significant press coverage of the now-yearly Tribal Canoe Journey that occurred in the name year this issue of *Tides of Flame* was published.

This dependence on both historical imagery and the lamentation of the loss of "once free" land (to say nothing of its proximity to the popular American descriptor "land of the free") illustrates anarchists as the occupants of the modern city while Native peoples exist in the wilderness, both temporal and ecological. What is more, this attempt to establish a direct genealogy between contemporary anarchists and Leschi enables anarchists to create the illusion that anarchist activists are inherently working alongside or within an Indigenous tradition, rather than reckoning with the realities of advancing a non-Native–led movement for an end to the state and capitalism on stolen land. Though this, as I'll discuss more below, isn't unique to anarchists in Seattle, it is particularly relevant for two reasons: first, because the 1999 Battle in Seattle holds such an important place in the New Anarchist imagination and, second, because (as Thrush points out) though "every American city is built on Indian land . . . few advertise it like Seattle."[26]

So much of how the writers for *Tides of Flame* depict the 1856 Battle of Seattle is bound up in the type of advertisements about indigeneity that Thrush identifies as the "central problem of Seattle's Native American History." By this, he means that though "there may be some historical truth to some of them" (such as the narrative of Leschi that is told in *Tides of Flame*), "for the most part, they are historical creations" that enable contemporary interlocutors to reframe Native history in ways that affirm our current expectations and perspectives (like absorbing Leschi into a longer genealogy of antiauthoritarian resistance of which we are a part).[27] In this way, anarchists follow in a long lineage of countercultural actors identifying their resistance to the mainstream through an emulation of or equivalence with Native peoples—what Dakota scholar Philip J. Deloria has famously termed "playing Indian."

For Deloria, this practice arises from the foundational paradoxes of American national identity, which lays claim to modernity by using "Indian play to encounter the authentic amidst the anxiety of urban industrial and postindustrial life."[28] In this way, Americanness depends on this desire for an authentic connection to place while being borne through the attempted eradications of those peoples, cosmologies, and epistemologies that may be able to provide such a connection. When the anarchists writing the history of the 1856 Battle of Seattle for *Tides of Flame* lament that they will "never get to experience what life in this region was like before colonization," this expresses precisely the type of desire to which Deloria points. Combined with the mourning for a land that "was once free" at the outset of the article, this jeremiad echoes the desire to find some connection with the land itself while simultaneously mourning the death of those whom the authors imagine could have provided it.

The anxiety of urban and postindustrial life concomitant in Deloria's tracing of playing Indian is centrally figured in *Tides of Flame*'s discussion of the 1856 Battle of Seattle. Written around the time that Seattle is again emerging in another boom, this time owing to the rise of Amazon, this piece from *Tides of Flame* evidences how local anarchists were reckoning with their place in a city dealing with new dimensions of urbanization and postindustrial development. There is an interesting deviation here from Deloria's frame—rather than articulating themselves as Indians, the authors of *Tides of Flame* instead articulate historical Indians as anarchists. In doing so, they position themselves as the necessary heirs of Indigenous resistance while relegating Native peoples to a time before modernity.

This invocation of indigeneity works to establish a lineage of resistance that can include Native peoples while simultaneously excluding them from the contemporary urban space of Seattle. Scholars like Thrush and Reyna Ramirez (Ho-Chunk) have demonstrated the problems with such approaches, which assume an inherent division between Native history and urban history.[29] Therefore, my interest is not in rehashing this point about the presumed mutual exclusion of urban and Native places—though this is certainly at work in the formulation of Native history as it is written in *Tides of Flame*. Rather, what I'm most interested in here is how this memorialization of Native history works alongside the memorialization of the 1999 Battle in Seattle in the anarchist milieu to articulate an approach to indigeneity and Native resistance that upholds settlement through a distinctly anarchist framework.

For Thrush, this memorialization of the "restless Indian dead" works to preclude the coexistence of Native peoples and urban spaces even though, since the mid-twentieth century, the majority of Native peoples in the United States have lived in cities.[30] His focus on Seattle helps us to connect the narratives of modernity, development, and indigeneity in *Tides of Flame* to the process of writing Native peoples out of modernity that White Earth Ojibwe historian Jean O'Brien locates in her study of nineteenth- century local histories in southern New England. Through her study of local historical ephemera in New England, O'Brien aims to "understand how non-Indians in southern New England convinced themselves that Indians there had become extinct even though they remained as Indian peoples—and do so to this day."[31] For her, this was enabled through a series of recurring narratives that "insisted that non-Indians held exclusive sway over modernity, denied modernity to Indians, and in the process created a narrative of Indian extinction that has stubbornly remained."[32] In *Tides of Flame*, we can see this process at work in the anarchist anxiety about Seattle as a city entrenched in escalating rounds of urban development and the consequences for the city at the turn of the twenty-first century.

In anarchist histories of New Anarchism, the 1999 Battle in Seattle offers a pivotal moment during which activist and organizers began coalescing a viable alternative to the trajectory of a neoliberal model of global economic development that threatened to define the twenty-first century. As celebrated organizer Grace Lee Boggs put it, "I think that at the Battle of Seattle in 1999, people began to understand something new. It was not only the World Trade Organization, not only those huge structures that have been created by corporate globalization that we have to replace. Especially with the climate crisis, we have to begin changing ourselves radically. That's the challenge of the twenty-first century."[33] At stake, in both the moment and in its ubiquitous retelling, was the very character of the postmodern future.

Anarchist scholar Mark Bray connects this directly to the 1999 Battle in Seattle, noting that "by the end of the twentieth century, the flaws of authoritarian, statist forms of socialism had been exposed, setting the stage for a new era of anarchist ascendancy of which Occupy Wall Street has been the most prominent example since . . . the 'Battle of Seattle.'"[34] Thus, the reiteration of the 1999 Battle in Seattle as a birth story of New Anarchism is part of the larger project of imagining the structure, strategy, and content of radical left movement in the postmodern moment. And, much in the same way that Native peoples were structurally written out of the narrative of modernity of which they were undeniably a part, as O'Brien and Thrush have demonstrated, the popular narrative of the 1999 Battle in Seattle continues to exclude

Native peoples from the alternative visions of *post*modernity espoused by New Anarchist movements that aim to assert another possible world against the assumed inevitability of a global neoliberal future. Moving beyond this particular text and its engagement with historical context, the persistence of this structure in New Anarchist narrativization of the 1999 Battle in Seattle is evident also in how these retellings omit important contemporaneous context from Washington State.

Home-Field Advantage

Undeniably, Native and Indigenous peoples were present and active at the 1999 Battle in Seattle. Perhaps most famously, Diné and Dakota activist and Executive Director of the Indigenous Environmental Network (IEN), Thomas Goldtooth "closed the Indigenous Forum at the WTO with a passionate talk about the threat of neocolonialism and the importance of waking up to corporate exploitation."[35] Ojibwe elder Esther Ogima geshig gwok quay Nahgahnub was also present at the forum, offering an address that asked participants and attendees to "talk about the treaties. Talk about them protecting the land."[36] However, we cannot read the prominence of Goldtooth and Nahgahnub's contributions as contrary to the argument that New Anarchism remains bound to a settler structure—rather, the fact that the presence and participation of Native and Indigenous peoples at the 1999 protests has not resulted in a shift toward a place-based method of social movement in New Anarchist movements demonstrates that this is an issue built into the structure of engagement rather than only the demographics of participants.

As Elizabeth Betita Martínez has carefully argued in her article "Where Was the Color in Seattle?," people of color (including Indigenous peoples) from around the world came together during the 1999 Battle in Seattle to create more cohesive and long-lasting relationships through which to build popular power. The array of constituencies whose close collaboration made the 1999 protests not only possible but also successful remains an enduring legacy of the events and of their possibilities for organized radical protest. However, this legacy is complicated by the fact that, according to Martinez, the mass mobilization in 1999 witnessed an "overall turnout of color in the U.S. [that] remained around five percent total."[37] Reconciling, or at least accounting for, the coexistence of this important legacy of the possibilities of building broad-based coalitions and what many activists (including Martínez) experience as the overwhelming whiteness of New Anarchism is at the root of my desire to use the 1999 Battle in Seattle as an important site for identifying the structure of settler anarchism.

In particular, it can help us to understand better the constellation of a broad social movement that can operate on a global scale while also retaining the structure of settlement locally. Indeed, one of the most enduring inspirations underpinning the memorialization of the 1999 Battle in Seattle in New Anarchist texts is the recognition of how broad a base it was able to build, especially across geographic borders. However, this focus on the global nature of the protests has often meant ignoring some important and influential context from Washington State that may help, in some way, to answer Martínez's question.

As activists and organizers began planning protests after the January 1999 announcement that Seattle would be the location for the third ministerial meeting of the WTO, Washington State was embroiled in the Makah whaling controversy. This controversy had reignited tensions over treaty rights that had characterized many Native and non-Native relationships in Washington State since the Fish Wars of the 1960s and 1970s.[38] After the gray whale was removed from the endangered species list in 1994, the Makah Nation began the process of appealing to the International Whaling Commission (IWC) for the right to resume their traditional whale hunt as secured in the 1855 Treaty of Neah Bay. As Makahs moved to hunt a gray whale in spring 1999, the backlash against their renewed hunting practices saw a willful collusion between right-wing anti-Native politicians, radical environmentalists, and animal rights organizations. As scholars like Zoltán Grossman and Joshua L. Reid (Snohomish) have documented, this resistance was characterized by a distinctly anti-Native sentiment at worst and an ignorance regarding sovereignty, indigeneity, treaty rights, and the law at best.[39]

This is the context in which the planning for the 1999 Battle of Seattle was occurring. This was a heated issue in Washington State at the time and was bringing to the fore debates about tribal sovereignty, indigeneity, and environmental conservation not only in both state and federal contexts but also on the international stage. It was closely covered by national news media, and was watched across Indian Country since the outcome promised to set precedent for other challenges to the limitation of Native treaty rights not only on national, but supranational stages. Despite both the intensity and prevalence of the Makah whaling controversy in Washington State in 1999, it rarely comes up in any of the materials reflecting on the emergence, the effects, or the legacy of the 1999 Battle in Seattle. This is especially strange, given that the late environmentalist and animal rights activist Ben White was intimately involved both in the WTO protests and activism against the renewal of the Makah whale hunt.

White was a long-standing and prominent part of the nearly year-long project of organizing against the WTO meeting in Seattle and the images of White's sea turtle brigade, with protestors decked out in cardboard sea turtle armor, are some of the most lasting from the protests.[40] During this time, he was also working with Makahs to try to prevent them from resuming the whale hunt, issuing advertisements in local newspapers from the organization People for the Makahs and Whales that offered money to stop the whale hunt as well as organizing presentations to the Makah Whaling Commission to provide "historical background" to the protests against Makahs that took place after the whaling permit was granted.[41] He appears often in interviews about the controversy, speaking as a "longtime environmental activist" who believed that Makahs had not "considered the worldwide social and political consequences of their actions."[42] In a story for the *Kitsap Sun*, White expressed skepticism that the hunt was being pursued in the interest of maintaining longstanding traditional practices, arguing, "I don't believe all traditions should be respected . . . If they don't need the meat, then why don't they just go out and touch the whale? If this need is truly spiritual, then why should the remedy be nutritional?"[43]

Nuu-chah-nulth scholar Charlotte Coté has argued that a lack of understanding about the centrality of whaling to Native communities like the Makah is, in effect, a denial of indigeneity itself. And as Keith Johnson (Makah), the president of the Makah Whaling Commission notes in his 1999 editorial for the *Seattle Times* "The Makah Manifesto," the Makah whale hunt was not the awakening of a sleeping tradition but rather a continuation of a still-living one: "We retain our whaling traditions today. It resonates through all of our people from the youngest to the oldest, and we don't take kindly to other people trying to tell us what our culture is or should be."[44] And though White's understanding of the topic isn't representative of the feelings of the diverse array of participants at the 1999 Battle in Seattle, his ardent participation in both the planning of the mass protests and the resistance to the revitalization of the Makah whale hunt demonstrates that these issues were overlapping.

The legacies of this context are lost in the collective recollection of the protests in New Anarchist texts. This absence is not only a problem of omission but one that demonstrates a lack of serious consideration of a core question: What was happening in Seattle and in Washington State during the lead up to the protests? This question gives way to other further reaching historical and contextual inquiries: Why had the WTO chosen to have its meeting in Seattle in the first place? What role did Seattle play in the development of a global neoliberalism? Neglecting this question in the fifteen or so years of commemoration has meant an extended disavowal of the important connections between trade, settlement, and neoliberalism at the turn of the twenty-first century. The fact that the Makah whaling controversy and the meeting of the WTO in Seattle were happening simultaneously is no coincidence. Rather, they rose together as part of the attempt to advance the long-lasting desire to secure for Seattle a position as a central locus of trade in the global world.

When Seattle beat out forty other cities to host the third ministerial meeting of the WTO, this was part of a broader arc of redevelopment in which multiple visions of what Seattle could be were coming into conflict as the city emerged from the Boeing Bust of the 1970s and 1980s into the twenty-first century. In fact, this cycle of depression and reemergence had characterized Seattle's identity since settlement, evidenced in the continual trajectory of boom-and-bust since the late nineteenth century. As Sam Howe Verhovek (the same journalist who covered the Makah whaling controversy) noted in an article covering the announcement of Seattle as the host city, "local leaders were exultant. Here in what is often called the most trade-dependent region of the nation, they said the meeting would be a chance to show off Seattle as a world-class center of high-tech innovation and a friend to global trade."[45] This sentiment echoes the political and economic motives underpinning other global-minded events in Seattle's history. Much like each of the cycles of boom-and-bust before, this desire to "show off" as a friend of global trade throughout the twentieth century was intimately connected to issues of Native sovereignty and land.[46]

Global trade was an important dimension of the public discussions surrounding the renewal of the Makah whale hunt. Both animal rights activist Paul Watson and White routinely focused their resistance to Makah whaling on their perception that the Makahs would attempt to sell whale meat to Japan—a charge that the Makah Whaling Commission consistently rejected. Citing this as a matter of international trade law, environmentalists like Watson invoked the sovereignty of the US settler state to intervene in the trade activities of Native nations. As Reid has pointed out, attempts to prevent tribes from developing or maintaining independent trade relationships with other nations was an essential part of the treaty process during the late nineteenth century in what was then Washington Territory. Reid reminds us that after the territorial governor Isaac Stevens was unable to muster strong military power through territorial militias, he "turned to the treaties to encode some method of control."[47]

Both the Treaty of Neah Bay, signed with Makahs, and the Treaty of Point Elliott, signed by representatives from across the Native nations of the Salish Sea region including Duwamish leader Chief Seattle, contained articles that explicitly prevented tribes from trading "at Vancouver's Island or elsewhere out of the dominions of the United States." According to Reid, this was Steven's attempt to "control Indian trade, redirecting it to benefit the US rather than British interests," as well as dislocating important kinship connections between Native nations newly divided by the 49th parallel.[48] In this sense, concerns about transnational trade were of great concern to agents like Stevens during a time when the US was trying to establish itself as a global economic power. Just as it was during the controversy over Makah whaling in 1999, concerns about global trade were central to the operation of the US settler state during the time when the 1856 Battle of Seattle took place.

In certain ways, however, the desire to show Seattle off as a global city, a sentiment grounded in the still oft-repeated representation of it as the most "trade dependent region" in the United States, was shared on both sides. For instance, organizers were showing off the globally minded nature of the city's progressive heart as well. As organizer Michael Dolan put it in 1999, "I was thrilled when Seattle was selected . . . It's almost like they're giving us home-field advantage. There are great labor unions here, great labor energy, all these environmentalists."[49] This sense of Seattle as a progressive, environmentalist city whose disposition linked into broader global sentiments was an essential one that the 1999 protests tapped into.

Rooted in a desire to confront the uniform image of global connection represented by the policies and practices of extranational organizations like the WTO, the IMF, and the World Bank, organizers of the 1999 protests sought to demonstrate an alternative vision of global connectivity that was rooted in justice. Because of this, many activists and organizers still bristle at referring to the series of protests of which 1999 was a part as the "anti globalization" movement, favoring instead terms like "alter- globalization" or "global justice," a point to which I return in my discussion of transnationalism and New Anarchism in chapter 5. This desire to situate Seattle as a locus of global resistance on the cusp of the twenty-first century is not coincidence. Rather, this new cycle of boom-and-bust resulted in what Thrush has described as a "sense of 'urban malaise' experienced by many Seattleites during the 1990s, when the phenomenal wealth and growth of the dot-com boom seemed to threaten the city's identity."[50]

These contexts add necessary texture to the story of the 1999 Battle in Seattle, adding complexity both by clarifying the circumstances of its emergence and by allowing for a critical engagement with its limitations. Considering the relationship between the story of the 1999 Battle in Seattle, the 1856 Battle of Seattle, and the Makah whaling controversy offers a place-based method for looking at the history of radical social movement in the area. What is more, it allows us to trace the structure of New Anarchist movements, and the embeddedness of settlement therein, through the impact of the 1999 protests on more contemporary examples of New Anarchism.

Reckoning with "Occupation"

The structure of settler anarchism evidenced in and maintained through the memorialization of the 1999 Battle in Seattle is apparent on a scale much greater than that of the milieu-focused *Tides of Flame* or the myriad mentions of the event and its legacy in New Anarchist texts. Both the specificity and breadth of these engagements cannot be disconnected from the broader interest in anarchism in North America spurred by the eruption of the Occupy Movement that began with Occupy Wall Street (OWS) in September 2011. In many ways, OWS serves as the emergent node in the genealogy of anarchist politics after 1999. Initially envisioned as a response to financial austerity and big banks, OWS came to represent a public embrace of the possibilities of anarchism as a viable method of political resistance in the twenty-first century.

As Nathan Schneider writes in *Thank You Anarchy: Notes from the Occupy Apocalypse*, even though public figures like Chris Hedges lamented the role that anarchists were playing in the OWS movement, "so many of OWS's most cherished institutions—the general assemblies, the leaderless structure, the diversity of tactics—had roots in anarchism and were being maintained by anarchists who'd been practicing them long before the movement began."[51] Along with Bray and Schneider, activists like Naomi Klein, Rebecca Solnit, and David Graeber have noted the genealogical connection between the 1999 Battle in Seattle and OWS by emphasizing the connection between some of the most definitive strategies and practices of both.[52] This genealogical connection is further solidified by the fact that Klein, Solnit, and Graeber are all relatively prominent activists who participated in and have written about their experiences in both mobilizations.

In this way, the connection between the 1999 Battle in Seattle and OWS is an intrinsic part of the structure of New Anarchism. However, just as the story of the 1999 Battle in Seattle neglects the broader historical context of place, flattens complicated relationships between anarchists and Native activists, and invokes histories of Native resistance to place anarchists in a parallel lineage, so too does the emerging memorialization of OWS. For instance, even though Lenape scholar Joanne Barker published a widely circulated blog post, "Manna-Hata," detailing the history of settlement in what is now Manhattan less than a month after the initial mobilization in Zuccotti Park, there is little sustained engagement in the extant literature on OWS with the question of settler colonialism in what is now New York City. As Barker notes in her post, the name "Wall Street" is derived directly from this history, named after a wall built by the Dutch to prevent Lenape people from attacking the settlement and torn down by the British after they asserted control over the territory in the late seventeenth and early eighteenth centuries.[53]

Thus, though both the name and space of Wall Street represent a literal and figurative structure of exclusion for local Native peoples, this history is not represented in the literature memorializing OWS either as a matter of fact or as a matter of critical reflection for what it meant for participants to occupy this space constructed expressly to dispossess Native peoples from their land.[54] Even Tom Goyens's place-specific exploration of anarchism in New York City from the mid-nineteenth century to OWS offers no reference to the history of the settlement of Manhattan or of Lenape peoples.[55] The absences are especially stark, since the critiques levied by activists like Barker ignited swift yet complicated conversations throughout the country.

For instance, a number of Occupy encampments took up the challenge of reckoning with the history of colonialism and responding to critiques that highlighted the use of the term *Occupy*, which many felt clearly signified a dependence on colonial claims to land by non-Native communities; the rhetoric of the 1% and the 99%, which Ojibwe poet Heid E. Erdrich has pointed out is ironic since Native peoples are the "original 100% who are also 1%, more or less"; and the focus on wealth disparity and redistribution without any critical engagement with the intertwined histories of land expropriation, resource extraction, and chattel slavery from which such wealth was derived.[56] Some of these difficult conversations yielded documents, manifestos, and statements focused on establishing solidarity with Native communities and peoples (ephemera to which I'll return in a moment). However, the complex, dynamic, and oftentimes frustrating conversations that resulted from these exchanges are flattened in texts reflecting on OWS, much as the controversial engagements between Native peoples (both locally and nationally) and environmentalists in Washington State in 1999 are absent from the literature reflecting on the 1999 Battle in Seattle.

Many of the collections that bring together writings from a range of activists, organizers, and intellectuals offer little representation of these complicated conversations and I found none that reproduced statements from local Occupy encampments on solidarity with Native communities that I discuss below. Though there are mentions of the critique of the word "occupy," these discussions tend to note this as a relevant point to mention in passing but rarely as one that figures centrally in the memorialization of OWS itself.[57] Rather, these kinds of discussions about settlement are posed as part of larger discussions about race and the radical left.[58] In addition to conflating discussions of race and indigeneity (a point to which I return more in-depth in the third chapter), this form of engagement doesn't take up the challenges of Native activists and organizers as transformative critiques that can determine new directions of social movement. Instead, it instrumentalizes the experiences of Native peoples both historically and in the contemporary moment to make broader points about wealth disparity.

For instance, in his *Occupy Nation: the Roots, the Promise, and the Spirit of Occupy Wall Street*, Todd Gitlin refers to the initial wave of campers at Zuccotti Park as "pioneers," depending on deeply colonial language to describe their project. Similarly, in his reflection on *Occupy*, noted anarchist linguist Noam Chomsky instrumentalizes Native peoples by invoking them only to make a broader point about corporate personhood.[59] Rebecca Solnit, whose reflections on the 1999 Battle in Seattle are central to the body of work that memorializes it, argues :

> Wall Street is a foreign country—and maybe an enemy country as well. And now it's occupied. The way that Native Americans occupied Alcatraz Island in San Francisco Bay for eighteen months four decades ago and galvanized a national Native American rights movement. You pick someplace to stand, and when you stand there, you find your other occupation, as a member of civil society. At this moment in history, occupation should be everyone's occupation.[60]

In this description, Wall Street is a country that rightfully belongs to the 99%, is occupied unjustly by the 1%, and, in the future, will be returned to its rightful inhabitants through the exercising of one's responsibilities to "civil society," to occupy this "foreign country." As Eve Tuck (Unangax) and K. Wayne Yang have pointed out, occupation, in this context, "is a move to innocence that hides behind . . . the elision of democracy with justice, and the logic that what became property under the 1% rightfully belongs to the other 99%."[61] Not only does Solnit instrumentalize the history of radical Native activism to make her point about OWS, she also positions OWS activists as inheriting the legacy of radicalism carved out by those who occupied Alcatraz. In doing so, she reiterates a claim of settler title to Native land, ignoring the fundamental differences between Native activists reclaiming land from the United States government under the rights ensured by a treaty (as was the case at Alcatraz) and predominantly non-Native activists claiming the right to space through a sense of disenfranchisement at the hands of big banks and other financial institutions who produce profit for a few at the expense of the many. Though the latter is certainly a commendable and necessary cause, its expression in these terms demonstrates not only the continued claim to Native land by non-Native peoples but also the expression of that claim in distinctly anarchist terms.

The evidence of the settler anarchism espoused in writings on OWS extends beyond the language of "occupy" or the invocation of Native resistance by radical writers reflecting on the movement. This rhetoric also reproduces in anarchist terms the methods by which Native peoples have been forcibly excluded from both modernity and postmodernity. In the case of both the 1999 Battle in Seattle and OWS, the failure to engage the history of settlement as an intrinsic part of the development of major urban landscapes, and of Native peoples' historical and contemporary centrality to US urban spaces, demonstrates how anarchists have written Native peoples out of modernity (to use O'Brien's term). As Thrush noted in his study of Native history in Seattle, "when native peoples occupied sites where the forces of urbanization were greatest, they found themselves becoming invisible—not to themselves, of course, but to their new neighbors—in the very places that had always been their homes."[62] And much like the memorialization of the 1999 Battle in Seattle excludes Native peoples from the envisioned future of postmodernity on the cusp of the twenty-first century, this process also can be seen in the ephemera from OWS. However, one notable difference between the memorialization of the 1999 Battle in Seattle and OWS was the dependence on the language and rhetoric of recognition to ameliorate critiques.

Radical Recognition

Though the term *recognition* has varying meanings within the Canadian and US contexts, in both cases it loosely refers to the process through which Native peoples are recognized by the settler state *as* Native peoples.[63] While the processes and structures of achieving recognition differ on either side of the colonial border, in both cases recognition represents the formal process through which Native peoples engage in nation-to-nation relationships with the US and Canadian states, assert both the political and economic rights reserved by Native nations and tribes as formalized through treaties, and access title to traditional and reserve territories. As scholars like Richard J. F. Day and Glen Sean Coulthard (Yellowknives Dene) have shown, casting Native self-determination in terms of recognition is a distinct feature of settler politics in the late twentieth and early twenty-first centuries.[64]

Thus, the rise of recognition as the primary method through which settler states attempted to reckon with the challenges of Native movements for self-determination is intimately tied to the rise of neoliberalism on which mass protest at the end of the twentieth century was centered. Along with Day and Coulthard, Lisa Duggan has shown how the rise of the multicultural state is intimately linked to a desire on the part of the US and Canadian states to manage swelling resistance to neoliberalism while maintaining their material structures. In this way, recognition is a historically specific approach linked to the rise of neoliberal multiculturalism in which logics of inclusion became sutured to the state rather than imagined in opposition to it.[65] Within this framework, recognition allows the structure of the settler state to remain intact while giving the appearance of respecting Native self-determination.

Despite its deep connections to the type of neoliberal policies and structures against which OWS tended to define itself, this is precisely the method of engagement that many Occupy encampments replicated in their statements on solidarity with Native peoples. In the wake of critical conversations about the language of "occupy" and the colonial foundations of economic inequality, Occupy encampments in Austin, Boston, Phoenix, Portland, and Santa Fe all issued statements in solidarity with Native peoples, while others, like Occupy Oakland and Occupy Seattle, created new terms and new working groups that embraced the term *decolonize* either alongside or instead of the term *occupy*. Much as the process of recognition in Canada sought, according to Coulthard, to "'reconcile' Indigenous assertions of nationhood with settler-state sovereignty via the accommodation of Indigenous identity claims in some form of renewed legal and political relationships with the Canadian state," these statements also attempt to reconcile critiques of the functioning of colonialism within the OWS movement via the accommodation of Native identity claims in a renewed relationship with Occupy encampments.[66] In the case of statements I have mentioned here, this often happened in three ways: by employing the language of recognition, by attempting to articulate a parallel relationship of resistance between OWS activists and Native communities, and by extending an invitation for Native communities to join the OWS movement rather than asking how OWS activists could contribute to already-existing Native movements.

Such statements often contained at least two forms of recognition: first, a recognition that Occupy encampments happen on (sometimes former) Native territories and, second, a recognition that colonization is something that must be resisted. For instance, Occupy Portland's statement "recognizes that the land now referred to as the Willamette Valley is already occupied . . . [and] recognizes that the injustice of colonization—whether by militarism, settlerism, statism, or corporatism—is a wrong that must ultimately be righted."[67] Similarly, Occupy Santa Fe's statement begins "by recognizing and affirming that we are all related . . . [and] acknowledging colonization and its harmful impacts, beginning with the genocide of the land-based peoples and the physical occupation of this land by the various European colonial governments and later by the government of the United States of America and the corporatocracy."[68] Occupy Boston's statement notes that "those participating in 'Occupy Boston' acknowledge that the United States of America is a colonial country, and that we are guests upon stolen Indigenous land that has already been occupied for centuries."[69]

These statements further obfuscate issues of settler amenability within OWS by entreating Native peoples to join and transform the movement, rather than considering the very structure of the movement to be at issue. For instance, in the "Declaration of Decolonize/Occupy Seattle" such an invitation follows a recognition that Occupy Seattle occurs "upon stolen indigenous land that has already been occupied for centuries, Seattle being the ancestral land of the Duwamish and Suquamish people":

> we hereby invite indigenous members of the Pacific Northwest . . . to collaborate with us in this event remembering and reawakening to our original identity as humane beings . . . We . . . implore Indigenous Peoples to share their knowledge and wisdom of stewardship of the earth, water, fire and air to inspire and guide us to restore pure democracy rather than representative democracy . . . and to initiate a new era of cooperation and peace that is cross-cultural, intergenerational, inclusive and universal in practical application upon Mother Earth with the original indigenous inhabitants of this land.[70]

This formulation sounds remarkably similar to that described by Coulthard as an essential component of the settler amenability of the politics of recognition: "in situations where colonial rule does not depend solely on the exercise of state violence, its reproduction instead rests on the ability to entice Indigenous peoples to *identify*, either implicitly or explicitly, with the profoundly *asymmetrical* and *nonreciprocal* forms of recognition either imposed on or granted to them by the settler . . . society."[71]

While these statements are the result of diverse and varied groups of people working together to produce collective documents, the resonance between them remains the dependence on the language and structure of recognition. And while this reflects the rise of recognition as the primary method through which the US and Canadian settler states have attempted to reconcile neoliberalism and liberal multiculturalism in the past few decades, as Coulthard has traced at length, it also demonstrates how the project of recognition is expressed in definitively anarchist terms. In these cases, Occupy activists bestow recognition, assert their shared collective radical identity, and thus invite Native peoples to identify with the Occupy movement. In doing so, they assert the resilience of Native peoples only in terms of their participation in the "occupation," much as the settler state paradoxically envisions the resilience of Native peoples only within the context of their identification with the state and its terms of recognition.

This, as a practice of engagement, replicates both the rhetorical and material structures of neoliberal approaches to Native sovereignty that define the era in which New Anarchism developed. And though this approach is markedly different from that evident in the memorialization of the 1999 Battle in Seattle, it represents a transformation of a distinctly anarchist tradition of settlement through the turn of the twenty-first century, rather than a critical engagement with the question of how radical activism becomes embroiled in the project of settler colonialism. In this, we can see both the edification and transformation of a settler anarchist tradition that is definitive of New Anarchism. In the heralding of the 1999 Battle of Seattle as an origin story, and the rise of OWS as part of its life history, New Anarchists have coalesced a settler anarchist project.

Conclusion: A Frontier Metropolis

Two years before the 1999 Battle in Seattle, Tom Robbins, the famed American author of cult classics like *Still Life with Woodpecker* and *Even Cowgirls Get the Blues*, was given the Golden Umbrella Award at Seattle's annual Bumbershoot festival, commemorating his lifetime achievement to the arts. In his acceptance speech, Robbins captures the multivalent mythologies of the city that animate my discussion here. Because his comments illustrate the commensurability of the seemingly discordant relationship between settlement and radicalism that forms the impetus to this chapter, I reproduce his reflection at some length:

> In Seattle, I soon found that my radical ideas and aesthetic explorations—ideas and explorations that in Richmond, Virginia, might have gotten me stoned to death . . . were not only accepted

> but occasionally applauded. In retrospect, that shouldn't be so astonishing, for the most fleeting overview of neurogeography reveals that for four or five thousand years, there has been a pattern of migratory movement of consciousness from east to west. The smartest people, the strongest, bravest, most adventurous, creative, open-minded, and advanced have pressed ever westward . . . and, now . . . Seattle represent[s] the end of terrestrial migration. Fulfilling its evolutionary destiny, our Emerald City has been populated by a significant number of migrants, mavericks, and mutants: seed people, future people, people on the edge of thought, the edge of discovery, the edge of tomorrow. To some extent, Seattle remains a frontier metropolis.[72]

Here, Robbins frames Seattle as the terminus of a naturalized westward migration, using the invocation of Seattle as a "frontier metropolis" to suture together the territorial expansion that is the foundation of US settler colonialism and a narrative of artistic and intellectual progress. What is more, he naturalizes this expansion through the concept of "evolutionary destiny," claiming "our" Emerald City as a place where his radicalism is valorized rather than condemned. Invoking without much subtlety both the language and rhetoric of manifest destiny, Robbins presents Seattle as a place that is at once a bustling metropolis and a lawless frontier town, bringing together narratives of American perseverance and ruggedness with a lauding of the prodigious ingenuity to which urbanization supposedly points.

I initially became interested in exploring the phenomenon of settler anarchism through the memorialization of the 1999 Battle in Seattle in the New Anarchist literature because of how often I encountered it being invoked as a generative moment. However, I *remained* interested in it because of what I initially found to be a peculiar line of illogic: why was there no reflection in these retellings on the intertwined histories of settlement and neoliberalism in Seattle? Wouldn't this argument inherently bolster an anarchist critique of the United States' role in furthering global neoliberalism, since it would locate neoliberalism not in the *actions* of the US state but in its very *structure*? The fact that anarchists writing today have not seized on the opportunity to draw connections between neoliberalism and the history of settlement in the US signaled to me that something else must be at work.

Throughout this chapter, I have argued that anarchists have avoided integrating a specific and place-based critique of settlement and its relationship to neoliberalism not because it isn't useful (it would be) but because the anarchist investment in settlement is more important. We can see the importance of this investment when we extend our scope to Occupy Wall Street, where we see anarchists cashing in on that investment through a claim to space on behalf of the anarchist-identified movement. Therefore, the lack of critical engagement with the history of settlement in the retelling of the 1999 Battle in Seattle as a generative event for New Anarchism lays the foundation for rallying cries like the mantra that appeared on materials consolidating the movement under the name "Occupy Together." Numerous posters distributed and plastered around US cities read:

> This is our country
> We will occupy it
> These are our streets
> We will occupy them
> We are here
> We are growing
> We are the 99%[73]

Here, we can see the extension of Robbins's vision of Seattle as a frontier metropolis in which radical ideas are part of the natural landscape. In the story of New Anarchism, its birth in 1999 and its maturation in 2011, we see the vestiges of settlement expressed in a distinctly anarchist form, rather than inherited and then replicated in an anarchist space.

In an interview with Kwakwaka'wakw artist and anarchist activist Gord Hill, the Crimethinc Collective asks, "How do you think non-indigenous anarchists can be informed by and supportive of Native struggles?" Hill's response is deceptively simple but is at the core of the way forward for addressing the structure of settler anarchism: "By knowing the history of European colonialism and incorporating this into their analysis and action."[74] In terms of the collective memorialization of the 1999 Battle in Seattle, this requires telling that story alongside and through the histories of settlement on which those structures were built both literally and rhetorically. Here, I've attempted to bring to the fore some of those covalent histories, sewing them together so that we can see them as one fabric while maintaining a focus on the seams that evidence a more complicated history.

How we tell and retell stories matters, the structures we use and the contours we choose to emphasize. Some of the most prolific writing on the 1999 Battle in Seattle centers on this recognition: reflecting on the ongoing struggle against simplistic, erroneous, and damaging depictions in the mainstream media, David Solnit asks, "Who has the power and resources to define our history and thus shape what people think?"[75] The question I've tried to emphasize here, however, is not only how our stories are told outside our movements, but how they continue to be told within them. In these spaces, *we* have the power and resources to define our history and to shape how we think. And this power is significant, shaping the way past movements are understood as predecessors of contemporary struggles.

In this chapter, I've taken up this question as it relates to New Anarchism. I've traced how the invocation of the 1999 Battle in Seattle as an origin story has enabled a settler amenability that extends into the Occupy era, revealing the structure of settlement as a constitutive part of New Anarchism itself. Returning to Goeman's understanding of place that I mentioned at the outset, we can use this attentiveness to the shape of stories to also rethink our relationship to place, since it requires that we understand stories as constitutive of place and vice versa. As Goeman argues, "seeing land as storied . . . rather than as a confined place within rigid boundaries will remind us of the responsibility to each other."[76]

In the next chapter, I turn to Cowlitz writer Elissa Washuta's memoir *My Body Is a Book of Rules* and Ohlone-Costanoan Esselen and Chumash writer Deborah Miranda's *Bad Indians: A Tribal Memoir* to explore how these writers have sought to see land as storied, demonstrating methods of memorialization and commemoration that do not depend on uprooting stories from their material contexts nor on limiting stories to rigidly imposed, static boundaries. Comparing two contemporary texts that creatively engage nonfiction forms, I emphasize how such experimentation acts as a method that can reckon with multiple, sometimes conflicting histories without either reifying or ignoring the complex structures through which such stories are formed and from which such stories give form.

CHAPTER 2

"Tell Me Where to Go and I Will"

Memorialization and Commemoration in Two Native Women's Memoirs

Indigenous peoples understand that there is no difference between the telling and the material. They understand how we all, in fact, live inside and through the narratives we tell and that the importance in telling stories is inseparable from the identity, community, and history they compose and the spiritual, economic, and political realities on which they depend and which they subvert or preserve.

—Teresia Teaiwa and Joanne Barker, "Native InFormation"

The task of memorialization and commemoration is a complicated one for building futures that contain within them the complexities of historical memory—what Mishuana Goeman has called "rememorative futures."[1] Realizing this challenge in a responsible way is at the core of the previous chapter's undertaking. There, I argued for the necessity of paying attention to the shape of stories, not only in the sense of formalist literary analysis but also in the sense of the shapes that stories give to us. Many writers, from Leslie Marmon Silko to Thomas King, have famously noted the centrality of stories and storytelling to Native sovereignty and self-determination. As Crow Creek Sioux writer Elizabeth Cook-Lynn has observed, "literature and storytelling are at the epicenter of all that . . . a nation intends to be."[2] What is more, as Teresia Teaiwa (I-Kirabati and African American) and Joanne Barker (Lenape) make clear in the epigraph above, storytelling is never separate from the form that storytelling takes—in their terminology, there can be no distinction between the "telling" and the "material."

In this chapter, I explore how two contemporary memoirs by Native women authors can help us understand how the connections between the telling and the material of New Anarchist stories work to fortify the structure of settlement within contemporary anarchist movements. By focusing on two memoirs that center experimentation with form, I aim to invoke the double meaning of "Native in/formation" of which Teaiwa and Barker speak in the article from which the epigraph comes. There, Teaiwa and Barker argue for a dynamic understanding of indigeneity (the Native "in formation") that confronts the ethnographic desire for information that situates the Native writer as the anthropologist's informant (Native "information").[3] Thus, I hope to highlight the authors' methods that demonstrate how we can reimagine the story of the 1999 Battle in Seattle in a way that reckons with the structure of settlement within New Anarchism while also recognizing the other worlds incumbent in its telling and its material.

My contention remains that we must recognize the generative power of stories like the 1999 Battle in Seattle, acknowledging that such stories do not merely reflect a static moment in history but rather give shape to the dynamic forms of intimate social, political, and intellectual relations that we seek to enact through its invocation. Whether we seek to maintain a longstanding, venerated structure or to instill a new method of telling into a familiar story, we must do so with the knowledge that the form we give to stories reciprocates the forms that stories give to us. In the shape of the story of the 1999 Battle in Seattle, I located the authoritative command of settler anarchism in New Anarchist movements. The focus on that particular story and its parlance throughout the next decade or so helped to illuminate how the structure of settler anarchism depends deeply on the reiteration of particular narratives through memorialization, or the preservation of memory, and commemoration, or the (usually public) recollection and honoring of that memory. In the case of New Anarchist movements, this has meant the preservation of a memory of the 1999 Battle in Seattle that severs it from the history of settlement in the Pacific Northwest and, thus, of the history of settlement from the rise of neoliberalism, and a commemorative practice that depends on constant reiteration of the story as a generative event. Or, in a sense both more sardonic and more ironic, as an origin story.

At issue, then, is how to develop a method that more thoughtfully engages the practice of storytelling through a lens attentive to such shapes—both the shapes of stories and the shapes that such stories give to us. How do we memorialize the history of radical social movements, provide evidence that these are genealogical struggles that emanate from longstanding physical, emotional, intellectual, and interpersonal labors rather than sporadic uprisings that respond only to proximate provocations? How do we commemorate successful organizing strategies and tactics, not just to provide moments of hope, but to reformulate the structures of relation and knowledge that are at the heart of settler structures? And, how do we do so in ways that reckon with the multiple histories imbricated therein, including the histories that live with the land and its people? These questions about the possibilities and practices of memory and the multiple ceremonies through which it is maintained are central to the field of Native and Indigenous Studies more broadly and to Native and Indigenous literatures more specifically, as authors work to solidify traditional methods of storytelling and the concomitant stories without marking such practices and their practitioners as static subjects of an ahistorical past.[4]

In this chapter, I explore two contemporary memoirs to bring forward some of the ways that Native authors are playing with form in creative nonfiction to provide alternative methods of memorialization and commemoration. Looking to Ohlone-Costanoan Esselen and Chumash writer Deborah Miranda's *Bad Indians: A Tribal Memoir* (2013) and Cowlitz writer Elissa Washuta's *My Body Is a Book of Rules* (2014), I explore how these authors are experimenting with form in creative nonfiction to exemplify methods of memorialization and commemoration that are able to reckon with multiple, conflicting histories without either reifying or ignoring the complex structures through which such stories are formed and to which such stories give form.

Building off my work in the previous chapter on the central constructions through which settler anarchism is expressed, I demonstrate how Miranda's and Washuta's methodological interventions can help to demonstrate the relationship between the telling of certain anarchist stories and the material of anarchist investment in settlement. As a reminder, I argued that the structure of settler anarchism is observable in three distinct ways: the invocation of anarchist stories without a grounding in both place-based and historical context, the flattening of rather than reckoning with histories of conflict between Native and non-Native communities, and the attempt to assert inherent parallel relationships between anarchist movements and Native sovereignty. In what follows, I explore the grounded approaches to memorialization in Miranda's and Washuta's genealogical methodologies; to commemoration through their appropriation of form; and to transformative methods of temporal and spatial navigation in their approaches to text, land, and movement. I begin by discussing briefly why Native women's memoir is a particularly apt site for examining some of these questions.

Why Memoir?

Memoir is an important though often overlooked part of the history of Native women's writing. Reflecting what Osage scholar Robert Warrior and Lisa Brooks have identified as the overarching trend of delimiting nonfiction work from the field of Native literatures, scholarly engagement with nonfiction work by Native women authors has been nominal. In this, I hope to take seriously Warrior's and Brooks's call to include nonfiction writing as an imperative part of Native literary history should we hope to understand its full scope and impact.[5] Most engagement with Native women's memoir has been focused on the work of Native writers who lived in the nineteenth and early twentieth centuries. Texts like Northern Paiute writer Sarah Winnemuca's *Life Among the Piutes* (1883), Yankton Dakota writer Zitkála-Šá's *American Indian Stories* (1921), and Okanogan writer Mourning Dove's *Mourning Dove: A Salishan Autobiography* (published posthumously in 1990) are considered foundational to the field of Native literatures itself alongside contemporaneous nonfiction texts like Pequot writer William Apess's *A Son of the Forest* (1829). And though the focus on nonfiction as a pivotal genre has dwindled in the scholarship on contemporary Native authors (as Warrior notes), the prevalence of memoir among contemporary Native women writers is notable. In fact, many of the most prominent contemporary Native women writers have written memoirs, including Janet Campbell Hale (Coeur D'Alene/Kootenai/Cree), Louise Erdrich (Ojibwe), Joy Harjo (Muscogee), Linda Hogan (Chickasaw), LeAnne Howe (Choctaw), Lee Maracle (Sto:lo Coast Salish), and Leslie Marmon Silko (Laguna Pueblo).[6] Taken together with work by writers like Ernestine Hayes (Tlingit) and Mary Brave Bird (Sincagu Lakota), who either work or worked primarily in memoir form, there is a significant body of work in the genre whose depth is simply not adequately reflected in the scholarship on Native literatures.[7]

The scholarship on such writing by Native authors has often focused on the genre of "autobiography."[8] Within this, the focus has usually been on exploring the assumed conflict between the form of autobiography, as a self-storied life narrative, and "traditional" Native storytelling practices. For instance, scholars like Arnold Krupat and Brian Swann have explored the challenges of the "as-told-to" model of many Native autobiographies, noting the complications of depending on a non-Native interlocutor to shape the story and its presentation, while others such as Warren Cariou (Métis) have commented on the relationship between oral storytelling and autobiography.[9] These discussions have raised important inquiries about power and self-storying, grounded in the acknowledgment that the power to shape stories is indelibly tied to the power to shape the work those stories do in the world. Little has been written, however, that places self-storying texts of Native nonfiction in conversation with broader explorations of literary nonfiction that have become so prevalent in the past twenty years or so.[10]

Dian Million's exploration of Native women's first-person narratives in *Therapeutic Nations* remains an unparalleled study of Native women's self-storying as political acts that transformed not only the rhetorical but the material bases on which discussions about First Nations communities took place in Canada in the late twentieth and early twenty-first centuries.[11] For her, this form is the epistemological basis of what she terms "felt theory," or an understanding of "felt experience as community knowledge, knowledge that interactively informs our positions as Indigenous scholars, particularly as Indigenous women scholars."[12] In what follows, I seek to delve more deeply into the space between Million's analysis of the centrality of Native women's first-person narratives and the profound interest in form that animates the field of creative nonfiction.

This interest is present throughout the history of Native women's memoir and echoes the way that Silko explored the relationship between literary form and storytelling in her 1989 collection *Storyteller*, which serves as an important genealogical precursor to the two memoirs I explore in this chapter. In the introduction, Silko observes that "if you think about it, nearly everything of consequence that we tell one another involves narration or story."[13] She ties this to the project of collective memorialization within Pueblo communities, noting that "the entire culture, all the knowledge, experience, and beliefs, were kept in the human memory of the Pueblo people in the form of narratives that were told and retold from generation to generation. The people perceived themselves in the world as part of an ancient continuous story composed of innumerable bundles of other stories."[14] Here, Silko emphasizes the genealogical dimensions of storytelling as a method of memorialization and connects that to nonfiction writing as literary genre: "For the Pueblo people, a collective truth resides somewhere within the web of differing versions, disputes over minor points, outright contradictions tangled with old feuds, and village rivalries" that come out in the telling of the story. Because of this, "the ongoing story or history of the Pueblo people continues endlessly," maintaining the ties between narrative form, collective memorialization, and place since "often it is impossible to determine which came first; the incident or the geographical feature that stirs the imagination."[15]

Silko's exploration of nonfiction writing within the context of literary form is an important node in the genealogy of Native women's memoir work that I want to center on here. In what follows, I extend Silko's discussion of the relationship between form, memorialization, and land into a discussion of Miranda's and Washuta's memoirs, which build on genealogies of Native women's memoir while even more explicitly playing with the formal possibilities of the genre. I begin my analysis with a focus on these two elements, providing both the foundation of the literary readings that I perform throughout the rest of the chapter while also making clear why I have chosen these two memoirs in particular as apt texts to which we can turn to rethink the approaches to memorialization and commemoration that I discussed in the previous chapter.

Genealogy in Native Women's Self-Storying

Centering the practice of genealogy in Native women's memoirs is essential for two reasons: first, it helps to engage Miranda's and Washuta's memoirs through Silko's work on stories and memorialization without denying the specificity of her grounding in Pueblo cosmologies and communities. And, second, because this is a primary formal method in both memoirs themselves. In the first case, Miranda and Washuta both invoke connections to earlier memoir work by Native authors. Miranda begins *Bad Indians* with the inscription, "For my mother and father, / who survived each other / 'I am the result of the love of thousands.'" The final line of the inscription invokes the final line of Hogan's 1995 memoir *Dwellings: A Spiritual History of the Living World*, which reads: "Suddenly, all my ancestors are behind me. Be still, they say. Watch and listen. You are the result of the love of thousands."[16]

Similarly, Washuta begins the first installment of her book's structuring series "A Cascade Autobiography" with an epigraph from Mourning

Dove's *Mourning Dove: A Salishan Autobiography*: "A girl who guarded her chastity was considered valuable in the eyes of our warriors. A man would willingly give many ponies and robes to her parents for such a wife."[17] At the outset, then, both Miranda and Washuta make clear the literary genealogies from which their works arise not only to signify their texts as part of a tradition of Native women's writing but also to center questions of genealogy as part of the formal foundation of the text itself. Both *Bad Indians* and *My Body Is a Book of Rules* use innovative approaches to and appropriations of form to emphasize how narrative form is related to the structure of settlement. Below, I discuss these approaches to and appropriations of form more in-depth. Here, I am first interested in how both Miranda and Washuta use this early invocation of genealogy to give structure to their texts through distinct formal elements.

According to Miranda, *Bad Indians: A Tribal Memoir* is a "belated offering" to the "Mission Unit, a part of the California public school curriculum that encourages parents and students to do a project that focuses on one of the twenty-one missions that line California's coast. Reflecting on how such projects serve to memorialize a sanitized imperial past, Miranda offers her project as a "space where voices can speak after long and often violently imposed silence."[18] For her, this is a project about both contemporary education and historical genealogies, bringing together a tribal history of the missionization of California that confronts the colonial one and a critical exploration of the processes of public memorialization and commemoration that enforce settlement through inherited colonial epistemologies.

Though the table of contents gives the appearance of a chronological text that begins with "The End of the World: Missionization, 1776–1836" and ends with "Teheyapami Achiska: Home, 1961–present," the temporal and spatial movement throughout the memoir question the structuring of a self-storying text through a linear progression. The first section of "The End of the World" illustrates for readers the clever methods that Miranda uses throughout the text of using formal familial structures to destabilize popular narratives of Native life. Titled "The Genealogy of Violence, Part I," this single page is laid out as a genealogy chart with "Spain" and "Catholic Church" occupying the generative parent positions. As Miranda follows the genealogy down through the generations, "Franciscans" and "Missionization/Land Theft" beget "Paternalism," "Slavery," "Mexican Invasion," and "Secularization/Abandonment," while "[Spanish] Soldiers" and "Rape" beget "Murder,"

"Flogging, Stocks, Manacles," "Syphilis," and "Measles/Small Pox." As the chart moves toward its broadest point, the two genealogical lines come together to beget sixteen descendants of Spain and the Catholic Church, including "Incarceration/Prison," "Domestic Violence," "United States Invasion," "Gold Rush/Environmental Rape," "Poverty," and "Homelessness." This genealogy of violence carries through to the end of the section, bookended with "Genealogy of Violence, Part II."

In this section, Miranda returns to the theme of inheritance by juxtaposing a memory of her father's physical abuse of her brother with blurbs taken from some of the twenty-one missions in California that describe the love that Native peoples have for their children.[19] Physically interspersing these quotations throughout her recollection of this violent incident, Miranda interrupts her memory with a more distant past. For instance, toward the end of the section, she writes of her father's use of physical violence:

> I know too well, the arc of leather, sharp edges of cured hide, instrument of punishment coming from two hundred years out of the past in a movement so ancient, so much a part of our family history that it has touched every single one of us in an unbroken chain from the first padre or the first *soldado* at the mission to the bared back of the first Indian neophyte, heathen, pagan, savage, who displeased or offended the Spanish Crown's representatives.[20]

Directly after this, she recounts a description from the Mission San Antonio: "They likewise love their children; in fact, it can be said that this love is so excessive that it is a vice, for the majority lack the courage to punish their children's wrongdoings and knavery."[21]

Though these two elements are placed together in the same physical space of the page, Miranda also uses formal play to distinguish the space between them. The quotations from the interpretative Mission narrations are bounded at the top and bottom by lines that cross the entire page and the font of that writing is slightly larger. The result is a memorialization of a genealogical history of violence, one that invokes and complicates the genealogical chart provided in this first part of the series. Miranda recognizes her father's acts of violence as "a part of our inheritance, our legacy" while also emphasizing that this means that it is "as much a part of . . . our culture as any bowl of acorn mush, any wild salmon fillet, *pilillis* fried and dipped in cinnamon and sugar, cactus fruit in a basket."[22] Her interspersing of language from the missions throughout her narrative of her own memory signifies the shared space of the two, rather than relying solely on a linear genealogical model. In this way, Miranda uses a genealogical form to critically engage with the memorialization of the California missions in public and in her own life. By offering a "tribal memoir" that interweaves the structures of colonial genealogies of violence, familial genealogy, and genealogies of memoir writing by Native women, Miranda expresses a dynamic approach to tribal history and self-narrativization that is able to begin answering her question: "Those who will not change do not survive; but who are we, when we have survived?"[23]

In *My Body Is a Book of Rules*, Washuta also uses a genealogical form to structure her book. Throughout the text are sixteen parts of what she titles "A Cascade Autobiography," the result of a single essay serialized to act as a thread suturing together the myriad forms with which Washuta works. Whereas Miranda's table of contents is laid out in an overt chronological structure, the parts of "A Cascade Autobiography" do not appear in Washuta's table of contents, formalizing them as an innate part of the skeletal structure of the text rather than individual pieces of its compound whole. Much like Miranda's "Genealogy of Violence," Washuta begins her memoir with the explicit engagement with historical documents that talk about her ancestors—in this case, the Cascade Indians from whom she, as a Cowlitz woman, is descended. After the epigraph invoking Mourning Dove, Washuta offers a long quotation from a letter written by Lawrence W. Coe (a member of a prominent family of Oregon pioneers) that describes the 1856 hanging of multiple Cascade leaders, including Washuta's great-great-great-grandfather Tumalth. Completing the first installment of "A Cascade Autobiography," the first words written by Washuta read, "Tumalth begat Mary who begat Abbie who begat Kathleen who begat Leslie who begat Elissa."[24] Here, she joins Miranda in placing her own birth within the context of a complex genealogy, one that cannot be described only through a lineage drawn through her ancestors but also must reckon with the legacy of settlement. In this way, it is not only Tumalth's *line* that begets Washuta but also his murder.

Throughout the memoir, the "A Cascade Autobiography" series serves as the anchor or the central node through which the other formal essays are routed. In the series, Washuta explores the complex methods of identification with indigeneity that are made ostensibly legible within a settler society. These early installments of "Cascade

Autobiography" focus on Washuta's experience as a child, illuminating the interplay between Washuta's own understanding of indigeneity and those given to her during her schooling on the East Coast, thousands of miles from her peoples' traditional territories. For instance, in the fourth installment, Washuta describes her experience in kindergarten, when the "teacher split the class into Pilgrims and Indians with construction paper costumes to teach us about our national heritage."[25] In quick succession, Washuta marks the years of her early life with other strange encounters with indigeneity as a conceptual, familial, and personal construction:

> When I was six, my dad taught me how to spell "Cowlitz," and I wrote it at the bottom of my drawings. When I was seven, I became obsessed with mermaids, certain that I could fuse my legs into a fin if I pressed them together firmly enough under my modest sub-desk plaid. At eight, I created dioramas of buildings where other Native people's ancestors slept, and though the teacher told me this was my heritage, I was not certain that I believed in cacti or mesas, having never seen them.[26]

Throughout the text, "A Cascade Autobiography" functions through these same core questions, allowing Washuta to trace the genealogy not only of her own experience but also the genealogy of settlement. As in Miranda's "Genealogy of Violence" series, these two genealogies cannot remain separate.

In this way, Washuta offers her structuring "autobiography" as a narrative of relational navigation, an exploration of the unstable edifice of indigeneity in her interactions with teachers, Native and non-Native peers, parents, ancestors, and herself. As Miranda does in *Bad Indians*, Washuta uses "A Cascade Autobiography" to refuse the temporal bounding of her own life as the foundation for personal memoir. By serializing the essay, rather than presenting it in full at the beginning, Washuta creates a genealogical form throughout the text, establishing nonlinear narratives of inheritance and bequest within an approach that recognizes descent and ancestry. In this sense, "A Cascade Autobiography" is an autobiography tied to place, to history, to ancestors, and to time. Washuta reimagines Native autobiography as an expansive genre, one that both eschews an individualist model and circumvents issues previously associated with the genre, especially the seemingly vexing dependence on non-Native interlocutors. Rather than articulate her written self as the authoritative voice of a definitive Native experience (devoid of the influence of tainted interlocutors), Washuta invites into the practice of self-storying a constant stream of interlocutors—perhaps most especially herself.

Neither Washuta nor Miranda is interested in an assumed purity of Native women's stories or, concomitantly, of Native people. Both refuse to narrate a pure indigeneity as a defense of themselves, their histories, their people, and their land against the multiple violences of settlement. However, neither do they merely accept settlement as a lamentable history to which they must acquiesce as part of their contemporary condition. Rather, *Bad Indians* and *My Body is a Book of Rules* use genealogical approaches to self-storying to imagine what a practice of memorialization can look like when it seeks to hold in one space multiple, conflicting histories whose synchronism refuses absolution, either personal or collective. In fact, this rejection of the assumed division between the individual and the collective is central to the employ of such a genealogical method in the first place.

In their discussion on Indigenous biography, Muscogee scholar K. Tsianina Lomawaima and Kanaka Maoli scholar David A. Chang describe this rejection in terms of relativity or an approach to life writing that centers on relationships rather than on individuals.[27] The terms that each author uses to describe their written form speaks to their structural methodology: for Washuta, this is "A Cascade Autobiography" and, for Miranda, this is a "tribal memoir"—neither is a singular self-storying but rather begins with a tribal or national history. Beyond indicating their appropriation of form in memoir work (to which I will turn next), this intervention provides an important methodology for thinking about the practice of memorialization.

In terms of the story of the 1999 Battle in Seattle, this methodology provides a structure to narrate the history of the uprising through a contention with the multiple histories of the place to which it is indelibly tied. Through Miranda's complex understanding of "culture," as a dynamic relationship defined by a constant movement forward and backward, we can better heed her warning that "culture is ultimately lost when we stop the telling the stories of who we are, where we have been, how we arrived here, what we once knew, what we wish we knew."[28] In order to sustain the task of maintaining collective memory that is accountable to the multiple histories through which is constituted, storytellers of the 1999 Battle in Seattle can honor the method developed by Miranda and Washuta by committing to a place-based accounting of the protests and their legacy. While this can make use of genealogy as a structure, it cannot depend on erasing complicated histories of interaction in favor of asserting only a parallel history of resistance. As Miranda's serialization of "A Genealogy of Violence" and Washuta's of "A Cascade Autobiography" demonstrate, such an approach provides a foundational inroad that is strong enough to hold multiple, sometimes seemingly contradictory histories simultaneously. The 1999 Battle in Seattle is part of a long genealogy of resistance in what is now Seattle. But this genealogy must bring to the fore the reality that those for whom it is an important generative event also participate in the structure of settlement. Both things, along with other worlds, are not only possible but are already here. Reckoning with this, rather than attempting to resolve it through either absolution or erasure, is essential to denying its replication in contemporary spaces.

Appropriating Form

Though Miranda and Washuta use epigraphs to place their works within larger genealogies of memoir writing by Native women, *Bad Indians* and *My Body Is a Book of Rules* also represent an important rupture in that genealogy. As memoirs, both Miranda and Washuta's texts focus on form not only as a structural element but as the primary mode of entry into the methodological work they pursue. In this sense, they extend the genealogy of works like Silko's *Storyteller*, which combines a variety of genres and forms, while more explicitly bringing such work into conversation with contemporary innovations in the field of creative nonfiction. As texts that are explicitly form-conscious, *Bad Indians* and *My Body Is a Book of Rules* explore the work that form does in terms not only of literary structure but also of social and political structure. This focus moves beyond a strict formalist approach that is concerned primarily with the function of form in the text. Instead, this method invokes an understanding of form more akin to that described by Caroline Levine, who suggests that while form is often understood in terms of either genre or aesthetics, it can also "be cast as historical, emerging out of particular cultural and political circumstances."[29] Reading form this way, she argues, works to expand "our usual definition of form in literary studies to include patterns of sociopolitical experience" and, in doing so, breaks down the assumed gap between formalist and historicist methods of literary analysis.

While Levine is primarily concerned with using this approach to analyze fiction, it also resonates with writing on form in the field of creative nonfiction. Concern with form has been central to the development of creative nonfiction as a distinct literary practice, especially clear in the explosion of interest in the lyric essay. Form, for foundational creative nonfiction writers Brenda Miller and Suzanne Paola, represents the practice of "placing your allegiance to artifact over experience" and is what distinguishes the art of creative nonfiction from "the intractable stuff of memory."[30] As Levine notes, though this focus on form is "precisely that which distinguished art objects from ordinary life," we must also recognize "how both aesthetic and social forms acted in the world, and how they interacted and overlapped with each other."[31] In what follows, I explore how Miranda and Washuta appropriate common forms of storytelling, especially those linked to formal education, to show how the social and political form of settler colonialism are commemorated and to ultimately resist those forms of commemoration.

Exploring how these two authors use literary form to interrogate and transform sociopolitical forms has important implications beyond the study of contemporary Native women's literatures. In fact, there has been some scholarly interest in the relationship between form and Native nonfiction, primarily in work on autobiography. In addition to some of the work I've mentioned already regarding the complexities of the as-told-to model of Native autobiography and the relationship between first-person narrative genre and orality, Crystal Kurzen has explored some of the formal dynamics of Native women's autobiography, tying form directly to activist intervention: speaking of works by Silko, Winnemucca, Bonnin, and Ki'che' activist Rígoberta Menchú, she argues that, "although their modes of telling are based primarily in practices of reconceptualizing conventional genre characteristics, these writers do not simply 'modify' or 'adapt' existing self-referential forms; rather, they make and remake an entire corpus of related genres . . . to carve out spaces of activism while offering a formal model of social change to other Native peoples."[32] I agree with Kurzen regarding the relationship between the invocation of literary form and the instantiation of new models of social change. However, my approach diverges from hers in my thinking on for whom the embedded methodologies might be useful. While Kurzen suggests that theses "formal models of social change" might be particularly useful to "other Native peoples," I see them as models whose protocols might also be honored by non-Native activists and organizers.

In both *Bad Indians* and *My Body Is a Book of Rules*, Miranda and Washuta critically engage the premise of the "allegiance to artifact" by employing form as a method through which to engage the relationship between artifact and knowledge. Both make use of popular educational forms, such as school projects, research papers, and annotated bibliographies, to not only assert alternative epistemologies and histories but also to also explore how colonial epistemologies and histories are commemorated through education. In the most general sense, this form of appropriation works against that of the settler state through a simultaneous reading and rejection of colonial forms. As Washuta and I have argued elsewhere, this act of appropriating form must be understood as a political gesture, since claiming an interior life on the page is an act of resistance for communities whose stories have been structured through an authority that has supposedly been yielded to the agent of literary expertise, whether literal or figurative. Rather, "to write form-conscious nonfiction is to undermine the idea of Native nonfiction as historic preservation by refusing to foreground the 'facts' of Native existence that have long been plundered and instead assert that which can never be stolen."[33]

One of the primary ways that Miranda and Washuta bring an epistemology to the page is through their appropriation of common educational forms. For both, the space of the classroom remains an important site of interrogation when considering the commemoration of colonialism as a process of settlement. As Washuta observes early on in *My Body Is a Book of Rules*, "my parents had explained to me that I was Indian, and the classroom taught me what that meant."[34] Throughout, Washuta uses the appropriation of form to explore the structural cohesion of epistemological contentions about indigeneity in spaces of formal education, particularly in the university. For instance, in "Preliminary Bibliography," she offers an annotated bibliography that follows a chronology of self-conception. Beginning with entries like "Various Picture Books About Mermaids," "Juvenile Nonfiction About Sharks," and "Juvenile Nonfiction About Shipwrecks," the essay moves through Washuta's formal and self-education, using texts as flashpoints through which to amplify significant moments not only of self-realization but also of engagement with the epistemological channels available in formal education in the United States.

For instance, Washuta writes entries for many canonical works of literature like Richard Wright's *Native Son*, Silko's *Ceremony*, Mark Z. Danielewski's *House of Leaves*, F. Scott Fitzgerald's *The Great Gatsby*,

William Faulkner's *Absalom, Absalom!*, Shakespeare's *King Lear*, Philip Roth's *American Pastoral*, Charles Dickens' *Hard Times*, and Joan Didion's *Run River*. Both working with and pushing against the common purpose of an annotated bibliography, Washuta's annotations speak to the relevance and quality of the texts to give a more cohesive image of the broader project at hand. However, these annotations also work to explore one's personal history of literary development as a form of epistemological excavation. In one of her first comprehensive entries on Francesca Lia Block's *I Was a Teenage Fairy* (1998), she locates definitive epistemological approaches:

> I wanted to be one of the most beautiful, underweight, tragic girls in a Block novel. I read Block's books after my bipolar mood canyons were carved, but before I fell all the way into them, hit by jagged rocks on the way down. After leaving home, after I grew to legal maturity, I became what I always wanted to be: starved, mentally ill, tortured from the outside in and the inside out, city-dwelling, fast-driving. I never regretted asking for this. Reading this book again, after the rape, the diagnosis, the drugs, the other assault, I understood that this book glimmers not because of a delightful magic; it is more like psychosis.[35]

These annotations mark a reflection on an epistemological trajectory: they reframe epistemology on the page not only by bringing the author's experience into a literary form but also by exploring the material connections between form, knowledge, page, and body through the forms of education.

In such a constellation, Wright's *Native Son*, which Washuta notes led to a forever-association with much older men and "dismembered bodies," sits alongside books like *The Okinawa Diet Plan: Get Leaner, Live Longer, and Never Feel Hungry*, which center how she understands the relationship between intellectual development and the body: "All books change me, but diet and self-help books try to force the change to show."[36] As part of *My Body Is a Book of Rules*, the annotated bibliography does the same. It seeks to show the epistemological change of engaging with canonical literature, to explore how the classroom teaches Washuta "what it means to be Indian," among other things and people. When Washuta writes of Silko's seminal novel *Ceremony*, which she read in an anthropology class on North American Indians, she describes not only her lack of connection to the text but also the sense of unindigeneity that comes along with that disconnect: "I read the first forty pages twice, and then caved and downloaded CliffsNotes. I felt like a bad Indian—this book was part of my canon."[37] Echoing the title of Miranda's own memoir, Washuta's sense of being a "bad Indian" comes not (only) from an implicit critique of the centrality of white voices to the canon but also from her sense that Silko's story of a Laguna Pueblo veteran of World War II who comes home to his reservation in the Southwest during a drought is supposed to teach her something about being Indian in the first place. Here, she emphasizes the way that Native women's literature is often read in the context of the canon of English literature: as singular text, as broadly applicable to a general "Native American" experience, and as an ethnographic voyage into the heart of indigeneity.

The form of the personal annotated bibliography is what anchors this critique in a critical study of literature and commemoration. It works out the critique from within, exploring not just the content of canonical power but its structure. As a form, the annotated bibliography acts both as an exploration of expectation and a study in the commemoration of the canon. Rather than offering a direct critique of the whiteness and maleness of the English canon of literature, Washuta's annotated bibliography instead explores what we might understand as the "skeleton architecture," to use Audre Lorde's term, of the work that canons do in the world.[38] In this, it confirms the work that canons do in shaping both epistemology and subject formation. As Roderick Ferguson has argued, "epistemology is an economy of information privileged and information excluded" and, as such, is an economy that gives rise to particular formations of racial and national subjects."[39] Such economies are built, according to him, through the development of canons, which become an educational method par excellence alongside narratives of American "progress and perfectibility."[40] As such, canons like those that Washuta both explores and infects work to commemorate subject formations to normalize them. By reappropriating this form, choosing to annotate both canonical and personally meaningful texts in a chronological study of her own epistemological stance, Washuta illuminates the structure of the canon and its purpose through a demonstration of how the structure of the canon works. Her writing of the annotated bibliography becomes a ceremony remade, the invocation of the practice of organizing, evaluating, and situating knowledge to confront the foundation that the canonization of knowledge provides to the structure of settlement. At once both reflective and assertive, Washuta's "Preliminary

Bibliography" reappropriates form to commemorate the collusion between the structure and content of settlement while simultaneously creating structures of resistance.

Miranda's *Bad Indians* uses form in a similar way. Much like Washuta reappropriates forms from academic contexts to expose how these structures espouse settler epistemological structures, Miranda's "tribal memoir" is also grounded in the reappropriation of an educational exercise. Only recently decommissioned as an essential part of the California public schools curriculum, the "Mission Unit" encourages students to create a project that focuses on one of California's twenty-one missions.[41] As Miranda notes, many of the missions now cater directly to this project, equipped with "gift shops well-stocked with CDs of *pre-researched* Mission Projects, xeroxed pamphlets of mission terms, facts and history (one for each mission), coloring books, packaged models of missions ('easily assembled in 10 minutes!') and other project paraphernalia for the discerning fourth grader and his or her worried parents."[42] Having moved to Oregon when she was young, Miranda never completed such a Mission Project herself. Ostensibly assigned to teach students the history of California, Miranda engages rather than banishes this project to explore what story precisely it is that is being reproduced through the Mission Project. Structuring her tribal memoir this way, Miranda explores not only the content but also the form of the Mission Project, emphasizing that the problem is not only the story itself but also the very ceremonial practices through which settlement is consistently commemorated and recommemorated as part of the foundational education curriculum.

Though Miranda offers a reappropriation of a rich number of forms associated with the Mission Project, I want to focus here on Miranda's "My Mission Glossary." In this piece, Miranda uses educational materials as the basis for literary collage to emphasize the dissonance between the seemingly virtuous attempt to learn more about local history and the practice of requiring young people to reproduce what Tuck and Yang call "settler moves to innocence," "which problematically attempt to reconcile settler guilt and complicity."[43] As Miller and Paola write, juxtaposition is the "key craft element" of collage and, in these piece, Miranda engages the form of a glossary to juxtapose the reproduction of a prideful common history of California through the Mission Project and the histories of violent colonialism, conversion, and captivity that remain part of the lived history for contemporary California Indians and their ancestors.[44] She resists the model of an "alternative history" by engaging directly with both the content and structure of the dominant history, refusing to simply cast it aside. Instead, she insists on reckoning with it by allowing it to inhabit her literary practice just as she must inhabit such structures in her life. In this, her history is not an "alternative" to anything but, rather, reifies the other worlds here while also engaging with those histories that have been laid on her body and the land to which it belongs.

Glossaries of popular words associated with the California missions abound in the myriad guides available to introduce visitors to the nomenclature and vocabulary that describes the physical, relational, and political dimensions of mission life. In her version of a mission glossary, Miranda takes on some of the most popular of these words, including "adobe bricks," "padre," "neophyte," and "mission." Much as Washuta reappropriated the form of the annotated bibliography to emphasize its claim over the ordering and evaluation of knowledge, Miranda uses the glossary form to highlight the way histories of violent settlement become both sanitized and normalized through the continuous attempt at a particular definition for common words. For instance, many students learn about adobe brick because it was made with local material, creating an economy through which Spanish padres could build the physical structures of the missions with materials that were widely available and cheap.

This basic building block has become one of the most enduring commemorations of the mission era in the California landscape, which continues to be defined by "mission architecture," often recognizable through this invocation of the adobe brick. As the first entry in her mission glossary, Miranda juxtaposes the popular practice of teaching students the "recipe" for adobe brick with the staunch reminder that padres actually built nothing with the material and, instead, depended on enslaved Native peoples. After describing the process of building the forms, mixing the materials, and curing the structure, Miranda writes: "All in all, adobe is cheap—the ingredients free for the taking—but you will certainly go through a lot of Indians. More lazy creatures on earth we have never seen."[45] As the glossary moves on, Miranda uses such apposing irruptions to begin interspersing less sanitized words and definitions throughout.

Though she continues to include words like "neophyte," "padre," and "mission" in her glossary, these words are forced into proximity with definitions of instruments of torture as described by Quechua nobleman Guamán Poma in his early-seventeenth-century letter on the treatment of Indigenous Andeans by the Spanish, later called *The First New Chronicle and Good Government*. Written alongside visual approximations, Miranda offers definitions of these instruments like the "cat-o'-nine tails" and the "cudgel," using the tone and language of a glossary. The juxtaposition of innocuous language and casual violence is startling, but it also works to unearth how the glossary form works to encourage young people to commemorate a valorized narrative of the mission era. By invoking this form, Miranda creates what Mary Louise Pratt has referred to as an "autoethnographic text . . . in which people undertake to describe themselves in ways that engage with representations others have made of them."[46]

As Pratt makes clear, autoethnography is about content and form: Poma's *New Chronicle* is notable not only because he demonstrates both an understanding of and resistance to the dominant modes of talking about Indigenous peoples among the Spanish invaders but also because he does so by taking up the form of the chronicle which "was the main writing apparatus through which the Spanish represented their American conquests to themselves." As Pratt argues, "in writing a 'new chronicle,' Guamán Poma took over the official Spanish genre for his own ends."[47] In writing her own mission project, including the ever-present mission glossary, Miranda engages in the same autoethnographic practice as Poma by appropriating the form through which claims to an innocuous history of settlement are cemented. Or, at least, are attempted.[48]

Washuta and Miranda's form-conscious memoir work encourages us, as Levine does, to expand "our usual definition of form in literary studies to include patterns of sociopolitical experience."[49] By structuring their engagements through the appropriation of form, Washuta and Miranda emphasize the connections between the shape of stories and the shape of settlement. Their work requires an understanding of form that rejects ahistorical versions of traditional formalist analysis that understand form as "transcending the specificities of history" and, instead, insist that "form can be cast as historical, emerging out of particular cultural and political circumstances."[50] Employing common forms like the annotated bibliography and the glossary that are used to arrange, evaluate, and transmit content and particular epistemologies, Washuta and Miranda expose the narrative structures through which settlement is maintained across generations. In this, they explore the interplay between the acquisition of knowledge on the individual level and structured orders of learning. Within this framing, the practice of commemoration is evidenced as a collective process of the continued ceremonial repetition of form. Being attentive to the formal dimension of stories and their transmission is essential to understanding how they preserve the structure of settlement.

The story of the 1999 Battle in Seattle has become such a commemorative event for contemporary anarchists. The shape of the story has taken form, becoming a ritual through which contemporary anarchist writers must locate themselves and their works in a lineage of New Anarchism. But the form of this story, as one tied to birth, nascence, and generation has created a formal structure that transmits settler moves to innocence. Though anarchists have criticized the invocation of the story as one of spontaneous generation, since this method neglects the histories of organizing to which it is related, the connections to settlement remain through the act of commemoration that the form of the story takes. So that we might adequately address the structure of settlement within New Anarchist movements, we must explore how settlement is commemorated through the form of its foundational stories and founding narratives, honoring the other worlds that live here already.

As rhetorical structures that, according to Tuck and Yang, "attempt to relieve the settler of feelings of guilt or responsibility without giving up land or power," settler moves to innocence are powerful methods through which individuals are interpellated into the broader structure of the settler state.[51] Several of these moves to innocence as described by Tuck and Yang can be identified in the story of the 1999 Battle in Seattle as the bequest of a larger settler structure, as well as a formal restructuring of these moves within an anarchist framework. For instance, they note settler nativism as one of the most prevalent moves to innocence, mostly popularly expressed as the claim to distant Native ancestry.[52] Within the story of the 1999 Battle in Seattle, we can see this at work not in the claim to individual Native ancestry but rather in the attempt to articulate an inherently overlapping relationship between Native and anarchist histories of resistance.

This claim works much like the individual claim to Native ancestry to "deflect a settler identity, while continuing to enjoy settler privilege and occupying stolen land."[53] Similarly, the story of the 1999 Battle in Seattle evinces what Tuck and Yang call "colonial equivocation" or the tendency to collapse resistance to the settler state as inherently part of larger antioppression or anti-imperialist movements.[54] Both Washuta's and Miranda's work appropriating form makes clear the structural work that stories do to fortify sociopolitical institutions and, concomitantly, substantiate Levine's contention that formalist analysis ends up being an effective analytic tool beyond reading literature.

In fact, we can look to literatures that employ form-conscious techniques like *Bad Indians* and *My Body Is a Book of Rules* to develop the skills necessary to effectively confront the ways that settler anarchism operates as a form that is fortified through a ritual commemoration of telling certain stories in certain ways. As Washuta and Miranda do, we must pay attention to the form that stories take—to what form *this* story takes and ask what work that form does. After such reflection, we can play with the form of the story of the 1999 Battle in Seattle as a birth story; working against the conventions of nativity by producing a birth story of the movement that refuses a linear narrative of progress, that refuses to memorialize singular histories within that narrative, and that works to identify then upend the forms of settlement rather than attempting absolution through disavowal. Building on the methodologies of memorialization and commemoration provided by Miranda and Washuta in their formal approaches that emphasize genealogy and the appropriation of epistemological forms, we can develop alternative approaches to narrating New Anarchism in ways that imagine futures rooted in Indigenous, rather than settler, futurity.[55]

New Navigation, Future Mythologies

Writers of speculative and science fiction have been doing this work of imagining Indigenous futures and thus have committed to an Indigenous futurity that rejects rather than assumes the future existence of the settler state.[56] Tuck and Yang describe this methodology as an "ethic of incommensurability" against the rhetoric of reconciliation, which they argue is "about rescuing settler normalcy, about rescuing a settler future."[57] Conversely, an ethic of incommensurability resists the attempt to resolve the conflicting political commitments of decolonization and settlement and, instead, insists on an understanding of the latter that renders it incompatible with Native peoples, cosmologies, and territories.

Within this framework, there can be no decolonization within a settler state. In this section on settler anarchism, I've sought to expand this recognition to argue that there can also be no decolonization within an antistatist anarchist movement that remains committed to the structure of settlement even if it is a movement that tacitly rejects the state as a sociopolitical institution. In the previous chapter, I followed the thread of the story of the 1999 Battle in Seattle to excavate the structure of settler anarchism that, for many, lives very close to the surface of contemporary radical social movements yet somehow remains obfuscated through a variety of structural and rhetorical mechanisms. Tuck and Yang's terminology gives us an effective way to articulate this attempted relationship in the simplest terms: settler anarchism aims to make commensurable settlement and anarchism because it refuses an approach to anarchism that insists on the destruction of settler structure *as a form*.

What I've explored throughout this chapter is how Miranda and Washuta use form-conscious nonfiction writing to explore what an ethic of incommensurability might look like in the practice of bringing together self-storying, settler history, and Indigenous futurity. Building on an analysis of their approaches to memorialization through genealogical structure and commemoration through the appropriation of educational form, I've demonstrated how they center incommensurability as a methodological tool capable of simultaneously exposing and resisting the structures of settlement without attempting to resolve their contemporaneity. In fact, these practices are what make *Bad Indians* and *My Body Is a Book of Rules* influential examples of studies in incommensurability that refuse to read coexistence as synchronicity.

Using Levine's discussion of form as a method of analysis able to account for both literary and sociopolitical forms, I asked what relationship these forms may have in movement spaces and what role literature might play in transforming that relationship. By way of conclusion, I move with Miranda's and Washuta's conclusions to demonstrate how they invoke decolonization as neither literary nor political metaphor (as Tuck and Yang warn against) and, instead, use epistemologies of temporal and spatial navigation to emphasize the worlds that live with the land and its people and to implore us to recognize these worlds as the responsibility through which we must conceptualize political intervention.

Both Miranda and Washuta's memoirs end with explorations of navigation systems. In the final section of *Bad Indians*, "To Make Story Again in the World," Miranda's tribal memoir coalesces into a triangulated montage of ancestor's stories, place-based cosmology, and what she calls "future mythology" or the practice of imagining the present through the vantage point of the future.[58] Threading the stories of her grandfather Thomas Miranda and Isabel Meadows, an Ohlone woman whose work with anthropologist J. P. Harrington provide some of the most foundational ancestral stories with which Miranda works through the text, Miranda connects the multiple histories that she has memorialized and commemorated throughout by grounding it in a sense of direction that we can read as an example of Million's "felt theory" or embodied knowledge:

> I think of my grandfather's stories; I think of Isabel's stories, and how their words survive, reach out for listeners. El Potrero lies in the shadow of Mt. Diablo's profile, the sacred place of emergence toward which my grandfather Tom Miranda yearned as a young man, knowing . . . that who we are is where we are from. . . . These are stories worth following home. Our bodies, like compasses, still know the way.[59]

In this sense, decolonization is not enacted as a literary metaphor toward which Miranda is being navigated through her engagement with historical exploration and future mythology. Rather, it is a place toward which her body (including those felt epistemologies she continues to inherit in the stories of her grandfather and Meadows) moves. The body-as-compass acts as a navigation system that is rooted in stories and the ways they manifest places and their worlds.

Washuta's *My Body Is a Book of Rules* ends in a similar way, with a focus on navigation systems and their connection to stories. In the final essay, "The Global Positioning Effect," Washuta is driving around Seattle feeling unfamiliar with the city despite having moved there years ago from Washington, DC, a place that she knows intimately. As she moves through the city, Washuta's interaction with her GPS navigation system becomes a locus point through which she reckons with the interiority of her experiences with bipolar disorder and the effect on her body, both its material form and her relationship to it. Much as Miranda understands the body as a compass through its embodiment of story, Washuta explores the contours of the body and its navigational epistemologies: "I try to remember that my body is not really the sum of what's visible . . . I don't know what happens beyond where the nerves end—maybe my body hurts but keeps it secret from my brain. It wouldn't be a surprise. My body keeps secrets all the time."[60]

For Washuta, unearthing these bodily secrets extends from her connection to the knowledge of her ancestors, much in the same way that Miranda's system of navigation worked through a connection between body and ancestral epistemologies. Washuta observes, with tentative hope: "I'm learning to talk to the ancestors, listen for answers, stay awake in dreams, and let those loved ones erase the muddy corners of my brain so I might learn all over again how to know anything at all."[61] These muddy corners are materially mirrored in Washuta's exploration of the city of Seattle using the voice of her GPS. Washuta ends the book with an acquiescence to the GPS as a navigational tool: "I tell my GPS, 'Fucking tell me where to go and I will.' Ten seconds later, she tells me."[62]

Miranda's and Washuta's self-storying, of themselves, of their ancestors, of their territories, end in this gesture toward the maps laid out by the navigational systems through which temporal and spatial movement are relationally determined, (re)shaped, and defined. In their configurations, these topologies are derived from and within stories, sometimes new stories and (more often) very old ones, especially those that they either hear repeated or continually repeat themselves. For Washuta, this is Tumalth's story; for Miranda, it is Isabel Meadows's stories of the missions.[63] Miranda's and Washuta's use of navigation systems as gestures out of the text offers a summation of the methodologies that their texts provide us, ones that articulate the material form on which such stores rest and the worlds to which they give shape. To confront the structure of settler anarchism, we must understand the forms that our most oft-repeated stories give to us. As it is memorialized and commemorated in the current body of literature, the story of the 1999 Battle in Seattle remains rooted in a settler future. In this, it doesn't provide a navigation system that can adequately account for place, history, and future mythology through an ethic of incommensurability or one that overtly and resolutely rejects settler futurity since it sees no other worlds here.

Miranda's and Washuta's memoirs provide formative methodologies through which to imagine alternative ways to navigate the complex webs of relation through which settlement is bound, whether to the state or to radical social movements that purport to work against the state. To reject the structure of settlement within an anarchist framework, anarchist scholars and organizers must recognize that the stories we tell provide material and relational topologies of the elsewheres of empire, both historical and futuristic.

Confronting settler anarchism means confronting the forms of such elsewheres and their narration on the land; it means writing stories like the 1999 Battle in Seattle through place, through multiple and sometimes contradictory histories, and through an awareness of navigational systems we create through storytelling. This method of dynamic, material storytelling emanates from the epigraph, to which I return here with the sense that the dynamic processes I explored in Miranda's and Washuta's texts are still best described by Barker and Teaiwa's term *Native in/formation*. As they note, "it's about process, not statis. It's not about romanticizing the dead of our history onto the sides of defaced mountains carved up for all time. It's about the way we move with time and with each other."[64] With this, stories must lead the way.

Part 2

Relocating Gendered Violence

CHAPTER 3

The Home from Which We Organize

Settlement, Feminism, and Gender in New Anarchism

In the wake of the one-year anniversary of the inauguration of Donald Trump as the forty-fifth president of the United States, the Black Rose Anarchist Federation released their online pamphlet "Below & Beyond Trump: Power and Counterpower in 2017." In it, members of the federation's Analysis and Strategy Committee argued that the numerous political crises induced by Trump's election had created particularly fertile ground for radical political intervention, especially the potential to "build popular power and social anarchism."[1] Alongside the increased interest in and attention to antifascist organizing in 2017, the statement from Black Rose points to another eruption of public interest in anarchism akin to that which followed both the Battle in Seattle in 1999 and Occupy Wall Street in 2011. In their estimation, the election and its aftermath was both a symptom and a cause of what they called "tensions at the top," which they defined as both a US ruling class in crisis and an eruption of distrust in the centrist ideology of the Democratic Party.[2]

For the Black Rose Anarchist Federation, this formed a powerful triad that created the conditions and motivations for the potential development of a strong anarchist movement in the United States. And, as the contemporary incarnation of a lineage of prominent anarchist federations like the Northeastern Federation of Anarchist Communists (NEFAC) and Common Struggle / Lucha Común, Black Rose was particularly well positioned to make such an observation. With over a dozen local chapters, Black Rose continues to build on the organizing work of its predecessors to establish a more centralized "political home from which to organize."[3] And though it is not representative of either the analysis or desires of every anarchist individual or organization in the United States, this statement from Black Rose offers a powerful window into the political mantra through which New Anarchism is being adapted and expressed in the contemporary moment. Of particular interest to me here is how a broad array of radical social movements figure into the platform presented by Black Rose and what this diagraming might tell us about why approaches to feminism, gender, and sexuality remain limited within New Anarchist analyses.

"Below and Beyond Trump" offers specific analyses of a variety of movements that reflect the more general political commitments through which the federation defines itself, including the Black Lives Matter movement, the labor movement, the feminist movement (the only one that has movement in scare quotes), the "indigenous and environmental movements," and the immigrant rights movement.[4] The assessment of these movements in the contemporary moment fits with the federation's "points of unity," which include critical orientation toward capitalism, the state, imperialism, white supremacy, patriarchy, and ableism.[5] Within this matrix, the concomitant focus on "revolution, anti-racism, internationalism, queer liberation, unionism, direct action, federalism, and libertarian socialism" indicates the interest in assessing the contemporary state of a variety of corresponding social movements. The statement argues that an array of movements including "labor, Black Lives Matter (BLM), immigrant, environmental, queer, or feminist struggles" are as fractured as the dominant political system.

Speaking about these movements, the authors contend that "most seem to be moving towards some type of retrenchment strategy in response to Trump" that depends on an "institutional left [that] has failed to build on deepening public outrage, offering little beyond symbolic demonstrations, 'get out the vote' efforts and militant reformism."[6] The statement implies that, within this political landscape, anarchism is uniquely positioned to offer a way out of the institutionalization of dissent. And though there is something to be said here regarding how the statement creates the illusion that such movements are defined solely by their supposed cooperation with state institutions rather than diverse movements that invoke a variety of organizing techniques across a spectrum of political radicalism, I am especially interested in how the statement classifies the array of movements that it invokes. This focus on taxonomy rather than the content of the analysis supports my larger project of illuminating some of the structural pieces of New

Anarchist politics that have made it so ill equipped to deal with the structure of settlement both in mainstream social and political institutions and within anarchist movements themselves. In this chapter, I pay particular attention to how issues of gender, sexuality, and feminism are invoked to ask how this treatment might form an important fulcrum that supports the structure of settler anarchism.

According to their mission statement, Black Rose is expressly "inspired by the traditions" of both feminism and queer liberation. In their point of unity titled "Patriarchy and Queer Liberation," they offer both an analysis of and statement against the exigencies of patriarchy noting that "we reject patriarchy: the system of male domination, heteronormativity, and gender oppression" and that "we intend to fight sexism both when it takes economic and non-economic form, such as through familial roles, rape culture, and unwaged labor." Importantly, they specifically note that they "challenge heteronormativity and the assumption of standardized expression of sexuality and gender, and support the free development of people's identity and relationships . . . by confronting patriarchy in social movement spaces [and] defending reproductive health for all genders."[7] It is this formulation of gender, sexuality, and feminism that reinforces the taxonomy provided in the "Beyond and Below Trump" statement.

In particular, we can see the seemingly paradoxical configuration of the recognition that gendered and sexualized hierarchy "intersects with other forms of oppression" alongside the attempts to distance it from such forms. For instance, it's unclear how and when sexism might take a "non-economic form," or one that is outside the purview of capitalist control. The examples they provide, particularly their emphasis on the family and unwaged labor, have a long history of engagement in materialist, Marxist, socialist, and even anarchist feminist work that asserts the intrinsically capitalistic nature of such gendered and sexual social arrangements.[8] But it is not only the lack of attention to these bodies of work that bolsters a taxonomical method through which the authors of the statement paint the question of feminism for New Anarchism. Rather, what is notable is how the attempt to assert at once a proximity and a distance between anarchism, feminism, and critical accounts of gender and sexuality is expressed.

In the "Beyond and Below Trump" statement, Black Rose defines the contemporary feminist movement through a dichotomy between the "Women's March" that took place on inauguration day on January 20 and the "Women's Strike" that followed on International Women's Day on March 8. For the statement's authors, this dichotomy highlights "a growing divide between reformist feminism and an increasingly militant antipatriarchal movement" that is defined by "a broader dialogue around feminism and the possibility for building a feminist/antipatriarchal movement aligned with the interests of working class women, trans, and queers, as well as inserting a feminist politics within social movements."[9] Within their taxonomy of movements, this is separate from the other analyses of Black Lives Matter, immigrant rights, labor, Indigenous, and environmental movements, despite how each of these movements has developed important gendered analyses, if to different degrees.[10] In fact, the Women's Strike itself is in part an outgrowth of gendered and sexual analysis of labor movements both in the contemporary moment and historically.[11] I see this tendency also at work in the simultaneous divorcing of questions of gender, sexuality, and feminism from other social movements and suturing of Native movements to environmentalism.

Within this taxonomy we can see how the structure of settler anarchism is maintained through common approaches to feminism, gender, and sexuality within New Anarchist approaches: the perfunctory pronouncement of engagement with Native movements is performed through its partition from questions of gender and sexuality and its location within "the environment." On this latter association, Potawatomi scholar Kyle Powys Whyte has argued that the association of Native movements only within environmentalism has led to a political approach in which "the conservation movement has been as damaging to Indigenous peoples as extractive industries" since this conflation "does not necessarily confront ongoing territorial dispossession and risks to health, economic vitality, lives, psychological well-being, and cultural integrity."[12] The limiting effects of considering Native movements in this way are mirrored in their partitioning from questions of gender, sexuality, and feminism, decentering them from consideration within the context of the issues to which Whyte points.

This is especially glaring since the statement makes particular mention of the Idle No More movement, which was founded by Native women and is indelibly connected to movements aimed at addressing the experiences that Native peoples have with gendered violence, such as #MMIWG2S (Missing and Murdered Indigenous Women, Girls, and Two-Spirit people) and #ItStartsWithUs, which work together to document, agitate, and organize against the epidemic of gendered violence against Native peoples in the United States and Canada.[13] This work also neglects the limited yet excellent work done by scholars like Laura Hall and Kathy Ferguson that asserts the connections between anarchist, feminist, and Native approaches to the development of social movements.[14] In what follows, I am interested in exploring how anarchist, feminist, and Native approaches are structurally kept apart rather than how they come together.

Coupled with the lack of any mention of the prevalence of or need to address gendered and sexual violence *within* anarchist spaces, the structure of inquiry in this statement invokes the broader methodologies of anarchist engagement with feminism, gender, and sexuality that limit the ability of anarchists to address the structure of settlement within our movements. I have written elsewhere on how anarchist approaches to gendered violence work to locate its origins outside of anarchist spaces, neglecting how anarchist politics create the conditions for the perpetuation and concealment of gendered violence within the movement.[15] In the formulation provided in the Black Rose statement on the contemporary political landscape, we can see this operating on an even broader scale—there is little evaluation of the state of anarchist movements themselves, especially recurring issues of antiblackness, colonialism, and gendered violence within those spaces.

What is more, anarchism is positioned as the nostrum to the limitations not only of particular movements but also of the debilitated left itself. In this way, the statement continues the tendency described in the first chapter of ignoring the specificity of the settler context of the United States and, concomitantly, it dispenses with any engagement of how settlement is intimately bound to gendered violence and how anarchism continues to depend on such structures. As Andrea Smith and J. Kēhaulani Kauanui (Kanaka Maoli) have pointed out, gendered violence and the ideology of heteropatriarchy in which it is rooted have fomented the naturalization of social hierarchy on which settlement is built.[16] In this chapter, I look to contemporary anarchist engagements with both feminism and studies in gender and sexuality to explore how the limitations of these approaches further bind New Anarchism to the settler structure of the US state.

I begin by performing a metareading of the common approaches to feminism within the anarchist milieu. Through this, I demonstrate how eschewing any engagement with Native feminisms is not a problem of either benign disregard or misunderstood pertinence, but rather is in line with the New Anarchist investment in a settler structure. I then analyze anarchist approaches to the study of gender and sexuality, exploring how these approaches are rooted in an account of gender and sexuality that remains unmoored to the material context of the US settler state and is often framed within broader discussions of identity politics. I have chosen to discuss anarchist approaches to feminism and anarchist approaches to gender and sexuality separately, not because they are unrelated but because these are distinct fields and, too often, their differences are supplanted by the assumption that they are interchangeable. Though there is significant overlap between the fields of feminist theory and gender and sexuality studies, these are not coterminous bodies of work. This is true in the broader scope of the fields as well as in the anarchist milieu.

Anarchism and Feminism

The discussion of feminism within the contemporary anarchist texts extends from the structure of settlement described in the first chapter in that it remains untethered to the specificity of the United States as a settler context. Defined by a relatively narrow focus on the overlap between feminist and anarchist thinkers, the assertion of an inherent similarity between feminism and anarchism, or the selective integration of insights from women of color and Native feminisms, the anarchist approach to feminism remains tied to a settler methodology that refuses to account for the material foundation on which it rests. I am concerned here, as I described in part I, not (only) with an in-depth critical analysis of particular anarchist texts on feminism but rather with a more metacritical approach that illuminates how the structure of inquiry is imbricated in the suturing together of settler anarchism and anarchist approaches to feminism. In contemporary texts, such approaches have tended to focus on the question of relationship between these two traditions. And, to be sure, the relationship between anarchism and feminism is a somewhat peculiar one, rooted in a paradox similar to that presented in the first chapter: that though the overarching assertion of anarchism as a political philosophy grounded in the rejection of hierarchy seems inherently compatible with a feminist politics that rejects gendered order, issues of misogyny and gendered violence persist in anarchist spaces. This is clear in the overall treatment of feminism in anarchist texts over the past twenty years.

Though engaging with feminism has become an ubiquitous enough concern that most contemporary anarchist texts make some reference to feminist politics, feminist history, or feminist movements, this imperative does not seem to have fundamentally transformed the foundation of anarchist social movement or lead to the production of a concomitant body of work focused exclusively on anarchism and feminism more specifically. In the works that do deal more explicitly with the relationship between anarchist and feminism, I have located a particular taxonomy of engagement that is defined by three approaches that dominate the structure of inquiry. These approaches include the genealogical approach, the equivalent approach, and the exchange approach. These common approaches have helped us better understand the history of feminist anarchists and anarchist feminists (the genealogical approach); the traits and practices that are shared by them both historically and today (the equivalent approach); and what they might be able to learn from each other (the exchange approach). Each approach makes important contributions to critically engaging the relationship between anarchism and feminism, but each is limited in its ability to adequately reckon with the contributions of Native feminists writing about the particularities of a feminist analysis and praxis that can account for the settler character of the US state. Here, I sketch out the overall structure of each approach and examine how each reinforces the structure of settlement within contemporary anarchism.

The Genealogical Approach

One of the most popular methods of attending to the relationship between anarchism and feminism is the genealogical approach. In this approach, the focus is on establishing a history of anarchist feminist thinkers, often presented chronologically. While each version of this approach may vary in what politics it highlights in its survey of thinkers, what they have in common is the goal of creating a distinct history of anarchist feminist thought.[17] This genealogy provides the architecture for many popular engagements, including the collection *Quiet Rumours*, which is the most well-known collection of anarchist feminist writings from the nineteenth to the twenty-first century. And though the most recent incarnation of *Quiet Rumours* doesn't follow in a chronological genealogy, it nonetheless aims to act as a "retrospective anthology" that "works not only as an essential collection of texts past but offers inspiration for future discussion and debate."[18] This imperative to maintain a history of anarchist feminist thought works within a genealogical approach since it seeks to establish a lineage of intellectual history that can be traced from the contemporary moment to assert a strong, long-standing tradition.

For instance, in her essay "Of What Is Anarcha-Feminism the Name?," Cinzia Arruzza attends to many of the same conceptual questions that I do here but by invoking a genealogical structure. Building on core questions that came out of the International Anarcha-Feminist meeting in Paris in 1992, Arruzza is similarly interested in the lack of theoretical development of anarchist feminism in the contemporary literature on New Anarchism. As she argues, "the reasons for this under-theorization are numerous and have to do with both the political marginalization suffered by anarchism and the resistance often offered by the anarchist movement itself to the autonomous organization and political elaboration of women."[19] And Arruzza and I have reached similar conclusions regarding this absence, namely, that it is bolstered by the mutual reinforcement of an anarchist investment in misogyny and the assertion that anarchism is already inherently feminist (a claim I take up below). However, here I am interested in how Arruzza's dependence on a genealogical approach limits her ability to adequately address the specific ways that anarchist investment in settlement, particularly for foundational anarchist feminist thinkers from the United States, has also contributed to the simultaneous limiting of the field of anarchist feminism.

Beginning with Emma Goldman and Voltairine de Cleyre, Arruzza moves through the twentieth century to writers like Carol Ehrlich, Peggy Kornegger, Lynne Farrow, and Marian Leighton, ending in the late twentieth and early twenty-first century by exploring the influences of poststructuralist feminism, queer theory, and ecofeminism to emphasize the "specificity of anarcha-feminism in the context of the flourishing of gender and sexuality theories from the 1970s onwards."[20] As it is invoked both here and elsewhere, the assertion of this genealogy has proven important for articulating anarchist feminism as a distinct and relatively cohesive theoretical tradition, especially since this genealogical approach provides a formulation that exists alongside and within the history of anarchism rather than arising as an ancillary concern. In this, it helps bolster the argument that feminist critiques of gendered hierarchy have an easy acquiescence with anarchist critiques of the state. For instance, Goldman's and de Cleyre's classic illuminations of the paradox in bourgeois sociality of the vilification and criminalization of prostitution alongside the glorification of heterosexual marriage remain central to anarchist discussions of marriage as a political institution of the state.[21] Interventions like these were also influential in developing radical approaches to sex work that consider it within the framework of gendered labor, rather than a test of moral fortitude whether of an individual or a social body.[22] In drawing a genealogical lineage, scholars engage this approach to more fully integrate feminist concerns within the history of anarchist political philosophy and to insist more forcefully on the necessity of its inclusion.

However, in attempting to illustrate a far-reaching tradition of anarchist feminist thought, this approach ignores the specificity of the US settler context and the unique challenges that it presents not only for imagining an antistate position on stolen land but also for understanding the relationship between the social and political institutions through which settlement is structured. Put another way, the focus on the long arc of anarchist feminist history neglects what Joanne Barker (Lenape) has called "the polity of the Indigenous," which she defines as "the unique governance, territory, and culture of Indigenous peoples in unique and related systems of (non)human relationships and responsibilities to one another."[23] The result is an elision of the question of settlement within the establishment of an anarchist feminist tradition. For instance, de Cleyre's and Goldman's analyses of marriage in a bourgeois system come together without any attention paid to how these two foundational thinkers represent an important distinction in the history of anarchism in the United States: work, like Goldman's, that emanated from and centered on immigrant communities, and work, like de Cleyre's, which heralded a distinct era of anarchist thought and organizing that is often called "native American anarchism." Originally coined by Eunice Schuster in 1932, the term was meant to account for the divergences of the work of native-born anarchists and immigrant anarchists, particularly the individualist strain of foundational thinkers like de Cleyre.[24] This term is still used without a sense of irony in reference to de Cleyre and her contemporaries, including in every edition of *Quiet Rumours*.[25]

This problem is not solely one of terminology. Rather, contemporary acquiescence to the term *native American anarchism* exemplifies how the attempt to create a genealogical approach to the study of anarchist feminism elides an approach that is attentive to the polity of the Indigenous. Though it's true that individualism became a hallmark distinguishing anarchist thought developed by people born in the United States, rather than those who had immigrated, the literature on

American anarchism does not engage the question of how that individualism was tied to the settler structure of United States. This lacuna is reflected in the literature on anarchist feminism as well, particularly as portrayed through the genealogical approach. For instance, suturing together Goldman and de Cleyre, who were not only contemporaries but eventually friends, ignores the important differences they had in their analysis of the US state and its treatment of Native peoples. Goldman, for example, once declared that "the only true Americans were the native Indians . . . who were cruelly robbed of their land and happiness by the ancestors of those who now rule the country," and noted, "I should think myself disgraced had my ancestors been amongst those who mercilessly slaughtered the Indians wholesale, pretending to do so in the name of civilization."[26]

De Cleyre's "Anarchism and American Traditions," written only four years before her death, offered a different estimation of the founding of the United States. In it, she insists on the "fundamental likeness between the Revolutionary Republicans and the Anarchists," lauding the "Boston Tea Party Indians," as well as citing Thomas Jefferson's 1787 letter to James Madison in which he laid out the three modes under which societies exist under government, of which "without government, as among our Indians" is the first. In "Breaking the Chains," she also lamented that "if the colonists had not resorted to direct actions, their scalps would have been taken by the Indians a year sooner."[27] Creating an anarchist feminist genealogical tradition that parallels these thinkers as progenitors neglects these disparate approaches to the history of settlement, eclipsing the settler structure of de Cleyre's estimation of American anarchism and its continued influence in anarchist feminism in the contemporary moment.[28]

What also remains uncritically adopted in this lineage is the adherence to a settler temporality that centers the arrival and progression of settler political institutions. Implicitly replicating the "wave" model of feminist theory, this genealogical model inherently illustrates anarchist feminism as a settler tradition or one that emerged as part of the history of settlement without any critical engagement with its legacy in New Anarchism more broadly or anarchist feminism in specific. This is particularly troubling since such a discussion is central to the field of Native feminisms. In fact, the question of the complicated relationship between feminism and settlement has been foundational to the development of Native feminist theory, as Native feminists have explored their relationship to a history of feminist movement that was founded on inclusion into a settler structure.[29] As scholars like Barker, Luana Ross (Confederated Salish/Kootenai), and Lisa Kahaleole Hall (Kanaka Maoli) have demonstrated, this doesn't mean that feminism is an inherently settler construct but rather that Native feminisms have "multiple intellectual and political genealogies within Indigenous communities that need to be remembered, not for the sake of feminism, but for the sake of Indigenous knowledge and the relationships and responsibilities it defines."[30]

This nuanced discussion about the history of feminism and settlement in the United States is lost in the untethered genealogy of anarchist feminism, particularly since the genealogy most often espoused in this approach includes examples of anarchist feminism that *are* attentive to historical and political context. For instance, Martha Acklesberg has given a powerful account of the *mujeres libres* or "free women" of Spain who aimed to address issues of misogyny and the subordination of women during the Spanish Revolution yet did not identify as feminists.[31] And, in an interview published in *Quiet Rumours*, members of the Bolivian group Mujeres Creando argue "we're not anarchists by Bakunin or the CNT, but rather by our grandmothers, and that's a beautiful school of anarchism."[32]

Both of these examples represent an approach to genealogies of anarchist feminism that are contextually grounded in a place-based model. Despite the celebration of these two examples within anarchist feminist texts, this model is nowhere replicated in the context of anarchist feminism in the US settler state. This is not only a methodological question but also a structural and material one—as Goeman has argued, though the politics of place remains a contested issue in Native Studies, "this grounding . . . is of utmost importance to the imaginative geographies that create the material consequences of everyday existence for Native people, even while the historical onslaught of legislation continues to rip that grounding out from under Native people."[33] Illuminating the connection between settlement and a genealogical approach to anarchist feminism is essential if we wish to adequately adhere to the type of materialist approach that anarchism supposedly espouses.

The Equivalent Approach

The limitations of the genealogical approach are mirrored in the equivalent approach to anarchism and feminism that became popular in the mid-twentieth century. Exemplified by Peggy Kornegger's 1975 pamphlet "Anarchism: The Feminist Connection," the equivalent approach articulates the relationship between anarchism and feminism as synonymous. As Kornegger famously argued, "It is my contention that feminists have been unconscious anarchists in both theory and practice for years."[34] Lynn Farrow echoed this sentiment the same year when she argued that "feminism practices what anarchism preaches," as did Marian Leighton the following year when she argued that "the refining distinction from radical feminist to anarcho-feminist is largely that of making a step in self-conscious theoretical development."[35] Though others like Carol Ehrlich offered more nuanced considerations of the relationship between anarchism and the radical feminism of the late twentieth century in the United States, there is relative accord in the literature that, as Julia Tanenbaum has put it, "many radical feminists shared anarchist goals such as ending domination, hierarchy, capitalism, gender roles, and interpersonal violence and utilized and influenced the key anarchist organizational structure of the small leaderless affinity group."[36] So, though some thinkers argued for a stauncher notion of one-to-one relationship between anarchism and feminism than others, the assertion of an inherent shared orientation remained paramount throughout.

This approach has proven important for emphasizing the theoretical consistency across the rejection of hierarchy by anarchists and the rejection of heteropatriarchy by feminists. In this way, the equivalent approach has proven a relatively productive way to reject claims to non- or antifeminist anarchism since it asserts, both implicitly and explicitly, that such an anarchist formation would not be anarchist at all. At the same time, proponents of the equivalent method argued that women were particularly well-positioned for anarchist practice because of their subordinated position socially, politically, and economically, presaging developing articulations of a Marxist feminist epistemology that arose a few years later in the early 1980s.[37] Kornegger described feminists of the time as "intuitive anarchists," which put "women in the unique position of being the bearers of a subsurface anarchist consciousness which . . . can take us further than any previous group toward the achievement of total revolution."[38] This approach, then, attempts not only to highlight a theoretical equivalence between the political philosophies of anarchism and feminism but also to suggest an operational advantage that women provide to the development of anarchist consciousness.

Mired in similar debates about the relationship between standpoint and essentialism that have been central to twentieth-century feminist theory, this approach is bound to a dependence on women as a universal category of analysis, a formulation that has served to uphold white supremacy and transphobia in feminist social movements.[39] For instance, Farrow replicates the popular narrative that it was Elizabeth Cady Stanton and Lucretia Mott's experience of exclusion at the 1842 World Anti-Slavery Convention that spawned the feminist movement, which she narrates as the fundamentally radical political position in nineteenth- century United States contra the "liberal" cause of abolition.

As Angela Davis has argued, this position ignores the investment that white women were making in a fundamentally antiblack and capitalist state as the means through which to achieve their liberation.[40] Similarly, Barker has documented the anger with which suffragettes responded to the US government's extension of property rights and, eventually, citizenship to Native peoples and the support that foundational suffragettes like Stanton and Susan B. Anthony manifested for US imperial projects in the Philippines during the Spanish-American War.[41] In depending on both this notion of womanhood and narrative of feminist history, the equivalent model maintains such investments in antiblack racism and the settler state while attempting to assert an inherently anticapitalist standpoint.

This content limits the equivalent approach to anarchism and feminism, as well as the structure through which it is enabled. Besides replicating some of the most critiqued elements of radical feminism, the equivalent approach also precludes a critical engagement with anarchism itself. Foregrounding equivalence, rather than the critical potential of feminism for anarchism, this approach to anarchist feminism creates the illusion that anarchism and feminism are inherently synonymous. In this, it prevents the use of feminism as a critical lens through which to assess how heteropatriarchal structures (and their relationship to the structure of settlement) become normalized within anarchist theory and practice itself, rather than only in dominant social and political structures. This dual method of critical feminist intervention is central to the prolific body of Native feminist work, in which Native feminists use an analysis rooted in the polity of the Indigenous to critically engage the maintenance of settlement through heteropatriarchy both within and without Native communities.

For instance, Kanien'kehá:ka scholar Audra Simpson explores the "gender of settler sovereignty" through the treatment of Attawapiskat activist Theresa Spence's hunger strike by the Canadian state and Inuk student Loretta Saunders's murder as well as popular eighteenth-century captivity narratives in the United States; Athabascan scholar Dian Million has written about the gendered, racial, and sexualized dimensions of settler state formation and maintenance, especially through attempts at reconciliation by the Canadian state; and Muscogee legal scholar Sarah Deer has demonstrated the settler structure of laws aimed at curbing gendered violence and how Federal Indian Policy creates a system of gendered violence against Native communities.[42] Scholars like these have done extensive work proving how gender and sexual hierarchies serve as justification for and continue to normalize the structure of the settler state.

Yet, these interventions also exist within a matrix of Native feminisms that critically engage the operation of heteropatriarchy within Native communities. For instance, Diné scholar Jennifer Denetdale has explored the connections between the Diné Marriage Act of 2005, which "restricted marriage to heterosexual couples," and the invocation of "Diné traditional values" to conflate "Navajo nationalism with American nationalism" after the World Trade Center attacks on September 11, 2001.[43] Similarly, writers like Paula Gunn Allen (Laguna Pueblo), Mary Crow Dog (Lakota), and Devon Abbott Mihesuah (Choctaw) have explored the devastating effects of patriarchy as a colonial structure in Native communities and movements, including the American Indian Movement.[44] These critiques of heteropatriarchy's influence within Native studies and within Native communities work alongside the critiques of such structures within the broader settler state to emphasize the insidious ways that such ideologies and practices become normalized within a variety of locations, even those to which they may seem inherently opposed.

The equivalent approach to anarchism and feminism is unable to make use of this model precisely because it obfuscates the possibility of such opposition. In this case, the assumption of an inherent correspondence between anarchism and feminism works to prevent a critical engagement with the question of how heteropatriarchy works to normalize the structure of settlement within anarchist politics in the United States.[45] In recent years, anarchist scholars have attempted to address some of these limitations of the equivalent approach by more carefully engaging the critical work of women of color and Native feminists to begin addressing the proliferation of some of these structures within anarchist politics.

The Exchange Approach

Influential and innovative articles like Deric Shannon and J. Rogue's "Refusing to Wait: Anarchism and Intersectionality" and J. Rogue and Abbey Volcano's "Insurrection at the Intersection: Feminism, Intersectionality, and Anarchism" seek to destabilize the invocation of a monolithic feminism in previous approaches to anarchism and feminism. For instance, drawing on the notion of "intersectionality" that was first coined by Black feminist legal scholar Kimberlé Crenshaw in her seminal study of violence against women of color, Shannon and Rogue argue that "anarchists could learn a lot" from feminists of color, especially "about the importance of addressing the needs of ALL sections of the working class and their attempts to check the tendency of the Left to ignore or dismiss the concerns, needs, ideas, and leadership of people living in the dangerous intersections of capitalism, white supremacy, patriarchy, etc."[46] In this evocation, Shannon and Rogue attempt to directly address the primary limitation of the equivalent approach described above by integrating feminist theory to critically engage anarchism itself. Drawing on the work of organizations like INCITE! Women of Color Against Violence, a "national activist organization of radical feminists of color advancing a movement to end violence against women of color and our communities through direct action, critical dialogue, and grassroots organizing," Rogue and Shannon bring the critiques that feminists of color have of white liberal feminism to bear on contemporary anarchism.[47]

In their article that appears in the extended third edition of *Quiet Rumours*, Rogue and Volcano offer a more deeply engaged exploration of the importance of integrating an intersectional analysis to attend to the limits of anarchist approaches that can't account for the ways that white supremacy and heteropatriarchy become integrated into the structure of anarchist politics. Focusing on the question of anarchist approaches to reproductive freedom to illustrate this broader point, Rogue and Volcano argue for an "anarchist intersectionality" that can account for the multiple ways that "capitalism, white supremacy, and heteropatriarchy . . . have required control over bodies."[48] Rogue and Volcano argue that an anarchist intersectionality is necessary to move from a paradigm of reproductive *justice* to reproductive *freedom*. For them, the latter represents an important shift since it offers a concept grounded in "an explicitly anti-state, anti-capitalist interpretation of reproductive justice," which requires a recognition of the point made by scholars like Dorothy Roberts and Andrea Smith that "a simple 'pro-choice' position is not sufficient for a revolutionary approach to reproductive 'rights'" since such an approach ignores the myriad ways that reproduction has been controlled and defined through settlement and antiblackness.[49]

Building on the work by such feminist scholars, Volcano and Rogue attempt to offer an approach to reproductive freedom that is attentive to the context of the United States:

> Looking at the history of colonialism in the Americas helps us understand the complexities of reproductive freedom in the current context. The state as an institution has always had a vested interest in maintaining control over social reproduction and in particular, the ways in which colonized peoples did and did not reproduce. Given the history of forced sterilization of Native Americans, as well as African-Americans, Latinos, and even poor white women, we can see that simply access to abortion does not address the complete issue of reproductive freedom.[50]

* * *

Here we can begin to see the limitations of the exchange approach. Rogue and Volcano's work offers an analysis that aims at a transformational approach to anarchism and feminism, attempting to integrate one of the key components missing from the previous approaches: a place-based approach that is attentive to the context of the United States and the gendered dimensions of its formation as a settler state. However, rather than being derived from a methodology that is attentive to the structure of settlement, this analysis replicates the liberal multicultural model of conflating racialization and colonialism that, as Chickasaw scholar Jodi Byrd has argued, is central to the normalization of the US settler state in the age of liberal multiculturalism.

According to Byrd, this "entanglement of colonization and racialization" is prevalent not only in work that lauds the US state but also in scholarly work that aims to critique it—much like anarchism. Though these systems work together to bolster the structure of US colonialism and imperialism on a global scale, to conflate them neglects "the distinctions between the two systems of dominance and the coerced complicities amid both."[51] And though I deal more in depth with the question of the anarchist engagement with US politics on a global scale in chapter 5,

I want to emphasize here how Rogue and Volcano's inclusion of Native peoples in this way imitates the structure that Byrd identifies.

For her, this conflation is pivotal as the United States attempts to retain the settler structure that fortifies its global empire while making claims to a liberal multiculturalism that centers inclusion for previously excluded groups. This structure is replicated in Volcano and Rogue's invocation of "the forced sterilization of Native Americans" as part of a list of other ethnoracial categories whose intertwined but different historical relationships to reproduction become flattened. Because of their conflation of colonization and racialization, Rogue and Volcano's approach to reproductive freedom is unable to account for the particular ways that settlement is structured through reproductive violence.

For instance, though they note that no discussion about access to abortion could be truly revolutionary without consideration of "access to health care, housing, education, and transportation, adoption, nontraditional families," as well as the actual cost of abortion procedures and recovery, they make no mention of the repatriation of land to Native communities, ecological protection of land and water, the accessibility of culturally specific birthing practices and centers, or the renewal of Native languages. Attending to these divergences is not a matter of specificity, but is essential to understanding how antiblack racism, settlement, and heteropatriarchy have been sutured together to create the fabric of the US state. The forced sterilization of Native women plays a very different though related role in the history of settlement than the controlling of Black women's reproduction, since the former was intrinsically bound to the claiming of land and thus the insidious limiting of Native people who could lay claim to such land and the latter to the violent reproduction of a racialized class of enslaved workers.[52]

Native activists and scholars alike have continuously emphasized the connection between reproductive violence and the theft of Native land.[53] For instance, the Native Youth Sexual Health Network has worked on a global scale to assert the "impacts of environmental violence including extractive industries . . . to our sexual and reproductive health, rights, and justice."[54] This lack of inclusion of any discussion of land within the framing of reproductive freedom demonstrates a tacit investment in settlement espoused within the structure of anarchist intersectionality. The focus on the body in Rogue and Volcano's discussion disconnects bodily violence from "violence over the land," to use Shoshone scholar Ned Blackhawk's term.[55] Because of this, it is unable to account for reproduction on a scale larger than the individual and thus neglects some of the most central issues of reproduction as it relates to settlement.

As a structure that requires continual and normalized claim over territory, settler colonialism compels not necessarily the eradication of Native bodies but the eradication of Native peoples *as indigenous* and, consequently, as peoples in relation to and (thus with claim to) the land. This recognition is central to Richard Henry Pratt's famous pronouncement that, to truly assimilate Native peoples into the polity of the United States, educators needed to work with Native students to "kill the Indian and save the man."[56] As Goeman has argued, to better understand the relationship between gendered violence and settlement, we must move beyond "the scale of the body."[57] Replicated in the anarchist approaches to gender and sexuality discussed below, this focus on the body without any reference to the polity limits the ability for this approach to account for the structural dimensions of US settlement and heteropatriarchy on both national and historical scales.

As was the case with the equivalent approach, this analytic problem is rooted in the structure of engagement enabled through the exchange approach to anarchism and feminism. In particular, this approach is often predicated on the idea of a bidirectional exchange enabled through a process of synthesis. As Rogue and Shannon put it, "We firmly believe that this learning process is a two-way street." Because of this, they argue that "when synthesizing our practice to include these concerns raised by feminists, feminism could stand to benefit from learning from anarchism as well."[58] This method is echoed in Rogue and Volcano's article, which attempts to use a synthetic method to develop an "anarchist intersectionality," implying that intersectional feminist approaches require the modification provided by an anarchist lens. In these formulations, the presumption is not only that anarchism needs feminism but also that feminism needs anarchism.

And, of course, there are many instances in which this seems to be the case—for instance, in schools of feminist thought that look to the state for liberation and which see advanced class status as an indication of progress against gendered oppression.[59] However, this element of the exchange approach is limited in its implication that feminists of color and Native feminists, in particular, require the insight of anarchism. Rogue and Shannon attempt to clearly articulate what this insight might be, arguing that "anarchism can provide a *radical* base from which to critique liberal interpretations of intersectionality," as well as "a critical analysis of the state."[60] But it is not clear why feminists of color or

Native feminists would need anarchism to provide a "critical analysis of the state," as Shannon and Rogue note, when such an analysis is foundational to some of the very feminist interventions they invoke.

For instance, INCITE!, the organization from which Rogue and Shannon draw their analysis, is expressly antistate, arguing for an understanding of sexual violence that views it as one example of statist violence enacted through systems of colonialism and militarism. Native scholars, and Native feminists in particular, have clearly developed analyses that are overtly critical of the existence of the US state, assert the connections between colonialism and capitalism, and offer alternative models of political and social formation.[61] This isn't to say that all Native peoples, or even all Native feminists, are anticapitalist and antistate. Rather, such work demonstrates the potent genealogies of resistance within Native communities on which Native feminist scholars are building—the other worlds in which Native feminists are grounding their analyses.

These genealogies of resistance to colonialism, capitalism, and the state need to be affirmed rather than supplanted to work against the naturalization of a structure of settlement that devalues Native epistemologies and cosmologies in anarchist spaces. The premise of exchange between Native feminists and anarchists precludes this affirmation, requiring instead an exchange that imagines a method of synthesis that makes no claims to or promises of reciprocity. In the simplest terms, Native feminists don't owe anarchists anything in exchange for the development of a critical approach to settlement that accounts for its gendered and sexualized dimensions. Instead, an approach to anarchism and feminism that does not replicate either an implicit or explicit claim to Native resources, whether land or knowledge, requires not an exchange or synthesis, but rather a transformational accounting for what it means to do anarchist feminist work on stolen land.

Anarchism, Gender, and Sexuality

The consequences of these limited approaches to anarchism and feminism are also evident in anarchist engagements with gender and sexuality. Without allowing for an engagement with feminism to act as a metonym for engagements with gender and sexuality, we must acknowledge the relationship between the two bodies of work. In particular, anarchist engagements with feminism should enable the integration of a critical approach to the study of gender and sexuality within anarchist politics by ensuring that such inquiry happens within a matrix of ethical commitments that refuse the normalization of the gender binary and heteronormativity. However, in the more prominent contemporary anarchist writing on gender and sexuality, we can see the effects of a methodology that remains deeply invested in the structure of settlement and its reproduction within anarchist spaces.

This is especially important to address since contemporary anarchist writings on gender and sexuality have proven to be some of the most transformative challenges to dominant anarchist politics in the past few decades. Indeed, as Acklesberg notes in her preface to the collection *Queering Anarchism*, "we have only just begun to understand the many possibilities offered by a queered anarchism, both with respect to critiques of existing institutions and practices and with respect to imagining alternatives to them."[62] As Jamie Heckert and Richard Clemison have pointed out, a significant amount of the contemporary anarchist work engaging with gender and sexuality comes out of an increased interest in the intersection between poststructuralism and anarchism, sometimes dubbed "postanarchism."[63]

This body of work follows alongside the trajectory of queer theory more generally, exploring questions of power, universality, and the body through a corpus that uses poststructuralist theory to develop an anarchist account of the contemporary operation of power, especially as it relates to gender and sexuality.[64] And though this body of work continues to be influential, its expression of a materialist analysis through a more abstract and universalist discussion of the body rather than the particularities of specific polities and nation-state contexts makes it ill-equipped to attend to the reproduction of settlement in anarchist approaches to gender and sexuality within the US context.[65] In addition, it does not accurately reflect the extent to which radical queer and anarchist politics have become aligned in the US context.

In recent years, anarchist writers and organizers have built on both the influence and the limitations of feminism to insist on nuanced and innovative gendered and sexual analyses of common topics of concern for anarchists, including the prison industrial complex, policing, health care, sex work, economic alternatives to capitalism, marriage, and family structure. Much of this work focuses on the affinity between radical queer movements and anarchist politics, building on genealogies of US-based organizations, like AIDS Coalition to Unleash Power (ACT UP), Queer Nation, and Lesbians and Gays Against Intervention (LGAI), to confront the attempts by the US state to interpellate queer politics into the state structure by redefining political demands through policies aimed at inclusion and representation. The bourgeoning popularity of organizations like Against Equality (which offers radical critiques and alternatives to the mainstream focus on marriage equality) and Black and Pink (a prison abolitionist organization working to support queer and HIV-positive people who are currently or formerly incarcerated) speak to the way such affinity between radical queer and anarchist politics in the United States has endured in the contemporary moment. These political, social, and intellectual interventions have been transformative for New Anarchist politics in the United States because they attempt to account for the particular ways in which the US state operates as a disciplinary structure exceptionally concerned with the regulation of gendered and sexual identities and practices.

For instance, Ryan Conrad's "Gay Marriage and Queer Love" explores how a movement grounded in equal inclusion in the institution of marriage is acquiescing to a "social contract that explicitly limits the ways in which we can organize our erotic and emotional lives" rather than a path toward "a radically equitable queer future."[66] Similarly, J. Rogue's "De-essentializing Anarchist Feminism: Lessons from the Transfeminist Movement" argues for the integration of approaches to gender and sexuality that reject essentialism since shifting this paradigm is necessary for coming to a more complete understanding of prevailing feminist and anarchist issues, including access to health care and mental health support services.[67] Stacy aka sallydarity's "Gender Sabotage" goes even further, offering an anarchist account of the formation of heteronormative gendered and sexual hierarchies that makes specific connections to the forming of the US state. These examples show how contemporary anarchist approaches to gender and sexuality in the United States are more attentive in their analyses to the context of the political and social structures of this particular nation-state.

But, these approaches continue to stop short of integrating a clear and concerted analysis of settlement as an intrinsic part of the structure of the US state. This is not only a failure to adequately account for settlement within anarchist analyses of gender and sexuality but also a reinscription of the structure of settlement within such analysis. Other scholars have evidenced such reinscription within queer movements. Building on Jasbir Puar's development of "homonationalism," Scott Morgensen has described the development of "settler homonationalism," a framing that he uses to confirm how "the imposition of colonial heteropatriarchy relegates Native people and all non-Native people of color to queered statuses as racialized populations amid colonial efforts to eliminate Native nationality and settle Native lands."[68] In developing an approach to the study of sexuality and queer modernity that is focused on the question of settlement, Morgensen is interested (as I am) in exploring how radical movements replicate the logic of settler colonialism by defining queer modernity "as not Native."[69] The precision of this work emanating from the intersection of feminist, queer, and settler colonial studies has not been addressed in contemporary anarchist studies of gender and sexuality, resulting in the reification of a settler structure within such inquiry.

For instance, in her discussion of the development of gender essentialism as a foundational component of the US nation-state, sallydarity argues that, "to understand the construction of a gender binary and hierarchy, we primarily look at Europe because of the ways in which, through colonization/imperialism, Europe violently exported its ideas throughout the world." Drawing on Silvia Federici's influential work on witch hunts and primitive accumulation, she goes on to argue that "it is no coincidence . . . that the witch hunts [in seventeenth-century United States] occurred in conjunction with the transition to capitalism and the colonization of the Americas."[70] And, of course, it is no coincidence. However, sallydarity's analysis does not offer an explicit analysis of the concurrence between the institution of a "gender binary and hierarchy" and the exigencies of the settler project. Many scholars working in Native gender, sexuality, and feminist studies have worked to articulate these connections, asserting the centrality of a normalized structure of the gender binary and heterosexuality to the project of expropriating Native land and resources.[71]

By invoking US colonialism as a generalized structure rather than reckoning with the specificity of the US settler context, sallydarity's mention of the connection between gender, sexuality, capitalism, and colonialism remains abstracted. Because of this, it is unclear how her vision of "gender transgression" can work to "transcend or destroy the gender-based power relations, as part of a sort of decolonizing."[72] Here, decolonization is invoked as a stand-in for all radical politics, a process that Tuck and Yang have articulated as an investment in the structure of settlement since it acts as a "form of enclosure, dangerous in how it domesticates decolonization." In this, the vision of an anarchist gender transgression that sallydarity proposes is rooted in "yet another form of settler appropriation," reproducing the structure of settlement within anarchist terms that simultaneously aim to address gendered and sexual hierarchy.[73]

This form is replicated in a number of anarchist texts on gender and sexuality, whether through the mention of two-spirit identity without any cultural grounding; identifying oneself as a settler without transforming one's method of analysis; the assertion of Indigenous movements as important influences without a critical examination of where such influence is either present or reciprocated; and the indiscriminating inclusion of terms like "indigenous," "colonization," or "decolonization" in larger litanies of seemingly related vocabularies.[74] As L. Cornum has noted, "Simply acknowledging 'two-spirit' peoples . . . does not account for the particular ways in which Western conceptions of gender have wreaked violence on Indigenous peoples" and neither can these other terms act as metonyms for the more concerted analysis required to make these structures legible within an anarchist framework.[75]

Accordingly, this formulation does nothing to locate an anarchist project of delimiting gendered and sexual boundaries in commitments to Native sovereignty or self-determination over land, territory, and nation (in addition to individual bodies). Here, the limitations of anarchist approaches to feminism are confirmed. Though analyses of gender and sexuality through an anarchist lens have become more rooted in the particular context of the US state, they have yet to adequately account for settlement both in their analysis of the state structure and in within the structures of anarchist movements themselves.

* * *

In their statement "Internationalism and Imperialism," the Black Rose Anarchist Federation argues that "our fight is both internal and external. Internally we fight the foundations of the imperialist economy and state which provides the basis for imperialism. Externally we seek to build concrete unity, through action and solidarity with movements that struggle to end imperialism and capitalism."[76] Much like the statement with which I began this chapter, which offers a more specific discussion of these points of unity by locating them in the particular context of the Trump Era, this statement on imperialism reveals the proliferation of an approach to heteropatriarchy that is grounded in a settler anarchist structure.

First, the anarchist investment in a settler structure is made obvious through the configuration of inside/outside that this point of unity provides. Replicating the narrative that US imperialism happens "out there" or in the external world, Black Rose implies that the "internal" work is to fight the domestic economic foundation of foreign intervention without any signal that some of this internal work may be to confront the structures of imperialism in anarchist spaces themselves. Without any mention of Native peoples in any of the Points of Unity, and only the briefest mention in reference to environmental movements in the "Beyond and Below Trump" statement, the configuration of imperialism offered by Black Rose reinforces the settler structure of the US state by locating the "foreign" as an "external" place rather than emphasizing that, in the context of North America, it is the United States that is the foreign empire.

In much the same way that the statement separates the "feminist movements" from "indigenous and environmental movements," so too do the Points of Unity evade any engagement of the relationship between gender, sexuality, and settler colonialism. In this, settlement is absolved as the material foundation of US empire, and feminism, gender, and sexuality are untethered from the material structures and discourses through which they acquire meaning in service of the state. As a result, anarchism is continually presented as the proprietary salve of radicalism in the United States. This structure of engagement is continually replicated in the contemporary anarchist writing on feminism, gender, and sexuality, wherein interventions from Native feminists and feminists of color are treated as niche oeuvres whose inclusion enriches anarchist analysis but does not transform it, when they are considered at all. Although a more rigorous engagement with how anarchist analyses of heteropatriarchy intersect with Native feminist critiques of the settler state would bolster the anarchist criticism of the US state, this obfuscation of the question of settlement remains tantamount to anarchist writings on feminism, gender, and sexuality.

In this chapter, I have focused especially on the structure of anarchist engagements with feminism, gender, and sexuality so that I may, again, emphasize issues of structure rather than a strict criticism of content. This approach attains a new valence when considering the body of work described here, since attempts to reckon with questions of feminism, gender, and sexuality remain one of the places in the milieu where anarchists have made important inroads to establishing a more concerted commitment to understanding the structure of settlement within the US context. Work like that of Shannon, Volcano, and Rogue demonstrate that anarchists are aware of and attempting to integrate the interventions of Native feminists and feminists of color, taking seriously the challenges they pose to more embedded formulations of radical politics. Above, I've traced both the rote taxonomy of anarchist engagements with feminism and the individualized rendering of gender and sexuality to prove how these approaches are restricted not through their intellectual intentions (which demonstrate a desire to willfully and thoughtfully engage with questions of settlement) but through the structure of their inquiry.

What becomes apparent when we apprehend anarchist engagements with feminism, gender, and sexuality in this way is how the structure of such inquiries mirror the structure of settlement and, in this, limit the ability of New Anarchism to account for some of the most pressing issues of gendered and sexualized violence that are incumbent within the processes of statecraft through which the US and Canadian settler states are constituted. Though I discuss this more in-depth at the end of this section on relocating gendered violence, I am thinking especially here of the campaign to address missing and murdered Indigenous women, girls, queer, and two-spirit communities. Without a methodology that can connect prevalent anarchist concerns like the militarization of borders, expansion of the prison industrial complex, and corporate capitalism to the processes of land dispossession, resource extraction, and suppression of the polity of the Indigenous as a cosmological edifice, anarchist feminism is unable to account for the particular dimensions of gendered and sexualized violence within the context of the settler state.

In the next chapter, I turn to poetry by two Native women authors to explore how they evidence the gendered structure of settlement through critical responses to monuments of American literature and alternative renderings of symbolized Native women in national American mythologies. Paying special attention to the way each author uses poetic form to confirm the gendered structure of settler claims to place, I demonstrate how this work might be of particular use as we begin to imagine new structures of inquiry for New Anarchist approaches to feminism, gender, and sexuality. In doing so, I highlight how such authors use literary intervention to provide methodologies capable of attending to the intimate connections between gendered and sexualized violence and the structure of settlement at the root of US and Canadian claims to sovereignty.

CHAPTER 4

"Some Elsewhere"

Poetic Transformations of American Monuments

Poetry, American Mythology, and Linguistic Performance

In her seminal study of the indiscernibility of Native women's poetry both within the study of Native literatures and the study of American literature more broadly, Deborah Miranda (Ohlone-Costanoan Esselen/Chumash) articulates the indelible connection between the mythology of American identity and the visibility of Native women. For her, the liminality of Native women's poetry is not due to a lack of material but rather is rooted in the danger that the centering of such work poses to what she calls "American mythology" or the stories through which the United States is constituted. She argues:

> if Native women, who bear the scars from five hundred years of erotic murder in this country, suddenly become visible, there is hell to pay. The crimes against humanity committed in the name of colonization become visible alongside these women, while the U.S. Constitution and Bill of Rights, as well as every treaty ever written and every protest against genocide in "other countries" suddenly become testimony that strangles American mythology and identity.[1]

The obfuscation of Native women's poetry, in Miranda's estimation, is the focal point of a collective and purposeful amnesia meant to justify the myth of the United States as a fully constituted, democratic, sovereign state. I want to emphasize here the scope of Miranda's illustration of the collusion between the neglect of Native women's poetry (operating here metonymically for Native women's presence more generally) and the sustenance of American mythology: she is concerned not only with how such amnesia is central to this mythology as it is invoked by the political documents through which the state is formed (such as the Constitution or the Bill of Rights) but also through the invocation of American democracy in critiques of "genocide in 'other countries.'" Emphasizing the irony of casting outrage at genocide outward into the world, Miranda's use of scare quotes emphasizes how the directionality of such rage reifies the settler claims of the United States.

In the previous chapter, I made a parallel argument focused on the structure of anarchist engagement with feminist, gender, and sexuality studies. There, I argued that the edifice of the US state remains intact within anarchist analyses of feminism, gender, and sexuality because they refuse to critically engage the question of settlement and its material dimensions. Much like Miranda locates the shoring up of US settler narratives through the structure of engagement with Native women's poetry, I located the expression of US settler sovereignty in anarchist spaces in the structure of engagement with questions of feminism, gender, and sexuality within the milieu. In this chapter, I examine two collections of poetry by Native authors to elucidate a methodological approach to feminism, gender, and sexuality that can more adequately account for the structure of settlement within anarchist spaces. In particular, I look to Ojibwe poet Heid E. Erdrich's 2008 collection *National Monuments* and Mohawk/Tuscarora poet Janet Rogers's 2017 collection *Totem Poles and Railroads* to see how they address some of the most foundational issues that plague the anarchist engagements I dealt with in chapter 3, including the material foundation of land, the gendered dimensions of settlement, and the role of the symbolization of Native women in maintaining settler sovereignty.

On one hand, this chapter continues the structure of this book more generally, which seeks to explore and expound on the uses of literature to shape anarchist political engagement. In this sense, I engage these two poetry collections as part of a wider arc of engagement with the place of Native women's writing in discussions of contemporary radical politics in the United States. On the other hand, this chapter also attempts to deal more specifically with the genre of poetry as one particular well-suited to revealing the complex methodologies that are necessary to address the structure of settlement within New Anarchism.

As Anishnaabe poet and scholar Molly McGlennen has argued, because it is "a genre that is attentive to the efficiency of language, poetry sustains a variety of shared spaces, which ultimately disrupt the linear, colonial narratives of violence that have been inscribed into the bodies and bodies of knowledge of Native peoples."[2] In chapter 2, I explored how Native nonfiction writers used form to address some of these linear colonial narratives. Here, I build on this work in a different genre by using McGlennen's focus on the inscriptions of violence that are written across both the physical and epistemological bodies of Native peoples, including the land and water, to explore how Erdrich and Rogers use poetry to re-mark these inscriptions in corrective ways. In doing so, I reveal more deeply the consequences of anarchist approaches to feminism, gender, and sexuality that are unable to read such inscriptions of violence beyond the individual body while also emphasizing how Native women poets provide generative ways of reading these inscriptions that aim to destabilize the gendered structures of settlement that such imprints uphold.

The relationship between the bodies and bodies of knowledge of Native peoples, of the other worlds that live here, are lost in the untethering of a New Anarchist politics from an engagement with settlement as constitutive of the US state and this particular form of dislocation is obvious in the treatment on feminism, gender, and sexuality. As McGlennen observes, poetry is an especially potent mechanism through which to address this untethering, since Native feminisms are central to the discourse of poetry because it "often redirects one's understanding of Indigenous women's response to colonialism by mapping routes beyond that enterprise of violence."[3] This echoes Sarah Dowling's recent argument that poetry is an essential radical political form.[4] Drawing on writing by Oglala Lakota poet Layli Long Soldier and Nisga'a poet Jordan Abel, Dowling argues that these "works show that when governments resort to linguistic performances like apology as substitutes for decolonization and material redistribution, poetry becomes a critical tool for response, intervention, and especially refusal" precisely because of its careful attention to and redistribution of language and linguistic performance.[5] And though Dowling is primarily concerned with how Long Soldier's and Abel's poetry confront *governmental* performances that reveal "the grounding of liberal multiculturalism in settler colonial theft," her insights are relevant to my project here as it explores how these performances are replicated in anarchist spaces using anarchist logics.[6]

Discourses on Indians in American Literature

So, if poetry is understood in this way, as a potent tool for addressing the gendered structures of settlement within claims to liberal multiculturalism both in mainstream and radical spaces, how does this intersect with the structure of the American literary canon? Miranda offered an important inroad to this question above, focusing on the obfuscation of Native women's poetry and the mythologization of Native bodies, stories, and literatures within the canon. This critique goes beyond recognizing the demographics of representation within the field to explore the gendered structures that underwrite it. It is one thing to recognize the deeply white and male character of the American literary canon—it is another to explore what this reveals about the gendered, sexualized, and racialized dimensions of the structure of settlement.

Other scholars of Native literatures have attempted similar projects in an attempt to underscore the dependence on tropes about Native peoples in the American literary canon. For instance, in *Muting White Noise: Native American and European American Novel Traditions*, James H. Cox uses Anishnaabe scholar Jill Carter's method of "red reading" to read foundational American texts in ways that "privilege a critical practice based on the work of Native creative writers and intellectuals and foreground the issues that they raise as important to Native people and communities."[7] Here, I am interested in extending this method beyond a critical practice that is *based on* the work of Native creative writers to explore how such theoretical intervention is *developed through* the creative work itself. What is more, I want to center the work of Native women writers in producing theoretical and methodological interventions through literary practice. I do this to address a limit in Cox's approach, which privileges a staunch division between literature and theory; which most resolutely focuses on canonical American authors; and which fails to address the relationship between gender and settlement.[8]

Cox's work draws deeply on a well of scholarly inquiry that addresses the question of Native presence in the history of American literature. This is not unexplored territory, to use a potent turn of phrase. Rather, numerous scholars have sought to understand how the foundations of the American literary canon depend on and reproduce particular assumptions about Native peoples through both prominent representation and conspicuous absence. For instance, in his study of early American literatures, Joshua Bellin has argued that "it is because

American literature emerges from contexts of encounter, from the interaction and intersection of peoples, that the presence of Indians is central to the literature."[9] Using this to reframe his analysis of key texts in canonical early American literature, Bellin argues for what he calls an "intercultural" approach that places these moments of encounter at the center of the study of American literature to, among other things, "refuse to reduce Indians to static antagonists or fodder for a Euro-American imaginary but to view them as actors in dynamic processes in which America and its literature were (and are) inescapably embedded."[10]

Similarly, Renée L. Bergland has argued that Native presence literally haunts American literature as a ghostly presence, a technique rooted in the "discursive removal of Indians from American physical territory and the Americanization of the imaginative territory into which Indians are removed."[11] For her, this process of "ghosting" is both a repressive and resistant one, since it "draws its ideological power from the sense of fait accompli (the Indians are already gone) and from reinforcing the intractable otherness of Indians" while also "present[ing] us with a host of doubts about America and American ideology."[12] As with Bellin's insistence on shifting to an intercultural approach, Bergland's articulation of ghosting emphasizes that she sees it operating within a rhetorical register that addresses the structures of power that underwrite, both overtly and duplicitously, American claims to Native land and the concomitant practices of narrating indigeneity within the canon. Along with other foundational approaches like Susan Scheckel's *The Insistence of the Indian* and Laura Mielke's *Moving Encounters*, Bellin's and Bergland's work prove the thinking that scholars have done about the foundational role that Indianness, as both corporeal and spectral presence, continues to play in the practice of American storytelling and the narrativization of the nation.

But, as Mark Rifkin has pointed out in his own study of nineteenth-century American literature, these texts focus "primarily on the ways non-native texts manifest Indian figures, the contours of those depictions, and the kinds of feelings and relations borne by them."[13] Therefore, such scholars locate the structure of settler colonialism, he argues, only as it "inheres in Native bodies" rather than "understanding it as a phenomenon that shapes non-native subjectivities, intimacies, articulations, and sensations separate from whether or not something recognizably Indian comes into view."[14] In his study of works by Nathaniel Hawthorne, Henry David Thoreau, and Herman Melville,

Rifkin eschews this reading of Native presence in early American literature as "indicative of a particular attitude, discourse, or ideology framing" and, instead, aims to highlight a "set of non-native inclinations, orientations, modes of perception, forms of network, and durable lived assemblages . . . experienced as the stability of the given."[15] In doing so, he explicitly explores the connections between settlement and the American literary canon but in canonization itself (to harken back to chapter 2) and the invocation of such a body of work to act as "the stability of the given."

My approach in this chapter shares many affinities with Rifkin's. Like him, I am also concerned with how previous approaches to the study of Native presence in American literature has tended to read Native bodies as the location on which to account for the structure of settlement, rather than understanding American literature itself as being marked by such a structure even in the (seeming) absence of Native presence. In moving toward a method that understands American literature otherwise, I ground my engagement in a series of questions that are obscured by what Rifkin calls the "stability of the given": if the structure of analytic engagement must be the moment of encounter, why? And on whose terms is this encounter set when it is reproduced as literary method? Whose protocols and methods of diplomacy are understood as the foundation of such encounter? Whose narratives are read as autonomous and whose are read as interventions in already established conversations?

I agree that, since Native land forms the literal foundation of the territory claimed by the United States, the question of settlement and the indelible history and persistence of Native writing must be included in discussions of American literature. However, in this chapter, I am interested in moving away from providing yet another reading of canonical American texts using the particular methods or insights enabled through an attentiveness to the presence of Indianness within their pages, whether Bellin's intercultural reading, Bergland's spectral presence, Cox's red readings, or Rifkin's settler common sense. Though I understand explanations like Rifkin's that such texts are "chosen *for* their canonicity, for the ways they continue to occupy an overdetermined place" within the field, I see no need to respond here by digging more deeply into that canon.[16] Instead, I am interested in centering texts by Native authors to explore such questions about canonicity, American literature, and Native presence. And I want to add to this a focus on how such authors center gender within discussions of the structure of settlement. This work draws on Rifkin's, which seeks to understand the relationship between what he calls a settler common sense and "specifically *queer* critiques of the state" in Hawthorne's *House of Seven Gables*, Melville's *Pierre*, and Thoreau's *Walden*.[17]

Just as Rifkin is interested in the tension of radicalism and settlement within these texts, I am interested in how texts by Native authors offer critical readings of particular practices of American radicalism to demonstrate their rootedness in settlement as a gendered and sexualized process. Whereas Rifkin explores this tension through an examination of the relationship between settler common sense and radical queer critiques of the state that he reads within these texts, I am interested in how Native authors have used to poetry to evidence how the creation of literary monuments within the canon depends on particular gendered and sexualized structures that bolster, rather than confront, the structure of settlement.[18] In what follows, I draw on Klamath scholar Angela Teresa Morrill's articulation of a "Native feminist reading methodology" to explore how contemporary Native authors use poetry to engage the structure of settlement and its rootedness in gendered violence within canonical American literary texts. These two elements of this chapter—the focus on readings of canonical American texts within Native women's poetry rather than *my own* rereading of such texts and the focus on contemporary writing rather than that of the nineteenth century—form the two pillars that distinguish this chapter from the body of scholarship mentioned above.

In invoking Morrill's approach, I also seek to draw a clear connection to the overall project of *Other Worlds Here*. As she observes, "what I am newly naming as a methodology is actually a legacy of practices that predates any such naming."[19] The forms of reading that Morrill identifies as a Native feminist reading methodology then, are not only preexisting, but draw on the existing worlds of stories that live with the land and its people. As Morrill insists, in this methodology, "there is a recognition of the knowledge of Indigenous peoples, there is an assumption of complexity and humanity."[20] So, by exploring how contemporary Native authors are using poetry *as* Native feminist reading methodology, we can see that such knowledge of complexity and humanity is not only *about* Native peoples, communities, and land but also about broader topics on which Native authors are rarely assumed to have expertise—including canonical American literature.

In this way, I move beyond reading Native literature through an autoethnographic approach, which Mary Louise Pratt describes as a "text in which people undertake to describe themselves in ways that engage with representations others have made of them."[21] Instead, I argue that the approach offered by Morrill, which I employ in my reading of poetry by Erdrich and Rogers's work below, evidences a method in which such authors undertake to describe *the United States and its literary monuments* in ways that engage with representations that American authors (as well as their critics, enthusiasts, and devotees) have attempted to make of themselves, their histories, and their legacies. This approach reframes Bergland's emphasis on the spectral presence of Indians in canonical American literature, then, through a rhetoric of haunting grounded in Native feminist readings: as Morrill observes, "reading is beyond words, it is hearing ghostly voices."[22] Rather than reading what Bergland calls the ghostly presence of Native people in American literature, this hearing echoes the process of haunting that Eve Tuck and C. Ree have explored in their "glossary of haunting," which "includes *the particular and the general*, violating the terms of settler colonial knowledge that require the separate of the particular from the general, the hosted from the host, personal from the public, the foot(note) from the head(line), the place from the larger narrative of nation, the people from specific places."[23] In what follows, I demonstrate how Erdrich and Rogers take up American literary monuments in ways that, especially, refuse this separation between place and the narrative of nation, people from place, and gender from settlement. In doing so, I insist on the role that Native women's poetry can play in deconstructing the assumptive links between anarchism, radical gender politics, and a resistance to settlement.

American Literary Monuments

Erdrich's 2008 collection *National Monuments* is such an exploration, focused on both illuminating the naturalization of settlement through literature and the body while investigating the construction of monuments that confront that process as well. Throughout the collection, Erdrich is concerned with the interconnected arc of monuments and Native peoples, from "monuments of literature that use indigenous figures as metaphor" to "sacred spaces and the risks we humans pose to the landscape" and to "the body itself [as] the place of monument."[24] As Abenaki poet Cheryl Savageau observes in her review of the collection, "this is poetry that matters . . . which grows out of the tribal voice of an Ojibway woman in this particular time in history, who reclaims her body, the land, and her vision as Native space."[25] Throughout the collection, Erdrich echoes approaches to canonical American literatures that I discussed at the outset, engaging with monuments of the tradition like Walt Whitman, William Carlos Williams, and Robert Frost to enact the structure of reclamation that Savageau describes as insisting on the inexpungible connection between body, land, and epistemology in the constitution of Native space. Erdrich's engagement moves beyond the cursory recognition that the American literary canon reflects a deep investment in whiteness and masculinity to explore how the gendered dimensions of settlement act as the foundation of both the United States and its literary monuments.

Erdrich's poetic response to Robert Frost's "The Gift Outright" is an impeccable example of Savageau's description of the collection's ability to bring together questions of body, land, and Native space. In "The Theft Outright," Erdrich reorders lines from Frost's poem, interjecting rejoinders to common settler responses to Native claims to territory. Frost's poem, most famously recited at John F. Kennedy's presidential inauguration in 1961 (a point to which I return below), begins, "The land was ours before we were the land's. / She was our land more than a hundred years / Before we were her people . . ."[26] Reorienting Frost's notion of the "gift" as "theft," Erdrich writes, "We were the land's before we were. // Or the land was ours before you were a land. / Or this land was our land, it was not your land. // We were the land before we were people."[27] Erdrich's reconfiguration insists on asserting a different understanding of the relationship between land and people, calling attention to how Frost's formation not only operates in a register of settler claims to space but also evidences the material of his own declaration's unmaking. Through this rearranging of Frost's words, Erdrich moves beyond the elementary recognition of US claim to territory as theft of Native land. Rather, throughout the poem, Erdrich uses the reordering of Frost's words to emphasize the ironic clash between his assertion of eternal prior claim to the land, his articulation of such land as a gift, and his sense that the presence of settlers is a gift to the land.

Here, she highlights the fundamental paradox at the heart of Frost's poetic rendering of the tie between American identity and place, wherein Frost imagines this relationship between the American polity and the land:

> Such as we were we gave ourselves outright
> (The deed of gift was many deeds of war)
> To the land vaguely realizing westward[28]

In her reworking of this passage, Erdrich taunts Frost's uses of parentheses to quietly recognize the legacies of violence through which the American polity supposedly gave of themselves to the land, which moved itself in the path of conquest. Her lines read:

> Such as we were we gave most things outright
> (the deed of the theft was many deeds and leases and claims and stakes
> and tenure disputes and moved plat markers stolen still today . . .)[29]

Erdrich's emphasis on the dual connotations of the term *deed* to refer to the gift of which Frost speaks extends beyond a neat interlude into a bigger narrative of inevitable westward conquest. Instead, the majority of her passage is contained within the parentheses, noting that contained within the claims that Frost attempts to make ancillary is the confirmation of the structure of settlement. In this sense, the "outright" theft to which Erdrich is pointing evokes a sense of directness, where such theft is not concealed but, rather, is an openly made and openly accepted part of the narrative of American history. This challenges the earnestness of the "outright" of Frost's poem, which evokes a sense of completeness, of a gift given without hesitation.

Erdrich's invocation of "theft" then mirrors Patrick Wolfe's famed description of settlement as a structure and not an event, underscored by her use of the ellipsis. Simultaneously, Erdrich centers indigeneity in her invocation of land, reaffirming Kanaka Maoli scholar J. Kēhaulani Kauanui's sentiment that one cannot speak of settlement without speaking of "enduring indigeneity," a concept that speaks to the concurrent resilience of Indigenous peoples and the sustenance of settlement against indigeneity.[30] Most importantly, Erdrich frames her contention with popular American rhetorics that attempt to regulate or deny indigeneity, such as the impulse to use DNA evidence or the Bering Strait theory, through gendered language.[31] As Cherokee scholar Rayna Green has argued, the ascription of both femininity and indigeneity to the territory of the so-called New World is essential to the structure of settlement. According to Green, the figure of the Native woman has long had a "symbolic, many-faceted life as a mother figure—exotic, powerful, dangerous, and beautiful—and as a representative of American liberty and European classical virtue translated into New World terms."[32] In "The Theft Outright," Erdrich unearths the ghost of this figure in Frost's formulation of American claim to Native land, echoing her inclusion of this poem in the section entitled "American Ghosts," invoking the type of haunting delineated by Tuck, Ree, and Morrill that arises from a centering of Native worlds.

Frost's gendering of the land "In Massachusetts, in Virginia" is deeply connected to his articulation of such space as uncivilized, void of any artistic or progressive merit. His use of "she" to refer to the land, as in his early declaration that "She was our land more than a hundred years / Before we were her people. She was ours," traces through to the end of the poem, in which he describes the land as "still unstoried, artless, unenhanced / Such as she was, such as she would become."[33] Invoking a constellation that links tropes of both feminine and Native passivity, Frost depends on an appeal to indigeneity that remains implied. In her reordering, Erdrich makes this dependence explicit, revealing a reconfiguration of this constellation through the lens of Native cosmology. The gendered language of "The Theft Outright" is indelibly connected to narrating Creation rather than the origins of Americanness:

> Red rocks, blood clots bearing boys, blood sands
> swimming being from women's hands, we originate,
> originally, spontaneous as hemorrhage.[34]

And later:

> We were the land before we were a people,
> earthdivers, her darling mudpuppies, so the stories go,
> or emerging, fully forming from flesh of earth—[35]

As in Frost's poem, Erdrich uses gendered language to engage the land. However, she does so within the context of Ojibwe creation stories, reframing Frost's use of gendered conceptions of land as an indication of passivity to emphasize Native cosmology. In Erdrich's poem, the feminine land is not passive but instead the site of dynamic creation.

In this way, Erdrich's focus on the gendered body evokes the body as Native polity, exhibiting Goeman's observation that "the focus on the gendered body . . . provides sites in which we can examine gendered, sexualized, and racialized differentiations in relation to imagined geographies that buttress colonialism and enact violence in our daily lives."[36] In this sense, the use of gendered language is evoked not as a stand-in for an engagement with "women" but rather speaks to the broader ways in which American claims to Native land are naturalized in monuments of American literature.

Such a critical reworking of "The Gift Outright" is essential not only because of the long shadow that Frost casts in the canon of American literature but also because of the role that this poem has played in the narrative of the United States as an ostensible monument to liberal democracy. Frost's recitation of it at Kennedy's inauguration speaks to the persistence of the structure of settlement even within a political discourse that makes claims to self-determination for Native peoples. Kennedy (and Lyndon B. Johnson, after him) is often considered to be a president whose political commitments signaled a positive change in how the federal government interacted with Native tribes and nations. Most notably, this era supposedly marked an end to the "termination era" of Federal Indian Policy, during which the US government enacted policies and practices aimed at assimilating Native peoples as US subjects, and moved instead into an era of "self-determination," during which the US government supposedly recognized the ability of Native tribes and nations to self-govern as sovereign polities. Partly owing to this shift, Kennedy is popularly regarded as friendly to Native interests, a legacy perhaps most famously solidified in his introduction to William Brandon's 1961 *The American Heritage Book of Indians*, in which he wrote, "For a subject worked and reworked so often in novels, motion pictures, and television, American Indians remain probably the least understood and most misunderstood Americans of us all."[37]

Frost's recitation of "The Gift Outright" at Kennedy's inauguration speaks to the ways in which Kennedy's political agenda, which as M. Annette Jaimes (Yaqui/Juaneño) has pointed out, was called the "New Frontier," a rhetorical device not exactly designed to reassure an indigenous population nearly obliterated during the US conquest of its first "wilderness," was bound to the assimilation of Native bodies, polities, and land into the fabric of the settler state.[38] For instance, though this era is referred to as one of "self-determination," the Kinzua Dam was also built during his presidency, flooding traditional territories of the Seneca Nation, which were protected through one of the country's oldest treaty agreements.[39] This connection to the political structure of US

Federal Indian Policy emphasizes the close relationship between the American literary canon and American political discourse.

"The Gift Outright" solidifies, through literary monument, the invocation of a gendered prior claim to land, naturalizing the US state within the context of a liberal commitment to inclusion. The connection to Kennedy's presidency evidences this as constant thread in the American political landscape, one whose presence is strong across the political spectrum. Accordingly, Erdrich's use of reordering to apprehend Frost's poem provides an important lens through which to understand both the place of literary monument in the maintenance of settlement and the continuity with which a naturalization of settlement is expressed in gendered terms throughout the political spectrum in the United States.

Mohawk/Tuscarora poet Janet Rogers similarly engages questions of land, the body, and literary canon as historical edifice in her collection *Totem Poles and Railroads*, which explores the relationship between Native nations and the structure of settlement in the postreconciliation era as still deeply connected to the histories of settlement marked on the land and its people. As the title indicates, Rogers is similarly concerned with Native monuments, such as totem poles, and the legacies of colonial monuments, such as the transcontinental railroad. And though much of her collection focuses on engaging the monuments of the Canadian settler state, her approach defies and criticizes the easy division of the 49th parallel, particularly when it comes to the artistic monuments with which she engages. Rogers's' collection emerges at the confluence of an engagement with moments in a dynamic current of justice on a transnational scale, bringing together poems that explore the 2014 murder in Ferguson, Missouri, of Michael Brown by police office Darren Wilson; the Haudenosaunee Great Law of Peace; the music and legacy of Nina Simone; the erasure of Laura Secord, a pivotal figure in the War of 1812, from the historical record; and the narrative construction of Native women like Pocahontas and Sacajawea in the American cultural imaginary. Within this constellation comes her poem "Bowel," a response to Allen Ginsberg's seminal poem "Howl."

First published in 1956, Ginsberg's poem is a pivotal monument in contemporary American literary history, partly due to its centrality in the midcentury counterculture that was also a definitive part of the Kennedy years and partly due to the ensuing obscenity trial.[40] A decisive part of the history of the Beat Generation, "Howl" emerged in the tense Cold War era as a poem both hated and revered, its reception confirming for its readers the very paradox of which the poem spoke—that the true creativity of America was to be found in those people most maligned by its elite and that the very political institutions meant to uphold the shining legacy of the "City Upon the Hill" (a phrase popularized again a few years later by Kennedy) were squelching its imaginative genius through their anticommunist suppression.[41] In this sense, Ginsberg's poem ignited a counterculture that was at once critical of the institutions of the US state, especially the CIA, but was also deeply committed to a sense of Americanness whose disintegrating inimitability was to be deeply lamented. Rogers's "Bowel," which she labels "My Answer to Howl," engages Ginsberg's work through this lens of the legacy of the Beat Generation and its political commitments, putting particular emphasis on its gendered dimensions.

Though Rogers's poem is an "answer" to rather than reordering of a classic monument of the American literary canon, much like Erdrich she explores Ginsberg's poem through the language of the original work. In Rogers's case, this form is most clearly engaged through the use of rhythm and beat. As a spoken work artist, Rogers has noted her indebtedness to the work of the Beat Generation of artists, whose invocation of the "beat" spoke to both a sense of rhythmic tempo and a sense of defeat.[42] This influence is palpable in "Bowel," which pulses forward with a tempo and rhyming scheme that is unmistakably focused on the breath as a unit of conception, structurally grounded in the practice of recitation. Through this inhabitation of the Beat style, Rogers is able to speak both to the influence of the literary canon and its limitations for her as a Native woman writer, exploring the connections between the political and aesthetic commitments of the countercultural movement alongside the exclusion of women from its canonization as an important American literary tradition.[43]

For instance, the poem begins: "hot tears roll / a forced letting go / critical gaze upon my / discontented soul / turns up in published / words."[44] Here, Rogers evokes the central themes associated with the Beat Generation, the sense of wayward dissatisfaction and restlessness being reflected on the page. Later, she breaks with this connection or, at least, with her sense of participation in its legacy, particularly its formalization in "published / words":

> there is no beat generation
> just rejection of convention
> bodies, breathing rhythms
> feeling the highs and lows

our brothers and sisters
bringing their best confessions
and burning them in the glow[45]

In Rogers's estimation, the canonization of the Beat Generation in the published word has severely limited the impact of its core interventions. For her, the connection between understanding Beat poetry as published word and its insulation as a generation represents a removal of the body as the central foundation of Beat practices. In this sense, it is the connection of breath, expressed through the rhythm of Beat poetry, which anchors the resistive work of the genre. Rhythm, as the beat of bodies, defies convention since it refuses canonization by "burning them in the glow," by being ever-present but also fleeting. In this erasure of the literary incarnation of the body in Beat poetry, Rogers locates the gendered dimensions of settlement that are reproduced in its structure as an American literary monument.

As "Bowel" continues, Rogers identifies the connections between masculinity and claims to territory as both a spatial and temporal process:

bricks scraping skies
informing personalities
giving definition
to whole societies
hand built with
masculinity
holding territories
being held
in place
with time[46]

Here, she emphasizes how the holding of territory, both in place and in time, is related to masculinity. In her construction, masculinity is not synonymous with settlement but rather is the structure through which territory is held and stabilized "in place" and "with time." This reflects the work of scholars like Scott Morgensen and Amy Kaplan who have demonstrated how the political, social, and economic structures of settlement are configured through gendered discourse.[47] By placing such analysis within a response to Ginsberg's "Howl," Rogers directs our attention to the reproduction of settlement through gendered discourse in countercultural monuments. Her simultaneous embodiment and critique of Ginsburg's poem reckons with the tension at the heart of *Other Worlds Here*: how can we honor the formative influence of radical politics while simultaneously addressing the way such politics reproduce the structure of the US settler state?

In the case of "Howl," Rogers invokes the connection between the body and the word, employing Beat-era techniques that take the breath as the rhythmic pace of the poem, to identify the promulgation of the gendered discourses of settlement within the politics of the Beat Generation and its legacy as an American literary monument. "Bowel," then, is not either a whole-scale rejection of or capitulation to Beat poetry as an American literary monument. Rather, it is a careful meditation on the confluence of influence and critique. Her invocation of masculinity and its connection to holding territory speaks back to the popular articulation of Beat literature in general and "Howl" in specific as definitive of a countercultural gender politics.

Working not against but within the paradigm that, as Ernest Smith has argued, the Beats "redefined American culture's notion of the male community," Rogers questions the limitations of the idea that writers like Ginsburg "insistently interrogated the American construction of the male and masculinity . . . establishing the counterculture voice as a powerful instrument in American discourse."[48] In "Bowel," Rogers pays homage to the way in which the Beat generation experimented with literary form as a way of confronting the gendered and sexual discourses of the postwar era while illuminating how such countercultural discourse depended on a holding on to both masculinity and Americanness, indelibly intertwined.

In "The Theft Outright" and "Bowel," Erdrich and Rogers offer critical reworkings of American literary monuments to illuminate how Native land forms both the literal and figurative foundation of the American literary canon. What is more, they employ a method of analysis that evidences the way such a foundation in constituted through gendered discourses. This intervention extends those I mentioned at the outset to demonstrate not only the influence of the American canon on Native authors but also the structure of settlement within the canon itself. By choosing texts that have distinct connections to American political structures, such as the shift in Federal Indian Policy during Kennedy's presidency and the development of lasting countercultural literary practices during the Beat Generation, Erdrich and Rogers demonstrate the significance of poetry for upending the structure of settlement within American political structures, both mainstream and radical. Their attention to the gendered dimensions of settlement within their poetic interventions amends previous Native literary scholarship that not only focuses on the work of Native men but also ignores the way that the political, economic, and cultural facets of settlement are expressed and upheld in gendered terms. Subsequently, the methodology espoused through these poems provides an analytic approach that extends beyond the page. This methodology is precisely what is missing, and thus needed, in anarchist approaches to feminism.

As I demonstrated in chapter 3, the structure of popular anarchist approaches to feminism preclude an apprehension of the structure of settlement within discussions of gendered violence, making New Anarchism ill-equipped to address such violence as constitutive of the settler state and vice versa. Because of this, such approaches also render anarchists incapable of reckoning with the structures of both settlement and gendered violence within our own spaces as well. What Erdrich's and Rogers's poems provide is both an analysis and a methodology, ones that speak from *within* forms of the American literary canon to illuminate its dependence on a gendered settler structure. In reformulating anarchist approaches to feminism, Erdrich's and Rogers's work provides a methodology through which to understand how the gendered structure of settlement persists within the *form* of engagement. Employing such a methodology forces contemporary anarchists to account for the specificity of the US settler state in their analyses of gender and sexuality. What is more, this methodology insists on the relationship between literary and national monuments. In this way, their work with American literary monuments confirms the relationship between the American literary canon and the maintenance of US settler sovereignty as a gendered structure.

Revisiting Elsie, Pocahontas, and Sacajawea

In both *Totem Poles and Railroads* and *National Monuments*, the authors' apprehension of the American literary canon is complemented by concurrent examinations of the figure of the Native woman as a national symbol of settler sovereignty. As Audra Simpson has pointed out, the construction of the settler state and its claims to sovereignty do not persist despite but rather depend on the death and disappearance of Native women. According to her, the bodies of Native women both literally and symbolically threaten settler claims to sovereignty and thus have been the requisite focus of eradication by the settler state. Drawing from examples such as the 1876 Indian Act in Canada, the public treatment of Attawapiskat activist Theresa Spence's 2012 hunger strike, and the 2014 murder of Inuk student Loretta Saunders, Simpson argues that public suffering borne on Native women's bodies is a central feature through which the Canadian settler state secures the material dispossession of Native land.[49] This focus on the bodies of Native women does not supplant an engagement with gender through a limited focus on "women," but rather explores how the figure of the Native woman has formed a central tenet of the gendered structure of settler discourse. And though Simpson's focus is on the Canadian context, I turn here to poems by Erdrich and Rogers to demonstrate how they use poetry to establish, as Simpson does, the indelible connection between the violent dispossession at the heart of the settler structure, its imbrication in gendered discourse, and such anchoring in the symbol of the Native woman in the US context. Focusing especially on prominent symbols of Native womanhood in the American imaginary, Erdrich and Rogers despoil American obsessions with the figure of the Native woman, releasing the ballast affixed to claims to sovereignty by the settler state.

As Cherokee scholar Rayna Green argues in her study of what she calls the "Pocahontas perplex," narratives about Native women are intrinsic to the structures of settler time and place, so much so that these narratives reify Native women as symbolic bearers of American affections while programmatically disposing of the histories of Native women themselves. For Green, the American preoccupation with Pocahontas represents the most vivid depiction of this process. She argues that the symbolic casting of Pocahontas's story, which she traces in depictions of the Americas from the sixteenth century forward, demonstrates how "the Indian woman began her symbolic, many-faceted life . . . as a representative of American liberty and European classical virtue translated into New World Terms."[50] In her study of La Malinche, Pocahontas, and Sacajawea as national symbols, Rebecca K. Jager extends this slippage between Native women as national symbols and their biographical history, noting that while "these women have been immortalized in the national consciousness . . . the authenticity of their stories has become irrelevant."[51] Both Green and Jager emphasize how Native women's stories are mythologized as a way to navigate the core paradoxes of American identity and history, acting as symbolic resolutions of the competing claims to democratic liberty and Native land.

In her poems "Pocahontas" and "Sacajawea," Rogers uses retellings of Pocahontas's and Sacajawea's stories to address how the symbolization of Native women has structured contemporary gendered violence in the context of the settler state, particularly against Native women. Taken together, these poems speak to her larger project of examining the structure of settlement through popular cultural and social mores, tropes, and objects. For instance, in both poems, Rogers employs the first-person narrative voice to tell each woman's story. Because of this, the use of each woman's name as the title for her respective poem evokes the sense of each as a theatric monologue, the text of which follows from the mark of the character's name in all capital letters. In Rogers's reframing, Pocahontas's name extends vertically along the right side of the page while Sacajawea's sits at the bottom left, signaling alternative directions of narrative telling that invoke yet reframe the traditions of the script as literary form.

This signals Rogers's exploration of the direction of narrative retellings of Pocahontas's and Sacajawea's lives, especially the way such stories become bound to what Mishuana Goeman has described as "imposed spatial ideologies" that are visible in "reterritorialization" or the "colonial bounding and renaming of land, bodies, and communities."[52] Placing Pocahontas's name vertically along the inside of the page and Sacajawea's horizontally along the bottom of the page, Rogers questions the strategies of colonial spatial ideologies that are implemented through the attempt to stabilize these two women as national symbols whose stories mimic the spatial mapping of the frontier. As Jager notes, centering a discussion of how Pocahontas and Sacajawea become symbols of American sovereignty in the national imaginary provides an opportunity to consider "the frontier through the lens of gender."[53] In Rogers's poems, the spatial dimensions of Pocahontas and Sacajawea's stories are literally reoriented through the placement of their names on the page, opening up the figurative space to reconsider their stories outside the spatial ideologies of settlement.

This is especially clear in Rogers's use of the poems to imagine and recreate the affective dimensions of colonial encounter, sitting uncomfortably in what Athabascan scholar Dian Million has located in the "agonistic heart to the self-determination Indigenous peoples affectively work out."[54] For both Million and Rogers, a focus on affect allows us to center the question of how colonialism is felt and, thus, to explore the reproduction of the "affective resonance" at the heart of colonial power.[55] In her poems, Rogers unsettles the affective conventions of

Pocahontas's and Sacajawea's stories, which are often mobilized to elicit a sense of connection between settlers and Native peoples who had to endure the exigencies of the frontier together.[56] Bringing together reflections that illuminate each woman's internal affective life with familiar autobiographical details, Rogers both indicts American mythologies of Pocahontas and Sacajawea as national symbols while imagining a richer engagement with their lived experiences. For instance, both poems begin with "My," signaling Rogers's intent to create life histories in which Pocahontas and Sacajawea have possessive claim over their own stories, rather than being narrated through colonial records and national mythologies. She continues with retellings of familiar details, such as Pocahontas's rescue of John Smith and marriage to John Rolfe and Sacajawea's journey with Lewis and Clark on their cross-continental expedition. Yet, these retellings are punctuated with affective insights. In "Sacajawea," the poem begins:

> My young eyes saw many unusual and exciting
> things.
> A life full of random circumstance.
> I decided to see each one as an adventure, lest I
> bury myself in pity.[57]

This sets the contours of Rogers's retelling of Sacajawea's experience on the Lewis and Clark expedition, framing her active participation not as an absolution of white settlement (for which it is often mobilized) but, instead, as a rejection of her mythologization as a pitiable figure whose participation in the mapping of the Western frontier is celebrated through collective lament.

"Pocahontas" is structured through a similar affective matrix, wherein the narrator acknowledges that, while "It was true I changed names / Pocahontas to Rebecca. / A consensual reinvention," she still recognizes how her story is wielded to justify the colonization of her people and the land to which they belong. Speaking of the famed encounter between Pocahontas and John Smith, the poem continues:

> We adopted him.
> And the stories that came forth hence
> were fiction and folly.
> Drama and disaster.
> I was the great child ambassador

sent to make many trades and
negotiate with his people . . .

I was the intoxicating elixir to their
common and hostile ways.
Everyone got what they wanted
after the visits I paid.[58]

This reading not only illuminates the narrator's own estimation of her internal affective world but also shows her awareness of the affective worlds that her presence (both symbolic and literal) are used to solidify. Much like she did in "Sacajawea," Rogers reframes the direction of pity in the colonial mythologization of Native women as symbolic figures of the nation. In "Pocahontas," the narrator observes of her affective reaction to being present in London, a center of empire in the seventeenth century: "My compassion turned confusion / watching people living every day / against their own nature."[59] Here, the colonial metropolis and its subjects become the locale of pity, forcefully denying what Kwagiulth scholar Sarah Hunt has described as the colonial impetus to frame Native women's bodies as sites of naturalized violence.[60] That is, in Rogers's poems, the constant inscription of Pocahontas and Sacajawea as symbols naturalizing American national identity is confronted not through an acquiescence to a patronizing lament of how their bodies and the land to which they belong become swept up in the centrifugal force of colonial movement across both the Atlantic and North America, but rather through an insistence on their affective lives both during and beyond their lifetimes.

For Rogers, attention to these affective lives and their legacy is what illuminates the connection between body and land. Much in the same way that she and Erdrich use American literary monuments to indicate their foundation in Native land, Rogers's "Pocahontas" and "Sacajawea" poems illuminate how control of Native women as symbols has been intrinsic to the attempt to claim Native territory and bodies. For instance, in "Sacajawea," Rogers writes, "My mind and spirit were my only true territory. / My body was another thing."[61] Here, the phrase "another thing" operates within two valences, as both an indication of the consolidation of the body as object and a signification of the body as something other than "true territory." Throughout these poems, Rogers explores this territory and its body not as something static but as something dynamic; not bounded but also not terra incognita. When, toward the end of "Sacajawea," the narrator signals her death as her move to "a map-less heaven" where she is set constantly to "travel / down rivers where I am a guide to no one," this is not only a breath of relief at no longer having to serve as a guide to white settlers attempting to create colonial maps of Native territory but also an aching recognition of the connection between her body and the histories of mapping held therein.[62] Working within this unresolved tension, Rogers reframes Pocahontas's and Sacajawea's stories as Native mediators whose relationships to white men have been used to justify settler incursion through gendered discourse.

As both Green and Jager note in their studies of these women as national symbols, the stories of Pocahontas and Sacajawea often metonymically represent the loving adoption of European political, cultural, and economic systems by Native communities.[63] Thus, settlement becomes justified through the mythologization of Native women as symbolic figures whose ability to navigate territory and community become the foundation of settler claims to space. Rogers's poems reorder this mapping, confirming what Goeman has described as the process of "imagining new geographies that account for the violence of gendered spatial restructuring."[64]

Through a focus on the role that Pocahontas and Sacajawea play in the construction of an American settler imaginary, she illuminates how the gendered discourses of settlement are observable in the constant narration of Native women as symbols capable of resolving some of the core tensions of settlement. Instead, Rogers reorients, both spatially and ideologically, the affective dimensions of Pocahontas's and Sacajawea's stories to emphasize these tensions rather than allowing them to be seemingly resolved. In this sense, her project is less about recovering the "true" stories of Pocahontas and Sacajawea than it is about insisting on a reckoning with how the invocation of Native women as central symbols in narratives about America undermines rather than bolsters settler claims to space through gendered discourse.

We can see this project at work in Erdrich's *National Monuments* as well, especially in her apprehension of the figure of the Native woman as symbol in the American literary imagination. Appearing throughout her collection are poems in which the figure of Elsie appears, a reference to William Carlos Williams's celebrated poem "To Elsie." One of Williams's most prominent poems, "To Elsie" ruminates on themes that extended to the Beat Generation, including Ginsberg's "Howl." Perhaps most notable is Williams's indictment of the desecration of an idyllic, bucolic America and the subsequent disconnection of Americans from the land through which such idyll is born.[65] Emanating from Williams's initial lament that "The pure products of America / go crazy," "To Elsie" ends with the famed metaphor of America as a car with no driver: "No one / to witness / and adjust, no one to drive the car." Speaking to a loss of authority, a loss of control, and a disconnection from the material world that ostensibly gives meaning to American national identity, this metaphor is one of the more resounding legacies of Williams's poem. The figure of Elsie is the symbolic anchor of Williams's' lament, a woman "with a dash of Indian blood" who has been

> rescued by an agent—
> reared by the state and
>
> sent out at fifteen to work in
> some hard-pressed
> house in the suburbs—
>
> some doctor's family, some Elsie—
> voluptuous water
> expressing with broken
>
> brain the truth about us—[66]

However, she (much like Pocahontas and Sacajawea) is also a historical figure, a maid who came from the state orphanage to work for Williams who was a medical doctor in addition to being a successful writer.[67] And, much like Rogers does in her imputation of Pocahontas and Sacajawea as national symbols, Erdrich uses poetic intervention to draw attention to how this dependence on the symbolization of Elsie signals the gendered structures of settlement within prominent literary constructions of American national identity.

In *National Monuments*, Erdrich offers three poems that center Elsie. In "Some Elsie," "Infinite Progression," and "Elsie Picks up the Dry Cleaning," Erdrich removes Elsie from the metaphorical role that she is called on to play in Williams's "To Elsie." In Williams's poem Elsie is reduced to a symbolic receptacle whose diminished mental capacity, unsightly physical appearance, lamentable upbringing, and obsession with "cheap / jewelry / and rich young men with fine eyes" become the looking glass through which Americans can see "the truth about us." Yet, in Erdrich's series Elsie is a figure who gazes back rather than merely reflects.[68] In "Some Elsie," Elsie is a college student in an American literature class "at the Community College or Harvard or the U." reading Williams's poem.[69] Titled after the line in Williams's poem where Elsie is transmuted into a symbol, "Some Elsie" traces Elsie's affective response to reading about William's Elsie whose story is presented through the "sleek New York TA."[70] It is this teaching assistant who insists to Erdrich's Elsie that she must consider Williams's Elsie as "*a text*," a move that she refuses.[71]

Just as Rogers insisted on limning the affective worlds of Pocahontas and Sacajawea, Erdrich uses the exploration of affective response to resist the pseudohomonymic rendering of Williams's' "some Elsie" into a generic "someone else." Rather than depending on the use of first-person, as Rogers does, Erdrich employs the refrain, "What if . . .":

> So what if she was hemmed all around with murder?
> Or if a few of her relatives had screws loose?
> She'd deny bathing in filth from Friday to Sunday.
> What a girl does on the weekend,
> come on now, that's her own affair.
>
> She endures the comments about her body,
> "the great ungainly hips and flopping breasts"
> What if her ample chest had been her pride?
> What if, at first, she flushed at the sound of
> "voluptuous water" and took it as a compliment?
>
> What if, at first she thought, *Ah, at last*
> a poem about someone I know.[72]

Framing her own Elsie's response to Williams's poem through this phrase of possibility, Erdrich rejects the authority of Williams's representation of the meaning that the details of Elsie's body, life, and character hold for diagnosing a diseased Americanness. Erdrich does not interrogate the details of Williams's description, but rather uses the refrain of "what if?" to question his sense of command over Elsie as a metaphorical reflection of American pathology. Here, Erdrich is not offering a rewriting but a rereading, one that rejects American acclimatization to its own history through a naturalization of the violence borne on Native women's bodies.[73] The "what if" of Erdrich's Elsie rejects naturalization by shedding light on alternative interpretations that emanate from Elsie's own feelings about the poem and, by extension, the tainted center of American identity. In this, Elsie is no longer the one who is either contaminated by "a dash of Indian blood" or "rescued by an agent—/ reared by the state." Instead, she is a self-reflexive subject in whose gaze she sees herself.

Extending into poetic motion the force of the question "What if?," Erdrich's Elsie lives far beyond the confines of the home where she serves the doctor's family. In "Elsie Drops Off the Dry Cleaning," Erdrich fills out Elsie's story, telling us how Elsie ends up in the American literature class in the first place. In tracing Elsie's progression (a pivotal term to which I'll return in a moment), Erdrich explores how the symbol of the Native woman becomes constitutive of the American literary canon (and national identity). For instance, when Erdrich asserts halfway through the poem "This is how Elsie winds up in American Lit.," she means both how the Elsie of "Some Elsie" found her way to college and how the figure of the Native woman became a reliant feature of canonical American literature.[74] In "Elsie Drops Off the Dry Cleaning," the Elsie who sits in a college course in American literature in "Some Elsie" is Williams's Elsie also: though "Her career / as a house-girl is long over," it is her appropriation of his prescription pad to write her poems that begins her literary path:

> If only she were bad, she'd write some 'ludes,
> but instead she thinks to pen a few lines,
> like the master himself, confine her desires
> to the square under his name and Rx.[75]

Here, Williams is the doctor whose name and prescription pad "confine her desires," those same desires to which Erdrich's refrain of "what if" pointed in "Some Elsie." In this poem, Elsie's authority over her affective and literary life strengthens, moving beyond the hesitation of the question "what if?" into an ability to find a path out of her confinement. Graduating from Williams's prescription pad (that one he uses to diagnose a diseased America in "To Elsie"), Elsie moves to "Big Chief tablets thick with lines" and, eventually, "in years, Son of Big Chief tablets," children's writing notebooks that were popular around the same time Williams first published "To Elsie" and which featured a Native figure with a Plains-style headdress on the cover. Eventually, the Elsie that once picked up the dry cleaning is hitchhiking across the country, "raising kids and hell for AIM." All the while, she writes in these tablets, "writes, and writes, straddles a canon, makes a name."[76] Here, Elsie is no longer contained within the canon, part of its own self-definition. Instead, she bestrides the canon, placing herself both inside and outside of it, effectively mirroring Erdrich's own engagement with it as well.

Returning to the notion of Elsie's progression, this question of directional development is central to the life that Erdrich gives Elsie. In "Elsie Drop Off the Dry Cleaning," Erdrich confronts the stagnancy of Williams's Elsie by following her through spatial and temporal movement beyond the literal and figurative confines of the doctor's home. In a third poem referring to Williams's "To Elsie," Erdrich extends this movement into a constantly replicating future, recasting Williams's ascription of pity to Elsie's "dash of Indian blood." Instead, in "Infinite Progression," Erdrich builds on Cherokee and Choctaw literary scholar Louis Owens's foundational work on the literary figure of the mixed Native to redirect Williams's formulation of Elsie's indigeneity as a refractory lens through which the reality of a despoiled America can be seen.

Erdrich begins with the following epigraph from Owens's *Mixed-Blood Messages: Literature, Film, Family, Place*: "If the mixed blood is a tragic mirror for Euroamerica, giving back a disturbing reflection, then the Euroamerican in turn would seem to offer no reflection at all for the mixed blood who gazes back."[77] The poem follows from these premises, exploring them in both literal and figurative terms with a special emphasis on the symbolic work of the mirror. At the outset, Erdrich centers the gendered dimensions of reflection, writing that "Like most girls, Elsie avoided the mirror. / It distorted her, brought out her flaws." As the poem continues, Erdrich's Elsie is beset by the same insecurities about her appearance that emerge in her reaction to Williams's poem in "Some Elsie": "She combed her hair a lot and primped / in window reflections that minimized imperfections / and lent her torso elongated proportion." These anxieties are bound to the mirror as both a literal and figurative object, one that reflects the interrelated settler anxieties about gender and indigeneity.

However, as the poem continues Erdrich reframes the mirror and Elsie's relationship to it:

> In the restroom once, Elsie saw how one mirror
> gives back another
> and that one gives another back

until dozens reflect in one frame.
That, she thought, is me:

Connected in all directions,
a walking picture of infinity.[78]

Following Elsie's rejection of the idea of splitting herself in two and dispelling with part of her, this reframing of the mirror speaks to Erdrich's reworking of Williams's Elsie whose "dash of Indian blood" is precisely what consigns her to a refractory object of settler society.[79] Rather, in "Infinite Progression," Elsie reflects an infinite version of herself. In Erdrich's version, when Elsie finally sees herself in a mirror she finds that she exists forever "in all directions." Rather than reflecting a slow melting away into the fabric of an America that has gone "crazy," as in Williams's poem, Erdrich's Elsie finds that her presence becomes boundless when she sees herself reflected. In this, Erdrich reshapes the figure of the Native woman as constitutive of an infinite Native world rather than a mechanism through which settler society can consider its own limitations. The position of "Infinite Progression" within the collection mirrors this process, since it sits between "Some Elsie" and "Elsie Drops Off the Dry Cleaning," favoring a structural model of infinite rather than linear progression.

Through this trio of poems, Erdrich takes up the deep-seated dependence on the figure of the Native woman in the settler imagination. Denaturalizing Williams's Elsie from her place as a tragic mixed figure, first abducted and reared by the state and then employed in the home of a wealthy white doctor who sees clearly in her the failures of his own social order, Erdrich simultaneous evidences and contests the appropriation of Native women as symbols in the American literary canon and the settler structure to which it is tied. She insists, instead, on a vision of Native women that centers possibility, the "what if" and the infinite. In "Infinite Progression," Elsie becomes infinite when her reflection reflects itself rather than acting as a looking glass for settler society; in "Elsie Picks Up the Dry Cleaning," she writes herself across the canon, transforming the degrading tools of American literary representation; and in "Some Elsie" she wears the scars of Williams's words while knowing her capacity to speak back against them "broken brain or not."[80] Just as Rogers did with "Pocahontas" and "Sacajawea," Erdrich dredges prominent invocations of Native women as symbols of an American national order to evidence the gendered dimensions of settler structure. In doing so, they also insist on a gendered approach to Native literary studies, offering an amendment to prominent methodologies in the field that similarly seek to apprehend the function of indigeneity within the American literary canon yet ignore its gendered dimensions.

Some Elsewhere

To return to the framework I presented in the introduction to this chapter, Erdrich's and Rogers's engagements with the American literary canon and the symbolization of Native women are rooted in a refusal to separate bodies and bodies of knowledge. Through deft poetic craft, Erdrich and Rogers offer important theoretical interventions that reveal more clearly the gendered dimensions of settler sovereignty. Taking up texts, authors, and figures that have been important to the mobilization of American identity and political discourse, these two authors provide a method that can help to address some of the central limitations of anarchist approaches to feminism, gender, and sexuality. In particular, Erdrich's and Rogers's poems offer a transformative methodology that insists on recognizing the foundational role that settlement plays in American politics (and literature), by demonstrating clearly how that structure is manifested through gendered discourse and by requiring that the centering of Native women be a transformative rather than inclusive move. Without such a methodology, anarchist approaches to feminism, gender, and sexuality remain structured through a settler frame that views such questions as removed from the material dispossession of Native land and the maintenance of settlement through gendered violence.

Perhaps a timely example can demonstrate the urgency of such a restructuring of anarchist approaches. Throughout the time I have been working on this book, frequent reports of missing and murdered indigenous women, girls, and two-spirit people have emerged through the #MMIWG2S and #ItEndsHere hashtags. The force of the heartbreak and sorrow accompanying each name has a depth that extends through the land and the history at the heart of US and Canadian claims to sovereignty. As I sat finishing this chapter, word had come down that Raymond Joseph Cormier was acquitted of the 2014 murder of fifteen-year-old Tina Fontaine, a young woman from Sagkeeng First Nation, despite his admission to authorities that he had a sexual relationship with her and a clearly stated motive to kill her.

His defense was so confident in his acquittal that they submitted no additional evidence.[81] Of thousands of missing and murdered indigenous women, girls, and two-spirit people in what is currently Canada and the United States, Fontaine is one of very few whose murder has led to a criminal trial and is the most prominent since Prime Minister Justin Trudeau established a National Inquiry into Missing and Murdered Indigenous Women and Girls in 2016. Coming on the heels of another not-guilty verdict for Gerald Stanley in the murder of Colton Boushie, a twenty-two-year-old from Red Pheasant Cree Nation, Cormier's acquittal underscored for many the interconnectedness of juridical structures, settlement, and gendered violence.

As Anishnaabe and Métis law professor Aimée Craft wrote of the decision, "I understand the law, but I don't see justice in it. The systems that purport to bring justice fail us over and over, time and again. Tina's case is a stark illustration of that terrible reality." But, beyond this, she argued, "We can't blame our sorrow solely on circumstantial evidence or failing systems. We must call to account the angry beasts of racism, sexism, patriarchy, misogyny, capitalism, and colonization that have allowed the devaluation of Indigenous women and girls."[82] It is precisely this "calling to account" that is evaded in the structure of anarchist approaches to feminism, gender, and sexuality. Without a cogent dedication to the distinctive structure of the settler state and the concomitant development of a precise approach to gendered violence that centers its connection to settlement, anarchist approaches are unable to account for an understanding that articulates Tina Fontaine's murder as colonial violence.

This recognition of gendered violence as colonial violence is at the heart of a vision of the future in which both are eradicated. This is why, in her pivotal study of sexual violence in Native America, Muscogee legal scholar Sarah Deer insists on speaking not only of the beginning of rape but also of its end: "we will not acquiesce until the end of rape arrives."[83] As Nishnaabeg scholar and artist Leanne Betasamosake Simpson has argued in her discussion of what she calls "indigenous radical resurgence," recognizing gendered violence as colonial violence is essential to illuminating new paths forward: "land and bodies are commodified as capital under settler colonialism and are naturalized as objects for exploitation. This has always been extremely clear to Indigenous women and 2SQ people, and it's why sexual and gender violence has to be theorized and analyzed as vital, not supplemental, to discussions of colonial dispossession."[84] The methodologies provided by Erdrich and Rogers contribute to such theorization and analysis. Not only because they emphasize the dependence on gendered structures of settlement at the core of American identity but also because they emphasize resurgent and insurgent approaches grounded in what Simpson calls decolonial love.[85] As Simpson publicly observed in response to calls for justice for Tina Fontaine and Colten Boushie, "we will build a different world full of indigenous joy, full of the very best parts of us. that's our revolution."[86]

This joy, the very best parts, are at the heart of Erdrich's and Rogers's poems that I've discussed here. Elsie loves her own infinite reflection; Sacajawea takes joy in her own sense of adventure; Pocahontas loves "watching mothers packing babies on their backs."[87] All love their land and its people, finding joy in it even in the lamenting tone through which their stories are often told. This methodology refuses a model of inclusion, of attaching a mention of settler colonialism to discussions of feminism, gender, and sexuality as an addendum to a list or as a fact mobilized to make a point about capitalism. Instead, as Tuck and Yang have pointed out, "decolonization is not an 'and.' It is an elsewhere."[88] Anarchists can more effectively work against the proliferation of a settler future within anarchist spaces by paying better attention to how writers like Erdrich and Rogers (and others like Simpson and Deer) build this elsewhere into the structure of their engagement, to watch how "some Elsie" becomes some elsewhere.

Part 3

The Limits of Anarchist Transnationalism

CHAPTER 5

"My Nationhood Doesn't Just Radiate Outwards"

Anarchist Transnationalism as Border Imperialism

I am not a nation-state, nor do I strive to be one.
—Leanne Betasamosake Simpson

In the previous chapters, I have argued that New Anarchism in North America has not developed a politics that reckons with the specificity of the US settler state as either a political, economic, or cultural structure. Native dispossession remains a momentary consideration of ancillary importance (when considered at all), rather than an issue of theoretical and material foundation whose consideration must necessarily transform well-established anarchist politics. By exploring the structure of settler anarchism and its rootedness in the anarchist approaches to feminism, gender, and sexuality, I've given a clearer picture of how New Anarchism remains rooted in the settler structure of the US, despite the seeming incommensurability of anarchist politics and the state. Throughout, my insistence has been on the urgency of holding anarchist politics accountable to the foundational principles of antistatism and anticapitalism and subsequently asking what forms these politics must take in the context of the United States as a nation-state founded in a settler structure that is intimately bound to both heteronormativity and racial capitalism. I have argued that, without this, anarchist politics are limited in their ability to reckon with those issues that cut to the heart of US settlement. In this final section, I extend this analysis to demonstrate how these limitations also prevent New Anarchism from developing a global approach that is able to address the structure of US empire.

I am acutely aware here of the danger of reproducing an approach that mirrors US exceptionalism, particularly one that depends on a narrow scope to reify the spatial and discursive ordering of the "domestic" and the "foreign." As Amy Kaplan has pointed out, the obfuscation of the United States as an empire has depended on this ordering.[1] This argument will resonate with scholars of New Anarchism, who will surely see the resonance between Kaplan's insistence on a transnational scope to apprehend the imperial character of the US nation-state and the centrality of cross-border solidarity to New Anarchist attempts to develop mass movements against capitalism and the state. In this final section, my goal is to clarify how the insistence in the previous chapters on centering the particularities of the US settler state squares with the anarchist insistence on a global frame of reference. To ignore the global dimensions of both historical and contemporary anarchism not only would limit our understanding of the breadth of anarchist politics but also would neglect the specific character of New Anarchism itself.

To harken back to chapter 1, the central place of the 1999 protests against the WTO in the New Anarchist imagination demonstrates the inextricability of New Anarchism from the imbrication of political activism and analysis on a global scale. As many scholars of anarchist history have demonstrated, internationalism has been a core tenet of anarchist activism since its inception. There is a plethora of work that follows from this exploration of the foundational role of internationalism in classical anarchist politics, including histories of the Industrial Workers of the World (IWW), the international dimensions of foundational classical anarchist theory, and the emphasis on immigration histories in the study of nineteenth and early twentieth century anarchism in the United States.[2] In recent years, we have also seen the proliferation of scholarship that seeks to emphasize the myriad places around the world where we see anarchism in practice, work that either implicitly or explicitly rejects the assignation of a European character to anarchism.[3] And though I offer below a more in-depth look at how these approaches attend to questions of scope, nation, and empire, I want to emphasize here the significance of this persistent global emphasis to understanding the particular character of the era and location of anarchist politics with which this book is fundamentally concerned.

New Anarchism is frequently tied to the rise of globalization, often leading to the erroneous application of the term *anti globalization* to

New Anarchist politics. As Thomas Friedman argued in his polemic against the 1999 Battle in Seattle, "what unites the anti-W.T.O crowd is their realization that we now live in a world without walls . . . the globalization system that we are now in is built around integration and webs. In this new system, jobs, cultures, environmental problems, and labor standards can more easily flow back and forth. The ridiculous thing about the protestors is that they find fault with this and blame the W.T.O."[4] As David Graeber pointed out in his article "The New Anarchists," this antagonistic rendering of anarchist politics misunderstands the way that activists at the 1999 protests, both against the WTO in Seattle and in the Carnival Against Capital in June of the same year, saw their relationship to a globalized world.

According to Graeber, the attempts by people like Friedman to paint the critique of neoliberalism as an insular approach to both economics and politics elided the fundamentally global nature of the emerging New Anarchism:

> If one takes globalization to mean the effacement of borders and the free movement of people, possessions and ideas, then it's pretty clear that not only is the movement itself a product of globalization, but the majority of groups involved in it—the most radical ones in particular—are far more supportive of globalization in general than are the IMF [International Monetary Fund] or WTO.[5]

Graeber's observation is important, since his sense of New Anarchist politics as inherently transnational in scope is reflected in the very language that the movement uses to speak of itself. For instance, the unofficial slogan of mass protests around the world in 1999 was "our resistance is as transnational as capital."[6] This sense of the intrinsic relationship between a resurgence of anarchism across North America and global movement against capitalism is the root of Graeber's sense of the "new anarchists," who have reframed "earlier internationalisms . . . [that] ended up exporting Western organizational models to the rest of the world" in favor of a model whose "signature techniques—including mass nonviolent civil disobedience itself—were first developed in the global South."[7]

Emphasizing this directionality has proven pivotal to contemporary anarchists in the United States, who insist the model of radical politics that developed out of the mass protests at the end of the twentieth century is connected to global movements against capital, such as the Zapatista uprising in 1994, the subsequent development of the Peoples' Global Action (PGA) beginning in 1996, and the establishment of the World Social Forum in 2001. In what follows, I explore how this insistence on a transnational movement community reveals again the structure of settlement within New Anarchism. I argue that current approaches to transnationalism in New Anarchism depend on the consummation of US settler sovereignty and therefore reinscribe the structure of settlement within the methods of engagement across borders. I explore the structure of settlement in anarchist approaches to transnationalism through three lenses: the anarchist mapping of the US in the world, the anarchist rejection of nationalism, and the failure to consider anarchist history within contemporaneous histories of US imperialism.

The Transnational Impetus

A significant portion of anarchist scholarship concerned with a global scope has focused on confirming Graeber's observation that the techniques, politics, and analyses that are characteristic of the global justice movement emanate from the Global South rather than being an imposed import of activists in the Global North. This has been a central feature of asserting the appeal and originality of this "movement of movements," as Naomi Klein has termed it, since it signals a method of political activism that is structured from the bottom-up.[8] This was especially important for activists who sought to emphasize the connections between neoliberalism and neocolonialism by underscoring how the former ushered in an allegedly postcolonial global financial order that continued to redirect wealth from the Global South to the Global North through paradigms of "development." For activists and intellectuals alike, this prominent feature of neoliberalism demonstrated the dangerous ways that the dominant political and economic order could be repackaged as a benevolent global system supposedly rooted in uplift. To this day, the World Bank presents itself as a transnational financial institution whose primary concern is alleviating global poverty.[9]

For New Anarchists, this lineage is particularly important. Although, as I mentioned in chapter 1, the movements that comprise what I refer to here as the global anticapitalist movement is not synonymous with New Anarchism, the centrality of anarchist tactics, politics, and aesthetics remains fundamental. In order to build a stronger sense of the lineage between the bottom-up focus of the global anticapitalist movement and its rootedness in New Anarchist politics, a significant body of anarchist scholarship manifests a transnational project by rejecting the paradigm of the nation-state in the study of resistance movements throughout the world. Regional studies eschewing the state as a paradigmatic organizing structure remain influential: classic texts in the genre, such as James C. Scott's *The Art of Not Being Governed: An Anarchist History of Upland Southeast Asia* and Benedict Anderson's *Under Three Flags: Anarchism and the Anti-Colonial Imagination*, join more contemporary texts like David Porter's *Eyes to the South: French Anarchists and Algeria* and Ángel Cappelletti's *Anarchism in Latin America* in demonstrating a method of anarchist engagement that rejects the state not only in principle but also in intellectual practice. Such texts engage a transnational practice by seeking to destabilize the hegemony of the nation-state as the primary ordering of historical analysis. In doing so, they elucidate anarchism as a global tradition emanating from the Global South, especially in historical context, solidifying its significance in the rise of global anticapitalist movements in the late twentieth and early twenty-first centuries.

However, this attempt to indicate a globalized history of anarchism is also embedded within an anxiety among US-based anarchists that anarchism is read as intrinsically tied to both whiteness and Europeanness—one which has yet to be sufficiently resolved, least of all because of the unwillingness of many anarchists to acknowledge the deeply white demographics of people working in the milieu. The emphasis on asserting a connection between anarchist politics and the Global South can be read as a response to the rootedness of classical anarchist theory, including the work of foundational thinkers like Pierre Joseph-Proudhon, Pyotr Kropotkin, Mikhail Bakunin, and William Godwin, in a distinctly European tradition, not solely in terms of the authors themselves but that their political theories are often centered on the material reality of the political and economic landscape of Europe during the time they were writing. In the United States, this indelible connection to Europe has brought up still-contentious questions about the racialized character of anarchism in the US context, particularly its whiteness. The attempt to solidify a global anarchist history has been instrumental in the pushback against this critique, wherein the profoundly white and European genealogy of anarchist history is understood as a historiographical problem rather than one that speaks to the fundamental character of New Anarchism itself.

For instance, in developing a more comprehensive history of global anarchisms, Jason Adams has argued that "the historiography of anarchism has focused almost entirely on these movements as they have pertained to the peoples of the West and the North, while movements amongst the peoples of the East and the South have been widely neglected."[10] This approach to anarchist transnationalism is rooted in an attempt to confirm the global movement of anarchist politics across borders, mirroring the slogan "our resistance is as transnational as capital." Therefore, despite the fact that Adam's analysis of "nonwestern anarchisms" is divided almost exclusively into nation-states, his project espouses a transnational paradigm in its attempt to illustrate a global history of anarchism that is characterized by exchange and movement across borders.[11] Though this approach provides a rich history that upends some of the silences that punctuate the milieu, it sidesteps the question of how whiteness is embedded in New Anarchism in the United States. Or, perhaps, vice versa.

Despite the generous and patient work of groups like Anarchist People of Color (APOC), Love and Rage, and Anti-Racist Action (ARA), many anarchists still bristle at the suggestion that the milieu is overwhelmingly white in demographic and imbricated through whiteness politically.[12] For instance, in their introduction to "Black Anarchism: A Reader," the Black Rose Anarchist Federation argue that the lack of attention to Black anarchism within the milieu "can be attributed to an inherent contradiction found within the Eurocentric canon of classical anarchism which, in its allegiance to a Western conception of universalism, overlooks and actively mutes the contributions by colonized peoples."[13] Despite critiques of the whiteness of anarchism within the reader from prominent Black anarchists like Lorenzo Kom'boa Ervin, Zoé Samduzi, and William C. Anderson, Black Rose still articulates the problem as one strictly related to canon rather than the persistence of white supremacy within anarchist communities themselves.[14]

This evasion is also evident in the literature on global anarchisms, most prominently in the controversy surrounding the popular book *Black Flame: The Revolutionary Class Politics of Anarchism and Syndicalism*, written by white South African anarchists Lucien Van Der Walt and Michael Schmidt. Touted as the first in a series of books that would offer a well-documented refutation of the claim that anarchism was inherently tied to European or Western traditions while applying stricter boundaries for naming the intellectual history of anarchist itself, *Black Flame* was one of the most popular books released by US-based anarchist publisher AK Press and was a widely read tome expected to spark a new interest in syndicalism among anarchists globally.[15] And though Van Der Walt and Schmidt were grounded in the South African context, their approach resonated within the milieu across the United States. Then, in September 2015, AK Press announced that they had put *Black Flame* out of print, along with other books by coauthor Michael Schmidt, after evidence surfaced that he was an avowed white supremacist and fascist.[16]

In their exposé on Schmidt's history of participation in white supremacist and fascist communities both online and in person, anarchists Alexander Reid Ross and Joshua Stephens provided ample evidence that Schmidt's interest in writing *Black Flame* was rooted in his commitment to bringing together anarchist and white supremacist movements.[17] Yet, many defended the continued use of the text and argued for its importance, casting Schmidt's influence as a lamentable aspect of his own thinking rather than embedded in the structural approach to anarchism that he and Van Der Walt presented. In this way, his avowed allegiance to white supremacy in the settler colonial state of South Africa was cast as a matter of personal rather than political belief, one that effectively sought to separate his simultaneous commitments to anarchism and whiteness.

This is the broader logic through which contemporary texts that explore the global reach of anarchism attempt to reckon with whiteness and anarchist transnationalism. That is, the implicit and explicit centering of whiteness in the milieu are expressed not as structural concerns, but as the failure of individuals to live up to the expectations of anarchist politics. In this way, the attempt to adopt a transnational approach that rejects the idea that anarchism is a movement bound to whiteness in the United States evidences a lack of engagement with the transformative dimensions of arguments, made by people like Ross and Stephens and the late Joel Olsen, that anarchists must reckon more seriously with the question of how anarchism becomes compatible with discourses of white supremacy and fascism in the US context.[18]

Recognizing this, I wonder whether this approach to anarchist transnationalism might be read as less concerned, actually, with producing a global understanding of anarchist history than about working out how to map the United States in the global context. Though at the outset, this approach appears to be rooted in a desire to decenter the United States from global histories of anticapitalism, I see in anarchist approaches to transnationalism the reification of the sovereignty of the US settler state. This is especially obvious in how attempts to develop anarchist transnationalism evade important criticisms of how violent structures such as whiteness and settlement, and their coconstitution, become amenable to New Anarchist politics. One of the places we can see this process most clearly is in the ubiquity of the Ejército Zapatista de Liberación Nacional (EZLN), popularly referred to as the Zapatistas, in scholarship on New Anarchism.

Indigeneity and the Mapping of the United States in Global Anarchisms

The Zapatistas brought their uprising into the public eye on January 1, 1994, emerging from the southern Mexican state of Chiapas on the day that the North American Free Trade Agreement (NAFTA) took effect. The Zapatista uprising appears in almost every text on New Anarchism in North America, heralded as one of the pivotal moments in the inauguration of a global movement against capitalism. As the Notes from Everywhere Collective noted in their introduction to the collection *We Are Everywhere: The Irresistible Rise of Global Anti-Capitalism*: "we chose to begin with the Zapatistas as we see their uprising on 1 January 1994 as heralding a new era of resistance movements."[19] The reading of the Zapatista uprising as an expressly indigenous movement remains a central feature of its import for New Anarchists, who applaud the connection that Zapatistas made between the proliferation of a neoliberal global order (exemplified by NAFTA) and the colonization of the Americas. In fact, this prolific engagement with Zapatismo and its origins remains one of the most prominent ways in which indigenous movements appear in New Anarchist literature. Rather than inspiring an interest in concomitant indigenous movements across North America, however, the anarchist fixation on Zapatistas has continually located indigeneity outside the boundaries claimed by the United States and Canada, reifying US claims to territory and sovereignty within an anarchist paradigm.

By way of example, we can see a stark rendering of these features at work in the map developed by James Davis and Paul Rowley, which aims to provide a visual and geographical representation of resistance to capitalist globalization. In this "map of resistance," Davis and Rowley show that "the density of events on this map (especially in the global South) suggests that a web or matrix of anti-globalizing practices has been steadily taking shape over the last twenty years." Repeating the line of reasoning put forward by Black Rose in their discussion of the relative obscurity of Black anarchism, they go on to argue that the map demonstrates unequivocally that "the fact that [antiglobalization] has only been 'discovered' as a worldwide movement after Seattle in 1999 is an indication more of Eurocentric blindness in the North than of theoretical under-development in the South."[20] With a combination of symbols and dates, Davis and Rowley map strikes, summit demonstrations, "eco-resistance," and "resistance to globalization policies," providing a more comprehensive vision of anticapitalist resistance in the late twentieth and early twenty-first centuries as a movement intrinsically tied to uprisings in the Global South.

On this map, the Zapatista uprising is so significant that it is not only included but also given its own symbol—the only one to appear only once. Only three events are marked in the United States and Canada: the November 1999 protests against the WTO in Seattle, the April 2000 protests against the IMF and World Bank in Washington, DC, and the April 2001 protests in Quebec City against the Summit of the Americas during negotiations to develop the Free Trade Area of the Americas (FTAA) agreement. To demonstrate the prevalence of resistance in the Global South, Davis and Rowley located indigenous resistance outside the United States and Canada, ignoring the myriad forms and instances of indigenous uprising that characterize the period of colonization within these settler nation-states.

Initially, this may seem to be the result of their self-imposed limitations in developing the map. As they note, "we have limited ourselves here to demonstrations, riots and events that are specific responses either to SAPs (structural adjustment programs) or summit/fulcrums of capitalist globalization."[21] However, in exploring the differences between moments of resistance in the Global North and Global South, they suggest that there are substantially less deaths associated with movements in the Global North and that, while such movements focus mostly on summit demonstrations, movements in the Global South are characterized by a much more comprehensive character of rebellion:

> The crosshair icon represents rebellions, ranging from spontaneous uprisings to general strikes, against the neo-liberal policies . . . [including] the displacement of communities due to the privatization of land and water, the clearcutting of forests to pay off foreign debt, the murderous immiseration of urban populations through fuel and food staple price increases, and the dismantling of public health care and education.[22]

To those familiar with the history of settlement in what is currently the United States and Canada, these policies will resonate as foundational methods through which the structure of settlement, especially the dispossession of Native land from its people, have been attempted. Continuous uprisings against the US and Canadian settler states as occupying foreign governments are completely whitewashed (pun intended) from Davis and Rowley's map of resistance to global capitalism. Because of this, the connection between neoliberal policies and colonialism are located outside the United States and Canada, situated instead within the invocation of the Zapatista uprising. Accordingly, Native claim to territory across North America is visually extinguished, naturalizing both US and Canadian settler sovereignty both visually and rhetorically.

In this attempt to illustrate a "resistance as transnational as capital" through the articulation of a global history of struggle that is centered in the Global South, anarchists have cemented the claims to spatial, temporal, and political fullness on which US claims to sovereignty rest. This model remains popular, as in the collection *No Gods, No Masters, No Peripheries: Global Anarchisms*, which begins with a section on "Learning from Indigenous Experience: Anarchism and Indigeneity." Drawing on the history of the collection, which emanated from a conference that happened in Cayuga territory at Cornell University in 2012, this framing signals a desire to begin from a form of global engagement that is grounded in a consideration of traditional territories. This desire is amplified by the inclusion of an epigraph from Kanien'kehá:ka scholar Taiaike Alfred (who coined the term *anarcho-indigenism*) that reads: "Is there a Native philosophical alternative? And what might one achieve by standing against the further entrenchment of institutions modeled on the state?"[23] Coupled with the inclusion of a still from Tuscarora artist Jolene Rickard's 2012 installation *Fight for the Line*, which depicts a sign that reads "Cayuga Territories" below Tuscarora language, this attempt to acknowledge the foundation of Native land is used to instantiate the refusal of peripheries in the study of global anarchism.

However, the acknowledgment of Native territory as a framing device has the opposite effect than is intended. Rather than center the question of settlement in an exploration of the global dimensions of anarchist movement, the placing of such an acknowledgement at the beginning of a text that contains within it no dedicated explorations of settlement in the US and Canadian contexts, or its implications for constructing an archive of global anarchism, reveals the specter of settlement as a peripheral concern. This structure is exacerbated by the fact that a consideration of the implications of Rickard's work doesn't appear until Maxwell's "Afterword," in which he uses a short discussion of her installation to assert that "much of what the contributors do in this book grows from the need to *un-settle*, both materially . . . and imaginatively when and where possible. Otherwise, *we can't breathe*."[24]

Though his implication is that this project, then, follows from Rickard's description of her piece as one that "responds to the duplicitous political and legal 'lines' between these nations as un-settled," the United States remains settled within the question of "un-settling," since such a project is delinked from a material engagement with the question of settlement as constitutive of a global approach emanating from the US context.[25] This same process is evinced in Maxwell's invocation of Eric Garner's last words that he spoke while being choked to death by NYPD officer Daniel Pantaleo in 2014, which is claimed as a broad revolutionary imperative despite that a discussion of Garner's murder, and the foundation of antiblack racism in the establishment of the US state, appears nowhere in the text itself.[26] In this way, the figurative periphetical treatment of settlement within global approaches to anarchism is confirmed in the literal way in which the question of settlement remains on the periphery of the text, present only in the first and last pages. Discussions of indigeneity therein, including Maia Ramnath's discussion of indigeneity in India, Silvia Rivera Cusicanqui's discussion of Ch'ixi identity in Bolivia, and Hilary Klein's discussion of indigenous tradition in the Zapatista movement, remain untethered from the foundational consideration of how the question of indigeneity in the US context transforms transnational approaches to global anarchism.[27]

None of this is to say that considering indigeneity outside North America is immaterial or inherently obfuscating. That is, I am not suggesting that all anarchist texts emanating from the US context must only be *about* indigeneity within that space and history. Rather, by ignoring the specificity of Native uprising within settler states (particularly alongside a contemporaneous centering of uprisings that are understood as expressly indigenous centered, such as the Zapatistas), this model of transnational engagement replicates the demarcation of space through the lens of "domesticity" and "foreignness," in which the primary ordering of activism is either "without" or "without" the United States. Of course, the political and social status of Native nations does not fit neatly within this ordering. As Kevin Brunyeel has noted, "the political relationship between the United States and indigenous people, especially tribes, has always eluded easy definition" since "U.S.-indigenous politics, at its core, is a battle between an American effort to solidify inherently contingent boundaries and an indigenous effort to work on and across these boundaries."[28] In this way, insisting on a fundamental rather than peripheral ordering of Native nations within the transnational approach to global anarchism is not about locating such nations within the "domestic" space of the United States but is rather about using such an approach to incipiently trouble such an ordering altogether.

As Amy Kaplan and Chickasaw scholar Jodi Byrd have argued, this work is meant to foreground how the category of "domestic" operates first to solidify US empire on both material and discursive levels and then to simultaneously deny the imperial character of the US state. Addressing some of the limitations of Kaplan's work, Byrd points out that this rendering of Native nations "has supplied, in the slip between *with* and *among* rather than 'foreign nations' and 'Indian tribes,' the rule of law through which the United States enacts its imperialist agenda."[29] It is in what she calls this "prepositional possibility" that indigeneity becomes the "transit of empire" or "a site through which U.S. empire orients and replicates itself by transforming those to be colonized into 'Indians' through continual reiterations of pioneer logics, whether in the Pacific, the Caribbean, or the Middle East."[30] Centering the anarchist engagement with indigeneity through this lens helps to illuminate why the approach to transnationalism that I described above especially attempts to map anarchist genealogies in the world and resonates in ways that reify rather than resist the US state. By either locating indigenous resistance outside the borders claimed by the United States or relegating them to the periphery of global anarchist inquiry emanating from the US context, anarchists obscure the connections between the economic and political processes at the core of neoliberalism and settlement, envisioning a transnational model that solidifies rather than overwrites US empire.

This approach to evidencing anarchism as a transnational movement extends into the contemporary moment, perhaps most observable in the US anarchist fascination with the Democratic Federation of Northern Syria (DFNS), popularly referred to as Rojava. Since it was established in 2012, the autonomous region of Rojava has attracted attention from anarchists in the United States, some of whom have traveled to Rojava to take up arms in the conflict.[31] Numerous solidarity networks have sprung up among anarchists and other antiauthoritarians, with local chapters of Rojava Solidarity groups appearing in Seattle, New York City, Portland, Los Angeles, and Vermont. Because of its articulation as a "Kurdish region in Northern Syria that's ruled by militant feminist anarchists," Rojava has become a fixation of US anarchists who see it as the preeminent contemporary example of the attempt to establish an autonomous anarchist community.[32] What is more, Rojava is often invoked among anarchists as an indigenous struggle. And though there is more to say about how this fixation is bound to a valorization of a particular form of highly militarized armed conflict among US anarchists, I want to emphasize here how the specter of Rojava is bound to the model of anarchist transnationalism that I described above.

Interest in Rojava among US anarchists is profound, often rooted in a critique of US intervention in the region that emanates from broader analysis of Western intervention in Southwest Asia and the rise of Daesh. Thus, support for Rojava becomes intimately bound to a critique of US imperialism throughout the region, complicated by the fact that DFNS is supported by the United States in this military conflict. Attempts to develop networks of support are articulated as the development of strong transnational anarchist linkages, revealing the global dimensions of contemporary anarchist resistance that transcends nation-state boundaries. There are important critiques of this fascination, including Razan Ghazzawi's important piece "Decolonising Syria's So-called 'Queer Liberation,'" in which she notes pushback from Syrian activists on the ground who highlight the imperial texture of US anarchists traveling to fight in Syria.[33]

The First of May Alliance's (M1) "Toward an Anarchist Policy on Syria" also garnered a response from an unnamed Syrian anarchist who gently critiques the misrepresentations of the conflict's political roots and also questions M1's reading of US imperialism.[34] Read alongside the lack of consideration of settlement within New Anarchism, this focus on building transnational solidarity networks in support of Rojava can be read as an eschewal of a critique (or recognition) of settlement as the literal foundation of US empire. From the available literature, it appears that many anarchists in the United States are more familiar with (and interested in) the intricacies of Syrian politics than with the history of settlement in the places they call home. The point here is not to suggest that anarchists working in the United States must ignore global politics (especially a humanitarian crisis that emerges from a clash between various imperial powers) but rather that to develop a transnational approach that ignores the connection between US interventions in the Southwest Asia and the United States claiming of continental territory is to limit our apprehension of US empire so severely that we end up reifying it through a naturalization of its claims to sovereignty.

Excluding Native Nationalisms

The reification of the US settler state is one of the most persistent issues in contemporary anarchist approaches to transnationalism, all the more frustrating because of how contradictory this outcome seems from its impetus. As Constance Bantman and Bert Altena note in their introduction to the collection *Reassessing the Transnational Turn: Scales of Analysis in Anarchist and Syndicalist Studies*, the transnational turn in anarchist studies (as in other fields) extended from a need to expand the scale of anarchist analysis without relying on a paradigm that naturalizes the nation-state. They observe that "what unites transnational scholars . . . is a shared awareness of the limitations of an exclusive national angle in approaching their field of expertise, as well as the determination to look beyond national borders in their analyses."[35] This determination is central to some of the most exciting transnational anarchist work of the past, including Anderson's *Under Three Flags* and the new English translation of Cappelletti's *Anarchism in Latin America*, which seek to destabilize the nation-state as the primary demarcation through which global anarchist history is told. However, within Bantman and Altena's observation, the conflation of "nation" with nation-state reveals another jagged edge that reformulates US settler sovereignty within the language of anarchist transnationalism.

The question of nationalism has long been a contentious discussion within anarchism and a resolution to this debate is not the focus of my inquiry here. Rather, I am interested in how the parameters used to structure the debate around the commensurability of anarchism and nationalism have effectively debarred the consideration of Native nationalisms, making it difficult to imagine a connection between New Anarchist and Native movements in North America. As Davide Turcato has argued, the debate about anarchism and nationalism has often been focused on the space between idealism and practicability since, while nationalism may seem incompatible with anarchist principles, it is nonetheless an important dimension of the history of militant, radical struggles around the world.[36] Thankfully, Turcato's thoughtful consideration of anarchist approaches to nationalism represents a shift away from more hardline rejections of nationalism that had previously defined the conversation within the milieu.[37] Using Italian anarchist Errico Malatesta as an example, Turcato argues that nationalism and anarchism are not incommensurable since anarchists "can nurture both a group identity and an ideal of universal cooperation without being inconsistent."[38] This approach seems to resolve anarchist discomfort with nationalism in general and with nationalist movements in particular, a move that is of some urgency since it undergirds discussions of anarchism's applicability in the postcolonial era, especially to nationalist independence movements.[39]

However, the limitations of Turcato's genealogy of both nation and nationalism evince the exclusion of Native nationalisms from even this more charitable framework. As is the case for both Anderson and Cappelletti, Turcato's genealogy of nationalism is inherently tied to European modernity.[40] In her study of Native nationalisms, Oneida scholar Lina Sunseri has argued that such a genealogy "dismisses those experiences of nationalism that existed prior to and/or outside of modernity and that in many cases preceded the time of contact with Europeans and colonialism."[41] Using the example of the Haudenosaunee Confederacy, Sunseri argues that the confederation of the initial five nations (Onondaga, Mohawk, Seneca, Oneida, and Cayuga) by the Peacemaker sometime between the fifteenth and sixteenth centuries and the inclusion of the Tuscarora in 1722 provide an example of Native nationalisms prior to the timeline laid out by scholars of nationalism who tie it to European modernity.[42]

Both Sunseri and Onondaga scholar Theresa McCarthy emphasize the connection between this understanding of Haudenosaunee nationhood and confronting the gendered structure of settlement, since "heteronormative thinking and homophobia are rooted in the same patriarchal outlooks used to alienate us from our land and our rights."[43] What is more, it's easy to see the threat that such an assertion of nationhood poses for US and Canadian claims to a singular nationalism rooted in modernity. As McCarthy's compelling study of Haudenosaunee reclamation at Grand River points out, both scholarly and political discourse about the Haudenosaunee have often repeated rhetoric about factionalism among the Six Nations of Grand River to destabilize claims to a unified sovereignty made through confederation. This denial of the possibility of Native nationalisms that exist in conflict with European modernity, rather than as an adaptation of its structure, is also reflected in anarchist approaches to transnationalism. As Sunseri points out in her critique of Anderson's famous formulation of nationalism in terms of "imagined communities," this genealogy of nationalisms is not tied only to European modernity but to the colonial demarcation of North America as the "New World."[44]

Of course, the question of nationalism is widely debated in Native and Indigenous Studies as well, forming an especially pivotal role in Native literary studies. And though I'll offer a more in-depth engagement with the question of Native literary nationalism in the next chapter, I bring forward another view of Native nationalisms to make a broader point here about how anarchist approaches to transnationalism reproduce the structure of settlement. In his book *X-Marks: Native Signatures of Assent*, Ojibwe scholar Scott Lyons offers a critique of what he terms the traditionalist perspective on Native nationalism made by scholars like Alfred (and perhaps Sunseri, though her work postdates Lyons's book). Instead, Lyons agrees with a genealogy of nationalism that ties it to modernity. However, this doesn't mean that Native nationalisms are simply adaptations of a European model of belonging. As Lyons argues, "the nation isn't 'Western,' it's modern" and, in this sense, "the idea of an Indian nation may be as modern as anyone else's nation, but that doesn't mean its origins aren't as old as the hills."[45] For him, Native nations represent the historical transformation of *ethnie* (or "human groups that formed coherent entities and achieved solidarity") into a modern structure. Nationalism, then, "is the political movement that makes the transformation happen."[46] I bring up Lyons's alternative rendering of Native nationalism not to dismiss Sunseri or McCarthy's arguments but rather to show what a transnational approach to the question of nationalism looks like.

As all three authors I've noted here make clear, their analysis of Native nationhood and nationalisms draw from their own national locations. In this sense, this conversation about Native nationalisms is deeply transnational in that it is working across national borders. What is more, none of these approaches deny, either overtly or through implied exclusion, the nationhood or claims to sovereignty of any Native nations. Instead, they debate the character and histories of the concept of Native nationhood precisely because it is so important to contemporary movements. Both the transnational conversations about Native nationalism and the centrality of Native nationhood to contemporary movements are lost in anarchist approaches to transnationalism. For instance, in their article "Why Anarchists Oppose Militarism and

Nationalism," which appeared in the third issue of the NEFAC newsletter *The Northeastern Anarchist*, members of the Boston chapter and the Boston Anarchists Against Militarism (BAAM) conflate a critique of US imperialism with a rejection of nationalism. They write, "anarchists oppose the idea of nationalism, believing that America is a superior nation, and even patriotism, blind devotion to America." They go on to note that "Nationalism is a choice: You may either follow the military or the president blindly, or you may think for yourself."[47] Though an example that belies the thoughtfulness with which other anarchist theorists like Turcato have approached the question of nationalism, this sentiment brings into sharp relief how the US state becomes reified through the invocation of American nationalism, as a formulation rooted in settlement and as a metonym for nationalism more generally. This move precludes the consideration of Native nations, which Sunseri's, McCarthy's, and Lyons's work (despite their divergences) confirm as central tenets of the transnational dimensions of Native movements.

Addressing this limit of anarchist approaches to transnationalism is essential to confronting the structure of settler anarchism since it requires a more concerted engagement with the importance of Native nationhood. Denaturalizing a paradigm of nationalism that conflates it with the colonial nation-state is the foundation of this transformation. As Leanne Betasamosake Simpson (Nishnaabeg) has argued in her reflection on the Indigenous Nationhood Movement,

> I believe my ancestors expected the settler state to recognize my nation, our lands and the political and cultural norms in our territory . . . Our politics and our nationalism are not based on enclosures defended with violence, yet we still have homelands. We've had them for thousands and thousands of years. My nationhood doesn't just radiate outwards, it also radiates inwards. It is my physical body, my mind, and my spirit. It is our families—not the nuclear family that has been normalized in settler society, but big, beautiful, diverse, extended multi-racial families of relatives and friends that care very deeply for each other.[48]

This project has begun taking shape in the work of prominent anarchist scholars like Uri Gordon, who has attempted to untangle anarchist rejections of nationalism from questions of "ethnocultural identity" and concomitant movements "in which anarchists are participants or accomplices, from indigenous and black liberation in North America to national liberation movements in Chiapas, Palestine, and Rojava."[49] Much as I argued in the previous section that the reproduction of settlement within anarchist approaches to feminism, gender, and sexuality was not an issue of intent (since numerous scholars have addressed the question of settlement) but rather one of structure, the current approaches to anarchist transnationalism limit our ability to draw the connections of which Gordon speaks.

Here I emphasize the importance of considering these questions within conversations about transnationalism, since this is one of the defining dimensions of New Anarchism. In this way, we cannot assume that the recognition of anarchism as rooted in a transnational model of global engagement, both historically and contemporarily, inherently aligns it with Native and Indigenous movements. Instead, we must vigilantly explore how the anarchist discussion of nationalisms (regardless of stated claims to support Native movements) reify the US settler state and preclude an apprehension of Native nationalisms on the (sometimes contested) terms set by Native nations themselves.

Contemporaneous Resistance

The limits of the approaches to anarchist transnationalism that I've discussed thus far are rooted in the obfuscation of the structure of settlement in attempts to articulate histories of global anarchism and to theorize nationalism within anarchist political philosophy. In what follows, I explore how the limits of these approaches also restricts the ability of contemporary anarchists to account for the connection between pivotal events in the history of anarchism in the United States and the contemporaneous construction of US empire. Turning to an earlier time period than that which has thus far been my main focus, I explore how the narrow scope with which anarchists have approached the question of transnational history have lasting impressions that extend into the period under consideration in *Other Worlds Here*.

Broadening the scale of inquiry that I introduced in chapter 1, I expand my consideration of the failure to consider the 1999 Battle in Seattle alongside the 1856 Battle of Seattle to demonstrate a large-scale disregard for the place of anarchist history in the history of US empire. There, I was focused on the unexplored link between two temporally distant events that happened in close spatial proximity. Here, I am interested in a related though different frame. By tracing contemporaneous events across a wide geographic scope, I explore how anarchist approaches to transnationalism ignore the spatial dimensions of US empire within shared temporal contexts. In particular, I am interested in how contemporary considerations of the transnational dimensions of the 1886 Haymarket Affair articulate it as a formative moment in the history of US anarchism while ignoring contemporaneous events that structured US empire during the same period in the late nineteenth century. In doing so, I pay special attention to how this approach to anarchist history reifies the structure of settler anarchism in the articulation of the particular character of present-day New Anarchism.

By uncovering histories of the transnational movement of both anarchist ideas and anarchists themselves, contemporary scholars have sought to evidence the long-standing transnational character of an anarchist tradition that has aimed to destabilize the hegemony of nation-state borders. This has proven to be an important mechanism for demonstrating the transnational character of anarchist movements throughout their histories. For instance, Anderson's *Under Three Flags* "attempts to map the gravitational force of anarchism between militant nationalisms on opposite sides of the planet." Tracing the connections between "Natives of the last important remnants of the fabled Spanish global empire," Anderson asserts that these groups "did not merely read about each other, but had crucial personal connections and . . . coordinated their actions."[50] Similarly, Porter's *Eyes to the South* explores the interaction between French and Algerian anarchists moving between France and Algeria from the period spanning the Algerian War in the 1950s to the early twenty-first century.

These two influential texts are examples of the broader impulse to trace the movement of anarchist ideas, anarchist individuals, and anarchist movements on a global scale in approaches to anarchist transnationalism. Such studies do an excellent job of employing a methodology that refuses to acquiesce a static spatial frame defined by nation-state borders and thus give a better sense of how anarchism translated across linguistic, religious, political, and cultural divides. However, this limited focus on tracing *anarchist* ideas, individuals, and movements on a global scale has obscured contemporaneous histories whose consideration would bolster an anarchist analysis of the US state as inherently rooted in empire. The failure to consider these contemporaneous histories has bolstered instead the structure of settlement within New Anarchism.

Much like the 1999 Battle in Seattle, the Haymarket Affair looms large in the history of anarchism in the United States. On May 1, 1886, labor unions in Chicago staged the first May Day strike as part of their agitation for the eight-hour workday. During a protest meeting a few days later, a bomb exploded as police attempted to disrupt the meeting of organizers and workers and one police officer was killed. In the ensuing trial, eight men were brought to trial, seven of whom were sentenced to death. Albert Parsons, August Spies, Adolph Fischer, and George Engle were hanged in Chicago and eventually became known among the radical left as the Haymarket Martyrs. As historian Timothy Messer-Kruse has argued, "the Haymarket bombing and trial marked a pivotal moment in the history of American social movements" since, along with the 1901 assassination of William McKinley by anarchist Leon Czolgosz, "it sparked the nation's first 'red scare' . . . drove the nation's labor unions onto a more conservative path . . . [and] began a tradition within the American left of memorializing the Haymarket defendants as martyrs to the cause of the eight-hour workday, free speech, and the cause of labor generally."[51]

For instance, in a 2007 post to their website, the Industrial Workers of the World (IWW), an anarchist labor union that Lucy Parsons helped found after her husband Albert was executed, honors the legacy of the Haymarket Four as martyrs: "Regardless of the consequences we must find within ourselves the same kind of spirit, dedication and resolve as those four Anarchists, who gave their lives in the name of social justice and freedom and anarchy."[52] Messer-Kruse's study of Haymarket rejects this analysis, asserting instead his controversial contention that the trial was fair by the standards of its day, rather than a politically motivated show trial.[53] Anarchists, on the other hand, assert the fundamental bias of the trial and see it as a scheme to curb the rising power of radical labor unions made up primarily of immigrant workers, a legacy that figures prominently into the drawing of a direct lineage between Haymarket and anarchist resistance to neoliberal globalization.[54] For instance, in the same statement, the IWW asserts: "the anti-globalization movement for us must be an anti capitalist movement and an anti state movement, for as this case only too well demonstrates the state is the hand maiden of the rich and powerful."[55]

Unsurprisingly, I share the latter interpretation, especially since Messer-Kruse acknowledges that "the prosecution took full advantage of the public's nativism and anti-leftist bias" and dismisses the integration of such tactics by arguing that they were "hardly necessary" since the prosecutor brought strong eyewitnesses and metallurgical evidence.[56] However, during the trial "prosecutors festooned the courtroom with anarchist and socialist flags and banners seized from workers' meeting halls," while "incendiary passages from anarchist books and newspapers were read into the record [and] as the trial progressed, an arsenal of weapons was heaped on tables in front of the jury, including loaded bombs."[57] Though the proceedings themselves may not have been a scripted drama, these performative aspects of the prosecution demonstrate how intrinsic the show was to securing a formal conviction.

Despite this, I do find his estimation of the reasons for the subsequent martyrdom of Parsons, Spies, Fischer, and Engle illuminating, especially since claiming the Haymarket Four as martyrs continues to be invoked as part of the legacy of anarchist resistance in the twenty-first century.[58] For Messer-Kruse, this memorialization arose most prominently in the 1960s "not because of its inherently historical importance, but because it served well as the symbol of state repression and indigenous radical dissent."[59] Albert Parsons, in particular, was a figure who, as a "Texan, a former Confederate, great-grandson of Bunker Hill Revolutionary War hero, namesake of a family whose lineage stretched back to the *Mayflower*" perfectly espoused "the indigenous roots of an American radicalism."[60] In this way, the Haymarket Martyrs represented the pinnacle of a radical American tradition that had developed its "radical tactics not from Europe but from their own hard experiences in the politically corrupt and economically exploitative cities of the Gilded Age."[61] Because Messer-Kruse reads this contra the development of American anarchism prior to Haymarket through developed transatlantic networks of radicals, he misses the connections between this development of an "indigenous American radicalism" and other contemporaneous events that defined the political, social, and economic structure of the US settler state during the same era—a lacuna that is replicated even in more favorable discussions of Haymarket among anarchist scholars. The result is a failure to consider contemporaneous histories of US empire alongside those of US anarchist movements whose legacies continue to be formative for New Anarchism.

The late nineteenth century was a pivotal moment in the solidification of US empire, rooted in the simultaneous projects of the closing of the continental frontier and extending the reach of US empire into the Pacific and Caribbean. In the same year that Parsons, Spies, Fischer, and Engle were executed, the Dawes Act ushered in the assimilation and allotment era of US Federal Indian Policy, fomenting the legal and political structure that cemented the appropriation of ninety million acres of Native land.[62] Putting into place a system of individual, rather than collective, land ownership that favored male heads of households organized around a nuclear family, the Dawes Act was also an intensely gendered policy with lasting implications.[63] Three years later, the Wounded Knee Massacre occurred in Lakota territory when the US Seventh Cavalry murdered 150 Native people after attempting to disarm them. Often considered the last in the series of conflicts collectively referred to as the Indian Wars, the Wounded Knee Massacre is regularly invoked as the event that closed the Western frontier, representing the "final chapter of Indian history."[64]

This process of aggressively and violently appropriating Native land on the continent cannot be considered apart from the US occupation of territory off the continent. Within fifteen years of the Haymarket Affair, the United States also occupied numerous sovereign nations following the 1898 Treaty of Paris, including Cuba, the Philippines, Puerto Rico, and Guåhan. That same year, the United States officially annexed the Kingdom of Hawai'i and, a year later, signed the Tripartite Convention with Germany, partitioning Samoa and claiming five islands and two atolls as unincorporated territory belonging to the United States.[65] As Yup'ik scholar Shari Huhndorf has argued, during this period "both thought and action shifted, facilitating the emergence of imperial forms that reshaped popular understandings of the nation's identity and its role in the world as they also transformed the lives of indigenous people in these new colonies."[66] She notes especially how drawing both implicit and explicit connections between indigenous peoples on the continent and in the Pacific became an important part of the justification of US empire as a civilizing mission.

However, the interest in reclaiming the Haymarket Affair as an important moment in the development of what Messer-Kruse calls an "indigenous radicalism" serves to obscure these connections in the New Anarchist era. Therefore, contemporary anarchists have been unable to make important connections between the quelling of radical transnational labor movements, the appropriation of large swaths of Native territory, and the expansion of US empire in the late nineteenth century. In both anarchist and more mainstream liberal incarnations, the transnational dimensions of the Haymarket Affair's legacy is largely expressed in terms of the connections between immigrant and labor movements in US history.[67] For instance, Peter Marshall argues that both before and after Haymarket "anarchism remained principally a movement of immigrants among the Italian and Jewish populations, and the Russian refugees in the larger cities," citing especially the presence of prominent figures in anarchist history like Alexander Berkman and Emma Goldman, who were immigrants.[68] Messer-Kruse's estimation of the transnational dimensions of anarchism during this time is similar, arguing that it "was divided not by geography but by ideological schools, and radicals of the same mind on either continent were more closely associated with one another than they were with their factional rivals across town.[69]

This emphasis on the centrality of transatlantic migration to the transnational character of anarchism during this period limits the study of anarchism in both temporal and spatial ways. First, the omission of the consideration of Haymarket within a transnational approach to US empire is particular jarring, since contained within this history are some of the most central political concerns of anarchism more generally: enclosure through the imposition of individual land ownership rather than collective land stewardship; the consolidation of imperial power to solidify capitalist enterprise; and the repression of diverse communities of radical activists who were connected to movements across the globe. Second, the emphasis on the transatlantic movement of immigrants as the primary means by which contemporary anarchists apprehend the transnational dimensions of the era obfuscates the Pacific as an essential theater of US empire with continued resonances for considering US imperialism today.

The remaking of those executed after the Haymarket Affair as part of a genealogy of American anarchism is an import node in the genealogy of settler anarchism that I have discussed throughout *Other Worlds Here*. In particular, the emphasis on using a transnational approach to connect anarchist movements across the globe and throughout history has precluded an approach that attends to the global dimensions of US empire and its historical foundations. For instance, the absence of a prominent discussion of US intervention in the Pacific is a glaring omission in the development of anarchist opposition to militarism that developed after the invasion of Afghanistan in 2001 and Iraq in 2003. Especially during the era of Occupy Wall Street, the legacies (and persistence) of the wars in Afghanistan and Iraq under President Obama proved to be an important node in the argument for a more radical approach to political change. As Ryan Harvey observed in his piece "Occupy Before and Beyond," "Afghanistan, now the longest and most expensive war in US history, is still raging, and attempts by Obama to market the withdrawal from Iraq as a 'profound' success have been met with an almost universal cynicism."[70] Opposition to militarism was also a central tenet of prominent anarchist organizations like NEFAC and BAAM, whose statement against militarism I discussed in the previous section.

Considered alongside the absence of a discussion of militarism in the Pacific within anarchist scholarship, this focus on militarism in New Anarchist movements substantiates the inability to reckon with the complex ways that US empire has functioned through the consolidation of "domestic" and "foreign" space. This limitation is exacerbated by the dependence on a transatlantic frame as a metonym for transnational engagement. As Chamoru scholars Tiara Na'puti and Michael Lujan Bevacqua have argued, the obscurity of the Pacific in the study of American politics is not a result of its liminality but rather because it "reveals . . . where the enduring presence of settler colonialism has created a seemingly impossible colonial bind that positions indigenous peoples as 'domestic to the United States in a foreign sense.'"[71] For them, this is particularly evident in the case of Guåhan, which is often painted as a tiny, obscure territory even while it remains a pivotal stronghold in US military strategy, often referred to as "America's spear-point." This came into even sharper relief in 2017, when North Korean state media suggested that they could launch a missile that would reach Guåhan.[72] Despite this, anarchist critiques of militarism in the contemporary moment focus almost exclusively on US interventions in Southwest and Central Asia, collapsing sovereign nations under occupation like Guåhan and Hawai'i, which remain some of the most densely militarized places on earth.[73]

Rather than being a newly constituted lacuna of New Anarchist engagements, this legacy persists through the lack of considering foundational events like the Haymarket Affair within a transnational approach that recognizes the sovereignty of Native nations and pays attention to the transpacific dimensions of US empire.[74] For instance, in the contemporary moment, this is evident in the lack of discussion of Hawaiian sovereignty movements among anarchist scholars in the United States, despite the development of these connections in Hawai'i and in Hawaiian studies. Kanaka Maoli scholars and activists like Noelani Goodyear-Ka'ōpua, Mary Tuti Baker, Kahala Johnson, Uahikeaikalei'ohu Maile, and J. Kēhaulani Kauanui have explored Hawaiian sovereignty movements in terms of decolonization outside of state-centered models that draw on Kānaka Maoli epistemologies and histories.[75] With the exception of Jacqueline Lasky's discussion of Hawaiian taro farming, anarchists working in the US context have not developed a concomitant attention to the issue of Hawaiian sovereignty.[76]

This is not only a problem of omission but also a process of obfuscation that Kanaka Maoli scholar Lisa Kahaleole Hall has called "strategies of erasure," which is a "phenomenon of separate spheres that distorts our understanding of the relationship between race, imperialism and indigeneity that have so profoundly shaped the development of the U.S. nation-state."[77] I locate the persistence of settlement precisely in this reification of "separate spheres" in anarchist approaches to transnationalism. Tracing anarchist histories from the vantage point of New Anarchism without also paying attention to contemporaneous histories of US empire reifies the structure of the settler state by accepting a hegemonic ordering of "domestic" and "foreign."

What is at stake in each of these approaches to transnationalism is the ability of New Anarchist politics to effectively address how borders, both figuratively and materially, are used to support US empire. And, of course, to recognize within anarchist praxis temporalities and geographies that are grounded in Indigenous worlds. In this chapter I've demonstrated how this call remains unanswered within the most prominent approaches to transnationalism of anarchists working in the United States, leading to the reformation of the US settler state as a constitutive whole within anarchist logics, its imperial claims over territory remaining unquestioned. Though I've offered more specific analyses of contemporary anarchist attempts to map the United States in the world, to reckon with the question of nationalism, and to engage contemporaneous histories of US empire, these three approaches are not separate. Rather, they remain bound together as anarchists work through the foundational question of how to engage local context while operating on a global scale. As Bantman and Altena point out in their study of anarchist transnationalism, this is one of the primary purposes of a transnational approach.[78] For anarchists, especially, this question of how federation will work on a global scale has proven especially important throughout anarchist history.

And, to be sure, focusing on a transnational scale is an important mechanism for confronting the type of internationalism to which Graeber alluded in the introduction, in which activists attempt to export an international approach rooted in the structure of the nation-state and expressed on a unidirectional axis of Global North to Global South. I agree with Graeber that, in many ways, New Anarchism has been much more carefully attentive to and invested in restructuring the paternalistic models of previous attempts to internationalize global radical movements. Elucidating the transnational dimensions of global movements against capitalism has proven an important part of this process, since such approaches have rejected and upended the nation-state as the naturalized structure of global politics. However, New Anarchists have not adequately accounted for the structure of the settler state in our approaches to transnationalism. As a result, the prolific work on transnational anarchism in the contemporary moment has yet to fully develop an approach that can engage in what Harsha Walia has called "undoing border imperialism."

For Walia, "an analysis of border imperialism interrogates the modes and networks of governance that determine how bodies will be included within the nation-state, and how territory will be controlled within and in conjunction with the dictates of global empire and transnational capitalism."[79] In this configuration, "undoing border imperialism" is not merely the process of moving across borders to build transnational movements. Rather, it requires an embedded analysis of how these borders function as part of the construction of global empire, paying special attention to how such borders also define the contours of struggle. And though Walia is primarily concerned with reimagining immigrant justice work within the context of settler colonialism, her framework is also useful for attending to the limits of anarchist transnationalism. As she observes, "at the global level, anti-imperialism goes beyond just expressing opposition to Western militarization," and, I add, it must also go beyond drawing connections between movements across national borders.[80]

Instead, a transnational approach that can confront the structure of settlement must account for how border imperialism is established through the claim to consistently demarcate the spaces of "domestic" and "foreign." I emphasize here the claim to control the malleability of these categories rather than to define them, since the ability to shift what territories and peoples are read as "domestic" and "foreign" has been intrinsic to the maintenance of US settlement. As Brunyeel has argued, "the invocation of spatial and temporal boundaries is a common practice of American political actors and institutions when trying to secure and impose the political rule of American colonial power . . . on indigenous people."[81] For him, recognizing this central dimension of US settlement opens new possibilities to conceptualize decolonizing political praxis. He argues that confronting the particular ways in which US settlement is defined through control of both territorial and political space "requires a decolonization of our spatial imaginations to reveal forms of political space that cannot simply be mapped onto the boundary lines of the international state system . . . instead [we must] imagine a postcolonial supplemental remapping of sovereign relationships that can include but not be dictated to or contained by state boundaries."[82]

This remapping is precisely what is missing from anarchist approaches to transnationalism. The result is a reinscription of the colonial ordering of both territorial and political space, one which silently subsumes Native resistance and self-determination within the borders (again, both territorial and political) claimed by the US settler state. Developing a transnational approach that undoes border imperialism requires centering a definition of the transnational that accounts for the sovereignty of Native nations and their complicated status within US articulations of domesticity and foreignness. In the following chapter, I explore how a rereading of Laguna Pueblo author Leslie Marmon Silko's influential work *Ceremony* as a transpacific novel provides a methodology through which to do this work of confronting US exceptionalism without erasing the sovereignty of Native nations.

CHAPTER 6

"Where Ocean Herself Was Born"

Transpacific Currents in Leslie Marmon Silko's *Ceremony*

> During the 1964 elections Indians were talking in Arizona about the relative positions of the two candidates, Johnson and Goldwater. A white man told them to forget about domestic policies and concentrate on the foreign policies of the two men. One Indian looked at him coldly and said that from the Indian point of view it was all foreign policy.
>
> —Vine Deloria Jr., *Custer Died for Your Sins: An Indian Manifesto*

These concerns regarding the limits of anarchist approaches to transnationalism echo similar anxieties in Native literary studies about the easy adoption of a transnational paradigm. Scholars like Chadwick Allen and Robert Warrior (Osage) have questioned the use of the category "transnational" to account for Native nationhood within a global paradigm, especially in the way it could serve to reify the structure of the US settler state.[1] And, as Muscogee scholar Craig Womack has pointed out, the shift toward the transnational has the uneasy effect of casting doubt on the utility of nationalist models of interpretation, which remain an important paradigm through which to consider Native and Indigenous literatures.[2] Though I more directly engage with these apprehensions about the paradigm of transnationalism in Native literary studies below, I begin with this recognition to situate some of the parallel concerns in anarchist studies that I articulated in the previous chapter.

In both cases, the uses of transnationalism for considering what Aloysha Goldstein has called the "formations of United States colonialism," nationalisms and nationalist paradigms, and global spatial geographies come into sharp relief. As Goldstein argues, "bridging the study of North American settler colonialism and U.S. overseas occupation provides a means with which to address both the incongruities and fault lines of the U.S. nation-state and the determined construction of national singularity, coherence, and continuity."[3] However, scholars like those mentioned above have especially wondered about the emergence of transnationalism from an American Studies paradigm, signaling an important questioning of whether such a conceptual turn is able to destabilize the US settler state as the central pivot of analysis or whether it serves to reassert US settler sovereignty in ways that paradoxically reify its claims to territorial and political space.

In this chapter, I offer a rereading of Laguna Pueblo writer Leslie Marmon Silko's *Ceremony* that emphasizes its transpacific dimensions. I argue that what emerges when we read it this way is a model of transnational engagement that decenters the US settler state while insisting on a critique of US empire that is grounded in a Native nationalist model. Drawing on original research in Silko's papers, I argue that the transpacific dimensions of *Ceremony* emerge when it is placed within the context of her contemporaneous literary production and her experiences while writing the novel. Building on this demonstration of the transpacific dimensions of the novel's creation, I move to a close reading of a few pivotal scenes in *Ceremony* to demonstrate how popular readings of the novel might be reframed through a transindigenous lens that offers a method of comparison similar to that developed by Alice Te Punga Somerville (Te Ātiawa/Taranaki) in her study of Māori connections to Oceania. There, Te Punga Somerville offers a rich study in "how Māori and other Pacific people talk about each other" rather than how they talk about the settler state of New Zealand. Emphasizing interaction across Indigenous communities, Te Punga Somerville argues that this method of comparative analysis "does not cut out the European gaze completely, but it certainly sidelines that gaze and produces spaces where its power is decentered."[4] This use of a comparative analysis capable of decentering while also apprehending the settler state is precisely what I locate through a transpacific reading of *Ceremony*.

My emphasis on the novel's Pacific dimensions builds on my use of Chamoru scholars Tiara Na'puti and Michael Lujan Bevacqua's argument that the Pacific represents a pivotal inroad for understanding how US settlement and empire are coconstructed through the demarcation of "domestic" and "foreign" spaces, as I discussed in the previous chapter. Within the scope of the Pacific, we can see the shared proximity of the myriad territorial and political claims through which US empire is structured: the US settlement of the Pacific Northwest; the overthrow of the sovereign kingdom of Hawai'i and subsequent statehood; the transformation of Alaska from organized territory to US state; the integration of the unincorporated territories of Guåhan, Samoa, and the Northern Marianas Islands; the US government's development and testing of nuclear weapons in the Marshall Islands and Kiribati; the use of nuclear weapons in Hiroshima and Nagasaki; and the US militarization of Okinawa. So central is the Pacific Ocean to US claims to territory that, in military parlance, it is often referred to as "The American Lake."[5] Scholars like Kaplan, Paul Lyons, and Yunte Huang have extended this recognition into the literary realm, demonstrating the central place of the Pacific within the American literary imagination.[6] Here, I extend this framework by asking how it might inform our reading of a pivotal work of Native literature, a body of work that is absent from studies like those of Kaplan, Lyons, and Huang.

Tracing the transpacific dimensions of both Silko's experience writing *Ceremony* and the world of the novel itself, I suggest a clear version of an approach to transnationalism that is commensurable with Native nationalisms, including Native literary nationalism.[7] What is more, by foregrounding the connection between the transpacific dimensions of both the novel itself and the context of its creation, I employ Womack's vision of a Native literary criticism that "attempts to find Native literature's place in Indian country, rather than Native literature's place in the canon."[8] Through my analysis, I explore the connections between Womack's call for a vision of Native literatures that reorients the focus on literary canon and Karin Amimoto Ingersoll's assertion that "indigeneity is both a local and a global interaction." Though she recognizes that this "appears to be a tension," she argues that it "is ultimately a continuous negotiation between roots and routes."[9] My rereading of *Ceremony* as a transpacific novel explores the connection between Womack's and Ingersoll's appeals, demonstrating how literary works develop an approach to the transnational that is attentive to questions of indigeneity, sovereignty, and place. In undertaking this work, I provide an approach to *Ceremony* that takes seriously the point made by Standing Rock Sioux scholar Vine Deloria Jr. in his joke that appears in the epigraph: that the function of the "domestic" and "foreign" is altered in both territorial and political terms when interpreted through Native epistemologies and cosmologies.

My decision to take up an analysis of *Ceremony*, one of the most prominent texts to come out of what Kenneth Lincoln famously termed the Native American Renaissance, extends from the commitments I describe above.[10] Though I return more in-depth to the question of popular analyses of *Ceremony* below, I am interested in revisiting it because of its prominent place in the study of Native literatures. Citing *Ceremony* as one specific example, Womack makes note of the relative popularity of "Native-written fictional stories about reconnection to Native culture," compared to the relative obscurity of Native-written texts that are overtly engaged in work "concerning their tribe's land claims or politics." The tension between these patterns of validation lead him to wonder whether the canonization of the Native American Renaissance, "in addition to its many positive qualities, also plays, in troubling ways, into the vanishing notion by allowing Native people to be fictional but not real."[11] This echoes Daniel Heath Justice (Cherokee) and James H. Cox's observation that the interpretation and reception of works considered foundational to the renaissance-era were dominated by "ethnographic methodologies that generated questions about identity and cultural authenticity."[12] In an effort to move away from such a method, I follow Cherokee scholar Sean Kicummah Teuton's articulation of *Ceremony* as an example of a practice in Renaissance-era novels "in which experiences are capable of yielding theory-mediated knowledge of the Indian world," a method he calls "tribal realism."[13]

By employing this approach to trace what emerges through such a methodological shift, I am interested in how *Ceremony* illuminates mappings of indigeneity on a global scale that serve to destabilize the US state as the hegemonic paradigm through which all Native literatures must be read while still offering a critical appraisal of its settler structure. Hsinya Huang has provided the impetus for a transpacific reading of *Ceremony* in her article "Towards Transnational Native American Literary Studies," in which she argues that Silko's focus on uranium mining creates a paradigm that evidences indigeneity connected across the Pacific:

> As he locates the mine, bomb factory, and atomic test sites on the reservations, [the main character] Tayo envisions his connection with other lands and people across the Pacific Ocean. The mining destroys lives across time and distance, connecting people in Hiroshima and Nagasaki with tribal indigenes in the Americas, virtually enclosing human beings in a "cycle of death" from which no escape is possible . . . this sets the ground for relevance and sympathy, and Tayo's epiphanic vision bespeaks an interconnectedness across the Pacific.[14]

I build on Huang's sense of the transpacific dimensions of *Ceremony* while moving away from her focus on violence and death as the primary transit through which indigeneity operates on a global scale. Instead, I read Tayo as a character whose experience signals a disidentification with the US settler state, suggesting a model of transnational engagement that disrupts the Indigenous/settler paradigm to move toward what Chadwick Allen has called a "transindigenous" methodology. Here, I find José Esteban Muñoz's articulation of disidentification as a "mode of dealing with dominant ideology . . . that neither opts to assimilate within such a structure nor strictly opposes it" to be particularly useful for attending to the territorial and political dimensions of the "third space of sovereignty" described by Brunyeel, which I introduced in chapter 5.[15] And in reading *Ceremony* through this lens, I draw out a vision of transnationalism capable of attending to these limits of anarchist approaches.

From Transnational to Transindigenous

My attempt to offer a rereading of *Ceremony* that seeks to intervene into discussions of transnationalism in both anarchist studies and Native literary studies requires an accounting for the complicated array of conversations in which this analysis is interjecting. As I mentioned in chapter 5, the ways that anarchists are grappling with the question of transnationalism reflect comparable (though not identical) conversations within Native literary studies. In this field, as in Native and Indigenous Studies more broadly, scholars have approached the topic of transnationalism with care, least of all because of its embeddedness in the field of American Studies, a field with which Native and Indigenous Studies (NAIS) has had a complicated relationship.[16] Warrior has offered an insightful reflection on the reception of transnationalism within NAIS, suggesting an interplay between "a strong practice of warily regarding various theoretical trends" and an unease with the implications for Native literary paradigms that center nationalist approaches.[17] However, drawing on the work of earlier theorists of transnationalism, such as Inderpal Grewal, Caren Kaplan, and Wai Chee Dimock, Warrior also recognizes the uses of transnationalism especially as it attends to the rise of neoliberal capitalism.[18] Within this tension between utility and legacy, the possibilities and limitations of transnationalism for Native literary studies emerge.

For preeminent scholars of Native literatures like Warrior and Womack, the dismissal of nationalist approaches is one of the greatest worries about the adoption of a transnational method of analysis. In his study of book-length Native literary criticism, Womack worries about the reification of "nationalism as a pathology," which runs contrary to "the tendency in Native studies to view it in terms of the survival of tribes."[19] Extending from conversations about the place of popular theoretical approaches like postmodernism and cosmopolitanism in the study of Native literatures, the emphasis on Native literary nationalism emerged as an insistence on the necessity of tribally specific approaches to literary criticism and an understanding of a concomitant commitment to Native sovereignty as the political valence of this diverse and growing body of creative work.[20]

The development of this approach has been pivotal to the bourgeoning of a Native literary criticism that works against the integration of token Native literary texts into the fabric of American literatures or the multicultural integration of Native literatures within the broader category of "multiethnic literatures." In her study of the transnational politics of contemporary Native cultures, Yup'ik scholar Shari Huhndorf has worried that "nationalist criticism . . . disregards global social dynamics and colonial critique, often opposing struggles for sovereignty to the interrogation of European ideologies and practices (even though these projects . . . are inseparable in Native culture)."[21] However, what would happen if we interpreted nationalist criticism within a framework that invoked a comparative analysis that centered not solely on Native interaction with settler structures but on the operation of indigeneity on a global scale?

This conversation about Native literary criticism is what I am most interested in highlighting here: its ability to emphasize the commensuration of Native nationalist and transnational approaches while demonstrating how this commensuration challenges claims to sovereignty by the US settler state. In particular, I am interested in exploring how Native literary nationalism, as an approach that attends to the specific political, territorial, and cultural contexts of Native literatures, might be able to at once emphasize the specificity of tribal and national locations while also considering how such texts operate on a broader scale. Such a method of critical engagement had been cultivated among scholars who seek to disentangle the settler state as the required point of reference for a comparative approach to Native literatures.

For instance, Chadwick Allen has offered a method of comparative literary engagement that he terms a "transindigenous approach," following from his disbelieving question of "whether we now require the rubric of the 'transnational' to recognize that Indigenous signs and sign systems travel?"[22] Allen's inquiry aligns with Hsinya Huang, Philip Deloria, Laura Furlan, and John Gamber's assertion that the possibilities of transnationalism for Native studies lie in "the significance of perceiving the Native as an active agent and of conceptualizing a comparative/trans-Indigenous paradigm for crossing over national, regional, and international boundaries to imagine a shared Indigenous world."[23] This emphasis on using a comparative method to evidence a "shared Indigenous world" is at the root of Allen's call to move from a transnational to transindigenous approach. For him, this shift signals a decentering of the nation-state as the primary method of comparative literary analysis while emphasizing the "necessary, invigorating study of specific traditions and contexts."[24]

This methodology, along with that of Huang et al., evidences a way of practicing a transnational approach that rejects the association of indigeneity with inertia and asks us to consider instead how a focus on indigeneity and global movement might destabilize the settler state as the necessary central anchor of comparative analysis. Work like that in the collection *The World, the Text, and the Indian: Global Dimensions of Native American Literature* have offered a diverse demonstration of the breadth of this approach, offering studies of the circulation of Native peoples and texts across the world through both literary and historical analysis. In his introduction to the collection, Scott Lyons emphasizes the distinction of transnationalism from the paradigm of globalization (which he describes as "the process by which a single world system is consolidated").[25] Noting the interplay between the two, he argues that transnationalism enables us to narrate the history of Native literatures "without endless recourse to American literary and cultural history," whereas globalization requires that we "observe . . . that this history is by no means 'separate' from non-tribal influences, forces, cultures, and people."[26]

My transpacific reading of Silko's *Ceremony* emerges precisely in this interplay between transnationalism and globalization. In contrast to Arnold Krupat's assertion in the same volume that Allen's transindigenous approach "relegate[s] national boundaries, borders, and treaty statuses to the background," leading to a transindigenous methodology that cannot "claim the more immediate political force that nationalist studies do," I suggest that reading *Ceremony* in this way evidences a transnational Native literary practice in which Native figures operate in the global world *as* national subjects, not of the settler state but of Native nations.[27] In fact, where Krupat (drawing on Huhndorf's analysis) cites

Ceremony as an example of a novel "about national return and integration," I argue that a transpacific reading reorients this directionality away from "return" toward one of circulation.[28] In doing so, I suggest that a transindigenous methodology attends to the limits of previous approaches to global Native literary studies, most notably those that center on cosmopolitanism or questions of authenticity, by demonstrating an approach wherein Native nationalisms are not discounted but are rather strengthened through a rejection of the settler state as the primary national formulation through which Native subjects interact with the global world.[29]

Reading *Ceremony* as a Nationalist Novel

Ceremony is a particularly engaging text to (re)read through this lens since the critical scholarship on it remains relatively ambiguous about its status as a nationalist novel. For instance, early on in the development of a theory of Native literary nationalism, Dakota writer Elizabeth Cook-Lynn questioned whether Silko's body of work could be understood as nationalist literature while a few years later Womack mentioned *Ceremony* as an example of a text whose engagement should include "a study of the primary cultures that produced them."[30] This sense of a nation-specific grounding in Laguna Pueblo epistemology and cosmology is also present in more critical receptions of her work, such as Laguna Pueblo writer Paula Gunn Allen's "Special Problems in Teaching Leslie Marmon Silko's *Ceremony*," in which she worries about Silko's dissemination of Laguna stories meant only to be told in certain contexts.[31] However, the novel is just as often read as one whose primary insistence is on reckoning with "mixed-blood" identity, a feature that Justice and Cox note was a central feature of early literary criticism on Native-authored texts from the Renaissance era. And though there has been significant focus on the protagonist Tayo's experience returning home to Laguna Pueblo after having been deployed abroad by the US military, this hasn't necessarily translated into a more concerted transindigenous reading of the novel.[32] For this reason, I want to linger here for a moment on the relevance of this array of interpretive models as an in-road to considering *Ceremony*'s transindigenous and transpacific dimensions.

First published in 1977, *Ceremony* is often read through the same foci that animate the study of Renaissance-era Native literatures more generally, including the study of the "mixed-blood" as a central figure through which questions of traditionalism are explored.[33] This focus forms the through line of scholarship on *Ceremony*, which follows protagonist Tayo during his tumultuous return to the reservation after serving in the Japanese-occupied Philippines during World War II. The relationship between Tayo's physical return home after serving abroad and his metaphysical return home to Laguna traditions has been a prominent focus of the novel, so popular that it has become almost pedestrian.[34] For instance, Kathleen M. Donovan has described *Ceremony* as a "classic 'homing in' [novel]," in which "the protagonist achieves a sense of identity by returning home to be healed with tradition, myth, and the land."[35] This connects to other popular readings of *Ceremony* through the lens of the exegetical function of the "mixed-blood" figure, as in Choctaw and Cherokee scholar Louis Owens's prominent study of such characters in Native literatures and film. He argues that, with *Ceremony*, Silko returns to the figure of the "mixed-blood" as it was explored in earlier texts like Mourning Dove's *Cogewea* (1927), D'Arcy McNickle's *The Surrounded* (1936), and John Joseph Matthews's *Sundown* (1934).[36] According to Owens, Silko's protagonist Tayo "inverts the tragic image of the halfbreed, constructing a novel that argues for hybridization and heterogeneity as sources of power and rich potential."[37] In his preface for the 2006 edition of *Ceremony*, famed writer of the American West Larry McMurtry echoes this reading and extends it into a connection with Silko's own experience. He writes that Silko, "like her hero Tayo, is of mixed blood" and, because of this, "most of her work could be said to explore those border-lands of identity experiences by mixed-blood people" or people who "find themselves stuck between cultures, neither wholly in nor wholly out of what may be their native society."[38]

This emphasis in the scholarly literature on Tayo as both a "mixed-blood" and "homing-in" character offers some insight into the ambiguous reading of *Ceremony* as a novel exemplifying Native literary nationalism. Tayo's experience as a mixed-blood veteran returning home invokes parallels to the history of pan-Indian movements and their connections to communities of Native veterans, especially since the novel takes place during the Termination and Relocation era of Federal Indian Policy directly following World War II.[39] But, as Huhndorf has pointed out, Tayo's salvation through Laguna Pueblo ceremonies also speaks to the centering of a tribally specific method of storytelling.[40] Rather than argue for or against a nationalist reading of *Ceremony*, I am interested in what this ambiguous approach can tell us about how the novel is read through a transnational lens, invoked either implicitly or overtly in the scholarly analysis. Read through a transnational approach, both the "mixed-blood" and "homing-in" approaches to *Ceremony* replicate the type of comparative approach that Allen argues against in his development of a transindigenous methodology since the axis of analysis hinges on comparing a dominating settler society to a dominated indigenous one. In thinking through its utility as a transnational approach, this reading maintains the US settler state as the pivot of comparative analysis, effectively obscuring the novel's transindigenous dimensions.

The delimiting of a possible transindigenous reading of *Ceremony* stems not only from the methods of engagement described above but also in how it is placed within Silko's broader body of work. Of special note here is *Ceremony*'s relation to Silko's successive novels, *Almanac of the Dead* (1991) and *Gardens in the Dunes* (1999), both of which are read as works grounded in a transnational framework. An epic and far-reaching novel, *Almanac of the Dead* follows the development of a hemispheric revolutionary Indigenous movement, connecting Indigenous struggles across the Americas, echoing especially the Zapatista uprising through which anarchists often invoke indigeneity in their articulations of a transnational approach, though it was published four years before the uprising. Goeman has pointed out how *Almanac* "provides us a critique of a faltering present in stories that (re)map the narratives of the past . . . not just [as] unfortunate accounts of a temporal past, but [as] part and parcel of events that have led to current geopolitical formations not only in the Northern Hemisphere, but globally."[41] Similarly, *Gardens in the Dunes* follows the protagonist Indigo as she is taken from her home among the fictional Sand Lizard people in the Southwest and adopted by a worldly white couple that bring her to Europe and South America. In her analysis of the novel, Huhndorf argues that through Indigo's story, Silko reframes the captivity narrative as a foundational American literary form by using the global scale to reveal the legacies of settlement intrinsic to the US settler state. By following Indigo on "a journey from west to east, it reverses the direction of conventional frontier narratives" on a global scale.[42]

Though Silko is a prolific writer whose work moves through and plays with multiple genre forms, these remain Silko's only novels. Yet, *Ceremony* is rarely read within the same contours as *Almanac of the Dead* or *Gardens in the Dunes*, isolated especially in the lack of attention to its transnational dimensions. In the most general sense, I am interested here in placing *Ceremony* within this lineage of Silko's work in the novel form because doing so might illuminate the connection between her turn to the novel as literary form and her evincing of a transnational approach to Native nationalism. In the analysis I provide below, I aim for an even more specific engagement of transnationalism by exploring the connection between a transindigenous and transpacific reading of *Ceremony* and how this might prove useful to the issues I discussed in chapter 5. In what follows, I build on the work of scholars like Huhndorf, Huang, and Kyoko Matsunaga who have emphasized the transpacific dimensions of *Ceremony* through their exploration of the connections between the American Southwest and Japan that emerge in the novel's focus on uranium mining and nuclear weapons.[43] I am interested in adding more texture to this apprehension of the novel's transpacific dimensions by bringing into sharper relief the connections to Alaska and the Philippines that emerge when we read *Ceremony* through a transindigenous lens.

Locating *Ceremony* in the Pacific

In my use of Allen's model of transindigenous reading to locate the transpacific dimensions of *Ceremony*, I am interested in two related scopes of analysis. First, I place *Ceremony* back into conversation with contemporaneous writing that Silko was producing while she was writing the novel, including literary writing and personal correspondence. Second, I analyze the transpacific dimensions of pivotal scenes in *Ceremony* to better establish how the transindigenous connections I emphasize in the context of its creation and Silko's contemporaneous literary output inform a reading of the novel. I begin with this consideration of Silko's contemporaneous writing to bring out some of the other ways she was thinking about the Pacific during this time. This engagement with the space of the Pacific extends far beyond a consideration of the connections between uranium mining at Laguna Pueblo and the use of nuclear weapons at Hiroshima and Nagasaki, speaking to broader transpacific currents that underscore the spatial and temporal dimensions of *Ceremony*.

Within her body of work, *Ceremony* remains deeply connected to some of Silko's earliest writing for which she began garnering critical attention. Along with her collection of stories and poems *Laguna Woman* (1974), the acclaimed critical reception of *Ceremony* led to

Silko becoming one of the inaugural recipients of the MacArthur Foundation Grant in 1981. Included within *Laguna Woman* (and later republished in her 1981 collection *Storyteller*) is the poem "Prayer to the Pacific," which Silko was working on as early as 1971.[44] Appearing in collections published before and after *Ceremony*'s debut, this poem represents an important bookend to the novel, evidencing especially a preoccupation with the Pacific during the time that it was written. The poem begins:

> I traveled to the ocean
> Distant
> from my southwest land of sandrock
> to the moving blue water
> Big as the myth of origin

As the poem goes on, Silko extends her invocation of water as a connective force between her home in the Southwest and the broader Pacific, collapsing the sense of juxtaposition between the arid desert of Laguna Pueblo territory and the vast moisture of the Pacific Ocean, the largest body of water in the world. Instead, she establishes a transpacific connection that connects "sun floating west / to China / where ocean herself was born." The ocean is not a static place on the map but becomes a method of interaction between landscapes, in which "Clouds that blow across the sand are wet."[45] For Silko, this "Prayer to the Pacific" is not concerned with offering ruminations on the qualities and properties of water as a metaphor for global diffuseness. Rather, Silko evinces the type of comparative transindigenous approach described by Allen in the way she positions transpacific movement as central to indigeneity.

Silko centers the Pacific Ocean in her narrative of origin, directly confronting the Bering Strait theory in her spatial and temporal rendering of movement across the Pacific, writing: "Thirty thousand years ago / Indians came riding across the ocean / carried by giant sea turtles." Here, she uses a transpacific approach to reorient a settler narrative about Indigenous movement across the Pacific through a distinctly Indigenous worldview that invokes North America as "Turtle Island," continuing:

> And so from that time
> immemorial,
> as the old people say,

rain clouds drift from the west
gift from the ocean

Green leaves in the wind
Wet earth on my feet
swallowing raindrops
clear from China."[46]

Instead of using an appeal to notions of indigeneity as a static relationship to place—to resist settler invocations of the Bering Strait theory that discount Native claims to territory—Silko establishes an alternative rendering of movement across the Pacific that is rooted in Native temporality ("from that time immemorial") and storytelling ("as the old people say"). This focus in "Prayer to the Pacific" is an especially compelling connection to the transpacific dimensions of *Ceremony* since it highlights some of the themes that Silko discusses in her reflection on living on the Pacific coast in Ketchikan, Alaska, while writing the novel's first draft.

In the same Penguin Classic edition in which McMurtry's introduction appears, Silko also provided a preface that details her experience writing *Ceremony* on the Pacific Coast in the town of Ketchikan. This proved to be a pivotal experience for Silko, not only because of her experience dealing with the unique climate in the temperate rainforest of Southeast Alaska (which I discuss below) but also because it initiated her contact with Alaska Native peoples. The lasting impressions of this experience are echoed in *Storyteller* (published four years after *Ceremony*), whose titular story follows a young Yup'ik girl as she seeks revenge for the murder of her parents by a government agent and her subsequent banishment to a residential school.[47]

Inspired by her time in Bethel, a city in mainland Alaska about four hundred miles west of Anchorage, *Storyteller* explores the complicated constellation of physical isolation, ecological devastation, inherited trauma, and gendered violence.[48] In this way, its themes and structure also echo those most central to *Ceremony*. Early drafts of "Storyteller" appear in Silko's personal files which also contain drafts of *Ceremony*, signaling the transindigenous connections between these two pieces. When placed within a transpacific scope, we can see the conversation that Silko is drawing out between Native peoples at Laguna Pueblo and Yup'ik people in mainland Alaska. And though, in each, she reckons with the continuing structure of settlement in these locations, placing these texts in conversation destabilizes the US settler state as the primary locus of comparative analysis, bringing relationships between Yup'ik and Laguna Pueblo peoples and territories to the fore.

For instance, in "Storyteller," Silko explores how the tenuousness of settler presence in a rugged, unfamiliar territory continually adapts to maintain control of the land through resource extraction. During a conversation with the young Yup'ik protagonist, the "storyteller" character of the story's title, whom Silko names only "the old man," observes of the white settlers: "They only come when there is something to steal. The fur animals are too difficult for them to get now, and the seals and fish are hard to find. Now they come for oil deep in the earth."[49] This resonates with similar themes of resource extraction with which scholars interested in the transnational dimensions of *Ceremony* have thus far been concerned. After his return to the Laguna Pueblo reservation, Tayo remembers "years before" when the US government "paid the land-grant association five thousand dollars not to ask questions about the test holes they were drilling" to mine the uranium that was central to the US nuclear program during World War II and the subsequent Cold War.[50] What is more, Tayo experiences the legacy of the mines, not only through memory but through water, verifying a connection to the methodology Silko began developing in "Prayer to the Pacific."

After crawling through the "strands of barbed wire" that still enclose the abandoned mine, Tayo drinks water that is "still warm from sun and taste[s] bitter." As he sits and drinks, Tayo surmises that "maybe the uranium made the water taste that way."[51] Echoing the focus on water that connects *Ceremony* to "Prayer for the Pacific," the invocation of the history of uranium mining contemporaneously with Silko's writing about oil extraction in Yup'ik territory demonstrates the connection that she is drawing between Alaska Native and Laguna Pueblo people's experiences during the time she spent writing in Ketchikan. This remained a preoccupation for Silko throughout her career, as she made multiple attempts to create a film based on "Storyteller," even working on a short film treatment based on it during a filmmaking seminar with Robert Redford during a Sundance Institute in 1982.[52]

Though her experiences in Alaska, particularly in Yup'ik territory on the mainland, clearly influenced Silko's writing for years to come, her difficulty navigating the climate of Southeast Alaska is also significant to reading *Ceremony* as a transpacific text. Initially intended as a collection of short stories that focused on the "funny story about Harley, the World War II veteran whose family tried but could not keep him away from liquor," Silko's difficulty in navigating the wet climate helped her develop *Ceremony* into the story of Tayo, a World War II veteran who struggles after returning home from serving in the Japanese-occupied Philippines.[53] In her preface to the third edition, Silko describes at length how deeply intertwined the writing of *Ceremony* was with her struggle to adapt to rainy Ketchikan, noting that she "was accustomed to the bright sunlight of the Southwest" and found the average yearly rainfall of 180 inches almost unbearable. According to her, the beginning of her time in Ketchikan was characterized by her "fighting off the terrible lethargy of a depression caused in large part by the absence of sunlight."[54] During those early months in Ketchikan, Silko wrote a never-published short story called "Returning," the story of an Alaska Native woman who drowns in the Thomas Basin in Ketchikan, presumably by suicide. In organizing her papers for acquisition by the Beinecke Rare Book and Manuscript Library at Yale University, Silko described "Returning" as "an unpublished short story written just before I began CEREMONY."[55] This story resonates with the literal and figurative darkness that Silko struggled with during her time there—a darkness from which she emerges through the writing of *Ceremony*.

Silko credits *Ceremony* with helping her recover from the debilitating headaches associated with this lethargy, noting that she healed along with the main character Tayo and crossed vast space through her literary journey. She describes the novel as her "refuge, [her] magic vehicle back to the Southwest land of sandstone mesas, blue sky and sun."[56] She describes writing the geographic space and contours in *Ceremony* as a transnational connection across space and time:

> As I described the sandstone spring, the spiders, water bugs, swallows, and rattlesnakes, I remade the place in my words; I was no longer on a dark rainy island thousands of miles away. I was home, from time immemorial, as the old ones like to say to use children long ago.[57]

For her, *Ceremony* itself acts as a transnational connection, an embodiment of how storytelling materializes multiple spaces simultaneously. These connections are echoed in the experience of Silko's main character Tayo. Much like Silko, Tayo struggles in the wet climate of the Philippines during his deployment. He describes the rain as unending, growing "like foliage from the sky, branching and arching to the earth."[58] For him, the rain is so severe that he comes to see it, with its persistence and pervasiveness, as responsible for the death of his cousin Rocky:

> Tayo hated this unending rain as if it were the jungle green rain and not the miles of marching or the Japanese grenade that was killing Rocky. He would blame the rain if the Japs [*sic*] saw how the corporal staggered; if they saw how weak Rocky had become, and came to crush his head with the butt of a rifle, then it would be the rain and the green all around that killed him.[59]

Tayo's struggle with the extremes of wetness and dryness are central to his understanding of himself as a transnational subject, a point to which I will return below. What is more, Silko's emphasis on her similar experience of invoking the arid desert while writing *Ceremony* in the rainforest of Southeast Alaska demonstrates the transnational dimensions of the novel as both a literary narrative and cultural object. The connections between Silko's and Tayo's experiences in rainforest climates on either side of the Pacific demonstrate how the geographic and atmospheric contexts of Silko's writing experience mediate the Pacific as a space of transnational exchange. Again, the focus here is not on the political or territorial space of US sovereignty, but on the meteorological connections across wide swaths of space.

This decentering of the US settler state is also present in Silko's reflections on the difficulties of navigating the wet weather of Ketchikan. She emphasizes the transpacific dimensions of her experience, noting that Ketchikan has a "mild climate by Alaskan standards due in large part to a warm ocean current named the Japanese Current."[60] Silko mentions the connection between the temperate weather and this "Japanese current" as early as 1975 in a letter to her longtime friend and Norwegian scholar Per Seyersted, in connection to her trip to Bethel (fig. 2):

> Later this week, I will fly 1,300 miles to the north of Ketchikan, to the tundra country of the Kuskokwim River at Bethel, Alaska. This will be my first opportunity to meet Eskimo [*sic*] people, since the native people in the Ketchikan area are Athabascan peoples such as the Haida and Tlingit tribes. It will also be my first exposure to the freezing weather which most people associate with Alaska. Ketchikan is on the sea coast, and it is warmed by the Japanese current, so the temperatures here rarely go below the freezing level. In fact, our weather is very similar to the weather in Seattle, Washington.[61]

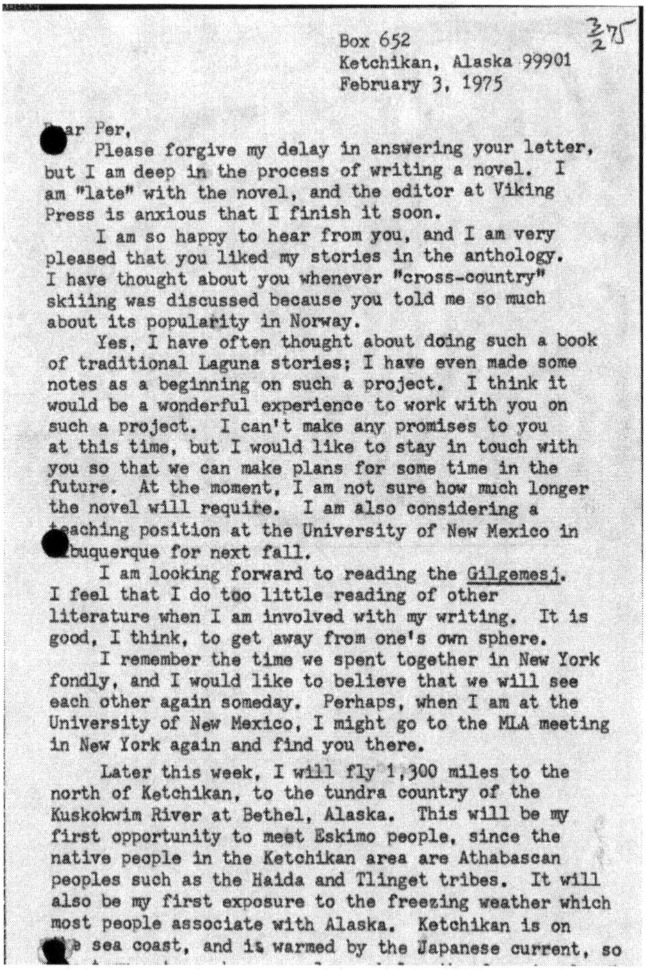

Box 652
Ketchikan, Alaska 99901
February 3, 1975

Dear Per,

Please forgive my delay in answering your letter, but I am deep in the process of writing a novel. I am "late" with the novel, and the editor at Viking Press is anxious that I finish it soon.

I am so happy to hear from you, and I am very pleased that you liked my stories in the anthology. I have thought about you whenever "cross-country" skiiing was discussed because you told me so much about its popularity in Norway.

Yes, I have often thought about doing such a book of traditional Laguna stories; I have even made some notes as a beginning on such a project. I think it would be a wonderful experience to work with you on such a project. I can't make any promises to you at this time, but I would like to stay in touch with you so that we can make plans for some time in the future. At the moment, I am not sure how much longer the novel will require. I am also considering a teaching position at the University of New Mexico in Albuquerque for next fall.

I am looking forward to reading the Gilgemesj. I feel that I do too little reading of other literature when I am involved with my writing. It is good, I think, to get away from one's own sphere.

I remember the time we spent together in New York fondly, and I would like to believe that we will see each other again someday. Perhaps, when I am at the University of New Mexico, I might go to the MLA meeting in New York again and find you there.

Later this week, I will fly 1,300 miles to the north of Ketchikan, to the tundra country of the Kuskokwim River at Bethel, Alaska. This will be my first opportunity to meet Eskimo people, since the native people in the Ketchikan area are Athabascan peoples such as the Haida and Tlinget tribes. It will also be my first exposure to the freezing weather which most people associate with Alaska. Ketchikan is on the sea coast, and is warmed by the Japanese current, so

Fig. 2. Letter from Leslie Marmon Silko (Laguna Pueblo) to Per Seyersted, February 3. Copyright © 1975 Leslie Marmon Silko, reproduced by permission from the Wylie Agency LLC.

In this letter Silko makes a point to engage with the specificity of multiple national and tribal locations across Alaska Native communities, distinguishing between Haida and Tlingit peoples as she informs Seyersted of the immense differences in climate between Southeast and mainland Alaska while connecting their differing climates to the movement of water across and within the Pacific. What is more, the letter itself is written on stationery adorned with a formline representation of

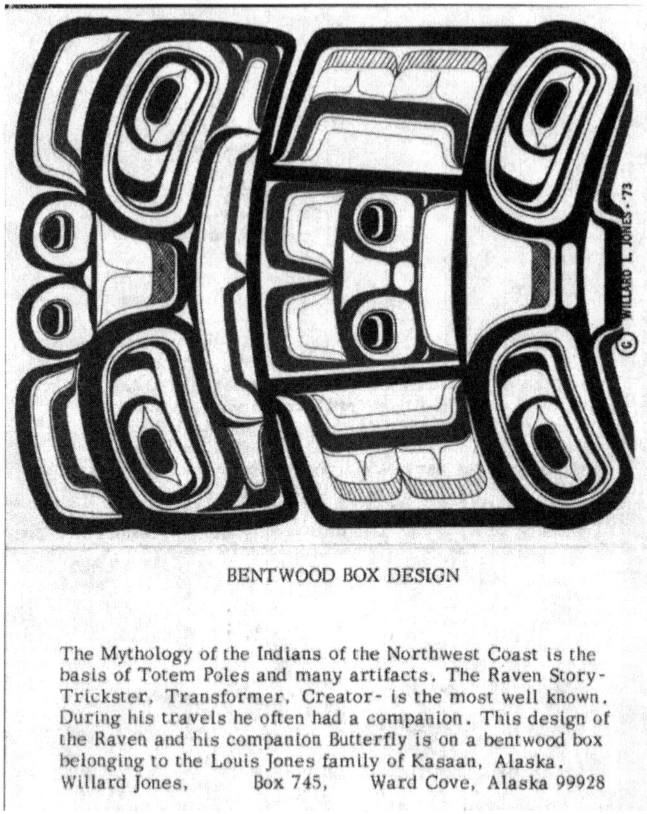

Fig. 3. Stationery with a Raven bentwood box design.

Raven (see fig. 3), symbolizing further connection between Southeast Alaska and the Pacific Northwest of the United States, which she also invokes through comparing the climate to that of Seattle.[62]

In both cases, Silko is referring to the Kuroshio or "Black Current," which is the northeasterly flowing continuation of the Pacific North Equatorial Current between Luzon, the most populous island of the Philippines, and the coast of Japan. The route of this transpacific movement is particularly relevant when considered alongside *Ceremony*'s focus on Tayo's experience being taken as a prisoner of war (POW) by the Japanese military during their occupation of the Philippines during World War II. As I discuss more at length in the following section, Tayo's struggle throughout *Ceremony* is tied to this space of overlapping national locations following the Bataan Death March of 1942, in which Laguna, Filipino, Japanese, and American contexts are brought together in the same space. The transpacific dimensions of Silko's invocation of the Kuroshio in both her personal correspondence and her description of her experience writing *Ceremony* are significant in both her lamentation of the weather and the very grace through which she is able to overcome it.

For instance, in that same preface to *Ceremony*, Silko speaks also about her friendship with a local Japanese restaurant owner, describing the strength she drew from the noodles and tea she consumed at the café where she ate her daily lunch, run by Mrs. Hirabayashi and her mother who, "like other Japanese Americans, were imprisoned in internment camps" during World War II.[63] This recalls the specter in *Ceremony* of both Tayo's own experience in a Japanese prison and Japanese internment in the United States, drawing again intimate connections between Alaska, Japan, the Philippines, and Laguna Pueblo.[64]

Charting the transpacific connections of *Ceremony* through both these contemporaneous writings and Silko's experience writing them while living in Alaska helps to anchor a transindigenous and transpacific reading of the novel itself. When placed within this context, *Ceremony* becomes clearly connected to Silko's understanding of Laguna Pueblo as being connected to the Pacific world as one that extends beyond the intervention of the United States across that expanse. Without circumventing or obscuring this history, Silko invokes water, currents, and transindigenous connections to decenter the influence of the US settler state from her sense of a transpacific world. In this transnational approach, she remains rooted in the specificities of tribal and national location as well. This transindigenous and transpacific methodology in terms of Silko's experience writing the novel are mirrored in pivotal scenes from the text itself.

"Great Swollen Grief": Transpacific Currents in *Ceremony*'s Pivotal Scenes

Early in the novel, Silko depicts Tayo's return to the United States after being hospitalized in a military facility following his tour of duty in the Japanese-occupied Philippines. A scene that echoes the themes of "returning" evoked by Silko's never-published short story that I mentioned above, Tayo's arrival at the train depot in Los Angeles is one of the first places that we see the transpacific currents of *Ceremony* emerge. In this scene, Tayo struggles with memories of his experience in the prison camp to which he is taken after the Bataan Death March. Depicted as his struggle with voices while waiting for his train at the depot, Tayo appears as a fragile, silent shell. His arrival at the depot leads him to recognize that "for a long time he had been white smoke." This was a state that he failed to recognize "until he left the hospital, because white smoke had no consciousness of itself."[65] As he stands in the Los Angeles depot, Tayo moves between remembering that "his body has density again and the world was visible" to the devastating memory of his cousin Rocky's death.[66] This memory threatens to bring him back into the fog, to make him into white smoke all over again: as he walks towards his train, Tayo "felt weak, and the longer he walked the more his legs felt as though they might become invisible again; then the top part of his body would topple, and when his head was level with the ground he would be lost in smoke again, in the fog again."[67]

As Tayo struggles through this transformation from density to ambiguity, he laments that it is "too late to ask for help," and he waits to "die the way smoke dies, drifting away in currents of air, twisting in thin swirls, fading until it exists no more." The only thing that brings him back to density after laying on the concrete floor, waiting to become smoke, are the "voices that surrounded him, voices that were either soft or distant."[68] These voices speak to Tayo first in English, and then in Japanese. And when he hears the Japanese words, "he wasn't sure where he was any more, maybe back in the jungles again." As he fights to emerge from the place of smoke to which he has retreated "he expected a rifle barrel to be shoved into his face."[69] For Tayo, hearing Japanese voices is a spatial experience, invoking a specific memory that immediately connects the Los Angeles train depot to the Pacific. Silko's use of voices here to indicate the coexistence of multiple Pacific spaces is echoed throughout the text.

For instance, in this early appearance of Tayo's experience with multivalent voices, she uses the invocation of Japanese language in the Los Angeles train depot to begin her complicated reckoning with the legacy of Japanese internment in the United States and Tayo's internment in a Japanese prison camp. As the Japanese voices initiate an expectation of the barrel of a rifle and of being pulled back into the Philippine jungle, Tayo is confronted instead with group of "Japanese women holding small children by the hands," one of whom asks him if he is sick. After Tayo fails to reply, the women leave him in the care of "white man in a train uniform," who helps him to his feet. Once standing again, Tayo watches the women and their children walk away, feeling "a current of air from the movement of their skirts" and notices one of the little boys "wearing an army hat" turn back and smile at Tayo before disappearing "through the wide depot doors." As he watches the small boy walk away, Tayo observes to the depot man, "Those people . . . I thought they locked them up." The man responds, "Oh, that was some years back. Right after Pearl Harbor. But now they've turned them all loose again."[70]

This early rumination on the intersection of Tayo's "return" and that of Japanese citizens interred in concentration camps during World War II is even more pronounced in an earlier draft of *Ceremony*. In one earlier version, the man in the train uniform suggests that the Japanese women and children that Tayo encounters are at the train depot because they are "coming back from the camps," bringing the proximity of their experiences of incarceration even closer so that it seems as if they were incarcerated in the United States while Tayo was in the Japanese prison camp in the Philippines. The small boy is even more present in this version, reminding Tayo of his cousin Rocky as a child—a realization that brings him to tears "because it was true nothing about thousands of miles or high ocean waves or green could change who people were." His encounter with the Japanese women and children in the train depot reminds him that "people were cut loose from their places and wandered anywhere—Japanese in the L.A. depot and an old Laguna man in the Phillipine [*sic*] jungles."[71] Here, Silko invokes the transpacific as a space not only of connection but of overlay. In doing so, she explores Tayo's connection to Japanese Americans during World War II to emphasize it as a war between two empires, rather than their subjects. In this way, Silko highlights the connection between the *subjects of* empire, rather than considering only their relationship to empire itself.

This particular transpacific and transindigenous method is echoed throughout the text, made particularly evident in one of the most prominent scenes in the novel, the scene in which Tayo is unable to erase the detection of his Uncle Josiah's face in that of a dead Japanese soldier. Immediately before the depot scene, *Ceremony* shifts to a series of memories from the Pacific Theater of World War II. We learn that as Tayo struggles to sleep, he attempts to think of something benign—in this case, a deer. However, this image quickly shifts to "become the deer that he and Rocky had hunted," a memory that quickly "unwind[s] into the last day they had sat together, oiling their rifles in the jungle of some nameless Pacific Island." For Tayo, this recollection moves seamlessly into his memory of being unable to kill a group of Japanese prisoners because "in that instant he saw Josiah standing there."[72] Connected in his dreams to Laguna Pueblo traditions of deer hunting (and the practice of relation to land and family therein), the constant uncanny familiarity of the faces of Japanese soldiers is a powerful fixation for Tayo. Though he is, in some sense, intellectually persuaded by Rocky that the face is not Josiah's, he remains disturbed by his inability to draw that distinction in his own intuition. Here, the transpacific connections of Tayo's experience are rooted in his sense of himself as embedded in Laguna Pueblo practices.

The transnational dimensions of this encounter exist in both Tayo's internal and external worlds. Externally, Tayo's recognition of Josiah in the face of a Japanese soldier emphasizes the relationship he sees between his Laguna Pueblo community and the Japanese soldiers against which he is supposed to be fighting as a member of the US armed forces. Tayo's difficulty in reckoning with these connections is exacerbated by learning that Josiah did, in fact, die while he was at war. Though this is a common reading of this climactic moment in *Ceremony*, I want to emphasize how Silko uses this moment not solely to draw a connection between Laguna Pueblo and Japanese soldiers but also to center movement across and within the Pacific that emanates from Tayo's location in a Laguna Pueblo national context.

Internally, Tayo is unable to rectify the emotional pull of these transnational connections despite Rocky's insistence on the use of logic to disentangle them. After Tayo breaks down when he sees Josiah's face in that of the Japanese soldier, Rocky "had reasoned it out with him," emphasizing that "it was impossible for the dead man to be Josiah, because Josiah was an old Laguna man, thousands of miles from the Philippine jungles and Japanese armies."[73] Here, Rocky attempts to interrupt the transpacific connection that Tayo experiences by highlighting the physical distance between Laguna Pueblo and the Philippine jungle. Despite his acknowledgement of the infallibility of Rocky's logic, Tayo begins shivering, "because all the facts, all the reasons made no difference any more [. . .] he could follow the logic of what Rocky said, but he could not feel anything except a swelling in his belly, a great swollen grief that was pushing into his throat."[74] This "great swollen grief" can be read as an indication not only of his intuition of Josiah's death a world away but also of the connection between the imposition of settler colonialism on Native nations in the United States and US imperialism abroad during World War II. Though it takes place during the World War II period, the transpacific connections between East

Asia and Indian Country that Silko draws in *Ceremony* speak also to the connections being drawn during the 1970s, when the book was published, by Native activists who fought in Vietnam only to return home and experience continued violence at the hands of the country for which they had fought.[75]

This connection to Vietnam is an important part of Silko's use of a transpacific narrative to emphasize Native disidentification with the US settler state as a definitive dimension of Native resistance throughout the twentieth century. As Paul Chaat Smith (Comanche) and Robert Warrior (Osage) make clear in their study of the American Indian Movement (AIM), Native veterans' recognition of their relation to the US settler state became a powerful method through which Native activism played against it. This is reflected in Tayo's experience in *Ceremony*. As Sharon Holm argues, "Tayo quickly learns that the uniform provides an illusory effect; while it is worn it effaces Indian identity in a white world, but the minute the war is over they become 'Indians' again, with all the associated negative and racially prejudiced connotations." As Tayo and Rocky experience the power of the uniform to either inculcate or disassociate them from belonging in the US settler state, "the uniform acts as a signifier that hides and deflects their Indianness under the guise of allegiance to as well as being included in the idea of the American nation-state and the democratic ideal."[76] This disidentification with the US settler state is countered in the novel with Tayo's deeper engagement with Laguna Pueblo traditions and language. In this way, *Ceremony* offers a transindigenous approach that demonstrates a commensuration between commitments to nationalism and transnationalism.

Through a return to the beginning of the novel, we can see the embeddedness of such a transindigenous and transpacific approach both in the depot scene and in Tayo's dream. In the opening scene of the novel, Tayo awakens to sunrise after having slept poorly the night before. As he tosses and turns in his bed, he remembers the "humid dreams of black night and loud voices rolling him over and over again like debris caught in a flood."[77] Here, the specter of water is present in movement, gesturing to how oceans connect seemingly disparate places through waves and through flood. The transnational dimensions of this movement are emphasized by how these voices reverberate in both this particular dream and in Tayo's dreams more generally in a number of languages and voices, including Spanish, Japanese, and Laguna. Our introduction to Tayo, then, is marked by his navigation of voices crossing space and time within his dreams. Like "the coiled springs [that] kept squeaking even after he lay still again," Tayo's dreams make transpacific noise even as he is sedentary.[78]

Alongside the Laguna song that opens the novel, these voices create a dynamic aural image of shifting space. Tayo's own understanding of the various voices he encounters in his dream reflects the geographic movement incumbent in the shift between voices:

> Tonight the singing had come first, squeaking out of the iron bed, a man singing in Spanish, the melody of a familiar love song, two words again and again, "Y volveré." Sometimes the Japanese voices came first, angry and loud, pushing the song far away, and then he could hear the shift in his dreaming, like a slight afternoon wind changing its direction, coming less and less from the south, moving into the west, and the voices would become Laguna voices.[79]

Tayo experiences the voices as movement emanating from and pointing toward specific directions, like wind. Even the "familiar love song" he hears is imbued with this spatial contour—"Y volveré," or "I'll return." The reference to the bachata "Y Voleré" made famous in 1969 by Chilean band Los Ángeles Negros also calls forth General MacArthur's famous 1942 avowal after landing in Australia following the Japanese conquest of the Philippines that "I came through and I shall return," offering a powerful connection to the operation of US imperialism in the Pacific at the height of World War II.[80] At the outset of the novel, then, Tayo's understanding not only of his physical position but of his own composition is presented through his reckoning with the multiple places and voices he carries with him. Though the temporal setting of *Ceremony* is singularly located in Tayo's experience of returning to Laguna Pueblo after serving in the Philippines, with his experiences abroad being established through memory, his experience of himself continues to be imbued with voices from multiple geographic, temporal, and cultural locations.

The transpacific dimensions of these pivotal scenes from *Ceremony* are embodied through Tayo's experience across the Pacific and through his encounter with other peoples navigating the complicated interplay of national and imperial structures throughout. Often read as a "mixed-blood" character struggling to understand his relationship to his Laguna Pueblo community, Tayo is misunderstood as a provincial figure. Rather, his experiences abroad and his coping with them at home signal a broader argument about Native people in the global world. In this way, *Ceremony* can be read as a novel that works against the depiction of Native peoples as immobile, isolated groups and, instead, illustrates the centrality of movement to a global Indigenous worldview. Though, as Te Punga Somerville has noted, the emphasis on movement is often taken to negate claims to indigeneity, the requirement that indigeneity be tied to immobility is a colonial idea that requires the enclosure of Indigenous space and the stasis of Indigenous peoples.[81] Instead, Silko uses the coexistence of voice, atmosphere, and memory to emphasize a transpacific world whose apprehension through a transindigenous lens offers a vision of transnationalism that connects Tayo's experiences as a Laguna Pueblo man, steeped in the language and ceremony of his people, who reckons with indigeneity in the context of multiple empires. In doing so, Silko is able to provide an approach to transnationalism that grounds Native nationalisms within a global world.

* * *

This rereading of *Ceremony* as a transpacific novel evidences the possibilities of Allen's transindigenous methodology for conceptualizing how Native nationalist paradigms operate on a transnational scale. In this sense, the transnationalism of Silko's most famous work pushes against notions of transnationalism that paint it as diametrically opposed to the type of tribal specificity incumbent within Native literary nationalisms. Throughout *Ceremony*, Tayo calls up direct and distinct grounding in his relationship to Laguna Pueblo territory, language, and practices as he travels both physically and metaphysically across the Pacific. And though, as the most prominent readings of the novel have pointed out, Tayo's return to the Laguna Pueblo reservation is essential to his healing, it is never temporally or spatially separate from his experiences in the Philippine jungle. Rather than engaging a transnational scale to erode Native nationhood, Tayo's experience draws such nationalism together through a disidentification with the US state that offers a critique of US empire that is fomented through decentering it as the pivot of any comparative analysis. This approach to transnationalism acts as an important corrective to limits of anarchist approaches described in chapter 5.

To refresh, in outlining the limits of anarchist approaches to transnationalism, I pointed out three ways in which anarchists have reified the structure of the US settler state in attempts to account for US imperialism and US exceptionalism: by subsuming Native nations under the auspices of US settler sovereignty in attempts to map the

United States in the world; by conceptualizing nationalism in ways that preclude a consideration of Native nationalisms; and by emphasizing global histories of anarchism that neglect contemporaneous histories of US empire. A transindigenous reading of Silko's *Ceremony* as a transpacific text addresses each of these limitations in its own way, beginning from Deloria's sentiment in the epigraph that "from the Indian point of view [American politics is] all foreign policy." Destabilizing a paradigm that subsumes Native nations under a US territorial and political ordering, the specificity of Laguna Pueblo as a spatial, epistemological, and cosmological location is the foundation of *Ceremony*'s methodological structure. Throughout the novel, Tayo travels across a global world while remaining rooted to Laguna Pueblo place and knowledge, revealing an approach to Native nationalisms that refuses an easy acquiescence to US nationalism. And the covalent crises of drought, environmental degradation, resource extraction, and imperialism, as well as the communal and personal legacies of global war, exhibit an approach that refuses the easy extraction of contemporaneous global histories.

In each of these cases, Tayo's operation as a character whose simultaneous rooting in Laguna Pueblo and his disidentification with the US state is figured through his exemplification of how indigeneity functions as what Byrd has called the "transit of empire." As a Native soldier who voluntarily enlisted in the US military and was deployed to a territory that had been under US occupation only a few decades earlier, Tayo is both the literal and figurative transit through which US empire is expressed. And though the novel takes place during World War II, its publication in the post-Vietnam era connects Tayo's experience to the experiences of Native veterans leading up to and throughout the Vietnam era.

For instance, Ojibwe activist Dennis Banks's description of his experience serving in the Air Force while stationed in Japan echoes Tayo's experience in *Ceremony*. In his memoir *Ojibwe Warrior*, Banks describes his experience during a 1956 protest at the Tachikawa Air Base in Sunagawa, Japan, during which members of his unit where instructed to "shoot to kill" protestors confronting the expansion of the US base. After the incident, Banks observed:

> I felt sick at what I had seen and ashamed of the uniform I was wearing. I remembered Sergeant Johnson firing and yelling for the beating to stop . . . That terrible scene has remained with me all of these years. I shall never forget those demonstrators

> were peaceful people literally being beaten to death. Since that time, during my struggles in the American Indian Movement, I have seen BIA [Bureau of Indian Affairs] police wield their clubs at Indians like that. Each time my memory flashed back to what I saw that day in Japan.[82]

Banks describes this time as his "hour of awakening," when he realized that he "had been guarding the ramparts of the American Empire." In his reflection, he draws connections between settlement and US empire across the Pacific, noting that "I felt like those Crow and Arikara Indians who, after scouting for Custer and fighting on behalf of the whites, were pitted against their own brothers, the Cheyenne and Lakota."[83]

When triangulated through Banks's reflections, Silko's rendering of Tayo's experience as a transnational subject resonates across Native experience throughout settlement and into the present, confirming a transindigenous approach that is grounded especially in the encroachment of US empire in the Pacific throughout the twentieth century. As Banks observed of the protestors at Sunagawa, "these were Native people, fighting for their land."[84] Reframing *Ceremony* through this transpacific and transindigenous lens offers a transnational methodology that does not either reify or ignore the structure of US settler sovereignty and US empire. Instead, this reading of *Ceremony* responds to Warrior's argument that transnational approaches should be taken up not because they are *de rigueur* but must instead be grounded in the goal of "seeking surer ways of addressing the intellectual needs of the Indigenous world."[85] For Warrior, this is intimately connected to Native literary production, since these literatures evidence that "Native nations and Indigenous peoples have persisted . . . by being ungovernable." For him, Native literatures "give voice" to this ungovernability by "unsettling a history that in the minds of many is already complete."[86] It is precisely the assumed completeness of the history (and thus political and spatial ordering) of the United States that limits the ability of anarchist approaches to transnationalism to effectively confront the persistence of the structure of settlement with anarchist spaces and to account for the operation of US empire in their global inquiries. Warrior's invocation of "ungovernability," though, speaks to the possibilities that remain for connections between Native literatures and anarchist movements. And it is to these possibilities that I turn now.

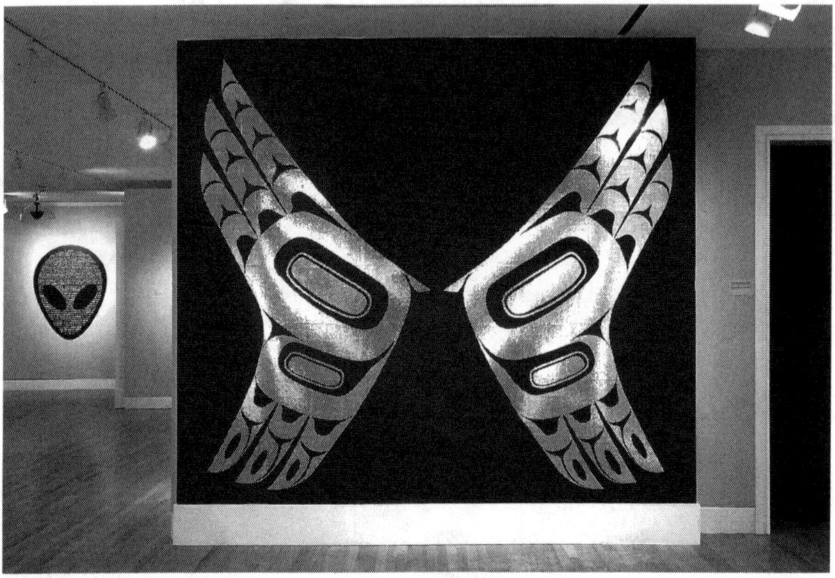

Fig. 4. Installation of Alison Marks's (Tlingit) *One Gray Hair,* Frye Art Museum, Seattle, WA, November 11, 2017, to February 14, 2018. Photograph by Mark Woods.

CONCLUSION

Other Worlds Here

Many words walk in the world. Many worlds are made. Many worlds are made for us. There are words and worlds which are lies and injustices. There are words and worlds which are truths and truthful . . . In the world we want many worlds fit. The Nation which we construct is one where all communities and languages fit, where all steps may walk, where all may have laughter, where all may live the dawn.

—EZLN, Fourth Declaration of the Lacandon Jungle (January 1, 1996)

Space Bear on Heaven and Earth

As part of her 2017 exhibition *One Gray Hair*, Tlingit artist Alison Bremner installed two interacting visuals, *Space Bear* and *Heaven and Earth*. The former took up an entire wall, which was painted black and overlaid with an incandescent silver formline representation of a Tlingit bear mask. While you stand and look at *Space Bear*, you can see to the left another wall installation looming in the background. This is the face of an alien that, even from that distance, seems haunting yet familiar. Rendered in a simplistic black oval shape, the creature's eyes emerge from a sea of white words that are written in a small font. As you get closer, you see that these are Tlingit words coupled with their English translations. The first word at the top of the alien's head is "abandon": the last is "accuse." In the author's commentary provided alongside *Heaven and Earth*, Bremner notes that the Tlingit language is critically endangered, with only between "seventy and one hundred fluent speakers left." Along with Tlingit language specialist Paul Marks, Bremner took entries from the Tlingit language dictionary and used a free star-naming site to name stars using Tlingit words. She notes that, "symbolically, I am sending the language into space so it may survive there if we don't save it on earth."[1] It seems that she is doing so literally, too.

And just as *Heaven and Earth* interacts spatially in the exhibit with *Space Bear*, so, too, do the stars named with Tlingit words interact with the object on which the latter is based. Alongside the installation is a brief lesson in a moment that brings together Tlingit, Russian, and American histories, long intertwined in the colonization of Tlingit territory in what is currently Southeast Alaska: "In October 2000, American astronaut William Shepherd flew a Tlingit bear mask into space aboard the Russian Soyuz spacecraft, headed to the International Space Station. The mask orbited Earth for four months before being returned to Alaska."[2] What happens to a traditional Tlingit mask that is taken and brought into space by an American astronaut in a Russian spacecraft, agents of the two colonial powers that traded Tlingit territory among themselves as if it were theirs to give? What does it look like when it comes back, when it comes home? How does Tlingit language sound different if the material world to which it is connected is not only the memory of Tlingit territory, but the literal material of all universal being? What is it able to name, and who is able to recognize it and as what?

In *Heaven and Earth*, Alison Bremner insists on the persistence of the Tlingit language, suturing its futurity to the naming of stars in the present moment so that, like those stars, the language will continue despite what might otherwise be lost. Though, of course, some of those stars could be dead already. *Space Bear* takes the Tlingit mask out of the hands of Russian and American governments and, instead, makes it phosphorescent, glimmering in multiple colors against the stark black backdrop. A larger than life mask carved not out of wood, but out of space itself. Here, Bremner crafts a Tlingit future as a series of both existing and possible worlds that live with the land even when it is jettisoned into a "new frontier," as the US government named their early twenty-first-century explorations into the far reaches of the solar system.[3] Fusing traditional aesthetics (like formline) with "nontraditional material, tools, and technique," Bremner explores the coexistence of many worlds without disregarding the palimpsestic structures of power that determine how such worlds are related.[4] As the Zuni/Tlingit curator Miranda Belarde-Lewis at the Frye observes, Bremner's "art is a testament to the extraordinary possibilities of today, when we have the confidence and the power to reclaim our Native languages and icons. She draws the past into the present, charting possibilities for the future."[5]

Throughout *Other Worlds Here*, I have insisted on the importance of bringing together calls and desires for other possible worlds with the recognition that there are many other worlds that live here already and, what is more, have done so since time immemorial. Such a recognition is often read through White Earth Chippewa author Gerald Vizenor's famous portmanteau "survivance," which remains famously imprecise, with scholars arguing that it is a combination of the word survival with a host of others, including endurance, presence, and resistance.[6] In his book *Manifest Matters: Narratives on Postindian Survivance* (which was published the same year as the mass protests against the WTO with which I began), Vizenor narrates survivance as a practice of what he calls "postindian simulations," which, he argues, can "counter the manifest manners of domination."[7] For him, the use of the term *simulation* does not signal a reference point devoid of meaning or that no longer exists but, rather, as a set of narrative practices that "arise from the silence of heard stories." In this, Native storytellers "create a new tribal presence in stories."[8] In using the term *other worlds here* to describe what Bremner does, along with the other Native women artists with whom I've engaged in the previous chapters, I aim to draw attention to the connection between Vizenor's vision of such simulations and how the ways that they are tied to land require our reckoning with their existence in the work we do in this place.

Though Bremner's *Space Bear* can be read as a simulation of the bear mask that went to space on a collaborative mission of two imperial powers to practice empire in a new frontier, the luminous and imposing installation through which she brings it into being is explicitly rooted in the same artistic and narrative practices that are the formal basis of Tlingit cosmology. In this way, *Space Bear* highlights the empty simulation of empire on the part of Russian and American aeronautics programs contra the grounded simulation of her reproduction of the Tlingit bear mask. Similarly, in *Heaven and Earth* Bremner uses a widespread facsimile of an "alien" face mapped with Tlingit words and their English translations to call into question how Native languages and peoples are read as "foreign" within settler empires. Engaging the image of the "extraterrestrial," Bremner's *Heaven and Earth* explores what happens when Native languages are disconnected from land while simultaneously refusing the removal of language from place by formally suturing Tlingit words to interstellar bodies.

In each of these cases, the practice of recognizing "other worlds here" is not a provincial one nor one rooted in a parochial navel gazing.

Instead, Tlingit language, cosmology, and artistic practice is articulated as relevant not only to this world but also to the myriad worlds that exist beyond—and to worlds not yet imagined or known. Bremner's work beautifully exemplifies the foundational argument in *Other Worlds Here* that, if New Anarchism is to engage in resistance movements on a global scale, we must do so by practicing a methodological and pedagogical imperative that centers a responsibility to place. This is essential to the very politics that New Anarchism espouses, since any attempt to confront the US state without addressing settlement is not to confront the US state at all. In fact, to do so reinforces some of the very foundational claims to sovereignty on which the US state depends.

Where We All May Live the Dawn

In these final moments, I want to return to the phrase "another world is possible," to which my own history of engagement with anarchist politics and the impetus of the concept of other worlds here is deeply connected. This phrase is ubiquitous in anarchist organizing around the world: it is the title of a 2002 film by Mark Dworkin and Melissa Young about that year's meeting of the World Social Forum, which adopted the phrase as its slogan the next year; the title of David McNally's 2006 book on globalization and anticapitalism; the name of an organizing coalition that arose from the Direct Action Network (DAN), which was instrumental to the 1999 protests; and is invoked innumerable times in articles about social movements in the late twentieth and early twenty-first centuries.[9] And, often, this phrase is connected to the uprising of the Zapatistas in 1994, a moment to which many contemporary anarchists point in their establishment of a genealogy of New Anarchism, as I noted in chapter 5.[10]

However, even in the connection of this phrase to the Indigenous uprising of the Zapatistas and in its ubiquitous adoption as a symbol of New Anarchist politics, we can see the elision of questions of settlement that necessitates a shift to the paradigm of other worlds here that I've suggested throughout. This phrase appears in the Sixth Declaration of the Lacandon Jungle, issued by the EZLN (Ejército Zapatista de Liberación Nacional, or Zapatista Army of National Liberation) in June 2005. The passage reads:

> If you look at one of those studies the governments make, you will see that the only indigenous communities which have

> improved their living conditions—whether in health, education, food, or housing—were those which are in Zapatistas territory, which is what we call where our villages are. And all of that has been possible because of the progress made by the Zapatista villages and because of the very large support which has been received from good and noble persons, whom we call "civil societies," and from their organizations throughout the world. As if all of these people have made 'another world is possible' a reality, but through actions, not just words.[11]

Here, the EZLN makes a direct connection to global radical politics not through calls to global solidarity but through a rooting in a place-based focus on local Indigenous communities. This is the first place, however, that this phrase appears in the official communications of the EZLN, twelve years after the First Declaration was issued. The association of the phrase "another world is possible" with the Zapatistas seems to come, in some ways, from a conflation of this phrase with another that appeared in the Fourth Declaration in 1996 that appears in the epigraph above.

In this declaration, released two years after the First Declaration and nine years before the Sixth Declaration in which the phrase "another world is possible" appears, the EZLN use the description "a world where many worlds fit" to describe their radical political vision. Though this shares numerous qualities with the more pervasive "another world is possible," this phrase and the larger quote from which it is extracted above illuminates a functionally and formally different approach to the question of (an)other world(s). It signals the need to imagine not a singular new future world, but to create the conditions for many worlds, both nascent and existing, to flourish; it emphasizes the relationship between words and worlds; it centers the role of the nation as a foundation of Indigenous worlds; and it hails us as people who "all may live the dawn" within the framework of the expressly Indigenous foundations of the EZLN's uprising.

The difference between these two phrases, "another world is possible" and "a world where many worlds fit" may seem inconsequential, but the effect of these words in shaping the radical political visions of New Anarchism is significant. When, as radical activists and scholars, we invite ourselves and others to imagine "another world is possible," one without the state, without capitalism, without settlement, without prisons, without police, this encourages us to stop normalizing these structures and their seeming perpetuity on the physical and social landscapes of our world. But we must also recognize that, in other ways, such imagining may not be the most difficult or imperative part of the process. What is more, framing our radical praxis this way can support the structure of settlement by obscuring the myriad worlds that have lived with the land and its people since time immemorial. Because, in fact, there have been and continue to be worlds that are without the state, without capitalism, without settlement, without prisons, without police. These worlds don't exist in a pure past to which we must return, but rather continue to exist within the words, the land, and the people that are constituted through and of these worlds.

Those worlds, the "other" ones that we are searching for, are here. And if we look at this place—at North America, at Turtle Island—and can only ask the question, "Can we *imagine* what this place might look like without those things?," then we are doing precisely that which Silko warns against in the epigraph to *Other Worlds Here*. If we look at the land and its people and think "there are no politics here," that those politics must be created to imagine a world without the structures that we work to oppose—then we are wrong. Again, recognizing "other worlds here" is not about trying to go back to a time before these things. Rather, it is about understanding that the practices these worlds require, the practices for the kinds of relationships we need to have to ensure their existence—those practices that anarchists are searching for through our praxis, already live here. Yes, another world is possible. One of the reasons we can even know this, though, even entertain this thought, is because there are other worlds *here*—if only we would honor them.

ACKNOWLEDGMENTS

I am grateful for the initial support of Gianna Francesca Mosser, who believed in this project from its very beginning. Thank you also to the *Critical Insurgencies* series editors, Jodi Byrd and Michelle Wright, for their vision. Numerous people at Northwestern University Press put time into supporting this project, including Trevor Perri, Maia Rigas, and Patrick Samuel. This book was greatly improved by the thoughtful comments from my anonymous reviewers and I am grateful for their careful attention. The research that went into this project was generously supported by the Walter McClintock Visiting Postdoctoral Fellowship from the Beinecke Rare Book and Manuscript Library at Yale University, the Mellon Postdoctoral Fellowship in Native Literature and Culture at Brown University, and a Manuscript Completion Grant from the Office of Research and Sponsored Programs at Western Washington University. An early grant from the Institute for Anarchist Studies gave me the resources to write an earlier version of chapter 3, which appeared in *Perspectives on Anarchist Theory*'s issue on Anarcha-Feminisms.

When I was young, my parents moved us from Colorado to Massachusetts so that my brother and I could be closer to family. I am grateful now for the complex web they brought us into, one that continues to teach me about the expansive arc of time. Being in that place brought me into closer relation with a wide network of extended family and friends while also teaching me how to say the first Indigenous word I probably ever learned—Massachusetts, a Wampanoag word. These two outcomes seem related to me now and I find this to be such a curious thing.

This owes much to the fact that my parents, Kathy and Bob Warburton, created a home where curiosity was valued and have always supported me in ways that enabled the possibility of pursuing it. My brother, Bob(by) Warburton, has been a lifelong partner in that pursuit and his presence has continuously given me permission to not take that pursuit too seriously. Rami, Hank, and Frances Warburton have continued in this tradition, adding softness to my life when I need it most.

In Hartford I was blessed to meet Jennifer Perrone who is my oldest friend. It is with sheer joy that I feel more related to her (and now, to Martin Layne and Rorie Layne-Perrone) every year that's passed since our meeting. Around that time, I also benefitted immensely from knowing Jen Michael-Stevens, Stephen Goldberg, Megh Bryan, Katrina Loyer, and Elizabeth Perrella. Nick Bazin was an unforgettable roommate and friend, whose periodic drop-ins in my life continue to be a delight whose recurrence I will always await. Josh Cerretti was also there, but I'll circle back to him later.

In Chicago, Em Lawler made moving to a new place easier during a difficult transition time in my life. I was fortunate during this time to be supported in my growing intellectual interests by Nicole Guidotti-Hernández and Jessica Cattelino, whose generosity gave me the confidence to embrace humility as the pathway to being a better scholar.

In Buffalo I met the people who taught me that good relationships, ethical commitments, and intellectual pursuits must be one and the same if they are to mean something to the world. At the University at Buffalo, Deborah Pierce-Tate's support made my life possible and I was always grateful to catch up with her. I had the immense honor of being guided early on by Theresa Runstedtler, who taught me how to be generous in my thinking, and Alexis De Veaux, who taught me how to love literature again. I was fortunate to learn alongside a great cohort of people, including Kyem Asa, Kritika Agarwal, Justin De Senso, Steve Demchak, Dan Elkan, Adrianna Hernandez, Jessi Lee Jackson, Chelsea Jones, Paul McCutcheon, Laticia McNaughton, Shannon O'Sullivan, Aleksandra Szaniawska, and Lou Williams. I am still appreciative of Drew Friedfertig's willingness to discuss both postanarchism and strange vegan recipes with me. And though there is a lot of physical distance between us now, my love for Fernanda Glaser and Harold Dumke has never waned. And though there has always been a lot of physical distance between us, I was also lucky during this time to forge friendships with T. J. Tallie, Katie Walkiewicz, and Chris Dixon.

This book is, in part, an attempt to honor the immense gift of being introduced to a community of Haudenosaunee intellectuals at UB, especially Jodi Maracle and Theresa McCarthy. There is still no medicine as good as Jodi's laugh. And there are no words to express my gratitude to Theresa, a person for whom the words advisor, mentor, or colleague will never suffice. I am grateful to have had the opportunity to work from the beginning with someone who showed me so clearly that one can and must be committed to an ethical center to do good work.

There are many people and places that helped me develop and keep an ethical center during my time in Buffalo, but most especially the folks who were part of the Buffalo Prison Abolition Reading Group, Defend Our Education Coalition, GSEU-CWA Local 1104, and UB CLEAR. Out of this constellation of things came the Buffalo Portal that keeps me connected to Adam Drury, Robin Jordan, and Cayden Mak, all of whom I love deeply. When Leslie Pickering, Theresa Baker, and Nate Buckley opened Burning Books in the sweltering summer of 2011, I learned what a real radical community space looked like and it still feels like home whenever I get the chance to return.

My friendship with Erin Sharkey emerged at a confluence of all these things. More than anyone else, she has taught me what it means to be a good friend and has modeled the kind of care that I want to be able to give in the world. Knowing her has also brought Zoe Hollomon and Junauda Petrus into my life, two people who fill my heart with sweetness whenever I see them which is never often enough.

Leaving Buffalo was incredibly difficult, but I was lucky enough to land in a place where I could forge new relationships with friends and comrades alike. At Western Washington University, Jane Wong, Katie Vulić, Travis Tennessen, Lysa Rivera, Ely Shipley, Trula Nicholas, Brenda Miller, Ricardo López-Pedreros, Tiana Kahakauwila, Vicki Hsueh, Stefania Heim, Nini Hayes, Angi Fillingam, Dolores Calderón, Rich Brown, and Natalie Baloy have all been wonderful colleagues who I am thankful to work alongside. Erica Dean-Crawford, Jemma Everyhope-Roser, Linda Flanagan, Tina Nelson, Pam Race, and Michelle Stach helped me adapt by answering every single question I could have possibly had. Solidarity forever with the UFWW, one of the very best parts of working at Western. And though they are no longer at WWU, Kristin Mahoney, Kaveh Askari, and AB Brown remain fantastic friends who I miss every day. All have supported me beyond even my own comprehension, especially Kristin who read the proposal for this book and helped me imagine what it could be.

In Bellingham, I've been grateful to learn from the important work of Michelle and Michael Vendiola, Junga Subedar, Edward Alexander, Tina McKim, Liisa Wale, Neah Monteiro, Maru Mora Villalpando, Chelsea Thaw, and Silky Shah. It is an honor to work with them to build a better community here. Kendall Dodd seems to always know what I need hear, which she often shares along with some form of carbohydrate. I could never say enough about Zoe Redwoman's friendship, which brings me such solace and calm. Living in the PNW has also enabled me to develop closer friendships with Laura De Vos and Paul, Lara, and Silas Messersmith-Glavin and I look forward to seeing these flourish. It also brought me to Elissa Washuta, my cosmic relative and often-twin, whose friendship means many worlds to me.

For a few years there, my life spanned the continent and I'm grateful for the community I was able to build during my time back on the East Coast. Carrie Cardoso was my first friend at Brown University and some days, I would come to campus just to spend a half hour laughing in her office. Matt Guterl, Adrienne Keene, Liz Hoover, Niyo Moraza-Keeswood, Ruth Miller, and Elena Shih also made me smile during times that might have otherwise felt too difficult. Under the guidance of Amanda Anderson and Damien Mahiet along with the constant support of Melissa Shein and Traude Kastner, I was thrilled to build lasting connections through the Cogut Seminar. What you hold in your hands is indebted to the guidance I received there, most notably from a wonderful cohort of peers including Ketaki Pant, Lakshmi Padmanabhan, Tuti Baker, Anna Thomas, Nic Ramos, and Iris Monteiro Sobrevilla. Nishant Upadhyay indulged my proclivity for strange New England tourism and also offered pivotal feedback on the introduction. I am also grateful for the time that I got to spend in the Northeast with J. Kēhaulani Kauanui, who has not only continued to support my intellectual work but who also took care of me when I showed up at her house with a broken foot. I will always be thankful for her generosity and kindness.

Being back in New England after having been gone for so many years also reinforced for me the deep connections I have there that have sustained me as a whole person, beyond any academic project. I have immense love for all of the Cerrettis, especially the Cerretti cousins including Aaron, Jamie, Jared, Joey, Kayla, and Lauren. Diane and Jimmy Cerretti have always made me feel welcome and loved. I am grateful to all of them, but especially to Jamie, for teaching me the meaning of chosen family. I am also thankful to Tate Williams, someone with whom to share the experience of being brought into this infamous group of magnificent people.

There's this lyric from an obscure Gainesville hardcore band called Army of Ponch that has rattled around my brain the entire time I've been working on this book: "If this holds the weight of one of us, it can take the weight of all of us." It used to unnerve me because it seemed patently untrue—surely, just because something can hold one of us doesn't mean it could hold us all. But when I think about how much I learned about caring for each other from Vern Avola, Adam and Risa

Caires, Rachel Chandler, Jarrod and Danielle Delong, Adam Garcia, Andre Hester, Matt McCarthy, Matty McGuire, Katie Sapp, Rick Stec, and Mike Tucker, I understand that it is a barometer for measuring what we take on together. If something is only good for one of us, it isn't good at all. What's right is what's good for all of us.

And then there's Josh Cerretti. In those moments that I doubted that this book would ever come into the world, he reminded me that no one else has my mind and he made me feel that that was a blessing. On my best days, I believe that and, on my worst, I still believe that he believes that. What an immense gift he is to this world.

NOTES

Introduction

1. Melanie Patten, "Elsipogtog First Nation Sees Violence as RCMP Moves To End Protest," *Huffington Post*, October 17, 2013.

2. Out of the Woods Collective, "Goodbye to the Future," Libcom.org, February 24, 2014, https://libcom.org/blog/goodbye-future-24022014.

3. McCarthy writes about similar events at Grand River a few decades earlier: "At three a.m. on March 13 [1959], over five hundred RCMP personnel used billy clubs to beat [protesters] out of the building and several protesters were arrested. In 1970, instead of occupying the building outright, the second Council House reclamation transpired as a lockout, which prohibited the elected band council from accessing the building. During June and July, participants guarded the Council House grounds for almost a month, until they were eventually dispersed by police intimidation, arrests, and court injunctions." Theresa McCarthy, *In Divided Unity: Haudenosaunee Reclamation at Grand River* (Tucson: University of Arizona Press, 2016), 164.

4. Leanne Betasamosake Simpson, "Elsipogtog Everywhere," October 20, 2013, https://www.leannesimpson.ca/writings/2013/10/20/elsipogtog-everywhere.

5. "I find it immensely important to put an analysis of affect and emotion, a felt theory, back into our quest to understand both classic colonialism and our present in neoliberal governance, because affect is now so profoundly implicated in these neoliberal relations." Dian Million, *Therapeutic Nations: Healing in the Age of Indigenous Human Rights* (Tucson: University of Arizona Press, 2013), 30.

6. See David Graeber, "The New Anarchists," *New Left Review* 13 (Jan.–Feb. 2002): 61–73; Staughton Lynd and Andrej Grubačić, *Wobblies and Zapatistas: Conversations on Anarchism, Marxism, and Radical History* (Oakland, CA: PM Press, 2008); Andrej Grubačić and David Graeber, "Anarchism, or the Revolutionary Movement of the Twenty-First Century," *Z-Net*, January 6, 2004, https://theanarchistlibrary.org/library/andrej-grubacic-david-graeber-anarchism-or-the-revolutionary-movement-of-the-twenty-first-century.

7. Thanks especially to Jodi Maracle, who served as a language consultant for the writing and use of Kanien'keha words throughout. On using "Kanehsatà:ke" rather than "Oka": "Although the 'Oka Crisis' is known to most Canadians as the 'Oka Crisis,' the term is offensive to many involved in the struggle because it refers to the non-Native town, and because the term was manufactured by the mainstream media." Kiera L. Ladner and Leanne Simpson, eds., *This Is an Honour Song: Twenty Years Since the Blockades* (Winnipeg: Arbiter Ring Publishing, 2010), 8–9.

8. See *Kanehsatake: 270 Years of Resistance*, directed by Alanis Obomsawin (1993; National Film Board of Canada: Montreal), streaming at http://workforall.nfb.ca/film/kanehsatake_270_years_of_resistance/.

9. Audra Simpson, *Mohawk Interruptus: Political Life Across the Borders of Settler States* (Durham, NC: Duke University Press, 2014), 148. On the spectacularizing of the images from the confrontation, Ladner and Simpson argue: "While all of these nations threw stones in the water that generated ripple effect, Kanasatà:ke was different. Not because of the ripple, but because we saw those powerful images every night on the news for months . . . the mobilization of Kanien'kehaka that summer was such a powerful image and such a defining moment for so many of us (Indigenous and Canadian alike)." See Ladner and Simpson, *This Is an Honour Song*, 3.

10. Canadian Broadcasting Company News, "Elsipogtog Chief Appoints 'Peacekeeper' in Shale Gas Dispute," *CBC News*, June 27, 2013, http://www.cbc.ca/news/canada/new-brunswick/elsipogtog-chief-appoints-peacekeeper-in-shale-gas-dispute-1.1365143.

11. This linking of Croatan and the Lost Colony at Roanoke as a progenitor of contemporary anarchist movements is replicated in the literature on contemporary anarchism. For instance, see James Koehnline, ed., *Gone to Croatan: Origins of North American Dropout Culture* (New York: Autonomedia, 1994).

12. Croatan, "Who Is Oakland?: Anti-Oppression Activism, the Politics of Safety, and State Co-Optation," *Anarchist Library*, 2012, https://escalatingidentity.wordpress.com/2012/04/30/who-is-oakland-anti-oppression-politics-decolonization-and-the-state/.

13. Corey Allen, "Canada's Image of Oka, 24 Years Later," *UBC News*, September 22, 2014, http://news.ubc.ca/2014/09/22/oka/.

14. Croatan, "Who Is Oakland," 32.

15. Croatan, "Who Is Oakland," 33.

16. This work is inspired by that of Roderick Ferguson and Scott Morgensen, both of whom explore how radical social movements end up

replicating the structures they seek to oppose. Just as Morgensen has explored how "Non-Native queer modernities naturalize settler colonialism," so too am I interested in elucidating how non-Native anarchist modernity naturalizes the same (Scott Morgensen, *Spaces between Us: Queer Settler Colonialism and Indigenous Decolonization* [Minneapolis: University of Minnesota Press, 2011], 2). As Ferguson has noted, considering the possibilities and limits of radical political intervention requires "investigating how intersecting racial, gender, and sexual practices antagonize and/or conspire with the normative investments of nation-states and capital" (Roderick Ferguson, *Aberrations in Black: Towards a Queer of Color Critique* [Minneapolis: University of Minnesota Press, 2003], 4).

17. Mishuana Goeman, *Mark My Words: Native Women Mapping Our Nations* (Minneapolis: University of Minnesota Press, 2013), 213.

18. I am especially thankful to Nishant Upadhyay for urging me to clarify this point. For more on the distinction of "settler" as a term that is linked directly to whiteness and white people, see Jodi Byrd's use of Kamau Brathwaite's term *arrivant* to refer to "people forced into the Americas through the violence of European an Anglo-American colonialism and imperialism around the globe" in *The Transit of Empire* (Minneapolis: University of Minnesota Press, 2011), xix; Eve Tuck and K. Wayne Yang's analysis of the "triangular" structure of settler organization in "Decolonization Is Not a Metaphor," in *Decolonization: Indigeneity, Education, and Society* 1, no. 1 (2012): 1–40 ; the discussion of Blackness and the term *settler* in the Canadian context among Bob Joseph, Chelsea Vowell, and Ashley Marshall in "Who Is a Settler, According to Indigenous and Black Scholars: Descendants of Slaves Don't Fit into Our Common Definition of Settlers," *VICE Canada*, February 15, 2019, https://www.vice.com/en_us/article/gyajj4/who-is-a-settler-according-to-indigenous-and-black-scholars; Manu Karuka's scrutiny of the relationship between Indigenous nations and Chinese workers during the building of the transcontinental railroad in *Empire's Tracks: Indigenous Nations, Chinese Workers, and the Transcontinental Railroad* (Oakland: University of California Press, 2019); Iyko Day's examination of Asian racialization and settler colonial capitalism in Canada and the United States in *Alien Capital: Asian Racialization and the Logic of Settler Colonial Capitalism* (Durham, NC: Duke University Press, 2016); Harsha Walia's work on the relationship between refugee and immigrant support work in Canada in *Undoing Border Imperialism* (Oakland, CA: AK Press, 2013); and Maylei Blackwell, Floridalma Boj Lopez, and Luis Urrieta Jr., eds., "Critical Latinx Indigeneities," special issue, *Latino Studies* 15, no. 2 (July 2017).

19. This echoes Patrick Wolfe's famed assertion that settler colonialism is "a structure not an event." Patrick Wolfe, "Settler Colonialism and the Elimination of the Native," *Journal of Genocide Research* 8, no. 4 (Dec ember 2006): 387–409.

20. See chap. 6 titled "The Gender of the Flint: Mohawk Nationhood and Citizenship in the Face of Empire," in Simpson, *Mohawk Interruptus*,147–77; McCarthy's discussion of women's roles during reclamations at Caledonia in McCarthy, *In Divided Unity*; and Martha Troian, "Mi'kmaq Anti-Fracking Protest Brings Women to the Front Lines to Fight for Water," *Indian Country Today*, November 10, 2013, https://indiancountrymedianetwork.com/news/first-nations/mikmaq-anti-fracking-protest-brings-women-to-the-front-lines-to-fight-for-water/.

21. Richard J. F. Day, *Gramsci Is Dead: Anarchist Currents in the Newest Social Movements* (London: Pluto Press, 2005).

22. Day, *Gramsci Is Dead*, 9.

23. See Andrew Cornell, *Unruly Equality: U.S. Anarchism in the Twentieth Century* (Oakland: University of California Press, 2016).

24. Chris Dixon, *Another Politics: Talking Across Today's Transformative Movements* (Oakland: University of California Press, 2014), 3–4.

25. Todd May, *The Political Philosophy of Poststructuralist Anarchism* (University Park: Penn State University Press), 2.

26. Day, *Gramsci Is Dead*, 67.

27. For a more comprehensive discussion of this history, see David Graeber, *Direct Action: An Ethnography* (Oakland, CA: AK Press, 2009).

28. For instance, see Susan Faludi, *Backlash: The Undeclared War Against American Women* (New York: Broadway Books, 1991).

29. Jodi A. Byrd, *The Transit of Empire: Indigenous Critiques of Colonialism* (Minneapolis: University of Minnesota Press, 2011), xiv.

30. Byrd, *Transit of Empire*.

31. David Graeber, *Possibilities: Essays on Hierarchy, Rebellion, and Desire* (Oakland, CA: AK Press, 2007), 304.

32. Dixon, *Another Politics*, 4.

33. Montgomery and bergman describe "rigid radicalism" as "the pleasure of feeling more radical than others and the worry about not being radical enough; the sad comfort of sorting unfolding events into dead categories; the vigilant apprehension of errors and complicities in oneself and others; the anxious posturing on social media with the highs of being liked and the lows of being ignored; the suspicion and resentment felt in the presence of something new; the way curiosity feels naïve and condescension feels right." Montgomery and carla bergman, *Joyful Militancy: Building*

Thriving Resistance in Toxic Times (Oakland, CA: AK Press, 2017): Kindle edition, loc. 56 of 3833.

34. Day observes this tendency in, for instance, in the mainstream attempts "to belittle the well-known Canadian activist Jaggi Singh [after protests against the Organization of American States in 2000] by noting that, before he sits down to talk with reporters, he orders a coffee from a Canadian doughnut-shop chain." Day, *Gramsci Is Dead*, 1.

35. Alexis Shotwell, *Against Purity: Living Ethically in Compromised Times* (Minneapolis: University of Minnesota Press, 2016), 4.

36. Cindy Milstein, *Anarchism and Its Aspirations* (Oakland, CA: AK Press, 2010), 68.

37. See Lisa Brooks, *The Common Pot* (Minneapolis: University of Minnesota Press, 2008).

38. Milstein, *Anarchism and Its Aspirations*, 68.

39. Alix Olson, "The Promise(s) of Resilience: Governance and Resistance in Complex Times," PhD diss., University of Massachusetts, Amherst, 2018.

40. See Derrick Jensen, *Listening to the Land: Conversations about Nature, Culture, and Eros* (White River Junction, VT: Chelsea Green Publishing, 2002); and Aric McBay, Lierre Keith, and Derrick Jensen, *Deep Green Resistance: Strategy to Save the Planet* (New York: Seven Stories Press, 2011).

41. For more on Aric McBay's decision to leave DGR, see his "DGR and Transphobia," *Aric McBay* (blog), May 14, 2013, http://www.aricmcbay.org/2013/05/14/dgr-and-transphobia/.

42. In a 2014 talk, Ivey says, "This isn't only my opinion; this represents DGR's policy and it has happened that people have joined DGR with the intention of specifically shifting our view of gender. And it failed miserably. It will again if it's tried again because that is the core of DGR." See "End of Gender, Revolution, Not Reform," *Medium* (blog), posted on September 16, 2015, https://medium.com/@deepgreenresist/end-of-gender-revolution-not-reform-cf5f23fd29c7.

43. Keith wrote this analysis in an email response to activists inquiring about her gender politics. For an account of that exchange, see Be Scofield, "How Derrick Jensen's Deep Green Resistance Supports Transphobia," *Decolonizing Yoga*, May 14, 2013, http://www.decolonizingyoga.com/how-derrick-jensens-deep-green-resistance-supports-transphobia/.

44. Taiaike Alfred, *Wasasé: Indigenous Pathways of Action and Freedom* (Peterborough, ON: Broadview Press, 2005), 45.

45. Alfred, *Wasasé*, 46.

46. Alfred, *Wasasé*, 47.

47. Joshua B. Nelson, *Progressive Traditions: Identity in Cherokee Literature and Culture* (Norman: University of Oklahoma Press, 2014), 37.

48. Glen Coulthard, Jacqueline Lasky, Adam Lewis, and Vanessa Watts, eds., "Working across Difference for Post-Imperial Futures: Intersections between Anarchism, Indigenism, and Feminism," special issue, *Affinities: Theory, Culture, Action*, August 31, 2011, https://ojs.library.queensu.ca/index.php/affinities/issue/view/572/.

49. Richard Day, "Who Is This We That Gives the Gift? Native American Political Theory and *The Western Tradition*," *Critical Horizons: A Journal of Philosophy and Social Theory* 2, no. 2 (2001): 173–201. See also Day, *Gramsci Is Dead*.

50. Stephen Arthur, "Where License Reigns with All Impunity: An Anarchist Study of the Iroquois Polity," *Northeastern Anarchist* 12 (Winter 2007).

51. Adam J. Barker, "Already Occupied: Indigenous Peoples, Settler Colonialism, and the Occupy Movements in North America," *Social Movement Studies* 11, no. 3–4 (August 9, 2012): 327–34; "The Contemporary Reality of Canadian Imperialism: Settler Colonialism and the Hybrid Colonial State," *American Indian Quarterly* 33, no. 3 (Summer 2009): 325–51; and "From Adversaries to Allies: Forging respectful alliances between Indigenous and Settler Peoples," in *Alliances: Re/Envisioning Indigenous Non-Indigenous Relationships*, ed. Lynne Davis (Toronto: University of Toronto Press, 2010), 316–33. See also Adam J. Barker and Jenny Pickerill, "Radicalizing Relationships To and Through Shared Geographies: Why Anarchists Need to Understand Indigenous Connections to Land, Sea, and Place," *Antipode* 44, no. 5 (August 17, 2012): 1705–25; and Adam J. Barker and Emma Battell Lowman, *Settler: Identity and Colonialism in 21st Century Canada* (Halifax: Fernwood Press, 2015).

52. Craig Fortier, *Unsettling the Commons: Social Movements Within, Against, and Beyond Settler Colonialism* (Winnipeg: Arbiter Ring Publishing, 2017); Adam Lewis, "Imagining Autonomy on Stolen Land: Settler Colonialism, Anarchism, and the Politics of Decolonization?" *Settler Colonial Studies* 7 (2017): 474–95.

53. Nick Montgomery and carla bergman, *Joyful Militancy: Building Thriving Resistance in Toxic Times* (Oakland, CA: AK Press, 2017), 73.

54. Maia Ramnath, *Decolonizing Anarchism: An Anti-Authoritarian History of India's Liberation Struggle* (Oakland, CA: AK Press, 2011). Here, I am most interested in Ramnath's emphasis on the double meaning of the term "decolonizing anarchism," though I recognize that there

are important critiques of the way she positions decolonization in India throughout. For more, see Dhruv Jain, "Maia Ramnath and the Search for a Decolonised Antiauthoritarian Marxism: A Review of *Haj to Utopia* and *Decolonizing Anarchism* by Maia Ramnath," *Historical Materialism* 25.2 (2017): 196–213.

55. For instance, see prolific anarchist writer Wayne Price, "Anarchist Organisation not Leninist Vanguardism," 2006, https://theanarchistlibrary.org/library/wayne-price-anarchist-organisation-not-leninist-vanguardism.

56. Jeff Shantz, *Against All Authority: Anarchism and the Literary Imagination* (Charlottesville, NC: Imprint Academic, 2011). Shantz, for instance, has collected writings on the anarchist dimensions of canonical literary figures like Oscar Wilde, Ralph Waldo Emerson, Henry David Thoreau, James Joyce, Ursula K. LeGuin, and Octavia Butler to evidence "constructive anarchist visions, which provide examples of politics . . . [and] offers needed insights into real world attempts by individuals and collectives to radically transform social relation in the here and now of everyday life"; see Shantz, *Spectres of Anarchy: Literature and the Anarchist Imagination* (New York: Algora Publishing, 2015), 2.

57. Allan Antliff, *Anarchism Modernism: Art, Politics, and the First American Avant-Garde* (Chicago: University of Chicago Press, 2001); and *Anarchy and Art: From the Paris Commune to the Fall of the Berlin Wall* (Vancouver: Arsenal Pulp Press, 2007).

58. André Breton, *Manifestoes of Surrealism* (Ann Arbor: University of Michigan Press, 1969); and Herbert Read, *Poetry and Anarchism* (Freeport, NY: Books for Libraries Press, 1938).

59. Shelley Streeby, *Radical Sensations: World Movements, Violence, and Visual Culture* (Durham, NC: Duke University Press, 2013).

60. Jesse Cohn, *Underground Passages: Anarchist Resistance Culture, 1848–2011* (Oakland, CA: AK Press, 2014), 14.

61. See Sandra Jeppesen, "Becoming Anarchist: the Function of Anarchist Literature," *Anarchist Developments in Cultural Studies*, no. 2 (2011): 189–213; Dani Spinosa "Postanarchist Literary Theory and the Experiment: Some Preliminary Notes," *Journal for the Study of Radicalism* 11, no. 1 (Spring 2017): 83–112; Lewis Call, *Postmodern Anarchism* (New York: Lexington Books, 2003); and Margaret Killjoy, ed., *Mythmakers and Lawbreakers: Anarchist Writers on Fiction* (Oakland, CA: AK Press, 2009).

62. In the appendices for *Mythmakers and Lawbreakers*, Killjoy offers bibliographies of "many authors who, while not anarchists themselves (or having been anarchists only for select periods of their lives), seem important enough to mention" and "anarchist representation in fiction" (208).

63. Brooks, *Common Pot*, 229.

64. Mishuana Goeman, "From Place to Territories and Back Again: Centering Storied Land in the Discussion of Indigenous Nation-Building," *International Journal of Critical Indigenous Studies* 1, no. 1 (2008): 23.

65. Goeman, "From Place to Territories and Back Again," 24.

66. Daniel Heath Justice, *Why Indigenous Literatures Matter* (Waterloo: Wilfred Laurier Press, 2018), xx.

67. Inés Hernández-Avila, "'It Is What Keeps Us Sisters': Indigenous Women and the Power of Story," *Frontiers: A Journal of Women Studies* 23, no. 2 (2002): x.

68. See Paula Gunn Allen, *The Sacred Hoop: Recovering the Feminine in American Indian Traditions* (Boston: Beacon Press, 1992); *Reinventing the Enemy's Language: Contemporary Native Women's Writings of North America*, ed. Joy Harjo and Gloria Bird (New York: W. W. Norton, 1998); and *A Gathering of Spirit: A Collection by North American Indian Women* (Toronto: Women's Press, 1992).

69. Leslie Marmon Silko, *Yellow Woman and a Beauty of the Spirit* (New York: Simon and Schuster, 1997), 49

70. Laura Tohe, "Introduction," in *Sister Nations: Native American Women Writers on Community* (Saint Paul: Minnesota Historical Society Press, 2002), xiv

71. As Jacqueline Keeler has argued, the recent controversy surrounding famed Coeur-D'Alene and Spokane author Sherman Alexie has confirmed the way this devaluation is bound up in the persistence of settler structures and gendered violence in the broader publishing world. See Jacqueline Keeler, "Why Reading Sherman Alexie Was Never Enough," *Yes! Magazine*, March 12, 2018.

72. Mishuana Goeman, *Mark My Words: Native Women Mapping Our Nations* (Minneapolis: University of Minnesota Press, 2013), 4.

73. Goeman, "From Place to Territories and Back Again," 24.

74. McCarthy, *In Divided* Unity, xv. See also Susan M. Hill, "'Travelling Down the River of Life Together in Peace and Friendship, Forever': Haudenosaunee Land Ethics and Treaty Agreements as the Basis for Restructuring the Relationship with the British Crown," in *Lighting the Eighth Fire: The Liberation, Resurgence, and Protection of Indigenous Nations*, ed. Leanne Simpson (Winnipeg: Arbeiter Ring, 2008), 23–46.

75. Brooks, *Common Pot*, 10.

76. Alicia Elliott, *A Mind Spread Out on the Ground* (Toronto: Double-Day Canada, 2019), 120.

77. Pauline Hillaire, "Bellingham Centennial History Pole," in *A Totem Pole History: The Work of Lummi Carver Joe Hillaire*, ed. Gregory P. Fields (Lincoln: University of Nebraska Press, 2013), 137.

78. Dawn Dove, "In Order to Understand Thanksgiving, One Has to Understand the Sacredness of the Gift," in *Dawnland Voices: An Anthology of Indigenous Writing from New England*, ed. Siobhan Senier (Lincoln: University of Nebraska Press, 2014), 526.

79. Dove, "In Order to Understand Thanksgiving."

80. See Coulthard, *Red Skin, White Masks*; Simpson, *Mohawk Interruptus*; Kevin Brunyeel, *The Third Space of Sovereignty: The Postcolonial Politics of US-Indigenous Relations*; and Shiri Pasternack, *Grounded Authority: The Algonquins of Barriere Lake against the State* (Minneapolis: University of Minnesota Press, 2017).

81. See Nick Estes, *Our History is the Future* (New York: Verso, 2019); and Leanne Betasamosake Simpson, *As We Have Always Done* (Minneapolis: University of Minnesota Press, 2017).

Chapter 1

1. Alexander Cockburn and Jeffrey St. Clair, *5 Days That Shook the World: Seattle and Beyond* (New York: Verso, 2000), 1.

2. Clare Hemmings, *Why Stories Matter: The Political Grammar of Feminist Theory* (Durham, NC: Duke University Press, 2010).

3. Hemmings, *Why Stories Matter*, 32.

4. Coll Thrush, *Native Seattle: Histories from the Crossing-Over Place* (Seattle: University of Washington Press, 2008), xiii

5. Hemmings, *Why Stories Matter*, 1, original emphasis.

6. Janet Thomas, *The Battle in Seattle: The Story Behind and Beyond the WTO Demonstrations* (Golden, CO: Fulcrum Publishing, 2000), 12. For more on television and violence in Seattle, see Kevin Michael DeLuca and Jennifer Peeples, "From Public Sphere to Public Screen: Democracy, Activism, and the 'Violence' of Seattle."

7. Uri Gordon, *Anarchy Alive!: Anti-Authoritarian Politics from Practice to Theory* (London: Pluto Press, 2008), 79–80.

8. Gordon, *Anarchy Alive!*, 80.

9. Solnit, "The Battle of the Story of the Battle in Seattle," in *The Battle of the Story of the Battle of Seattle*, ed. David Solnit and Rebecca Solnit (Oakland, CA: AK Press, 2009), 15.

10. In his article for the *Guardian*, John Vidal described scenes of interaction between delegates and protestors: "On the front line of the protest

a small debate was taking place. Two African delegates were trying to get through the lines of protesters. An argument was raging. 'Look,' said the Kenyan, 'this round is vital to us. We need world trade. We need development. We respect that you are standing up for your rights and are trying to help, but the talks must go on.' 'The protesters were very well informed,' said one of the delegates later. "I was quite surprised. I thought trade was something no one understood in America"" John Vidal, "Real battle for Seattle," *Guardian*, December 4, 1999, https://www.theguardian.com/world/1999/dec/05/wto.globalisation. Similarly, in an op-ed, Klein emphasizes the anticorporate message of the protests against Friedman's claims of naivete. See Naomi Klein, "Rebels in Search of Rules," *New York Times*, December 2, 1999, https://www.nytimes.com/1999/12/02/opinion/rebels-in-search-of-rules.html; and Thomas Friedman, "Senseless in Seattle," *New York Times*, December 1, 1999.

11. Chris Dixon, "Five Days in Seattle," in *The Battle of the Story of the Battle of Seattle*, ed. David Solnit and Rebecca Solnit (Oakland, CA: AK Press, 2009), 105.

12. For more on the history of protest movements against SAPs, see George Caffentzis and Silvia Federici, "A Brief History of Resistance to Structural Adjustment," in *Democratizing the Global Economy: The Battle Against the World Bank and the IMF*, ed. Kevin Danaher (Monroe, ME: Common Courage Press, 2002).

13. David Solnit, "Battle of the Story of the Battle in Seattle," 19.

14. Dixon, "Five Days in Seattle," 105.

15. Dixon, "Five Days in Seattle," 105.

16. Thrush, *Native Seattle*, 46–47. For more on Chief Seattle's famous speech, see Albert Furtwangler, *Answering Chief Seattle* (Seattle: University of Washington Press, 2011).

17. See Christopher Frizelle, "Nightstand: My New Favorite Newspaper," *The Stranger*, August 3, 2011, https://www.thestranger.com/seattle/nightstand/Content?oid=9322085; and Brendan Kiley, "Anarchy is Boring: The May Day Smashup Was the Spectacular Tip of a Mundane Iceberg," *The Stranger*, May 9, 2012, https://www.thestranger.com/seattle/anarchy-is-boring/Content?oid=13597692.

18. This description is present at the beginning of each issues of *Tides of Flame*, all of which are available at tidesofflame.wordpress.com.

19. "Forgotten History: 1856; The Battle of Seattle," *Tides of Flame* 20 (June 2012): 4, https://tidesofflame.files.wordpress.com/2012/06/tof20.pdf.

20. "Forgotten History," 4.

21. "Forgotten History," 4.

22. Scott Richard Lyons, *X-Marks: Native Signatures of Assent* (Minneapolis: University of Minnesota Press, 2010), 1.

23. See Richard Walker, "Failed Treaty of Point Elliott [*sic*] Promises Spotlighted in Play," *Indian Country Today*, September 23, 2013, https://indiancountrymedianetwork.com/history/events/failed-treaty-of-point-elliott-promises-spotlighted-in-play/.

24. Lyons, *X-Marks*, 1.

25. See Lisa Blee, *Framing Chief Leschi: Narrative and the Politics of Historical Justice* (Chapel Hill: University of North Carolina Press, 2014).

26. Thrush, *Native Seattle*, 3.

27. Thrush, *Native Seattle*, 7.

28. Philip Deloria, *Playing Indian* (New Haven, CT: Yale University Press, 1999), 5–7.

29. In addition to creating a fictional history of Native peoples on which to build our understanding of the present, this persistent method of articulating Native history in Seattle confirms the prevalent idea that "Native history and urban history—and indeed, Indians and cities—cannot coexist, and one must necessarily be eclipsed by the other." Thrush, *Native Seattle*, 8. See also Reyna Ramirez, *Native Hubs: Culture, Community, and Belonging in Silicon Valley and Beyond* (Durham, NC: Duke University Press, 2012).

30. Thrush, *Native Seattle*, 8.

31. Jean M. O'Brien, *Firsting and Lasting: Writing Indians Out of Existence in New England* (Minneapolis: University of Minnesota Press, 2010), xii.

32. O'Brien, *Firsting and Lasting*, xiii.

33. Stevie Peace, "The Power Within Us to Create the World Anew: A Discussion with Grace Lee Boggs," in *Uses of a Whirlwind: Movement, Movements, and Contemporary Radical Currents in the United States*, ed. Team Colors Collective (Oakland, CA: AK Press, 2010), 351.

34. Mark Bray, *Translating Anarchy: The Anarchism of Occupy Wall Street* (Winchester, UK: Zero Books, 2013), 52.

35. Thomas, *The Battle in Seattle*, 202.

36. Thomas, *The Battle in Seattle*, 201.

37. Elizabeth Betita Martínez, "Where Was the Color in Seattle? Looking for Reasons Why the Great Battle Was So White," *Colorlines*, March 10, 2000, https://www.colorlines.com/articles/where-was-color-seattlelooking-reasons-why-great-battle-was-so-white.

38. I am thankful to Zoltán Grossman for challenging me to think through this interplay between the Battle in Seattle and the Makah whaling

controversy, which is informed by his work on Native and non-Native alliances during the Fish Wars in both Washington and Wisconsin. See Zoltán Grossman, *Unlikely Alliances: Native Nations and White Communities Join to Defend Rural Lands* (Seattle: University of Washington Press, 2017).

39. Zoltán Grossman, *Unlikely Alliances: Native Nations and White Allies Join to Defend Rural Lands* (University of Washington Press, 2017); and Joshua L. Reid, *The Sea Is My Country: The Maritime World of the Makahs* (New Haven, CT: Yale University Press, 2015). Opponents like Republican US representative Jack Metcalf and Sea Shepard's Paul Watson were joined by journalists like Richard Blow (writing for *Mother Jones*) in demonstrating an extreme lack of knowledge not only about the issue at hand, but also about the history of treaties in Washington in general. Metcalf repeatedly depended on the claims that the right to whale is a "special right" granted to Makahs by the US government, rather than rights secured and reserved by Makahs during the signing of the treaty. Joining Metcalf's project of preventing Makahs from exercising their treaty rights, Watson consistently decried the hunts by positioning himself as the arbiter of traditionalism, pointing repeatedly to Makah whalers' use of contemporary tools as evidence that the whale hunt had no relationship to maintaining traditional cultural practices. And in his article "The Great American Whale Hunt," Blow describes the broader political issues at hand: "Challenging the whaling moratorium, and the [National Oceanic and Atmospheric Administration] would ignite international fury, not to mention the wrath of domestic environmental groups. But contest the Makah's treaty, and it would risk a political firestorm from all American Indians, all of whom live under similar treaties with the federal government." Of course, not all Native peoples in the US live under treaties with the federal government. But what is more, Blow (much like Metcalf) misunderstands the fundamental character of treaties themselves. Because the US signed the treaty with the Makah that reserved their rights to traditional whaling practices and grounds in 1855, they had no authority to give away those rights when they participated in either the International Convention for the Regulation of Whaling (ICRW) in 1946 or agreed to the moratorium on whaling through the IWC in 1982. As a sovereign nation, Makahs petitioned the IWC themselves, willfully participating in an international conversation that demonstrated their ongoing commitment to a balance between conservation and traditional whaling practices—something central to Makah whaling practices since time immemorial.

40. Thomas, *The Battle in Seattle*, 20. Graeber has mentioned White's turtles as a notable example of the use of puppetry in mass protests.

Graeber, *Direct Action: An Ethnography* (Oakland, CA: AK Press, 2009), 491; Marc Cooper of the *Los Angeles Times* noted White's turtles as a definitive image of the protests as well. Marc Cooper, "Teamsters and Turtles: They're Together at Last," *Los Angeles Times*, December 2, 1999, http://articles.latimes.com/1999/dec/02/local/me-39707.

41. Associated Press, "Protestors Leave, But What Hunt Is Still Planned: Makah Tribes Is Considering Alternatives," *Deseret News*, December 1, 1998, https://www.deseretnews.com/article/666150/Protesters-leave-but-whale-hunt-is-still-planned.html; and Jim Nollman, "Whaling Report to the Makah Tribal Council," *Interspecies Newsletter*, 1999, https://www.whaleweb.org/intersp/pages/makah.html.

42. Christopher Dunagan, "Hunters Become the Hunted," *Kitsap Sun*, October 5, 1998, http://web.kitsapsun.com/archive/1998/10-05/0056_hunters_become_the_hunted.html.

43. Dunagan, "Hunters Become the Hunted." See also Paul C. Rosier, *Native American Issues* (Westport, CT: Greenwood Publishing, 2003), 43.

44. Keith A. Johnson, "The Makah Manifesto," *Seattle Times*, August 23, 1998, http://community.seattletimes.nwsource.com/archive/?date=19980823&slug=2768010.

45. Sam Howe Verhovek, "For Seattle, Triumph and Protest," *New York Times*, October 13, 1999, https://www.nytimes.com/1999/10/13/us/for-seattle-triumph-and-protest.html.

46. As Yu'pik scholar Shari Huhndorf has argued, consolidating colonial representations of indigeneity was central to the Alaska Yukon Exposition, connecting Native communities in the Pacific Northwest to Alaska Native peoples and indigenous peoples in US colonies like the Philippines. See Shari Huhndorf, *Mapping the Americas: the Transnational Politics of Contemporary Native Culture* (Ithaca, NY: Cornell University Press, 2009).

47. Reid, *Sea Is My Country*, 133.

48. Reid, *Sea Is My Country*, 133.

49. Verhovek, "For Seattle, Triumph and Protest."

50. Thrush, *Native Seattle*, 201.

51. Nathan Schneider, *Thank You Anarchy: Notes from the Occupy Apocalypse* (Berkeley: University of California Press, 2013), 127.

52. See Bray, *Translating Anarchy*; Schneider, *Thank You Anarchy*; Naomi Klein, "The Most Important Thing in the World"; and David Graeber, "Enacting the Impossible: Making Decisions by Consensus."

53. Barker provides an extensive background in her essay "Territory as Analytic: The Dispossession of Lenapehoking and the Subprime Crisis," *Social Text* 36, no. 2 (2018): 19–39.

54. Craig Fortier offers a brief discussion, built on Barker's and Sandy Grande's work, of the history of settlement in Manhattan in *Unsettling the Commons*. Adam Lewis has also offered a mention of settlement and Manhattan in "Imagining Autonomy on Stolen Land: Settler Colonialism, Anarchism, and the Possibilities of Decolonization?," *Settler Colonial Studies*, 7, no. 4 (2017): 474–95.

55. In fact, Goyens's only discussion of Native peoples, land, or activism is within the history of a mid-twentieth century group based on the Lower East Side of Manhattan who called themselves The Motherfuckers. According to Goyens, this almost exclusively white group of political artists and activists embraced what he describes as "the symbolic markers of Native Americans" including "Native American warriors, totem poles, and tribal-inspired designs" which he notes are "by far the most common images in the Motherfuckers' leaflets and broadsheets." Goyens recognizes that though "Native Americans' supposed authenticity and willingness to fight for their culture attracted the Motherfuckers . . . [their] understanding of actual Native Americans was simplistic and even cartoonish." Tom Goyens, *Radical Gotham: Anarchism in New York City from Schwab's Saloon to Occupy Wall Street* (Champaign: University of Illinois Press, 2017), 168.

56. Heid E. Erdrich, "Pre-Occupied," http://heiderdrich.com/video/pre-occupied/.

57. There are even fewer discussions of the participation of Native peoples in OWS encampments themselves. Some exceptions include Chris Dixon's "Building a Mass Movement? Learning from the Occupy Sudbury Experience" and Michael Gourd-Wartofsky's brief mention of Isham Christie, "a Native American revolutionary from the Choctaw Nation, who went on to play a vital part in the formation of OWS" (24), in his book *The Occupiers: The Making of the 99 Percent Movement* (New York: Oxford University Press, 2015).

58. For example, in their piece "Occupy and the 99%," Lester Spence and Mike McGuire note: "For *Adbusters*, the term 'occupation' was a progressive term connoting reclamation . . . In North America, though, the term 'occupy' also has a deeply regressive meaning—it denotes the white settler colonialism that led to the brutal suppression of Indigenous peoples, and to the creation of the Atlantic Slave Trade. Furthermore, in the American context, the term also refers to the contemporary urban policy of gentrification—a policy that often ends up displacing poorer populations of color in favor of middle and upper income white populations. The nomenclature of Occupy and the decision to 'occupy' spaces that were (in many cases) already occupied led to the symbolic and physical displacement of

people of color. While understandably chosen, the use of the term 'occupy' largely ignores the role of historical occupations in subjugating people of color. Lester Spence and Mike McGuire, "Occupy and the 99%," in *We Are Many: Reflections on Movement Strategy from Occupation to Liberation*, ed. Kate Khatib and Margaret Killjoy (Oakland, CA: AK Press, 2012): 53–65.

59. "The indigenous population, for example. They didn't have any rights. In the U.S. Constitution there was a category of creatures called three-fifth humans—the enslaved population. They were considered persons. And in fact women were barely considered persons, so they didn't have rights . . . Over the following years, the concept of 'person' was changed by the courts in two ways. One was to broaden it to include corporations, legal fictions established and sustained by the state. In fact, these 'persons' later became the management of corporations, according to the court decisions. So the management of corporations became 'persons.'" Noam Chomsky, *Occupy: Reflections on Class War, Rebellion, and Solidarity* (Brooklyn: Zuccotti Park Press, 2013), 40–41.

60. Rebecca Solnit, "The Occupation of Hope: Letter to a Dead Man," in *This Changes Everything: Occupy Wall Street and the 99% Movement*, ed. Sarah Van Gelder and the staff of *YES! Magazine* (Oakland, CA: Berret-Koehler Publishers, 2011), 80.

61. Tuck and Yang, "Decolonization Is Not a Metaphor," 28.

62. Thrush, *Native Seattle*, ix.

63. For more on the legal and political structures of recognition in the United States, see Amy E. Den Ouden and Jean M. O'Brien, eds., *Recognition, Sovereignty Struggles, and Indigenous Rights in the United States: A Sourcebook* (Chapel Hill: University of North Carolina Press, 2013).

64. See Glen Sean Coulthard, *Red Skin, White Masks: Rejecting the Colonial Politics of Recognition* (Minneapolis: University of Minnesota Press, 2014); and Day, *Gramsci Is Dead*.

65. Lisa Duggan, *The Twilight of Equality?: Neoliberalism, Cultural Politics, and the Attack on Democracy* (Boston: Beach Press, 2012).

66. Coulthard, *Red Skin, White Masks*, 3.

67. Occupy Portland, "Working Draft of Occupy Portland Statement of Indigenous Solidarity," *Portland Occupier*, November 25, 2011, http://www.portlandoccupier.org/2011/11/25/working-draft-of-occupy-portland-statement-of-indigenous-solidarity/.

68. Occupy Santa Fe, "Statement of Solidarity with Indigenous Peoples," January 13, 2012, https://wiki.occupyboston.org/wiki/Decolonize_To_Liberate/declarations.

69. Occupy Boston, "Occupy Boston Declares Solidarity with Indigenous Peoples," OccupyBoston.org, October 10, 2011, http://www.occupyboston.org/2011/10/10/occupy-boston-declares-solidarity-with-indigenous-peoples/.

70. Passed on October 19, 2011, the statement can be read in its entirety at the following: https://blackorchidcollective.wordpress.com/2011/10/22/decolonize-occupy/.

71. Coulthard, *Red Skin, White Masks*, 25, original emphasis.

72. Robbins's acceptance speech was reproduced in print for the first time in 2006. Tom Robbins, "Here in Geoduck Junction," *Seattle Weekly*, October 9, 2006, http://archive.seattleweekly.com/2000-05-03/news/here-in-geoduck-junction/.

73. For an image of the flyer, see Dave Pollard, "The Occupy Movement: Don't Tell Us What to Do," *how to save the world*, November 12, 2011, http://howtosavetheworld.ca/2011/11/12/the-occupy-movement-dont-tell-us-what-to-do/.

74. CrimethInc., "Gord Hill, Indigenous Artist and Anarchist: An Interview," August 1, 2017, https://crimethinc.com/2017/08/01/an-interview-with-gord-hill.

75. Solnit, "Battle of the Story of the Battle in Seattle," 9.

76. Goeman, "From Place to Territory and Back Again," 32.

Chapter 2

1. "The rememorative words—that is, words that remind us of a past and its meaning in the present—carry important weight for our futures." Mishuana Goeman, *Mark My Words: Native Women Mapping Our Nations* (Minneapolis: University of Minnesota Press, 2013), 161–62.

2. Elizabeth Cook-Lynn, "Life and Death in the Mainstream of American Indian Biography," *Wicazo Sa Review* 11, no. 2 (Autumn 1995): 93.

3. Joanne Barker and Teresia Teaiwa, "Native InFormation," in *Reading Native American Women: Critical/Creative Representations*, edited by Inés Hernández-Avila (New York: AltaMira Press, 2005), 107–128

4. See Taiaiake Alfred, *Peace, Power, and Righteousness: An Indigenous Manifesto* (New York: Oxford University Press, 1999); and Mark Rifkin, *Beyond Settler Time: Temporal Sovereignty and Indigenous Self-Determination* (Durham, NC: Duke University Press, 2017).

5. Robert Warrior, *The People and the Word: Reading Native Nonfiction* (Minneapolis: University of Minnesota Press, 2005); Lisa Brooks, *The Common Pot: The Recovery of Native Space in the Northeast* (Minneapolis: University of Minnesota Press, 2010).

6. Lee Maracle, *Bobbi Lee: Indian Rebel* (Toronto: Women's Press, 1991); Janet Campbell Hale, *Bloodlines: Odyssey of a Native Daughter* (Tucson: University of Arizona Press, 1998); Linda Hogan, *The Woman Who Watches Over the World: A Native Memoir* (New York: W. W. Norton, 2001); Alison Hedge Coke, *Rock, Willow, Ghost, Deer: A Story of Survival* (Lincoln: University of Nebraska Press, 2004); Louise Erdrich, *The Blue Jay's Dance: A Memoir of Early Motherhood* (New York: Harper Perennial, 2010) and *Books and Islands in Ojibwe Country: Traveling Through the Land of My Ancestors* (New York: Harper Perennial, 2014); Leslie Marmon Silko, *The Turquoise Ledge: A Memoir* (New York: Penguin Books, 2010); Joy Harjo, *Crazy Brave: A Memoir* (New York: W. W. Norton, 2012); and LeAnne Howe, *Choctalking on Other Realities* (San Francisco: Aunt Lute Books, 2013).

7. See Ernestine Hayes, *Blonde Indian: An Alaska Native Memoir* (Tucson: University of Arizona Press, 2006) and *The Tao of Raven: An Alaska Native Memoir* (Seattle: University of Washington Press, 2017); Mary Crow Dog, *Lakota Woman* (New York: Harper Collins, 1990); and Mary Brave Bird, *Ohitika Woman* (New York: Grove Press, 1993).

8. I should note here the exciting special issue of *Biography*, edited by Alice Te Punga Somerville (Te Ātiawa/Taranaki), Noelani Arista (Kanaka Maoli) and Daniel Health Justice (Cherokee) on indigenous biography. Though my work here is more closely aligned with scholarship on *auto*biography or self-storying, I employ a mode of analysis that focuses on a critical engagement with the methodological work of Indigenous writers, rather than only life-writing texts focused on Indigenous subjects, "which are too often studied for how they engage colonial subjects rather than for the ways they center their own contexts and concerns both within and beyond settler colonialism." Alice Te Punga Somerville and Daniel Heath Justice, "Introduction: Indigenous Conversations about Biography," *Biography* 39, no. 3 (Summer 2016): 241.

9. Arnold Krupat and Brian Swann, introduction to *Here First: Autobiographical Essays by Native American Writers*, ed. Arnold Krupat and Brian Swann (New York: Modern Library, 2000), xi–xv; and Warren Cariou, "Life-Telling: Indigenous Oral Autobiography and the Performance of Relation," *Biography* 39, no. 3 (Summer 2016): 314–27.

10. For instance, see John D'Agata, ed., *The Making of the American Essay* (Minneapolis: Graywolf Press, 2016); Vivian Gornick, *The Situation and the Story: The Art of Personal Narrative* (New York: Farrar, Straus, and Giroux, 2002); Kevin Kerrane and Ben Yagoda, eds., *The Art of Fact: A Historical Anthology of Literary Nonfiction* (New York: Scribner, 1998); and Chris Anderson, ed., *Literary Nonfiction: Theory, Criticism, Pedagogy* (Carbondale: Southern Illinois University Press, 1989).

11. As she argues, Native women's first-person narratives "participated in creating new language for communities to address the real multilayered facets of their histories and concerns by insisting on the inclusion of our lived experience, rich with emotional knowledges, of what pain and grief and hope meant or mean now in our pasts and futures." Million, *Therapeutic Nations*, 57.

12. Million, *Therapeutic Nations*, 57.

13. Leslie Marmon Silko, *Storyteller* (New York: Penguin Books, Reprint Edition 2012), xvii.

14. Silko, *Storyteller*, xix.

15. Silko, *Storyteller*, xix.

16. Hogan, *Dwellings*, 195.

17. Elissa Washuta, *My Body Is a Book of Rules* (Los Angeles: Red Hen Press, 2014), 1.

18. Deborah Miranda, *Bad Indians: A Tribal Memoir* (Berkeley, CA: Heydey Books, 2013), xx.

19. Miranda, *Bad Indians*, 33–35.

20. Miranda, *Bad Indians*, 34. Here, Miranda refers to the *soldado de cuera* described by Conor McMahon as "the cavalry soldiers who manned the presidios" or military forts used by the Spanish as a line of defense in its territories throughout the Americas. See Conor McMahon, "The Espada Ancha in New Mexico: Conservation of a New World Sword," *El Palacio: New Mexico's Magazine of Art, History, and Culture of the Southwest* 111, no. 4 (Winter 2005): 23

21. Miranda, *Bad Indians*, 34.

22. Miranda, *Bad Indians*, 34. In her article for the *Los Angeles Times* on "California Parties—Past and Future," author of *California Rancho Cooking* Jacqueline Higuera McMahan notes that "*Pilillis* are another of the *Californios'* culinary inventions. The word, like *sarsa*, is untraceable, but *pilillis* are remarkably similar to *sopaipillas*, the puffy fried bread of the Southwest. Anyone who came for one of the great Sunday barbecues and snuggled into one of the ghostly rooms of the old ranch house for the night would wake up the next morning to the smell of *pilillis* and dark-roasted coffee."

23. Miranda, *Bad Indians*, xiv.

24. Washuta, *My Body Is a Book of Rules*, 1.

25. Washuta, *My Body Is a Book of Rules*, 27.

26. Washuta, *My Body Is a Book of Rules*, 27.

27. For more, see Lomawaima, "A Principle of Relativity through Indigenous Biography," and Chang's response, "Indigenous Biography, Genealogy,

and Webs of Relation," in "Indigenous Conversations about Biography," ed. Alice Te Punga Somerville, Daniel Heath Justice, and Noelani Arista, special issue, *Biography* 39, no. 3 (Summer 2016): 248–69, 274–76.

28. Miranda, *Bad Indians*, xiv. For Miranda, this understanding of culture is bound not (only) to individual identification with particular categories of race, ethnicity, or indigeneity, but rather with understanding oneself and one's community as the meeting place of complex, covalent histories and places. She refuses a static notion of culture that seeks a return to a pure time before colonialism. Instead, she observes: "By 1961, my father's family had been enduring and/or celebrating mixed-race unions for about two hundred years in one form or another: California Indian with Mexican Indian, Chumash with Esselen, Spaniard with Indian, and rich variations thereof."

29. Caroline Levine, *Forms: Whole, Rhythm, Hierarchy, Network* (Princeton, NJ: Princeton University Press, 2015), 2.

30. Brenda Miller and Suzanne Paola, *Tell It Slant: Creating, Refining, and Publishing Creative Nonfiction* (New York: McGraw Hill, 2012), 90.

31. Levine, *Forms*, xi.

32. Crystal Kurzen, "Toward a Native American Women's Autobiographical Tradition: Genre as Political Practice," in *The Oxford Handbook of Indigenous American Literatures*, ed. James Cox and Daniel Heath Justice (New York: Oxford University Press, 2014), 202–3.

33. Elissa Washuta and Theresa Warburton, introduction to *Shapes of Native Nonfiction: Collected Essays by Contemporary Authors*, ed. Elissa Washuta and Theresa Warburton (Seattle: University of Washington Press, 2019), 3–20.

34. Washuta, *My Body Is a Book of Rules*, 27.

35. Washuta, *My Body Is a Book of Rules*, 42.

36. Washuta, *My Body Is a Book of Rules*, 43.

37. Washuta, *My Body Is a Book of Rules*, 44.

38. Audre Lorde, *Sister/Outsider: Essays and Speeches* (Berkeley: Crossing Press, 1984), 36.

39. Ferguson, *Aberrations in Black*, ix.

40. Ferguson, *Aberrations in Black*, 25.

41. Antonie Boessenkool, "The California Missions School Project Is Becoming a Thing of the Past and Here's Why," *Los Angeles Daily News*, September 24, 2017, https://www.dailynews.com/2017/09/24/the-california-missions-school-project-is-becoming-a-thing-of-the-past-heres-why/.

42. Miranda, *Bad Indians*, xviii.

43. Tuck and Yang, "Decolonization Is Not a Metaphor," 3.

44. Miller and Paola, *Tell It Slant*, 124.

45. Miranda, *Bad Indians*, 8.

46. Mary Louise Pratt, "Arts of the Contact Zone," *Profession* (1991): 35.

47. Pratt, "Arts of the Contact Zone," 34.

48. This lineage of autoethnographic engagement with form is not only a literary one but also one that enables Miranda to emphasize the connections between the California missions and the Spanish invasion of South America, especially the Andes.

49. Levine, *Forms*, 1.

50. Levine, *Forms*, 2.

51. Tuck and Yang, "Decolonization is Not a Metaphor," 10.

52. For more on claims to indigenous ancestry, see Kim Tallbear, *Native American DNA: Tribal Belonging and the False Promise of Genetic Science* (Minneapolis: University of Minnesota Press, 2013); and Vine Deloria Jr., *Custer Died for Your Sins: An Indian Manifesto* (Norman: University of Oklahoma Press, 1969).

53. Tuck and Yang, "Decolonization Is Not a Metaphor," 11.

54. They use this term to refer to the "homogenizing of various experiences of oppression as colonization." Tuck and Yang, "Decolonization Is Not a Metaphor," 17.

55. I take this term from Eve Tuck and Rubén A. Gaztambide-Fernández's "Curriculum, Replacement, and Settler Futurity," in *Journal of Curriculum Theorizing* 29, no. 1 (2013): 72–89.

56. See Grace Dillon, ed., *Walking the Clouds: An Anthology of Indigenous Science Fiction* (Tucson: University of Arizona Press, 2012).

57. Tuck and Yang, "Decolonization Is Not a Metaphor," 35.

58. Miranda uses the term *future mythology* to refer to the practice of telling one's history from the vantage point of their descendants: "When I look toward the next seven generations, I imagine this is the kind of story that my descendants will tell, seven generations from now, in the future mythology of the Mestiza Nation." Miranda, *Bad Indians*, 123.

59. Miranda, *Bad Indians*, 208. Elsewhere, I've analyzed more extensively Miranda's exploration of her grandfather's attraction to the light at the top of Mount Diablo and the connection to Million's "felt theory": see my "A Similar Place: Resistance and Existence in 21st Century Black and Native Women's Memoir," *Critical Studies, Cultural Methodologies* 17, no. 1 (2017): 41–49.

60. Washuta, *My Body Is a Book of Rules*, 187.

61. Washuta, *My Body Is a Book of Rules*,180.

62. Washuta, *My Body Is a Book of Rules*, 189.

63. In her essay "Apocalypse Logic," Washuta writes of the story of Tumalth's murder: "I feel like I should say I'm tired of writing this again. I am always writing that Tumalth was hanged a year after signing the Kalapuya Treaty. I am always writing that his daughters were taken to Fort Vancouver when the Cascade leaders were hanged. I am always writing about the resistance of the women who hung tough along the Columbia River for generations, even after the disruption of the systems of hunting, fishing, and gathering our family maintained for thousands of years. Actually, I'm not tired of writing about this, and I may never be, but sometimes when I say once more that *my great-great-great-grandfather was hanged by the U.S. government* I can feel someone thinking, *God, she's back on that*." Washuta, "Apocalypse Logic," *The Offing*, November 21, 2016, https://theoffingmag.com/insight/apocalypse-logic/. In addition to the extensive material based on Meadow's stories in *Bad Indians*, Miranda has also written about her elsewhere; see Deborah Miranda, "'They Were Tough, Those Old Women Before Us': The Power of Gossip in Isabel Meadows's Narratives," *Biography* 39, no. 3 (Summer 2016): 373–401.

64. Barker and Teaiwa, "Native InFormation," 125.

Chapter 3

1. Black Rose Anarchist Federation, "Below and Beyond Trump: Power and Counter-Power in 2017," December 22, 2017, http://blackrosefed.org/below-and-beyond-trump/.

2. Black Rose Anarchist Federation, "Below and Beyond Trump."

3. Black Rose Anarchist Federation, mission statement, accessed January 29, 2018, http://blackrosefed.org/mission-statement/.

4. Black Rose Anarchist Federation, "Below and Beyond Trump."

5. Black Rose Anarchist Federation, "Points of Unity," accessed January 29, 2018, http://blackrosefed.org/points-of-unity/.

6. Black Rose Anarchist Federation, "Below and Beyond Trump."

7. Black Rose Anarchist Federation, "Patriarchy and Queer Liberation," accessed January 29, 2018, http://blackrosefed.org/points-of-unity/patriarchy-queer-liberation/.

8. For some foundational examples, see Zillah Eisenstein, "Constructing a Theory of Capitalist Patriarchy and Socialist Feminism," *Critical Sociology* 25, no. 2–3 (March 1999): 196–217; Gayle Rubin, "The Traffic in Women: Notes on the 'Political Economy' of Sex," in *Toward an Anthropology of Women*, ed. Rayna R. Reiter (New York: Monthly Review Press, 1975), 157–210; Shulamith Firestone, *The Dialectic of Sex: The Case for*

Feminist Revolution (New York: Farrar, Straus, and Giroux, 2003); Lise Vogel, *Marxism and the Oppression of Women: Toward a Unitary Theory* (New Brunswick: Rutgers University Press, 1987); and Eli Zaretsky, *Capitalism, the Family, and Personal Life* (New York: Harper Collins, 1986)

9. Black Rose Anarchist Federation, "Below and Beyond Trump."

10. From the Black Lives Matter main website: "We affirm the lives of Black queer and trans folks, disabled folks, undocumented folks, folks with records, women, and all Black lives along the gender spectrum. Our network centers those who have been marginalized within Black liberation movements; https://blacklivesmatter.com/about/. See also Noah Berlatsky, "The Women of #BlackLivesMatter," *Atlantic*, January 27, 2015, https://www.theatlantic.com/national/archive/2015/01/women-and-blacklivesmatter/384855/; Kaavya Asoka, "Women and Black Lives Matter: An Interview with Marcia Chatelain," *Dissent Magazine*, Summer 2015, https://www.dissentmagazine.org/article/women-black-lives-matter-interview-marcia-chatelain; and Kimberly Williams, "Black Lives Matter Gave Me the Confidence to Be Visible in Appalachia," *Slate*, June 27, 2017, https://slate.com/human-interest/2017/06/how-black-lives-matter-gave-a-black-queer-woman-the-confidence-to-be-visible-in-appalachia.html. For more on the immigrant rights movement, see important discussions regarding immigration, undocumented populations, and sexual assault in mainstream publications and rights organizations, including Human Rights Watch, "US: Sexual Violence, Harassment of Immigrant Farmworkers," May 5, 2012, https://www.hrw.org/news/2012/05/15/us-sexual-violence-harassment-immigrant-farmworkers#; Southern Poverty Law Center, "Sexual Assault Against Immigrant Women is a Human Rights Tragedy," April 5, 2011, https://www.splcenter.org/news/2011/04/05/sexual-assault-against-immigrant-women-hidden-human-rights-tragedy; and American Civil Liberties Union's map of sexual abuse since 2007 in immigration detention facilities, https://www.aclu.org/issues/immigrants-rights/immigrants-rights-and-detention/sexual-abuse-immigration-detention-0.

11. On the Women Strike website for the 2017 strike, the organizers note that strikers will halt myriad kinds of household work (www.womenstrike.org). For the call from the organizers of the 2018 Women's Strike, see Linda Martín Alcoff, Cinzia Arruzza, Tithi Bhattacharya, Rosa Clemente, Angela Davis, Zillah Eisenstein, Liza Featherstone, Nancy Fraser, Barbara Smith, and Keeanga-Yamahtta Taylor, "We Need a Feminism for the 99%," *Guardian*, January 27, 2018, https://www.theguardian.com/commentisfree/2018/jan/27/we-need-a-feminism-for-the-99-thats-why-women-will-strike-this-year.

12. Kyle Powys White, "White Allies, Let's Be Honest About Decolonization," *YES! Magazine*, April 3, 2018, http://www.yesmagazine.org/issues/decolonize/white-allies-lets-be-honest-about-decolonization-20180403.

13. For more, see the website It Starts with Us: http://itstartswithus-mmiw.com/.

14. See Laura Hall, "Indigenism Intersectionality: Decolonizing an Indigenous Eco-Queer Feminism and Anarchism," *Perspectives on Anarchist Theory* 29 (May 2016); and Kathy Ferguson, "Becoming Anarchism, Feminism, and Indigeneity," *Affinities: A Journal of Radical Theory, Culture, and Action* 5, no. 1 (2011): 96–109.

15. See Theresa Warburton, "Coming to Terms: Rethinking Popular Approaches to Anarchism and Feminism," *Perspectives on Anarchist Theory* 29 (May 2016).

16. Andrea Smith and J. Kēhaulani Kauanui, "Native Feminisms Engage American Studies," *American Quarterly* 60, no. 2 (June 2008): 241–49.

17. Throughout, I will use the term *anarchist feminism* rather than anarcha- or anarcho-feminism. I do this for two reasons: to emphasize my refusal to accept an easy, inherent synonymy between the two and to enable a coherence throughout, despite differing approaches to the relationships between them. When I use direct quotations from authors who use other configurations, I will leave their configuration.

18. "Foreword," in Dark Star Collective, ed., *Quiet Rumours: An Anarcha-Feminist Reader*, 3rd ed. (Oakland, CA: AK Press, 2012), 10.

19. Cinzia Arruzza, "Of What Is Anarcha-Feminism the Name?," in *The Anarchist Turn*, ed. by Jacob Blumfeld, Chiara Bottici, and Simon Critchley (New York: Pluto Books, 2013), 112.

20. Arruzza, "Of What Is Anarcha-Feminism the Name?," 113.

21. For Goldman, see "The Traffic in Women." For De Cleyre, see "Sex Slavery."

22. See Gayle Rubin's influential essays "The Traffic in Women: Notes on the 'Political Economy' of Sex" and "Thinking Sex: Notes for a Radical Theory of the Politics of Sexuality," the former of which takes its name from Goldman's essay of the same title which appears in *Anarchism and Other Essays*.

23. Joanne Barker, "Introduction: Critically Sovereign," in *Critically Sovereign: Indigenous Feminist, Gender, and Sexuality Studies*, ed. Joanne Barker, (Durham, NC: Duke University Press, 2017), 7.

24. For a more in-depth discussion of De Cleyre's relationship to individualist anarchism, see *Exquisite Rebel: The Essays of Voltairine De Cleyre: Feminist, Anarchist, Genius* (Albany: State University of New York Press, 2012).

25. See Marian Leighton's "Voltairine De Cleyre: An Introduction," in Dark Collective, *Quiet Rumours*, where she repeatedly uses the term *native American anarchism*.

26. *Emma Goldman: A Documentary History of the American Years, Vol. I: Made for America, 1890–1901*, ed. Candace Falk (Berkeley: University of California Press, 2003), 230.

27. Voltairine De Cleyre, "Anarchism and American Traditions," in *The Selected Works of Voltairine De Cleyre: Poems, Essays, Sketches, and Stories, 1885–1911* (Oakland, CA: AK Press, 2016), 127, and "Breaking the Chains: Changing Society Through Direct Action," in *Exquisite Rebel: The Essays of Voltairine De Cleyre* (Albany: State University of New York Press. 2005), 276.

28. For more on de Cleyre and New England in particular, see my article "What Looks Like a Grave: Native and Anarchist Place-Making in New England," *Studies in American Indian Literatures* 32, no. 1–2 (Spring–Summer 2020): 75–110.

29. See Joanne Barker's "Indigenous Feminisms," in *Oxford Handbook of Indigenous People's Politics*, ed. José Antonio Lucero, Dale Turner, and Donna Lee VanCott (pub. online, January 2015), http://www.oxfordhandbooks.com/view/10.1093/oxfordhb/9780195386653.001.0001/oxfordhb-9780195386653-e-007.

30. Joanne Barker, "Introduction: Critically Sovereign," 11. See also Luana Ross, "From the 'F' Word to Indigenous/Feminisms," *Wicazo Sa Review* 24, no. 2 (Fall 2009): 39–52; and Lisa Kahaleole Hall, "Navigating Our Own 'Sea of Islands': Remapping a Theoretical Space for Hawaiian Women and Indigenous Feminism," *Wicazo Sa Review* 24, no. 2 (Fall 2009): 15–38.

31. See Martha Acklesberg, *Free Women of Spain: Anarchism and the Struggle for the Emancipation of Women* (Oakland, CA: AK Press, 2004).

32. Mujeres Creando, "An Interview with Mujeres Creando," in Dark Star Collective, *Quiet Rumours*, 126.

33. Mishuana Goeman, "Notes Towards a Native Feminist Spatial Practice," *Wicazo Sa Review* 24, no 2. (Fall 2009): 170.

34. Peggy Kornegger, "Anarchism: The Feminist Connection," in Dark Star Collective, *Quiet Rumors*, 25–35.

35. See Lynn Farrow, "Feminism as Anarchism," and Marian Leighton, "Anarcho-Feminism and Louise Michel," also in Dark Star Collective, *Quiet Rumours*, 19–24, 47–51.

36. Julia Tanenbaum, "To Destroy Domination in All Its Forms: Anarcha-Feminist Theory, Organization and Action 1970–1978," *Perspectives on*

Anarchist Theory 29 (May 2016). Similarly, Carol Ehrlich has argued that "again, radical feminism and anarchist feminism have much more in common than either does with socialist feminism. Both work to build alternative institutions, and both take the politics of the personal very seriously. Socialist feminists are less inclined to think either is particularly vital to revolutionary practice." Carol Ehrlich, "Socialism, Anarchism, and Feminism," 58.

37. See Nancy Hartsock, *Money, Sex, and Power: Towards a Feminist Historical Materialism* (Boston: Northeastern University Press, 1985).

38. Kornegger, "Anarchism: The Feminist Connection," 31.

39. See Maya J. Golderberg, "The Problem of Exclusion in Feminist Theory and Politics: A Metaphysical Investigation into Constructing a Category of 'Woman,'" *Journal of Gender Studies* 16, no. 2 (July 2007): 139–53.

40. See Angela Davis, *Women, Race and Class* (New York: Vintage Books, 1983).

41. See Barker, "Indigenous Feminisms."

42. See Simpson, "From White into Red: Captivity Narratives as Alchemies of Race and Citizenship" and "The State Is a Man: Theresa Spence, Loretta Saunders and the Gender of Settler Sovereignty"; Million, *Therapeutic Nations*; and Sarah Deer, *The Beginning and End of Rape: Confronting Sexual Violence in Native America* (Minneapolis: University of Minnesota, 2015).

43. Jennifer Denetdale, "Securing Navajo National Boundaries: War, Patriotism, Tradition, and the Diné Marriage Act of 2005," *Wicazo Sa Review* 24, no. 2 (Fall 2009): 131–48.

44. See Allen, *The Sacred Hoop*; Crow Dog, *Lakota Woman*; and Devon Abbott Mihesuah, *Indigenous American Women: Decolonization, Empowerment, and Activism* (Lincoln: University of Nebraska Press, 2003), especially her chapters on the murder of Anna Mae Pictou-Aquash.

45. There has been some writing about this dealing with the anarcho-sexism of classical anarchist thinkers, most notably Proudhon, but this doesn't directly address the particularities of anarchism in the contemporary moment. For an example of such analysis, see Sharif Gemie, "Anarchism and Feminism: A Historical Survey," *Women's History Review* 5, no. 3 (1996): 417–444.

46. Shannon and Rogue, "Refusing to Wait: Anarchism and Intersectionality," 2009, http://www.anarkismo.net/article/14923.

47. "About INCITE!," INCITE!, https://incite-national.org/history/.

48. Rogue and Volcano, "Insurrection at the Intersection," in Dark Star Collective, *Quiet Rumours*, 45.

49. Rogue and Volcano, "Insurrection at the Intersection," 45. See also Dorothy Roberts, *Killing the Black Body: Race, Reproduction, and the Meaning of Liberty* (New York: Vintage, 2017); and Andrea Smith, *Conquest: Sexual Violence and American Indian Genocide* (Boston: South End Press, 2005).

50. Rogue and Volcano, "Insurrection at the Intersection," 45–46.

51. Jodi A. Byrd, *The Transit of Empire: Indigenous Critiques of Colonialism* (Minneapolis: University of Minnesota Press, 2011), xxiii.

52. For more on the comparative approach to Black and Native categories and blood quantum in US history, see Sissteon Wahpeton Oyate scholar Kim TallBear, *Native American DNA: Tribal Belonging and the False Promise of Genetic Science* (Minneapolis: University of Minnesota Press, 2013).

53. In addition to Deer, *The Beginning and End of Rape*, see Jane Lawrence, "The Indian Health Service and the Sterilization of Native American Women," *American Indian Quarterly* 24, no. 3 (Summer 2000): 400–19.

54. Native Youth Sexual Health Network, "Environmental Health and Reproductive Justice," http://www.nativeyouthsexualhealth.com/environmentalviolenceandreproductivejustice.html.

55. See Ned Blackhawk, *Violence Over the Land: Indians and Empires in the Early American West* (Cambridge, MA: Harvard University Press, 2008).

56. For more on the history of boarding schools, see Brenda Child, *Boarding School Seasons: American Indian Families, 1900–1940* (Lincoln: University of Nebraska Press, 2000).

57. Mishuana Goeman, *Mark My Words: Native Women Mapping Our Nations* (Minneapolis: University of Minnesota Press, 2013).

58. Rogue and Shannon, "Refusing to Wait."

59. For descriptions and critiques of transexclusive radical feminism, see Julia Serrano, *Excluded: Making Feminist and Queer Movements More Exclusive* (New York: Seal Press, 2013).

60. Rogue and Shannon, "Refusing to Wait," original emphasis.

61. See Naomi Klein's interview with Simpson, "Dancing the World into Being: A Conversation with Idle No More's Leanne Simpson," *Yes! Magazine*, March 5, 2013, http://www.yesmagazine.org/peace-justice/dancing-the-world-into-being-a-conversation-with-idle-no-more-leanne-simpson; and Glen Sean Coulthard, *Red Skin, White Masks: Rejecting the Colonial Politics of Recognition* (Minneapolis: University of Minnesota Press, 2014).

62. Martha Acklesberg, "Preface," in Daring et al., *Queering Anarchism*, 1.

63. Jamie Heckert and Richard Clemison, "Ethics, Relationships, and Power: An Introduction," in *Anarchism and Sexuality: Ethics, Relationships,*

and Power, ed. Jamie Heckert and Richard Clemison (New York: Routledge, 2011), 1–22.

64. In some cases, this has led to an antagonistic relationship with questions of race, gender, and sexuality within the contours of anarchist politics. For instance, in *From Bakunin to Lacan: Anti-Authoritarianism and the Dislocation of Power*, foundational postanarchist theorist Saul Newman laments: "We seem to be surrounded today by a multitude of new identities and lifestyle politics—'S/M' gays, 'separatist' lesbians, 'transgenders,' etc. . . . to think solely in terms of the oppression of women by men, gays by straights, blacks by whites, etc., is to severely limit our political possibilities. Perhaps this is why there certain inanity and definite sense of boredom that goes along with identity politics, with waving the banners of 'feminist struggles,' 'gay struggles,' 'black struggles' . . . Why is it that when someone is asked to talk about radical politics today one inevitably refers to this same tired, old list of struggles and identities" (171). This approach has not been popular in the broader literature on postanarchism and is not widely taken up by any other authors, though Newman remains an influential figure in the development of postanarchism.

65. For example, Iwona Janicka offers an in-depth analysis of Judith Butler's theory of performativity through the lens of mimesis. See Janicka, *Theorizing Contemporary Anarchism: Solidarity, Mimesis, and Radical Social Change* (New York: Bloomsbury Academic, 2017).

66. Ryan Conrad, "Gay Marriage and Queer Love," in Daring et al., *Queering Anarchism*, 19–20.

67. J. Rogue, "De-essentializing Anarchist Feminism: Lessons from the Transfeminist Movement," in Daring et al., *Queering Anarchism*, 25–32.

68. Scott Lauria Morgensen, *Spaces between Us*, 1.

69. Morgensen, *Spaces between Us*, 2.

70. sallydarity, "Gender Sabotage," in Daring et al., *Queering Anarchism*, 47.

71. See Amy Kaplan, "Manifest Domesticity," *American Literature* 70, no. 3 (September 1998): 581–606; Sarah Deer, "Decolonizing Rape Law: A Native Feminist Synthesis of Safety and Sovereignty," *Wicazo Sa Review* 24, no. 2 (Fall 2009): 149–67; Scott Morgensen, "Cutting to the Roots of Colonial Masculinity," in *Indigenous Men and Masculinities*, ed. Kim Anderson and Robert Alexander Innes (Manitoba: University of Manitoba Press, 2015); and Rayna Green, "The Pocahontas Perplex: The Image of Indian Women in American Culture," *Massachusetts Review* 16, no. 4 (October 1975).

72. sallydarity, "Gender Sabotage," in Daring et al., *Queering Anarchism*, 45.

73. Tuck and Yang "Decolonization Is Not a Metaphor," 3.

74. For example: "This appreciation [for processes and relationships] is one of many inheritances from anarchist, feminist, and indigenous traditions for which we are deeply grateful" (Hecker and Clemison, "Ethics, Relationships, Power: An Introduction," 2); "Queer peasants were disciplined by means of terror in Europe in particular . . . but also during colonization of the Americas as homosexuals and *two-spirit* people were killed, and the continuation of these identities and practices were averted or forced underground" (sallydarity, "Gender Sabotage," 47).

75. L. Cornum, "First Women, Then the Nation: Confronting Colonial Gender Violence," *LIES: A Journal of Materialist Feminism* 2 (August 2015): 79.

76. Black Rose Anarchist Federation, "Internationalism and Imperialism," http://blackrosefed.org/points-of-unity/internationalism-imperialism/.

Chapter 4

1. Deborah Miranda, "Dildos, Hummingbirds, and Driving Her Crazy: Searching for American Indian Women's Love Poetry and Erotics," *Frontiers: A Journal of Women's Studies* 23, no. 2 (2002): 145.

2. Molly McGlennan, *Creative Alliances: The Transnational Designs of Native Women's Poetry* (Norman: University of Oklahoma Press, 2014), 5.

3. McGlennen, *Creative Alliances*, 5.

4. Sarah Dowling, *Translingual Poetics: Writing Personhood under Settler Colonialism* (Iowa City: University of Iowa Press, 2018).

5. Dowling, *Translingual Poetics*, 152.

6. Dowling, *Translingual Poetics*, 152.

7. James H. Cox, *Muting White Noise: Native American and European American Novel Traditions* (Norman: University of Oklahoma Press, 2006), 12.

8. For instance, in his chapter on "red readings" and American literature, Cox analyzes books by American men and women, but the theoretical method he uses is based mostly on the work of Louis Owens, Gerald Vizenor, Thomas King, and Sherman Alexie, with some discussion of Elizabeth Cook-Lynn's work as well. See his chapter "Unmapping the Conquest: Red Readings of the European American Novel Tradition," in *Muting White Noise*, 203–50.

9. Joshua Bellin, *The Demon of the Continent: Indians and the Shaping of American Literature* (Philadelphia: University of Pennsylvania Press, 2008).

10. Bellin, *Demon of the Continent*, 4.

11. Renée L. Bergland, *The National Uncanny: Indian Ghosts and American Subjects* (Hanover: University of New England Press, 2000): 5.

12. Bergland, *The National Uncanny*, 5.

13. Mark Rifkin, *Settler Common Sense: Queerness and Everyday Colonialism in the American Renaissance*. (Minneapolis: University of Minnesota Press, 2014), 6.

14. Rifkin, *Settler Common Sense*.

15. Rifkin, *Settler Common Sense*, 7.

16. Rifkin, *Settler Common Sense*, xvii. My emphasis.

17. Rifkin, *Settler Common Sense*, xviii. Original emphasis.

18. Rifkin argues, for instance, that *House of Seven Gables*, *Walden*, and *Pierre* confront "dominant conceptions of household and family formation and feature identities, practices, and spaces deemed perverse, opening room for envisioning modes of occupancy and self-identification not dependent on state authorization" (*Settler Common Sense, xviii*).

19. Angele Teresa Morrill, "Toward a Native Feminist Reading Methodology," PhD diss. (University of California, San Diego, 2016), 1.

20. Morrill, "Toward a Native Feminist Reading Methodology," 13.

21. Pratt, "Arts of the Contact Zone," *Profession* (1991): 35.

22. Morrill, "Toward a Native Feminist Reading Methodology," 3.

23. Tuck and Ree. "A Glossary of Haunting," 640.

24. Heid E. Erdrich, *National Monuments* (East Lansing: Michigan State University Press, 2008), 94.

25. Cheryl Savageau, "The People and the Land," in *The Women's Review of Books* 27, no. 2 (March 2010): 26–27.

26. Robert Frost, "The Gift Outright," in *Robert Frost: Collected Poems, Prose, and Plays*, ed. Richard Poirier and Mark Richardson (New York: Penguin, 1995), 316.

27. Erdrich, *National Monuments*, 31.

28. Frost, "The Gift Outright," 316.

29. Erdrich, *National Monuments*, 31.

30. "Here I use it in two senses: first, that indigeneity itself is enduring—that the operative logic of settler colonialism may be to "eliminate the native," as the late English scholar Patrick Wolfe brilliantly theorized, but that indigenous peoples exist, resist, and persist; and second, that settler colonialism is a structure that endures indigeneity, as it holds out against it." J. Kēhaulani Kauanui, "'A Structure, Not an Event': Settler Colonialism and Enduring Indigeneity," *Lateral: Journal of the Cultural Studies Association* 5, no. 1 (2016), doi: https://csalateral.org/issue/5-1/forum-alt-humanities-settler-colonialism-enduring-indigeneity-kauanui/.

31. Of DNA evidence, she observes, "Dineh in documentaries scoff DNA evidence off. / They landed late, but canyons spoke them home. / Nomadic Turkish horse tribes they don't know." Referring to the Bering Strait theory, she writes, "Could be cousins, left on the land bridge, / contrary to popular belief, that was a two way-toll. / In any case we'd claim them, give them some place to stay." Erdrich, *National Monuments*, 31.

32. Rayna Green, "The Pocahontas Perplex: The Image of Indian Women in American Culture," *Massachusetts Review* 16, no. 4 (Autumn 1975), 703.

33. Erdrich, *National Monuments*, 31.

34. Erdrich, *National Monuments*.

35. Erdrich, *National Monuments*.

36. Goeman, *Mark My Words*, 13.

37. John F. Kennedy, introduction to William Brandon, *The American Heritage Book of Indians* (New York: Simon & Schuster, 1961)..

38. M. Annette Jaimes, "The Hollow Icon: An American Indian Analysis of the Kennedy Myth and Federal Indian Policy," *Wicazo Sa Review* 6, no. 1 (Spring 1990): 34.

39. For more on Federal Indian Policy during the Kennedy and Johnson administrations, see Thomas Clarkin, *Federal Indian Policy in the Kennedy and John Administrations 1961–1969* (Albuquerque: University of New Mexico Press, 2001). For more on the Kinzua Damn, see Joy A. Bilharz, *The Allegany Senecas and Kinzua Dam: Forced Relocation Through Two Generations* (Omaha: University of Nebraska Press, 2002); and Paul Lamont's film *Lake of Betrayal* (2017).

40. For more on the history of the obscenity trial, see Jake Ehrlich, *Howl of the Censor: The Four Letter Word on Trial* (London: Nourse Books, 1956); and the 2010 film *Howl*, directed by Rob Epstein and Jeffrey Friedman.

41. For a more complete history and analysis of the cultural significance of Ginsberg's "Howl," see Johan Raskin, *American Scream: Allen Ginsberg's* Howl *and the Making of the Beat Generation* (Berkeley: University of California Press, 2004).

42. See Rogers's interview with CBC News, "Janet Rogers on 'Totem Poles and Railroads,'" *CBC News*, September 11, 2017, http://www.cbc.ca/news/janet-rogers-on-totem-poles-and-railroads-1.4277258.

43. For more on the exclusion of women in the history of the Beat Generation, see *Women of the Beat Generation: The Writers, Artists, and Muses at the Heart of a Revolution*, ed. Brenda Knight (Berkeley: Conari Press, 1996); and Amy L. Friedman, "'Being Here as Hard as I Could': The Beat Generation Women Writers," in *Discourse* 20, no. 1/2 (Winter and Spring 1998): 229–44.

44. Janet Rogers, "Bowel," in *Totem Poles and Railroads*, n.p.

45. Rogers, "Bowel, n.p."

46. Rogers, "Bowel, n.p."

47. See Scott Morgensen, "Cutting to the Roots of Colonial Masculinity," in *Indigenous Men and Masculinities*, ed. Robert Alexander Innes and Kim Anderson (Winnipeg: University of Manitoba Press, 2015); and Amy Kaplan "Manifest Domesticity," *American Literature* 70, no. 3 (1998): 581.

48. Ernest Smith, "Beat Poets," in *Men and Masculinities: A Social, Cultural, and Historical Encyclopedia*, ed. Michael Kimmel and Amy Aronson (Santa Barbara: ABC-CLIO, 2003): 70–71. See also Dagmar Van Engen, "Howling Masculinity: Queer Social Change in Allen Ginsburg's Poetry," Gender, Sexuality, and Urban Spaces: Conference 2011, Working Papers Collection 2012, MIT, Cambridge, MA, March 2011, http://web.mit.edu/Gcws/pdf/2012ConfPublication/Papers/Drafts/VanEngen.pdf.

49. Audra Simpson, "The State Is a Man: Theresa Spence, Loretta Saunders, and the Gender of Settler Sovereignty," *Theory & Event* 19, no. 4 (2016).

50. Rayna Green, "The Pocahontas Perplex: The Image of Indian Women in American Culture," *Massachusetts Review* 16, no. 4 (October 1975): 703.

51. Rebecca K. Jager, *Malinche, Pocahontas, and Sacajawea: Indian Women as Cultural Intermediaries and National Symbols* (Norman: University of Oklahoma Press, 2015), 9.

52. Mishuana Goeman, "Notes Towards a Native Feminist Spatial Practice," *Wicazo Sa Review* 24, no. 2 (October 2009): 13

53. Jager, *Malinche, Pocahontas, and Sacajawea*, 8.

54. Dian Million, *Therapeutic Nations* (Tucson: University of Arizona Press, 2013). 3.

55. Million, *Therapeutic Nations*, 46.

56. As Jager observes, "Pocahontas and Sacajawea were originally mythologized to clarify how Natives and Europeans came together willingly. Nationalists in . . . the United States depicted a frontier experience that gave the illusion of a united citizenry; Native Americans and Euro-Americans endured the frontier together, and this shared experience became the ideological foundation for nationhood" (Jager, *Malinche, Pocahontas, and Sacajawea*, 9).

57. Rogers, *Totem Poles and Railroads*, n.p.

58. Rogers, *Totem Poles and Railroads, n.p.*

59. For more about Pocahontas's time in England, see Coll Thrush, *Indigenous London: Native Travelers at the Heart of Empire* (New Haven, CT: Yale University Press, 2016).

60. As Hunt argues, "structural violence is concealed through the naturalization of these spaces as degenerate, such that the places of 'Indians' can only be visible as spaces of expected violence." See Hunt's published roundtable with Cindy Holmes and Amy Piedalue : "Violence, Colonialism, and Space: Towards a Decolonizing Dialogue," *ACME: An International Journal for Critical Geographies* 14, no. 2 (2015): 12.

61. Rogers, *Totem Poles and Railroads*, n.p.

62. Rogers, *Totem Poles and Railroads, n.p.*

63. "The powerfully symbolic Indian woman, as Queen and Princess, has been with us since 1575 when she appeared to stand for the New World . . . Europeans easily adopted the Indian as the iconographic representative of the Americas"; see Green, "The Pocahontas Perplex," 701. Jager's book "deals with the symbolic roles of Malinche, Pocahontas, and Sacagawea in the ongoing construction of a satisfying national creation story. Analysis of their myths reveals how sensitive question regarding national origin, race, and gender have been negotiated in theory. Their pliable legends have been employed to justify or condemn European colonization, to explain Indian defeat or celebrate indigenous prehistory, and to serve as a forum for recurring discussions of race and gender"; see Jager, *Malinche, Pocahontas, and Sacagawea*, 6.

64. Goeman, *Mark My Words*, 205.

65. Williams and Ginsberg, of course, had a close relationship, perhaps best described as that of a mentor and a mentee. Williams eventually wrote the introduction to the first edition of *Howl and Other Poems* and included letters from Ginsberg in his epic five-volume collage poem *Paterson*.

66. William Carlos Williams, "To Elsie," in *The Collected Poems of Williams Carlos Williams, Volume 1, 1909–1939*, ed. A. Walton Litz and Christopher MacGowan (Cambridge, NY: New Directions, 1991), 317.

67. In their endnotes for *The Collected Poems of William Carlos Williams*, editors A. Walton Litz and Christopher MacGowan write a single line about Elsie: "Elsie was a retarded [*sic*] nursemaid from the State Orphanage who worked for the Williams family after Kathleen McBride left" (504).

68. For more on an analysis of the gendered analysis of "To Elsie," see A. Kinnahan's discussion in *Poetics of the Feminine: Authority and Literary Tradition in William Carlos Williams, Mina Loy, Denise Levertov, and Kathleen Fraser* (Cambridge: Cambridge University Press, 1994).

69. "The U." here refers to the shorthand used by locals, like Erdrich, to refer to the University of Minnesota, Minneapolis. However, this also speaks to a tripartite level of secondary education: community college, public state-centered university, and elite private university. The point is, it

doesn't matter at what level of prestige Elsie gains her education in American literature—Williams's presumptions about the symbolic work of Native women carry throughout.

70. Heid Erdrich, *National Monuments*, 18. As Roger Gilbert has argued, Williams's use of "some" here is "devastating, because it identifies individual and class in a way that leaves no room for the saving difference of selfhood . . . We may well conclude that Williams himself does as much to rob Elsie of selfhood as her culture . . . Yet it is also Williams, like the state, who has plucked Elsie out of her original context, who has made her an example, a special case, part anomaly and part specimen." Roger Gilbert "Some Parts of a World: Example as Trope in American Poetry," *Western Humanities Review* 48, no. 2 (Summer 1994): 144.

71. Erdrich, *National Monuments*, 18, original emphasis.

72. Erdrich *National Monuments*, 18, original emphasis.

73. For more on the "naturalization of violence," see Cindy Holmes, Sarah Hunt, and Amy Piedalue, "Violence, Colonialism, and Space: Towards a Decolonizing Dialogue," *ACME* (2015): 539–70.

74. Erdrich, *National Monuments*, 37.

75. Erdrich, *National Monuments*, 37.

76. Erdrich, *National Monuments*, 37.

77. Quoted in Erdrich, *National Monuments*, 25. For a critical engagement with Owen's work from a Native feminist perspective, see Cheryl Suzak, "Land Claims, Identity Claims: Mapping Indigenous Feminism in Literary Criticism and in Winona LaDuke's *Last Standing Woman*," in *Reasoning Together*, ed. Craig S. Womack, Daniel Heath Justice, and Christopher B. Teuton (Norman: University of Oklahoma Press), 169–92.

78. Erdrich, *National Monuments*, 25.

79. The stanza before this passage reads:

> But she wouldn't send anyone back across the ocean.
> Which ancestor would she let go? The one who lent her
> Her long second toe? Or the ancient one whose blood
> made hers the universal donor, safe for all others?

80. Erdrich, *National Monuments*, 18.

81. For more on his statements to authorities, see Katie May, "The Cormier Wiretaps: Crown and Defence Interpretations of Wiretap Audio," *Winnipeg Free Press*, February 21, 2018, https://www.winnipegfreepress.com/local/the-cormier-wiretaps----and-the-crown-and-defence-interpretations-474736623.html; Cameron MacLean, "Raymond Cormier's Defence Tried to Have Case Thrown Out Due to Lack of Evidence,"

CBC News, February 21, 2018, http://www.cbc.ca/news/canada/manitoba/raymond-cormier-trial-judge-instructs-jury-tina-fontaine-1.4544214.

82. Aimeé Craft, "Tina Fontaine's Story Shows There Is No Real Justice for Indigenous People in Canada," *Globe and Mail*, February 23, 2018, https://www.theglobeandmail.com/opinion/tina-fontaines-story-shows-there-is-no-real-justice-for-indigenous-people-in-canada/article38086537/.

83. Deer, *The Beginning and End of Rape*, 163.

84. Leanne Betasamosake Simpson, *As We Have Always Done: Indigenous Freedom Through Radical Resurgence* (Minneapolis: University of Minnesota Press, 2017), 41.

85. See Simpson's collection of short stories *Islands of Decolonial Love: Stories and Songs* (Winnipeg: Arbeiter Ring, 2013).

86. Leanne Betasamosake Simpson, Twitter, February 23, 2018, 1:48 p.m., https://twitter.com/betasamosake/status/967154280892452864, accessed April 6, 2018.

87. Rogers, "Pocahontas," in *Totem Poles and Railroads*, n.p.

88. Tuck and Yang, "Decolonization Is Not a Metaphor," 36.

Chapter 5

1. See Kaplan, *The Anarchy of Empire in the Making of US Culture* (Cambridge, MA: Harvard University Press, 2005), and *Cultures of United States Imperialism*, ed. Amy Kaplan and Donald E. Pease (Durham, NC: Duke University Press, 1994).

2. For a history of the IWW with a global focus, see *Wobblies of the World: A Global History of the IWW*, ed. Peter Coe, David Struthers, and Kenyon Zimmer (London: Pluto Press, 2017); Ruth Kinna, "Kropotkin's Theory of the State: A Transnational Approach," in *Reassessing the Transnational Turn: Scales of Analysis in Anarchist and Syndicalist Studies, ed. Constance Bantman and Bert Altena* (New York: Routledge, 2015): 43–61; Bert Altena, "A Networking Historian: The Transnational, the National, and the Patriotic in and around Max Nettlau's *Geschichte der Anarchie*," in Bantman and Altena, *Reassessing the Transnational Turn*, 62–80.

3. For instance, see Dongyoun Hwang, *Anarchism in Korea: Independence, Transnationalism, and the Question of National Development 1919–1984* (Albany: State University of New York Press, 2016); and Arif Dirlik, *Anarchism in the Chinese Revolution* (Berkeley: University of California Press, 1993).

4. Thomas Friedman "Senseless in Seattle," *New York Times*, December 1, 1999, https://archive.nytimes.com/www.nytimes.com/library/opinion/friedman/120199frie.html. This misreading of anarchist politics, which

leads Friedman to refer to anti-WTO protesters as "a Noah's ark of flat-earth advocates," is made especially ironic in the contemporary moment, since Friedman argued six years later that the dawn of the twenty-first century is characterized by a flattening of the world. See Thomas Friedman, *The World is Flat: A Brief History of the Twenty-First Century* (New York: Farrar, Straus, and Giroux, 2005)

5. David Graeber, "The New Anarchists," *New Left Review* 13 (January/February 2002): 63.

6. Paul Routledge, "'Our Resistance Will Be as Transnational as Capital': Convergence Space and Strategy in Globalising Resistance," *GeoJournal* 52, no. 1 (2000): 25–33.

7. Graeber, "New Anarchists," 65–66.

8. As Klein states in an interview during the protests at the Third Summit of the Americas held in Quebec in 2001: "I call it a movement just for shorthand. Really it's a movement of movements or coalition of coalitions. It's lots of movements and campaigns that converge every once in a while. It converged in Seattle during the World Trade Organization meeting, converged in Washington, [in] Prague, now in Quebec City, because there is a common target in a particular economic model that is reflected in trade agreements like the FTAA [Free Trade Areas of the Americas] and in World Bank and IMF policies and the types of ideas that come out of the Davos Economic Forum. But it's not one movement in the sense that everybody is part of a political party organized into neat little cells and locals. I mean, here we are in Quebec City and calling it 'the protest.' 'How do you think the protest is going?' There are thousands of autonomous protests going on in Quebec City that all happen to be here at the same time. It's kind of like this web that all comes together in one place, and it has to do with the fact that there are common themes that run through all of the campaigns that are converging in Quebec this week. I think the best way I would describe it is that there is a common concern about the privatization of every aspect of human life. So you have people entering this movement from lots of different places, but it's that theme you hear over and over again." Naomi Klein, interview with *Commanding Heights*, PBS, April 21, 2001, http://www.pbs.org/wgbh/commandingheights/shared/minitext/int_naomiklein.html.

9. The "What We Do" page on the World Bank's website reads: "Three priorities guide our work with countries to end poverty and boost prosperity for the poorest people. Helping create sustainable economic growth, the surest path out of poverty. Investing in people, through access to health care, education, water and sanitation, and energy. Building resilience to

shocks and threats that can roll back decades of progress." https://www.worldbank.org/en/what-we-do.

10. Jason Adams, *Non-Western Anarchisms* (Fordsburg, South Africa: Zabalaza Books, 2000), 1.

11. Adams divides his text into four sections, one each on Asian, African, Latin American, and Middle Eastern Anarchisms. Each of these is subdivided into nation-states, with the lone exception of "Igbo" being placed alongside "Egypt, Libya, Nigeria, and South Africa." See Adams, *Non-Western Anarchisms*.

12. For more on the works of such groups, see the interview with Ernesto Aguilar of APOC conducted by The Female Species, available at http://www.coloursofresistance.org/596/interview-with-ernesto-aguilar-of-the-anarchist-people-of-color-apoc/.

13. *The Black Anarchism Reader*, ed. Black Rose Anarchist Federation (self-pub., 2017).

14. "The very means of class control by the rich is the least understood. White supremacy is more than just a set of ideas or prejudices. It is national oppression. Yet to most white people, the term conjures up images of the Nazis or Ku Klux Klan rather than the system of white skin privileges that really under girds the Capitalist system in the U.S. Most white people, Anarchists included, believe in essence that Black people are 'the same' as whites, and that we should just fight around 'common issues ' rather than deal with 'racial matters,' if they see any urgency in dealing with the matter at all. Some will not raise it in such a blunt fashion, they will say that 'class issues should take precedence,' but it means the same thing. They believe it's possible to put off the struggle against white supremacy until after the revolution, when in fact there will be no revolution if white supremacy is not attacked and defeated first." Lorenzo Kom'boa Ervin, "Anarchism and the Black Revolution," in Black Rose Anarchist Federation, *Black Anarchism Reader*, 18. See also Zoé Samduzi and William C. Anderson, *As Black As Resistance: Finding the Conditions for Liberation* (Oakland, CA: AK Press, 2018).

15. From the introduction to *Black Flame*: "For anarchists, a worker in Bangalore has more in common with a worker in Omsk, Johannesburg, Mexico City, or Seoul than with an Indian elite." See Lucian Van Der Walt and Michael Schmidt, *Black Flame: The Revolutionary Class Politics of Anarchism and Syndicalism* (Oakland, CA: AK Press, 2009), 7.

16. The evidence that Schmidt has participated for years in fascist and white supremacist communities both in South Africa and globally were published by Alexander Reid Ross and Joshua Stephens in a four-part series:

"About Schmidt: How a White Nationalist Seduced Anarchists Around the World," *Medium*, October 12 (chapter 1), October 14 (chapter 2), October 16 (chapter 3), October 20 (chapter 4), 2015.

17. For instance, in the first installment of "About Schmidt," Ross and Stephens argue that the staunch commitment to platformism in which the authors rooted the overall argument of *Black Flame* was, for Schmidt, already embedded in his "attempts to reconstruct the platform" since it was here that he seemed to see "himself as leading the whites in laying out the 'task' of revolution for the 'ideologically less convinced' people of color whose 'inactivity' had brought about the failure of the anarchist movement in South Africa" (Ross and Stephens, "Chapter 1"). That is, by drawing extensively on Schmidt's own political writings leading up to the publication of *Black Flame*, Ross and Stephens demonstrate how his desire to assert the necessity of a rigid version of anarchist platformism was deeply rooted in a paternalistic belief that white anarchists had to use the platform in order to restore anarchism following its dilution at the hands of people of color who he saw as less intellectually capable.

18. See Joel Olsen, *The Abolition of White Democracy* (Minneapolis: University of Minnesota Press, 2004); and Alexander Reid Ross, *Against the Fascist Creep* (Oakland, CA: AK Press, 2017).

19. Notes from Everywhere Collective, *We Are Everywhere: The Irresistible Rise of Global Anti-Capitalism* (London: Verso, 2003): 15. The Zapatista uprising has also been the focus of some prominent anarchist texts like John Holloway, *Change the World Without Taking Power: the Meaning of Revolution Today* (London: Pluto Press, 2002); and Lynd and Grubačić, *Wobblies and Zapatistas*.

20. James Davis and Paul Rowley, "Internationalism Against Globalization: A Map of Resistance," in *The Battle of Seattle: The New Challenge to Capitalist Globalization*, ed. Eddie Yuen, George Katsiaficas, and Daniel Burton Rose (New York: Soft Skull Press, 2001), 25.

21. Davis and Rowley, "Internationalism against Globalization," 25.

22. Davis and Rowley, "Internationalism against Globalization," 25

23. Barry Maxwell and Raymond Craib, eds., *No Gods, No Masters, No Peripheries: Global Anarchisms* (Oakland, CA: PM Press, 2015), 11.

24. *Barry Maxwell, "Afterword, Beginning with 'A,'" in Maxwell and Craib, No Gods, No Masters,* 11.

25. *Maxwell, "Afterword, Beginning with 'A,'"* 11.

26. In the collection, Adrienne Hurley offers an analysis of the linkages between professors and police as agents of repression, but notes that her "examples are drawn from contexts I know in Japan and Québec." And

though she goes on to say that, despite this focus, "none [of her examples] are representative of anything especially Japanese or Québécois/e," her discussion of police includes no specific discussion of Black Lives Matter or any other public discourse that might connect it specifically to Maxwell's invocation of Eric Garner's murder in New York. Hurley, "Let's Ditch School and Be Unmanageable," in Maxwell and Craib, *No Gods, No Masters*, 116.

27. See Silvia Rivera Cusicanqui, "The Ch'ixi Identity of a Mestizo: Regarding an Anarchist Manifesto of 1929," in Maxwell and Craib, *No Gods, No Masters*,12–21; Hilary Klein, "The Zapatista Movement: Blending Indigenous Tradition and Revolution Praxis," in Maxwell and Craib, *No Gods, No Masters*, 22–43; and Maia Ramnath, "No Gods, No Masters, No Brahmins: An Anarchist Inquiry on Caste, Race, and Indigeneity in India," in Maxwell and Craib, *No Gods, No Masters*, 44–79.

28. Kevin Brunyeel, *The Third Space of Sovereignty: The Postcolonial Politics of U.S.-Indigenous Relations* (Minneapolis: University of Minnesota Press, 2007), 2–6.

29. Byrd, *Transit of Empire*, xxii.

30. Byrd, *Transit of Empire*, xiii.

31. For instance, see Megan Specia's profile of Robert Grodt who worked as a medic at the Occupy Wall Street protests in 2011 before traveling to Rojava, where he was killed. Megan Specia, "First, a Symbol of Occupy Wall Street. Then He Waded Into Syria," *New York Times*, July 12, 2017; see also Seth Harp, "The Anarchists vs. The Islamic State," *Rolling Stone*, February 14, 2017.

32. Michelle Goldberg, "American Leftists Need to Pay More Attention to Rojava," *Slate*, November 25, 2015, http://www.slate.com/blogs/xx_factor/2015/11/25/rojava_is_a_radical_experiment_in_democracy_in_northern_syria_american_leftists.html.

33. She quotes, "Syrian queer academic-activists Fadi Saleh," who wonders "[why] 'anarchists' go to a country devastated by war and chaos for years now and say they want to spread anarchism," noting that such a practice is "not only ridiculous, but also unethical and quite arrogant, because in a country that has been fighting for some sense of stability, peace, and belonging for years, their mission is nothing short of abhorrent." Razan Ghazzawi "Decolonising Syria's So-called ' Queer Liberation,'" *Al Jazeera*, August 5, 2017, https://www.aljazeera.com/indepth/opinion/2017/08/decolonising-syria-called-queer-liberation-170803110403979.html.

34. "Response by a Syrian Anarchist to the First of May Statement on Syria," libcom.org, September 17, 2013, https://libcom.org/news/response-syrian-anarchist-first-may-statement-syria-17092013.

35. Constance Bantman and Bert Altena, "Introduction: Problematizing Scales of Analysis in Network-Based Social Movements," in Bantman and Altena, *Reassessing the Transnational Turn*, 6.

36. David Turcato, "Nations without Borders: Anarchists and National Identity," in Bantman and Altena, *Reassessing the Transnational Turn*, 25–41.

37. See Murray Bookchin, "Nationalism and the 'National Question,'" *Democracy and Nature: The International Journey of Inclusive Democracy* 2, no. 2, issue 5 (1994); and Fredy Perlman, *The Continuing Appeal of Nationalism* (Detroit: Black and Red, 1985).

38. Turcato, "Nations without Borders," 40.

39. See Roger White, "Postcolonial Anarchism: Essays on Race, Repression, and Culture in Communities of Color, 1999–2004," *The Anarchist Library* (2005), https://theanarchistlibrary.org/library/roger-white-post-colonial-anarchism.pdf; J. Sakai, *Settlers: The Mythology of the White Proletarian from Mayflower to Modern* (Montreal: Kersplebedeb, 2014); and Ashanti Alston, "Beyond Nationalism But Not Without It," *Black Anarchism Reader*.

40. "Like the very ideas of nation and of a nationalistic ideology, anarchism comes to us from Europe." Ángel Cappelletti, *Anarchist in Latin America* (Oakland, CA: AK Press, 2018), 6.

41. Lina Sunseri, *Being Again of One Mind: Oneida Women and the Struggle for Decolonization* (Vancouver: UBC Press, 2010), 21.

42. Sunseri notes that the exact date of the forming of the initial Confederacy is still debated, though she notes that "the differences in opinion about the exact date can be partly due to the fact that one could view the formation of the league not as a single event but as a long process of resolution of the ongoing struggle between different nations, each joining the league at different times and/or having its own oral narrative of the coming of the Peacemaker. What I have been told personally by members of my community, Onyota:aka, is that the Peacemaker came before the Europeans arrived, hence supporting Porter's claim" (*Being Again of One Mind*, 52). See also Mohawk elder Tom Porter (Sakokweniónkwas), *And Grandma Said . . . Iroquois Teachings: As Passed Down Through the Oral Tradition* (New York: Xlibris Press, 2008).

43. Theresa McCarthy, *In/Divided Unity: Haudenosaunee Reclamation at Grand River* (Tucson: University of Arizona Press, 2016), 98.

44. Sunseri, *Being Again of One Mind*, 22–23.

45. Scott Lyons, *X-Marks: Native Signatures of Assent* (Minneapolis: University of Minnesota Press, 2010), 121.

46. Lyons, *X-Marks*, 119–21.

47. Boston Anarchists Against Militarism and Northeastern Federation of Anarchist Communists, "Why Anarchists Oppose Militarism and Nationalism," *Northeastern Anarchist* 3 (Fall 2001).

48. Leanne Betasamosake Simpson, "I Am Not a Nation-State," https://unsettlingamerica.wordpress.com/2013/11/06/i-am-not-a-nation-state/.

49. Uri Gordon, "Anarchism and Nationalism," in *The Brill Companion to Anarchism and Philosophy*, ed. Nathan Jun (Leiden: Brill Publishing, 2018), 197.

50. Anderson, *Under Three Flags*, 2.

51. Timothy Messer-Kruse, *The Haymarket Conspiracy: Transatlantic Anarchist Networks* (Champaign: University of Illinois Press, 2012), 4.

52. "Remembering the Haymarket Martyrs," accessed July 2019, https://www.iww.org/branches/US/CA/lagmb/lit/haymarket.shtml.

53. For more on the controversy surrounding Messer-Kruse's argument, see his article in the *Chronicle of Higher Education* regarding his attempts to edit the Wikipedia page on the Haymarket Affair. Timothy Messer-Kruse, "The 'Undue Weight' of Truth on Wikipedia," *Chronicle of Higher Education*, February 12, 2012. https://www.chronicle.com/article/The-Undue-Weight-of-Truth-on/130704.

54. For instance, in his foundational work *Demanding the Impossible: A History of Anarchism*, Peter Marshall argues that "seven anarchists were accused . . . despite the absence of evidence to link them to the bombing." Peter Marshall, *Demanding the Impossible: A History of Anarchism* (Oakland, CA: PM Press, 2010), 499.

55. "Remembering the Haymarket Martyrs," accessed July 2019, https://www.iww.org/branches/US/CA/lagmb/lit/haymarket.shtml.

56. Messer-Kruse, *Haymarket Conspiracy*, 2.

57. Messer Kruse, *Haymarket Conspiracy*, 2.

58. For instance, while Messer-Kruse acknowledges that "the prosecution took full advantage of the public's nativism and anti-leftist bias. Prosecutors festooned the courtroom with anarchist and socialist flags and banners seized from workers' meeting halls. Incendiary passages from anarchist books and newspapers were read into the record. As the trial progressed, an arsenal of weapons was heaped on tables in front of the jury, including loaded bombs," he dismisses the impact of these tactics on the verdict, arguing that they were "hardly necessary" since the prosecutor brought strong eyewitness and metallurgical evidence (Messer-Kruse, *Haymarket Conspiracy*, 2).

59. Messer-Kruse, *Haymarket Conspiracy*, 185.

60. Messer-Kruse, *Haymarket Conspiracy*, 4.

61. Messer-Kruse *Haymarket Conspiracy*, 4.

62. Goeman, *Mark My Words*, 91.

63. For more on the Dawes Act of 1887, see Katherine Ellinghaus, *Blood Will Tell: Native Americans and Assimilation Policy* (Lincoln: University of Nebraska Press, 2017); C. Joseph Genetin-Pilawa, *Crooked Paths to Allotment: The Fight over Federal Indian Policy after the Civil War* (Chapel Hill: University of North Carolina Press, 2014); and Carolyn Ross Johnson, *Cherokee Women in Crisis: Trail of Tears, Civil War, and Allotment, 1838–1907* (Tuscaloosa: University of Alabama Press, 2003).

64. Ned Blackhawk, *Violence Over the Land: Indians and Empires in the Early American West* (Cambridge, MA: Harvard University Press, 2008). See also Dee Brown *Bury My Heart at Wounded Knee: An Indian History of the American West* (New York: Open Road Media, 2012).

65. For more on the annexation of Hawai'i, see Tom Coffman, *Nation Within: The History of American Occupation in Hawai'i* (Durham, NC: Duke University Press, 1998).

66. Shari Huhndorf, *Mapping the Americas: The Transnational Politics of Contemporary Native Culture* (Ithaca, NY: Cornell University Press, 2009), 31.

67. "Haymarket resonates today more than it has at any other time in recent years. The original Haymarket affair of 1886 was part and parcel of a massive, national May Day rally and strike led, by and large, by America's immigrant workers. Today, precisely 120 years later, the May 1, 2006 Immigrant General Strike—also known as the 'Day without Immigrants ' and the 'Great American Boycott '—looks set to inherit and reinvigorate the legacy of Haymarket. Then, as now, employers launched an aggressive drive to undermine wages and living standards. In 1886 workers from around the world responded with an aggressive campaign of their own: an international movement for less work and more pay." Jonathan Cutler, interview by James Green, *All Things Considered*, NPR, April 29, 2006, https://www.npr.org/templates/story/story.php?storyId=5369420.

68. Peter Marshall, *Demanding the Impossible: A History of Anarchism* (Oakland, CA: PM Press, 2010), 393.

69. Messer-Kruse, *Haymarket Conspiracy*, 44.

70. Ryan Harvey, "Occupy Before and Beyond," in *We Are Many: Reflections on Movement Strategy from Occupation to Liberation*, ed. Kate Khatib, Margaret Killjoy, and Mike McGuire (Oakland, CA: AK Press, 2012), 123.

71. Tiara Na'puti and Michael Lujan Bevacqua, "Militarization and Resistance from Guåhan: Protecting and Defending Pågat," *American*

Quarterly 67, no. 3 (September 2015): 840. Here, they are drawing on Kevin Brunyeel's work on the "third space of sovereignty." See Kevin Brunyeel, *The Third Space of Sovereignty: the Postcolonial Politics of US-Indigenous Relations* (Minneapolis: University of Minnesota Press, 2007).

72. See Krishnadev Calamur, "Why North Korea Is Threatening Guam," *Atlantic*, August 8, 2017, https://www.theatlantic.com/international/archive/2017/08/north-korea-guam/536286/.

73. For instance, the third issue of *The Northeastern Anarchist*, published in fall 2001, is dedicated to the theme "Anarchists Against the War" and includes articles that focus predominantly on US intervention in Afghanistan. This focus makes sense giving the timing of the publication of this issue, but there is no discussion therein of the history of US militarism outside of the Middle East nor the connection of such militarism to the invasion of Afghanistan in 2001.

74. The limits of this approach to transnational anarchist history extend into the contemporary moment, where even interventions that bring together anarchist and Indigenous movements remain ancillary rather than transformative. Work like Richard Day's analysis of the Aboriginal Provisional Government (APG), Jeff Shantz's discussions of Haudenosaunee land reclamation projects at Six Nations, Jacqueline Lasky's consideration of the connections between Native sovereignty and anarchism, and Stephen Arthur's exploration of Haudenosaunee governance through an anarchist lens are not taken up in meaningful ways in the contemporary literature nor are they read through a transnational lens. See Richard Day, *Gramsci Is Dead*; Jeffrey Shantz, "Solidarity and the 6 Nation Struggle for Land," *Northeastern Anarchist* 12 (January 2007); and Jacqueline Lasky, "Indigenism, Anarchism, Feminism: An Emerging Framework for Exploring Post-Imperial Futures," *Affinities: A Journal of Radical Theory, Culture, Action* (August 2011): 3–36.

75. See Noelani Goodyear-Ka'ōpua, "'Kuleana Lāhui: Collective Responsibility for Hawaiian Nationhood in Activists' Praxis," *Affinities: A Journal of Theory, Culture, Action* (August 2011): 130–63. The work of the other scholars and activists mentioned were presented on the panel "Hawaiian Anarchist Praxis: Radically Reimagining Resurgence, Decolonizing and Rapprochement" at the 2016 meeting of the Native and Indigenous Studies Association at the University of Hawai'i, Mānoa, in Honolulu. Presentation topics were as follows: Baker, "Aloha 'Āina: Tool for Radical Anarchal Transformation or State-Centered Political Accommodation; Johnson, "Outlaw Sovereignties in the Break of the Event: Enacting Kanaka Maoli Anarcha-Indigenous Insurgence through Fugitive

Workshops; Maile, "Resurgent Refusals: Protecting Mauna a Wākea and Kanaka Maoli Decolonization"; and Kauanui, "Radical Rapprochement: Anarchism, Indigeneity, and Sovereignty."

76. Lasky, "Indigenism, Anarchism, Feminism."

77. Lisa Kahaleole Hall, "Strategies of Erasure: U.S. Colonialism and Native Hawaiian Feminism," *American Quarterly* 60, no. 2 (June 2008): 273–80.

78. As they ask, "How does the geographical basis that one adopts affect histories of the anarchist movement? What is missed when focusing on anarchism within certain state borders, and what is gained? The same questions apply to international or transnational, regional, and local angles of analysis. Conversely, can the anarchist and syndicalist movement be fully captured with a focus on transnational and national networks only? Should one start from the assumption of anarchism as a countercultural movement and a created space and follow its own rules, or does a particular geographical (or ethnic for that matter) scope add something to our understanding?" Bantman and Altena, *Reassessing the Transnational Turn*, 5.

79. Harsha Walia, *Undoing Border Imperialism* (Oakland, CA: AK Press), 14.

80. Walia, *Undoing Border Imperialism*, 253.

81. Kevin Brunyeel, *The Third Space of Sovereignty: The Postcolonial Politics of U.S.-Indigenous Relations* (Minneapolis: University of Minnesota Press, 2007), xiv.

82. Brunyeel, *The Third Space of Sovereignty*, 222.

Chapter 6

1. Robert Warrior, "Native American Scholarship and the Transnational Turn," *Cultural Studies Review* 15, no. 2 (2009): 119–30; and Chadwick Allen, "A Transnational Native American Studies? Why Not Studies That Are Transindigenous?," *Journal of Transnational American Studies* 4, no. 1 (2012).

2. Craig Womack, "A Single Decade: Book-Length Native Literary Criticism between 1986 and 1997," in *Reasoning Together*, ed. The Native Critics Collective (Norman: University of Oklahoma Press, 2008), 3–104.

3. Aloysha Goldstein, "Toward a Genealogy of the U.S. Colonial Present," in *Formations of United States Colonialism*, ed. Aloysha Goldstein (Durham, NC: Duke University Press, 2012), 2.

4. Alice Te Punga Somerville, *Once Were Pacific: Māori Connections to Oceania* (Minneapolis: University of Minnesota Press, 2012), xxviii.

5. See Hal M. Friedman, *Governing the American Lake: The U.S. Defense and Administration of the Pacific*, 1945–1947 (Lansing: Michigan State University Press, 2007).

6. Kaplan, *Anarchy of Empire*; Paul Lyons, *American Pacificism: Oceania in the U.S. Imagination* (New York: Routledge, 2006); and Yunte Huang, *Transpacific Imaginations: History, Literature, Counterpoetics* (Cambridge, MA: Harvard University Press, 2008).

7. The terminology for this approach to Native literary criticism has gone through numerous incarnations, including Womack's "American Indian Literary Separatism" and Womack, Weaver, and Warrior's "American Indian Literary Nationalism." Here, I refer to this critical approach as "Native literary nationalism" in fitting with my chosen nomenclature throughout the text and to draw clearer connections with my discussion of Native nationalisms in chapter 5. For Womack's discussion of "American Indian Literary Separatism," see Craig S. Womack, *Red on Red: American Indian Literary Separatism* (Minneapolis: University of Minnesota Press, 1999); and for more on "American Indian Literary Nationalism," see Jace Weaver, Craig S. Womack, and Robert Warrior, *American Indian Literary Nationalism* (Albuquerque: University of New Mexico Press, 2005).

8. Womack, *Red on Red*, 11.

9. Karin Amimoto Ingersoll, *Waves of Knowing: A Seascape Epistemology* (Durham, NC: Duke University Press, 2016), 27.

10. See Kenneth Lincoln, *Native American Renaissance* (Berkeley: University of California Press, 1985).

11. Womack, *Red on Red*, 11.

12. Daniel Heath Justice and James H. Cox, "Post-Renaissance Indigenous American Literary Studies," in *The Oxford Handbook of Indigenous American Literature* ed. James Cox and Daniel Heath Justice (New York: Oxford University Press, 2014), 3.

13. Sean Kicummah Teuton, *Red Land, Red Power: Grounding Knowledge in the American Indian Novel* (Durham, NC: Duke University Press, 2008), 120.

14. Hsinya Huang, "Towards Transnational Native American Literary Studies," *Comparative Literature and Culture* 12, no. 2 (2011): 5.

15. José Esteban Muñoz, *Disidentifications: Queers of Color and the Performance of Politics* (Minneapolis: University of Minnesota Press, 1998), 11.

16. See Warrior, "Native American Scholarship and the Transnational Turn"; and Philip Deloria, "American Indians, American Studies, and the ASA," *American Quarterly* 55, no. 4 (December 2003): 669–80.

17. Warrior, "Native American Scholarship," 120.

18. ". . . the effects of capitalism, which were once contained and constrained by the sovereignty of nations, now supersede and trump the power of states." Warrior, "Native American Scholarship," 119.

19. Womack, "A Single Decade," 37

20. For a discussion of Native literary criticism and postmodernism, see Elvira Pulitano, *Toward a Native American Critical Theory* (Lincoln: University of Nebraska Press, 2003); for a discussion of Native literary criticism and cosmopolitanism, see Arnold Krupat, *Red Matters: Native American Studies* (Philadelphia: University of Pennsylvania Press, 2002).

21. Huhndorf, *Mapping the Americas: The Transnational Dimensions of Contemporary Native Culture* (Ithaca, NY: Cornell University Press, 2009), 11.

22. Allen, "A Transnational Native American Studies?," n.p., https://escholarship.org/uc/item/82m5j3f5.

23. Hsinya Huang, Philip Deloria, Laura Furlan, and John Gamber, "Charting Transnational Native American Studies," *Journal of Transnational American Studies* 4, no. 1 (January 1, 2012), n.p.

24. Chadwick Allen, *Transindigenous: Methodologies for Global Native Literary Studies* (Minneapolis: University of Minnesota Press, 2012), 15.

25. Scott Richard Lyons, "Introduction: Globalizing the World," in *The World, the Text, the Indian: Global Dimensions of Native American Literature, ed. Scott Richard Lyons* (Albany: State University of New York Press, 2017), 1.

26. Lyons, "Introduction: Globalizing the World," 12.

27. Arnold Krupat, "Native American Literary Criticism in Global Context," in Lyons, *The World, the Text, the Indian*, 67–68

28. Krupat, "Native American Literary Criticism," 66.

29. For examples of Native cosmopolitanism, see Krupat's *Red Matters: Native American Studies* and Elvira Pulitano, "'The Right to Enjoy All Human Rights': The UN Declaration on the Rights of Indigenous Peoples and the Potential for Decolonial Cosmopolitanism," in Lyons, *The World, the Text, the Indian*, 257–82. For a discussion of Native transnationalism and authenticity, see Deborah L. Madsen, ed., *Native Authenticity: Transnational Perspectives on Native American Literary Studies* (Albany: State University of New York Press, 2010).

30. See Elizabeth Cook-Lynn, "The American Indian Fiction Writer: 'Cosmopolitanism, Nationalism, the Third World, and First Nation Sovereignty,'" *Wicazo Sa Review* 9, no 2 (Autumn 1993); and Womack, *Red on Red*, 25–26.

31. Paula Gunn Allen, "Special Problems in Teaching Leslie Marmon Silko's *Ceremony*," *American Indian Quarterly* 14, no. 4 (Autumn, 1990): 379–86.

32. Mi Sun Park has offered an excellent analysis of the gendered dimensions of *Ceremony* as a nationalist text in her dissertation "Reimagining the Nation: Gender and Nationalism in Contemporary U.S. Women's Literature." However, her analysis situates Silko's novel squarely within a United States paradigm, rather than a transnational one. See Mi Sun Park, "Reimagining the Nation: Gender and Nationalism in Contemporary U.S. Women's Literature" (PhD diss., Texas A&M University, 2007).

33. See Lincoln, *Native American Renaissance*.

34. For instance, see Diane Cousineau, "Leslie Silko's *Ceremony*: The Spiderweb as Text," *Revue française d'études américaines* 43 (February 1990): 19–31; Helen May Dennis, *Native American Literature: Towards a Spatialized Reading* (New York: Routledge, 2007); David A. Rice, "Witchery, Indigenous Resistance, and Urban Space is Leslie Marmon Silko's *Ceremony*," *Studies in American Indian Literatures* 17, no. 4 (Winter 2005): 114–43; and Lauren S. Cardon, *The White 'Other' in American Intermarriage Stories, 1945–2008* (New York: Palgrave MacMillan, 2012).

35. Kathleen M. Donovan, *Feminist Readings of Native American Literature: Coming to Voice* (Tucson: University of Arizona Press, 1998), 30.

36. "It would not be until the fictions of Gerald Vizenor and Leslie Marmon Silko in the 1970s that characters in Native American novels would begin to successfully inhabit the kind of frontier space first explored by Morning Dove. Silko's *Ceremony* (1977) delves into the realities of a protagonist who is half Pueblo and half white and who seemingly finds himself in the terminal condition of a Chal Windzer [of Matthews's *Sundown*] or Archile Leon [of McNickle's *The Surrounded*]." Louis Owens, *Mixedblood Messages: Literature, Film, Family, Place* (Norman: University of Oklahoma Press, 2001), 35.

37. Owens, *Mixedblood Messages*, 35.

38. Larry McMurtry, introduction to Leslie Marmon Silko, *Ceremony* (New York: Penguin Books, 2006), xxii.

39. This connection between pan-Indianism and veterans during this era is especially evident in the resurgence of powwows that often involved a strong component aimed at respecting Native veterans.

40. Huhndorf, *Mapping the Americas*, 8–10.

41. Goeman, *Mark My Words*, 157. See also the collection *Howling for Justice: New Perspectives on Leslie Marmon Silko's Almanac of the Dead*, ed. Rebecca Tillett (Tucson: University of Arizona Press, 2014). Elizabeth Cook-Lynn also had this to say about the transnational dimensions of *Almanac*: "Whatever may be said about Silko's earlier works, ALMANAC OF THE DEAD engages in and insists upon the nationalist's approach to historical events, and in the process, seems to put any so-called 'pandering'

ordinarily required of the writer/storyteller in its place. Her effort here, in her new work, is to create a Panindian journey toward retribution, not to appeal to non-indigenous mainstream readership nor to tell tribal secrets. While this is a heartening focus it, too, fails in this nationalistic trend since it does not take into account the specific kind of tribal/nation status of the original occupants of the continent. There is no apparatus for the tribally specific treaty-status paradigm to be realized either in the Silko fiction or in the Panindian approach to history. The explanation for that in tribal terms may be that Laguna falls under the Treaty of Guadalupe Hidalgo, very different circumstance from the Plains Indian Treaty program," Cook-Lynn, "American Indian Fiction Writer," 34.

42. Shari Huhndorf, *Going Native: Indians in the American Cultural Imagination* (Ithaca, NY: Cornell University Press): 191.

43. Huhndorf, *Mapping the Americas*, 15; Huang, "Towards Transnational Native American Literary Studies"; and Kyoko Matsunaga, "Leslie Marmon Silko and Nuclear Dissent in the American Southwest," *Japanese Journal of American Studies* 25 (2014): 67–87.

44. In an early draft of "Prayer for the Pacific" in her papers, there is a note at the top that reads "Revised Nov. 1971." Typescript of early draft of novel "Prayer to the Pacific" (YCAL MSS 637, box 1), Leslie Marmon Silko Papers, Yale Collection of American Literature, Beinecke Rare Book and Manuscript Library, Yale University.

45. Leslie Marmon Silko, *Storyteller* (New York: Penguin Books, 2012), 170.

46. For a discussion of the motifs of water in "Prayer to the Pacific" and other poems in *Storyteller*, see Linda L. Danielson, "Storyteller: Grandmother Spider's Web," *Journal of the Southwest* 30, no. 3 (Autumn 1988): 325–55.

47. Silko, *Storyteller*, 17–30.

48. Appearing also in the collection is a poem called "How to Write a Poem About the Sky," which is dedicated to "the students of the Bethel Middle School, Bethel, Alaska—Feb. 1975" (168).

49. Silko, *Storyteller*, 21.

50. Silko, *Ceremony*, 244.

51. Silko, *Ceremony*, 244.

52. Typescript of film treatment (YCAL MSS 637, box 18, August 2004 acquisition) and Notes from Sundance Workshop (YCAL MSS 637, box 12, August 2004 acquisition), Leslie Marmon Silko Papers, Yale Collection of American Literature, Beinecke Rare Book and Manuscript Library, Yale University.

53. Silko, "Preface," in *Ceremony*, xi.

54. Silko, "Preface," in *Ceremony*, xii.

55. Notes on Manila folder (Uncategorized ZA MS 232, 920504-g), Leslie Marmon Silko Papers, Yale Collection of American Literature, Beinecke Rare Book and Manuscript Library.

56. Notes on Manila folder, xv.

57. Notes on Manila folder, xv.

58. Silko, *Ceremony*, 11.

59. Silko, *Ceremony*, 11–12.

60. Silko, *Ceremony*, xi.

61. Correspondence from Leslie Marmon Silko to Per Seyersted, 3 February 1975 (YCAL MSS 87, folder 14), Per Seyersted Papers Concerning Leslie Marmon Silko, American Literature Collection, Beinecke Rare Book and Manuscript Library, Yale University.

62. For more on formline and Pacific Northwest Coast, see Bill Holm, *Northwest Coast Indian Art: An Analysis of Form* (Seattle: University of Washington Press, 2014); and Rico Lanaat' Worl, Shaadoo'tlaa, and Donald Heendei Gregoy, *A Basic Guide to Northwest Coast Formline Art* (Juneau: Sealaska Heritage Institute, 2014).

63. Silko, "Preface," in *Ceremony*, ix.

64. For more on the connections between Japanese internment and the structure of settler colonialism in the United States, see Iyko Day's *Alien Capital*.

65. Silko, *Ceremony*, 13.

66. Silko, *Ceremony*, 14.

67. Silko, *Ceremony*, 16.

68. Silko, *Ceremony*, 16.

69. Silko, *Ceremony*, 16.

70. Silko, *Ceremony*, 17.

71. Typescript of early draft of novel *Ceremony* (YCAL MSS 637, box 20, folder 5 of 5), Leslie Marmon Silko Papers, Yale Collection of American Literature, Beinecke Rare Book and Manuscript Library, Yale University.

72. Typescript of early draft of novel *Ceremony*, 7.

73. Typescript of early draft of novel *Ceremony*, 8.

74. Typescript of early draft of novel *Ceremony*, 9.

75. See Alvin M. Joseph Jr., Joane Nagel and Troy Johnson, *Red Power: The American Indians' Fight for Freedom* (Lincoln: University of Nebraska Press, 1999).

76. Sharon Holm, "The 'Lie' of the Land: Native Sovereignty, Indian Literary Nationalism, and Early Indigenism in Leslie Marmon Silko's *Ceremony*," *American Indian Quarterly* 32, no. 3 (Summer 2008): 256.

77. Silko, *Ceremony*, 5.

78. Silko, *Ceremony*, 5.

79. Silko, *Ceremony*, 5–6.

80. "On February 23, the same day he gave the chat, Roosevelt sent a second directive to MacArthur, informing him that his eventual destination was Australia, where he was to direct the American buildup as allied commander of the Southwest Pacific theater, which stretched north as far as the Philippines. MacArthur, with his wife, four-year-old son Arthur, Chinese nurse Ah Cheu, and sixteen staff officers, including a public relations specialist and one master sergeant, embarked from Corregidor about midnight on March 12 in four PT boats. They headed for Mindanao, which American forces still controlled. After a daylight layover on an uninhabited island, they concluded the six-hundred-mile journey just before daylight on March 14. From there a B-17 flew the party to Australia. By the time MacArthur arrived in Australia, Wavell's ABDA command had been dissolved after the Japanese victory in the Battle of the Java Sea. As Samuel Eliot Morison put it, this defeat "doomed" the Dutch Empire in Asia. On arrival MacArthur announced, 'I came through, and I shall return.'" Roger Daniels, *Franklin D. Roosevelt: The War Years, 1939–1945* (Urbana: University of Illinois Press, 2016), 258.

81. Alice Te Punga Somerville, *Once Were Pacific: Māori Connections to Oceania* (Minneapolis: University of Minnesota Press, 2012).

82. Dennis Banks with Richard Erdoes, *Ojibwe Warrior: Dennis Banks and the Rise of the American Indian Movement* (Norman: University of Oklahoma Press, 2011), 53–54.

83. Banks, *Ojibwe Warrior*, 55.

84. For more on Dennis Banks's role in the protests at Sunagawa, see Dustin Wright, "From Tokyo to Wounded Knee: Two Afterlives of the Sunagawa Struggle," *The Sixties: A Journal of History, Politics, and Culture* 10, no. 2 (October 2017): 133–49.

85. Warrior, "Native American Scholarship and the Transnational Turn," 125.

86. Warrior, "Native American Scholarship and the Transnational Turn," 127.

Conclusion

1. Alison Marks, *Heaven and Earth*, 2017, wall text, *Alison Marks: One Gray Hair*, 2017, Frye Art Museum, Seattle, WA.

2. Alison Marks, *Space Bear*, 2017, wall text, *Alison Marks: One Gray Hair*, 2017, Frye Art Museum, Seattle, WA.

3. According to NASA's website on "Planetary Missions: Unlocking the Mysteries of Our Solar System," "The New Frontiers Program represents a critical step in the advancement of solar system exploration. The missions in the program tackle specific solar system exploration goals identified as top priorities by consensus of the planetary community. The strategy is to explore the solar system with medium-class spacecraft missions that conduct high-science-return planetary investigations that add to our understanding of the solar system. Initiated in 2003, New Frontiers builds on the innovative approaches used in NASA's Discovery and Explorer Programs, but provides a mechanism for identifying and selecting missions that cannot be accomplished within the cost and time constraints of Discovery." https://www.nasa.gov/planetarymissions/newfrontiers.html.

4. Miranda Belarde-Lewis, "Alison Marks: One Gray Hair," curator's introduction, *Alison Marks: One Gray Hair*, 2017, Frye Museum, Seattle, WA.

5. Belarde-Lewis, "Alison Marks."

6. See Gerald Vizenor, *Manifest Manners: Narratives on Postindian Survivance* (Lincoln: University of Nebraska Press, 1999).

7. Vizenor, *Manifest Manners*, 4.

8. Vizenor, *Manifest Manners*, 12.

9. See David McNally, *Another World is Possible: Globalization and Anti-Capitalism* (Manitoba: Arbeiter Ring, 2006); *Another World is Possible*, directed by Mark Dworkin and Melissa Young (Moving Image Media, 2002).

10. For instance, see John Ross, *¡Zapatistas!: Making Another World Possible, Chronicles of Resistance 2000–2006* (New York: Nation Books, 2006).

11. Zapatista Army of National Liberation, "Sixth Declaration of the Lacandona Jungle," July 2005, https://schoolsforchiapas.org/library/sixth-declaration-lacandona-jungle/.

WORKS CITED

Acklesberg, Martha. "Preface." In Daring et al. *Queering Anarchism*, 1.

———. *Free Women of Spain: Anarchism and the Struggle for the Emancipation of Women*. Oakland, CA: AK Press, 2004.

Adams, Jason. *Non-Western Anarchisms*. Fordsburg, South Africa: Zabalaza Books, 2000.

Alcoff, Linda Martin, Cinzia Arruzza, Tithi Bhattacharya, Rosa Clemente, Angela Davis, Zillah Eisenstein, Liza Featherstone, Nancy Fraser, Barbara Smith, and Keeanga-Yamahtta Taylor. "We Need a Feminism for the 99%." *Guardian*, January 27, 2018. https://www.theguardian.com/commentisfree/2018/jan/27/we-need-a-feminism-for-the-99-thats-why-women-will-strike-this-year.

Alfred, Taiaike. *Peace, Power, and Righteousness: An Indigenous Manifesto*. New York: Oxford University Press, 1999.

———. *Wasasé: Indigenous Pathways of Action and Freedom*. Peterborough, ON: Broadview Press, 2005.

Allen, Chadwick. *Transindigenous: Methodologies for Global Native Literary Studies*. Minneapolis: University of Minnesota Press, 2012.

———. "A Transnational Native American Studies? Why Not Studies That Are Transindigenous?" *Journal of Transnational American Studies* 4, no. 1 (2012).

Allen, Corey. "Canada's Image of Oka, 24 Years Later." *UBC News*, September 22, 2014. http://news.ubc.ca/2014/09/22/oka/.

Alston, Ashanti. "Beyond Nationalism But Not Without It." In *The Black Anarchism Reader*, ed. Black Rose Anarchist Federation, 72–76. Self-published, 2017. https://www.blackrosefed.org/wp-content/uploads/2016/02/Black-Anarchism-A-Reader-4.pdf.

Altena, Bert. "A Networking Historian: The Transnational, the National, and the Patriotic in and around Max Nettlau's *Geschichte der Anarchie*." In Bantman and Altena, *Reassessing the Transnational Turn*, 62–80.

American Civil Liberties Union. "Sexual Abuse in Immigrant Detention." Accessed 1 September 2020. https://www.aclu.org/issues/immigrants-rights/immigrants-rights-and-detention/sexual-abuse-immigration-detention-0.

Amimoto Ingersoll, Karin. *Waves of Knowing: A Seascape Epistemology*. Durham, NC: Duke University Press, 2016.

Anderson, Benedict. *Under Three Flags: Anarchism and the Anti-Colonial Imagination*. London: Verso Books, 2007.

Anderson, Chris, ed. *Literary Nonfiction: Theory, Criticism, Pedagogy*. Carbondale: Southern Illinois University Press, 1989.

Anonymous. "Response by a Syrian Anarchist to the First of May Statement on Syria." libcom.org, September 17, 2013. https://libcom.org/news/response-syrian-anarchist-first-may-statement-syria-17092013.

Another World Is Possible: Impressions of the 2002 World Social Forum. VHS. Directed by Mark Dworkin and Melissa Young. 2002. Oley, PA: Bullfrog Films.

Antliff, Allan. *Anarchism Modernism: Art, Politics, and the First American Avant-Garde*. Chicago: University of Chicago Press, 2001.

———. *Anarchy and Art: From the Paris Commune to the Fall of the Berlin Wall*. Vancouver: Arsenal Pulp Press, 2007.

Arruzza, Cinzia. "Of What is Anarcha-Feminism the Name?" In *The Anarchist Turn*, edited by Jacob Blumfeld, Chiara Bottici, and Simon Critchley, 111–24. New York: Pluto Books, 2013.

Arthur, Stephen. "Where License Reigns with All Impunity: An Anarchist Study of the Iroquois Polity." *Northeastern Anarchist* 12 (Winter 2007).

Asoka, Kaavya. "Women and Black Lives Matter: An Interview with Marcia Chatelain." *Dissent Magazine*, Summer 2015. https://www.dissentmagazine.org/article/women-black-lives-matter-interview-marcia-chatelain.

Associated Press. "Protestors Leave, But What Hunt Is Still Planned: Makah Tribes Is Considering Alternatives." *Deseret News*, December 1, 1998. https://www.deseretnews.com/article/666150/Protesters-leave-but-whale-hunt-is-still-planned.html.

Banks, Dennis, with Richard Erdoes. *Ojibwe Warrior: Dennis Banks and the Rise of the American Indian Movement*. Norman: University of Oklahoma Press, 2011.

Bantman, Constance, and Bert Altena, eds. *Reassessing the Transnational Turn: Scales of Analysis in Anarchist and Syndicalist Studies*. Oakland, CA: PM Press, 2017.

Barker, Adam J. "Already Occupied: Indigenous Peoples, Settler Colonialism, and the Occupy Movements in North America." *Social Movement Studies* 11, no. 3–4 (August 2012): 327–34.

———. "The Contemporary Reality of Canadian Imperialism: Settler Colonialism and the Hybrid Colonial State." *American Indian Quarterly* 33, no. 3 (Summer 2009): 325–51.

———. "From Adversaries to Allies: Forging Respectful Alliances between Indigenous and Settler Peoples." In *Alliances: Re/Envisioning Indigenous Non-Indigenous Relationships*, edited by Lynne Davis, 316–33. Toronto: University of Toronto Press, 2010.

Barker, Adam J., and Emma Battell Lowman, *Settler: Identity and Colonialism in 21st Century Canada*. Halifax: Fernwood Press, 2015.

Barker, Adam J., and Jenny Pickerill. "Radicalizing Relationships To and Through Shared Geographies: Why Anarchists Need to Understand Indigenous Connections to Land, Sea, and Place." *Antipode* 44, no. 5 (August 2012): 1705–25.

Barker, Joanne. "Indigenous Feminisms." In *Oxford Handbook of Indigenous People's Politics*, edited by José Antonio Lucero, Dale Turner, and Donna Lee VanCott. Oxford: Oxford University Press, January 2015. http://www.oxfordhandbooks.com/view/10.1093/oxfordhb/9780195386653.001.0001/oxfordhb-9780195386653-e-007.

Barker, Joanne. "Introduction: Critically Sovereign." In *Critically Sovereign: Indigenous Feminist, Gender, and Sexuality Studies*, edited by Joanne Barker, 1–44. Durham, NC: Duke University Press, 2017.

Barker, Joanne, and Teresia Teaiwa. "Native InFormation." In *Reading Native American Women: Critical/Creative Representations*, edited by Inés Hernández-Avila, 107–28. New York: AltaMira Press, 2005.

Belarde-Lewis, Miranda. Curatorial statement displayed in Alison (Bremner) Marks's *One Gray Hair*, organized and presented at the Frye Art Museum, Seattle, November 11, 2017, to February 4, 2018.

Bellin, Joshua. *The Demon of the Continent: Indians and the Shaping of American Literature*. Philadelphia: University of Pennsylvania Press, 2008.

Bergland, Renée L. *The National Uncanny: Indian Ghosts and American Subjects*. Hanover, NH: University of New England Press, 2000.

Berlatsky, Noah. "The Women of #BlackLivesMatter." *Atlantic*, January 27, 2015. https://www.theatlantic.com/national/archive/2015/01/women-and-blacklivesmatter/384855/.

Bilharz, Joy A. *The Allegany Senecas and Kinzua Dam: Forced Relocation through Two Generations*. Omaha: University of Nebraska Press, 2002.

Black Rose Anarchist Federation. "Below and Beyond Trump: Power and Counter-Power in 2017." December 22, 2017. Accessed September 1, 2020. http://blackrosefed.org/below-and-beyond-trump/.

———. "Internationalism and Imperialism." Accessed September 1, 2020. http://blackrosefed.org/points-of-unity/internationalism-imperialism/.

———. Mission statement. Accessed January 29, 2018. http://blackrosefed.org/mission-statement/.

———. "Patriarchy and Queer Liberation." Accessed January 29, 2018. http://blackrosefed.org/points-of-unity/patriarchy-queer-liberation/.

———. "Points of Unity." Accessed January 29, 2018. http://blackrosefed.org/points-of-unity/.

Blackwell, Maylei, Floridalma Boj Lopez, and Luis Urrieta Jr., eds. "Critical Lantinx Indigeneities." Special issue, *Latino Studies* 15, no. 2 (July 2017).

Blackhawk, Ned. *Violence over the Land: Indians and Empires in the Early American West*. Cambridge, MA: Harvard University Press. 2008.

Blee, Lisa. *Framing Chief Leschi: Narrative and the Politics of Historical Justice*. Chapel Hill: University of North Carolina Press, 2014.

Blow, Richard. "The Great American Whale Hunt." *Mother Jones*, September 1998. https://www.motherjones.com/politics/1998/09/great-american-whale-hunt/.

Boessenkool, Antonie. "The California Missions School Project Is Becoming a Thing of the Past and Here's Why." *Los Angeles Daily News*, September 24, 2017. https://www.dailynews.com/2017/09/24/the-california-missions-school-project-is-becoming-a-thing-of-the-past-heres-why/.

Bookchin, Murray. "Nationalism and the 'National Question.'" *Democracy and Nature: The International Journey of Inclusive Democracy* 2, no. 2, issue 5 (1994). https://www.democracynature.org/vol2/bookchin_nationalism.htm.

Boston Anarchists Against Militarism and Northeastern Federation of Anarchist Communists (BAAM). "Why Anarchists Oppose Militarism and Nationalism." *Northeastern Anarchist* 3 (Fall 2001).

Brant, Beth, ed. *A Gathering of Spirit: A Collection by North American Indian Women*. Toronto: Women's Press, 1992.

Brave Bird, Mary. *Ohitika Woman*. New York: Grove Press, 1993.

Bray, Mark. *Translating Anarchy: The Anarchism of Occupy Wall Street*. Winchester, UK: Zero Books, 2013.

Breton, André. *Manifestoes of Surrealism*. Translated by Richard Seaver and Helen R. Lane. Ann Arbor: University of Michigan Press, 1969.

Brooks, Lisa. *The Common Pot*. Minneapolis: University of Minnesota Press, 2008.

Brown, Dee. *Bury My Heart at Wounded Knee: An Indian History of the American West*. New York: Open Road Media, 2012.

Brunyeel, Kevin. *The Third Space of Sovereignty: The Postcolonial Politics of US-Indigenous Relations*. Minneapolis: University of Minnesota Press, 2007.

Byrd, Jodi. *The Transit of Empire: Indigenous Critiques of Colonialism*. Minneapolis: University of Minnesota Press, 2011.

Caffentzis, George, and Silvia Federici. "A Brief History of Resistance to Structural Adjustment." In *Democratizing the Global Economy: The Battle Against the World Bank and the IMF*, edited by Kevin Danaher, 143–46. Monroe, ME: Common Courage Press, 2002.

Calamur, Krishnadev. "Why North Korea Is Threatening Guam." *Atlantic*, August 8, 2017. https://www.theatlantic.com/international/archive/2017/08/north-korea-guam/536286/.

Call, Lewis. *Postmodern Anarchism*. New York: Lexington Books, 2003.

Canadian Broadcasting Company News. "Elsipogtog Chief Appoints 'Peacekeeper' in Shale Gas Dispute." June 27, 2013. http://www.cbc.ca/news/canada/new-brunswick/elsipogtog-chief-appoints-peacekeeper-in-shale-gas-dispute-1.1365143.

Cappelletti, Ángel. *Anarchist in Latin America*. Oakland, CA: AK Press, 2018.

Cardon, Lauren S. *The White "Other" in American Intermarriage Stories, 1945–2008*. New York: Palgrave MacMillan, 2012.

Cariou, Warren. "Life-Telling: Indigenous Oral Autobiography and the Performance of Relation." *Biography* 39, no. 3 (Summer 2016): 314–27.

Child, Brenda. *Boarding School Seasons: American Indian Families, 1900–1940*. Lincoln: University of Nebraska Press, 2000.

Chomsky, Noam. *Occupy: Reflections on Class War, Rebellion, and Solidarity*. Brooklyn: Zuccotti Park Press, 2013.

Clarkin, Thomas. *Federal Indian Policy in the Kennedy and John Administrations 1961–1969*. Albuquerque: University of New Mexico Press, 2001.

Cockburn, Alexander, and Jeffrey St. Clair. *5 Days That Shook the World: Seattle and Beyond*. New York: Verso, 2000.

Coe, Peter, David Struthers, and Kenyon Zimmer, eds. *Wobblies of the World: A Global History of the IWW*. London: Pluto Press, 2017.

Coffman, Tom. *Nation Within: The History of American Occupation in Hawai'i*. Durham, NC: Duke University Press, 1998.

Cohn, Jesse. *Underground Passages: Anarchist Resistance Culture, 1848–2011*. Oakland, CA: AK Press, 2014.

Conrad, Ryan. "Gay Marriage and Queer Love." In Daring et al., *Queering Anarchism*, 19–20.

Cook-Lynn, Elizabeth. "Life and Death in the Mainstream of American Indian Biography." *Wicazo Sa Review* 11, no. 2 (Autumn, 1995): 90–93.

———. "The American Indian Fiction Writer: 'Cosmopolitanism, Nationalism, the Third World, and First Nation Sovereignty." *Wicazo Sa Review* 9, no. 2 (Autumn 1993): 26–36.

Cooper, Marc. "Teamsters and Turtles: They're Together at Last." *Los Angeles Times*, December 2, 1999. http://articles.latimes.com/1999/dec/02/local/me-39707.

Cornell, Andrew. *Unruly Equality: U.S. Anarchism in the Twentieth Century*. Oakland: University of California Press, 2016.

Cornum, L. "First Women, Then the Nation: Confronting Colonial Gender Violence." *LIES: A Journal of Materialist Feminism* 2 (August 2015): 75–93.

Coulthard, Glen Sean. *Red Skin, White Masks: Rejecting the Colonial Politics of Recognition*. Minneapolis: University of Minnesota Press, 2014.

Cousineau, Diane. "Leslie Silko's *Ceremony*: The Spiderweb as Text." *Revue française d'études américaines* 43 (February 1990): 19–31.

Cox, James H. *Muting White Noise: Native American and European American Novel Traditions*. Norman: University of Oklahoma Press, 2006.

Craft, Aimée. "Tina Fontaine's Story Shows There Is No Real Justice for Indigenous People in Canada." *Globe and Mail*, February 23, 2018. https://www.theglobeandmail.com/opinion/tina-fontaines-story-shows-there-is-no-real-justice-for-indigenous-people-in-canada/article38086537/.

CrimethInc. "Gord Hill, Indigenous Artist and Anarchist: An Interview." August 1, 2017. https://crimethinc.com/2017/08/01/an-interview-with-gord-hill.

Croatan. "Who Is Oakland?: Anti-Oppression Activism, the Politics of Safety, and State Co-Optation." May 1, 2012. https://libcom.org/files/whoisoaklandsyn.pdf.

Crow Dog, Mary. *Lakota Woman*. New York: Harper Collins, 1990.

Cusicanqui, Silvia Rivera. "The Ch'ixi Identity of a Mestizo: Regarding an Anarchist Manifesto of 1929." In Maxwell and Craib, *No Gods, No Masters*, 12–21.

Cutler, Jonathan. "The Haymarket Riot Remembered. Interview by James Green. "All Things Considered," *NPR*, April 29, 2006. https://www.npr.org/templates/story/story.php?storyId=5369420.

D'Agata, John ed., *The Making of the American Essay*. Minneapolis: Graywolf Press, 2016.

Daniels, Roger. *Franklin D. Roosevelt: The War Years, 1939–1945*. Urbana: University of Illinois Press, 2016.

Danielson, Linda L. "Storyteller: Grandmother Spider's Web." *Journal of the Southwest* 30, no. 3 (Autumn 1988): 325–55.

Dark Star Collective, ed. *Quiet Rumors: An Anarcha-Feminist Reader*. 3rd ed. Oakland, CA: AK Press, 2012.

Daring, C. B., J. Rogue, Deric Shannon, and Abbey Volcano, eds. *Queering Anarchism: Addressing and Undressing Power and Desire*. Oakland, CA: AK Press, 2012.

Davis, Angela. *Women, Race and Class*. New York: Vintage Books, 1983.

Davis, James, and Paul Rowley. "Internationalism Against Globalization: A Map of Resistance," in *The Battle of Seattle: The New Challenge to Capitalist Globalization*, edited by Eddie Yuen, George Katsiaficas and Daniel Burton Rose, 25–7. New York: Soft Skull Press, 2001.

Day, Iyko. *Alien Capital: Asian Racialization and the Logic of Settler Colonial Capitalism*. Durham, NC: Duke University Press, 2016.

Day, Richard J. F. "Journal Editor's Introduction." In "Anarch@indigenism," edited by Glen Coulthard, Jacqueline Lasky, Adam Lewis, and Vanessa Watts. Special issue, *Affinities: A Journal of Radical Theory, Culture, and Action* 5, no. 1, 1–2 (2011): 1–2.

Day, Richard J. F. *Gramsci Is Dead: Anarchist Currents in the Newest Social Movements*. London: Pluto Press, 2005.

Day, Richard. "Who Is This We That Gives the Gift? Native American Political Theory and the Western Tradition." *Critical Horizons: A Journal of Philosophy and Social Theory* 2, no. 2 (2001): 173–201.

De Cleyre, Voltairine. "Anarchism and American Traditions." In *The Selected Works of Voltairine de Cleyre: Poems, Essays, Sketches, and Stories, 1885–1911*, 118–35. Oakland, CA: AK Press, 2016.

———. "Breaking the Chains: Changing Society Through Direct Action." In *Exquisite Rebel: The Essays of Voltairine de Cleyre*, edited by Sharon Presley and Crispin Sartwell, 269–306. Albany: State University of New York Press, 2005.

———. "Sex Slavery." In *Exquisite Rebel: The Essays of Voltairine de Cleyre—Anarchist, Feminist, Genius*, edited by Sharon Presley and Crispin Sartwell, 225–38. Albany: State University of New York Press, 2005.

Deer, Sarah. *The Beginning and End of Rape: Confronting Sexual Violence in Native America*. Minneapolis: University of Minnesota Press, 2015.

———. "Decolonizing Rape Law: A Native Feminist Synthesis of Safety and Sovereignty." *Wicazo Sa Review* 24, no. 2 (Fall 2009): 149–167.

Deloria, Philip. "American Indians, American Studies, and the ASA." *American Quarterly* 55, no. 4 (December 2003): 669–80.

———. *Playing Indian*. New Haven, CT: Yale University Press, 1999.

Deloria, Vine, Jr. *Custer Died for Your Sins: An Indian Manifesto*. Norman: University of Oklahoma Press, 1969.

Deluca, Kevin Michael, and Jennifer Peeples. "From Public Sphere to Public Screen: Democracy, Activism, and the 'Violence' of Seattle." *Critical Studies in Media Communication* 19, 2 (2002): 125–51.

Den Ouden, Amy E., and Jean M. O'Brien, eds. *Recognition, Sovereignty Struggles, and Indigenous Rights in the United States: A Sourcebook*. Chapel Hill: University of North Carolina Press, 2013.

Denetdale, Jennifer. "Securing Navajo National Boundaries: War, Patriotism, Tradition, and the Diné Marriage Act of 2005." *Wicazo Sa Review* 24, no. 2 (Fall 2009): 131–48.

Dennis, Helen May. *Native American Literature: Towards a Spatialized Reading*. New York: Routledge, 2007.

Dillon, Grace, ed. *Walking the Clouds: An Anthology of Indigenous Science Fiction*. Tucson: University of Arizona Press, 2012.

Dirlik, Arif. *Anarchism in the Chinese Revolution*. Berkeley: University of California Press, 1993.

Dixon, Chris. *Another Politics: Talking Across Today's Transformative Movements*. Berkeley: University of California Press, 2014.

———. "Building a Mass Movement? Learning from the Occupy Sudbury Experience." In *We Are Many: Reflections on Movement Strategy from Occupation to Liberation*, edited by Kate Khatib, Margaret Killjoy, and Mike McGuire, 284–86. Oakland, CA: AK Press, 2012.

———. "Five Days in Seattle." In *The Battle of the Story of the Battle of Seattle*, edited by David Solnit and Rebecca Solnit, 73–107. Oakland, CA: AK Press, 2009.

Donovan, Kathleen M. *Feminist Readings of Native American Literature: Coming to Voice*. Tucson: University of Arizona Press, 1998.

Dove, Dawn. "In Order to Understand Thanksgiving, One Has to Understand the Sacredness of the Gift." In *Dawnland Voices: An Anthology of Indigenous Writing from New England*, edited by Siobhan Senier, 526–29. Lincoln: University of Nebraska Press.

Dowling, Sarah. *Translingual Poetics: Writing Personhood under Settler Colonialism*. Iowa City: University of Iowa Press, 2018.

Duggan, Lisa. *The Twilight of Equality?: Neoliberalism, Cultural Politics, and the Attack on Democracy*. Boston: Beach Press, 2012.

Dunagan, Christopher. "Hunters Become the Hunted." *Kitsap Sun*, October 5, 1998. http://web.kitsapsun.com/archive/1998/10-05/0056_hunters_become_the_hunted.html.

Ehrlich, Carol. “Socialism, Anarchism, and Feminism.” In Dark Star Collective, *Quiet Rumors*, 55–67.

Ehrlich, Jake. *Howl of the Censor: The Four Letter Word on Trial*. London: Nourse Books, 1956.

Eisenstein, Zillah. “Constructing a Theory of Capitalist Patriarchy and Socialist Feminism.” *Critical Sociology* 25, no. 2–3 (March 1999): 196–217.

Ellinghaus, Katherine. *Blood Will Tell: Native Americans and Assimilation Policy*. Lincoln: University of Nebraska Press, 2017.

Elliott, Alicia. *A Mind Spread Out on the Ground*. Toronto: DoubleDay Canada, 2019.

Erdrich, Heid E. *National Monuments*. East Lansing: Michigan State University Press, 2008.

Erdrich, Heid, and R. Vincent Moniz Jr., dir. “Pre-Occupied.” 2013. http://heiderdrich.com/video/pre-occupied/.

Erdrich, Louise. *The Blue Jay's Dance: A Memoir of Early Motherhood*. New York: Harper Perennial, 2010.

———. *Books and Islands in Ojibwe Country: Traveling Through the Land of My Ancestors*. New York: Harper Perennial, 2014.

Ervin, Lorenzo Kom'boa. “Anarchism and the Black Revolution.” In *The Black Anarchism Reader*, ed. Black Rose Anarchist Federation, 10–71. Self-published, 2017.

Esteban Muñoz, José. *Disidentifications: Queers of Color and the Performance of Politics*. Minneapolis: University of Minnesota Press, 1998.

Estes, Nick. *Our History is the Future*. New York: Verso, 2019.

Falk, Candace, ed. *Emma Goldman: A Documentary History of the American Years, Vol. 1: Made for America, 1890–1901*. Berkeley: University of California Press, 2003.

Faludi, Susan. *Backlash: The Undeclared War against American Women*. New York: Broadway Books, 1991.

Farrow, Lynne. “Feminism as Anarchism.” In Dark Star Collective, *Quiet Rumors*, 19–24.

Ferguson, Kathy. “Becoming Anarchism, Feminism, and Indigeneity.” *Affinities: A Journal of Radical Theory, Culture, and Action* 5, no. 1 (2011): 96–109.

Ferguson, Roderick. *Aberrations in Black: Towards a Queer of Color Critique*. Minneapolis: University of Minnesota Press, 2003.

Firestone, Shulamith. *The Dialectic of Sex: The Case for Feminist Revolution*. New York: Farrar, Straus, and Giroux, 2003.

“Forgotten History: 1856; The Battle of Seattle.” *Tides of Flame* 20 (June 2012): 4. https://tidesofflame.files.wordpress.com/2012/06/tof20.pdf.

Fortier, Craig. *Unsettling the Commons: Social Movements Within, Against, and Beyond Settler Colonialism*. Winnipeg: Arbiter Ring Publishing, 2017.

Friedman, Amy L. "'Being Here as Hard as I Could': The Beat Generation Women Writers." *Discourse* 20, no. 1/2 (Winter and Spring 1998): 229–44.

Friedman, Hal M. *Governing the American Lake: The U.S. Defense and Administration of the Pacific, 1945–1947*. Lansing: Michigan State University Press, 2007.

Friedman, Thomas. "Senseless in Seattle." *New York Times*, December 1, 1999. https://archive.nytimes.com/www.nytimes.com/library/opinion/friedman/120199frie.html.

———. *The World Is Flat: A Brief History of the Twenty-First Century*. New York: Farrar, Straus, and Giroux, 2005.

Frizelle, Christopher. "Nightstand: My New Favorite Newspaper." *The Stranger*, August 3, 2011. https://www.thestranger.com/seattle/nightstand/Content?oid=9322085

Frost, Robert. "The Gift Outright." In *Robert Frost: Collected Poems, Prose, and Plays*, edited by Richard Poirier and Mark Richardson, 316. New York: Penguin, 1995.

Furtwangler, Albert. *Answering Chief Seattle*. Seattle: University of Washington Press, 2011.

Gemie, Sharif. "Anarchism and Feminism: A Historical Survey." *Women's History Review* 5, no. 3 (1996): 417–44.

Genetin-Pilawa, C. Joseph. *Crooked Paths to Allotment: The Fight over Federal Indian Policy after the Civil War*. Chapel Hill: University of North Carolina Press, 2014.

Ghazzawi, Razan. "Decolonising Syria's So-called 'Queer Liberation.'" *Al Jazeera*, August 5, 2017. https://www.aljazeera.com/indepth/opinion/2017/08/decolonising-syria-called-queer-liberation-170803110403979.html.

Goeman, Mishuana. "From Place to Territories and Back Again: Centering Storied Land in the Discussion of Indigenous Nation-Building." *International Journal of Critical Indigenous Studies* 1, no. 1 (2008): 23–34.

———. *Mark My Words: Native Women Mapping Our Nations*. Minneapolis: University of Minnesota Press, 2013.

———. "Notes Towards a Native Feminist Spatial Practice." *Wicazo Sa Review* 24, no 2. (Fall 2009): 169–87.

Goldberg, Michelle. "American Leftists Need to Pay More Attention to Rojava." *Slate*, November 25, 2015. http://www.slate.com/blogs/xx_factor/2015/11/25/rojava_is_a_radical_experiment_in_democracy_in_northern_syria_american_leftists.html.

Golderberg, Maya J. "The Problem of Exclusion in Feminist Theory and Politics: A Metaphysical Investigation into Constructing a Category of 'Woman.'" *Journal of Gender Studies* 16, no. 2 (July 2007): 139–53.

Goldman, Emma. *Anarchism and Other Essays*. Mineola, NY: Dover Publications, 1969.

Goldstein, Aloysha. "Toward a Genealogy of the U.S. Colonial Present." In *Formations of United States Colonialism*, edited by Aloysha Goldstein, 1–31. Durham, NC: Duke University Press, 2012.

Goodyear-Ka'ōpua, Noelani. "Kuleana Lāhui: Collective Responsibility for Hawaiian Nationhood in Activists' Praxis." *Affinities: A Journal of Theory, Culture, Action* (August 2011): 130–63.

Gordon, Uri. "Anarchism and Nationalism." In *The Brill Companion to Anarchism and Philosophy*, edited by Nathan Jun, 196–215. Leiden: Brill, 2018.

———. *Anarchy Alive!: Anti-Authoritarian Politics from Practice to Theory*. London: Pluto Press, 2008.

Gornick, Vivian. *The Situation and the Story: The Art of Personal Narrative*. New York: Farrar, Straus, and Giroux, 2002.

Gourd-Wartofsky, Michael. *The Occupiers: The Making of the 99 Percent Movement*. New York: Oxford University Press, 2015.

Goyens, Tom. *Radical Gotham: Anarchism in New York City from Schwab's Saloon to Occupy Wall Street*. Champaign: University of Illinois Press, 2017.

Graeber, David. *Direct Action: An Ethnography*. Oakland, CA: AK Press, 2009.

———. "The New Anarchists." *New Left Review* 13 (Jan.–Feb. 2002): 61–73.

———. *Possibilities: Essays on Hierarchy, Rebellion, and Desire*. Oakland, CA: AK Press, 2007.

Green, Rayna. "The Pocahontas Perplex: The Image of Indian Women in American Culture." *Massachusetts Review* 16, no. 4 (October 1975): 698–714.

Grossman, Zoltán. *Unlikely Alliances: Native Nations and White Communities Join to Defend Rural Lands*. Seattle: University of Washington Press, 2017.

Grubačić, Andrej, and David Graeber. "Anarchism, or the Revolutionary Movement of the Twenty-First Century." *Z-Net*, January 6, 2004. https://theanarchistlibrary.org/library/andrej-grubacic-david-graeber-anarchism-or-the-revolutionary-movement-of-the-twenty-first-century.

Gunn Allen, Paula. *The Sacred Hoop: Recovering the Feminine in American Indian Traditions*. Boston: Beacon Press, 1992.

———. "Special Problems in Teaching Leslie Marmon Silko's *Ceremony*." *American Indian Quarterly* 14, no. 4 (1990): 379–86.

Hale, Janet Campbell. *Bloodlines: Odyssey of a Native Daughter*. Tucson: University of Arizona Press, 1998.

Hall, Laura. "Indigenism Intersectionality: Decolonizing an Indigenous Eco-Queer Feminism and Anarchism." *Perspectives on Anarchist Theory* 29 (May 2016): 81–94.

Hall, Lisa Kahaleole. "Strategies of Erasure: U.S. Colonialism and Native Hawaiian Feminism." *American Quarterly* 60, no. 2 (June 2008): 273–80.

———. "Navigating Our Own 'Sea of Islands': Remapping a Theoretical Space for Hawaiian Women and Indigenous Feminism." *Wicazo Sa Review* 24, no. 2 (Fall 2009): 15–38.

Harjo, Joy. *Crazy Brave: A Memoir*. New York: W. W. Norton, 2012.

Harjo, Joy, and Gloria Bird, eds. *Reinventing the Enemy's Language: Contemporary Native Women's Writings of North America*. New York: W. W. Norton, 1998.

Harp, Seth. "The Anarchists vs. the Islamic State." *Rolling Stone*, February 14, 2017, 42–49. https://www.rollingstone.com/politics/politics-features/the-anarchists-vs-the-islamic-state-109047/.

Hartsock, Nancy. *Money, Sex, and Power: Towards a Feminist Historical Materialism*. Boston, MA: Northeastern University Press, 1985.

Harvey, Ryan. "Occupy Before and Beyond." In *We Are Many: Reflections on Movement Strategy from Occupation to Liberation*, edited by Kate Khatib, Margaret Killjoy, and Mike McGuire, 123–33. Oakland, CA: AK Press, 2012.

Hayes, Ernestine. *Blonde Indian: An Alaska Native Memoir*. Tucson: University of Arizona Press, 2006.

———. *The Tao of Raven: An Alaska Native Memoir*. Seattle: University of Washington Press, 2017.

Heckert, Jamie, and Richard Clemison. "Ethics, Relationships, and Power: An Introduction." In *Anarchism and Sexuality: Ethics, Relationships, and Power*, edited by Jamie Heckert and Richard Clemison, 1–22. New York: Routledge, 2011.

Hemmings, Clare. *Why Stories Matter: The Political Grammar of Feminist Theory*. Durham, NC: Duke University Press, 2010.

Hernández-Avila, Inés. "'It Is What Keeps Us Sisters': Indigenous Women and the Power of Story." *Frontiers: A Journal of Women Studies* 23, no. 2 (2002): ix–xviii.

Higuera McMahan, Jacqueline. "California Parties—Past and Future." *Los Angeles Times*, January 2, 2001. https://www.latimes.com/archives/la-xpm-2002-jan-02-fo-topten2-story.html.

Hill, Susan M. "'Travelling Down the River of Life Together in Peace and Friendship, Forever': Haudenosaunee Land Ethics and Treaty Agreements as the Basis for Restructuring the Relationship with the British Crown." In *Lighting the Eighth Fire: The Liberation, Resurgence, and Protection of Indigenous Nations*, edited by Leanne Simpson, 23–46. Winnipeg: Arbeiter Ring, 2008.

Hillaire, Pauline. "Bellingham Centennial History Pole." In *A Totem Pole History: The Work of Lummi Carver Joe Hillaire*, edited by Gregory P. Field, 137–46. Lincoln: University of Nebraska Press, 2013.

Hogan, Linda. *The Woman Who Watches over the World: A Native Memoir*. New York: W. W. Norton, 2001.

Holloway, John. *Change the World without Taking Power: The Meaning of Revolution Today*. London: Pluto Press, 2002.

Holm, Bill. *Northwest Coast Indian Art: An Analysis of Form*. Seattle: University of Washington Press, 2014.

Holm, Sharon. "The 'Lie' of the Land: Native Sovereignty, Indian Literary Nationalism, and Early Indigenism in Leslie Marmon Silko's *Ceremony*." *American Indian Quarterly* 32, no. 3 (Summer 2008): 243–74.

Holmes, Cindy, Sarah Hunt, and Amy Piedalue, "Violence, Colonialism, and Space: Towards a Decolonizing Dialogue." *ACME* (2015): 539–70.

Howe, LeAnne. *Choctalking on Other Realities*. San Francisco: Aunt Lute Books, 2013.

Howe Verhovek, Sam. "For Seattle, Triumph and Protest." *New York Times*, October 13, 1999. https://www.nytimes.com/1999/10/13/us/for-seattle-triumph-and-protest.html.

Huang, Hsinya, Philip Deloria, Laura Furlan, and John Gamber. "Charting Transnational Native American Studies." *Journal of Transnational American Studies* 4, no. 1 (January 1, 2012): n.p.

Huang, Hsinya. "Towards Transnational Native American Literary Studies." *Comparative Literature and Culture* 12, no. 2 (2011). https://docs.lib.purdue.edu/cgi/viewcontent.cgi?article=1744&context=clcweb.

Huang, Yunte. *Transpacific Imaginations: History, Literature, Counterpoetics*. Cambridge, MA: Harvard University Press, 2008.

Huhndorf, Shari. *Going Native: Indians in the American Cultural Imagination*. Ithaca, NY: Cornell University Press, 2001).

———. *Mapping the Americas: the Transnational Politics of Contemporary Native Culture*. Ithaca, NY: Cornell University Press, 2009.

Human Rights Watch. "US: Sexual Violence, Harassment of Immigrant Farmworkers." May 15, 2012. https://www.hrw.org/news/2012/05/15/us-sexual-violence-harassment-immigrant-farmworkers.

Hunt, Sarah, Cindy Holmes, and Amy Piedalue. "Violence, Colonialism, and Space: Towards a Decolonizing Dialogue." *ACME: An International Journal for Critical Geographies* 14, no. 2 (2015): 539–70.

Hurley, Adrienne. "Let's Ditch School and Be Unmanageable." In Maxwell and Craib, *No Gods, No Masters*, 116–30.

Hwang, Dongyoun. *Anarchism in Korea: Independence, Transnationalism, and the Question of National Development 1919–1984*. Albany: State University of New York Press, 2016.

Ivey, Rachel. "End of Gender: Revolution, Not Reform." *Medium* (blog), September 16, 2015. https://medium.com/@deepgreenresist/end-of-gender-revolution-not-reform-cf5f23fd29c7.

Jager, Rebecca K. *Malinche, Pocahontas, and Sacajawea: Indian Women as Cultural Intermediaries and National Symbols*. Norman: University of Oklahoma Press, 2015.

Jaimes, M. Annette. "The Hollow Icon: An American Indian Analysis of the Kennedy Myth and Federal Indian Policy." *Wicazo Sa Review* 6, no. 1 (Spring 1990): 34–44.

Jain, Dhruv. "Maia Ramnath and the Search for a Decolonised Antiauthoritarian Marxism: A Review of Haj to Utopia and Decolonizing Anarchism by Maia Ramnath." *Historical Materialism* 25, no. 2 (2017): 196–213.

Janicka, Iwona. *Theorizing Contemporary Anarchism: Solidarity, Mimesis, and Radical Social Change*. New York: Bloomsbury Academic, 2017.

Jensen, Derrick, Aric McBay, and Lierre Keith. *Deep Green Resistance: Strategy to Save the Planet*. New York: Seven Stories Press, 2011.

Jensen, Derrick. *Listening to the Land: Conversations about Nature, Culture, and Eros*. White River Junction, VT: Chelsea Green Publishing, 2002.

Jeppesen, Sandra. "Becoming Anarchist: the Function of Anarchist Literature." *Anarchist Developments in Cultural Studies* 2 (2011): 189–213.

Johnson, Carolyn Ross. *Cherokee Women in Crisis: Trail of Tears, Civil War, and Allotment, 1838–1907*. Tuscaloosa: University of Alabama Press, 2003.

Johnson, Keith A. "The Makah Manifesto." *Seattle Times*, August 23, 1998. http://community.seattletimes.nwsource.com/archive/?date=19980823&slug=2768010.

Joseph, Alvin M., Jr., Joane Nagel, and Troy Johnson. *Red Power: The American Indians' Fight for Freedom*. Lincoln: University of Nebraska Press, 1999.

Justice, Daniel Heath. *Why Indigenous Literatures Matter*. Waterloo, ON: Wilfred Laurier Press, 2018.

Justice, Daniel Heath, and James H. Cox. "Post-Renaissance Indigenous American Literary Studies." In *The Oxford Handbook of Indigenous American Literature*, edited by James Cox and Daniel Heath Justice, 1–14. New York: Oxford University Press, 2014.

Kaplan, Amy. *The Anarchy of Empire in the Making of US Culture*. Cambridge, MA: Harvard University Press, 2005.

———. "Manifest Domesticity." *American Literature* 70, no. 3 (September 1998): 581–606.

Kaplan, Amy, and Donald E. Pease. *Cultures of United States Imperialism*. Durham, NC: Duke University Press, 1994.

Karuka, Manu. *Empire's Tracks: Indigenous Nations, Chinese Workers, and the Transcontinental Railroad*. Oakland: University of California Press, 2019.

Kauanui, J. Kēhaulani. "'A Structure, Not an Event': Settler Colonialism and Enduring Indigeneity." *Lateral: Journal of the Cultural Studies Association* 5, no. 1 (2016). https://csalateral.org/issue/5–1/forum-alt-humanities-settler-colonialism-enduring-indigeneity-kauanui/.

Keeler, Jacqueline. "Why Reading Sherman Alexie Was Never Enough." *Yes! Magazine*, March 12, 2018.

Kennedy, John F. Introduction to *The American Heritage Book of Indians*, by William Brandon. New York: Simon & Schuster, 1961.

Kerrane, Kevin, and Ben Yagoda. *The Art of Fact: A Historical Anthology of Literary Nonfiction*. New York: Scribner, 1998.

Kiley, Brendan. "Anarchy is Boring: The May Day Smashup Was the Spectacular Tip of a Mundane Iceberg." *The Stranger*, May 9, 2012. https://www.thestranger.com/seattle/anarchy-is-boring/Content?oid=13597692.

Killjoy, Margaret, ed. *Mythmakers and Lawbreakers: Anarchist Writers on Fiction*. Oakland, CA: AK Press, 2009.

Kinna, Ruth. "Kropotkin's Theory of the State: A Transnational Approach." In Bantman and Altena, *Reassessing the Transnational Turn*, 43–61. New York: Routledge, 2015.

Kinnahan, A. *Poetics of the Feminine: Authority and Literary Tradition in William Carlos Williams, Mina Loy, Denise Levertov, and Kathleen Fraser*. Cambridge, MA: Cambridge University Press, 1994.

Klein, Hilary. "The Zapatista Movement: Blending Indigenous Tradition and Revolution Praxis." In Maxwell and Craib, *No Gods, No Masters*, 22–43.

Klein, Naomi. "Rebels in Search of Rules." *New York Times*, December 2, 1999. https://www.nytimes.com/1999/12/02/opinion/rebels-in-search-of-rules.html.

———. Interview with Commanding Heights. PBS, April 21, 2001. http://www.pbs.org/wgbh/commandingheights/shared/minitext/int_naomiklein.html.

Klein, Naomi, and Leanne Simpson. "Dancing the World into Being: A Conversation with Idle No More's Leanne Simpson." *Yes! Magazine*, March 5, 2013. http://www.yesmagazine.org/peace-justice/dancing-the-world-into-being-a-conversation-with-idle-no-more-leanne-simpson.

Knight, Brenda ed. *Women of the Beat Generation: The Writers, Artists, and Muses at the Heart of a Revolution*. Berkeley: Conari Press, 1996.

Koehnline, James, ed. *Gone to Croatan: Origins of North American Dropout Culture*. New York: Autonomedia, 1994.

Kornegger, Peggy. "Anarchism: The Feminist Connection." In Dark Collective, *Quiet Rumors*, 25–35.

Krupat, Arnold. "Native American Literary Criticism in Global Context." In Lyons, *The World, the Text, the Indian*, 49–102.

———. *Red Matters: Native American Studies*. Philadelphia: University of Pennsylvania Press, 2002.

Krupat, Arnold, and Brian Swann. Introduction to *Here First: Autobiographical Essays by Native American Writers*, edited by Arnold Krupat and Brian Swann, xi–xv. New York: Modern Library, 2000.

Kurzen, Crystal. "Toward a Native American Women's Autobiographical Tradition: Genre as Political Practice." In *The Oxford Handbook of Indigenous American Literatures*, edited by James Cox and Daniel Heath Justice, 202–3. New York: Oxford University Press, 2014.

Ladner, Kiera L., and Leanne Simpson, eds. *This Is an Honour Song: Twenty Years Since the Blockades*. Winnipeg: Arbiter Ring Publishing, 2010.

Lamont, Paul, dir. *Lake of Betrayal: The Story of the Kinzua Dam*, 2017.

Lasky, Jacqueline. "Indigenism, Anarchism, Feminism: An Emerging Framework for Exploring Post-Imperial Futures." *Affinities: A Journal of Radical Theory, Culture, Action* (August 2011): 3–36.

Lawrence, Jane. "The Indian Health Service and the Sterilization of Native American Women." *American Indian Quarterly* 24, no. 3 (Summer 2000): 400–419.

Leighton, Marian. "Anarcho-Feminism and Louise Michel." *Our Generation* (Summer 1990): 22–29.

———. "Voltairine de Cleyre: An Introduction." In Dark Collective, *Quiet Rumours*, 47–50.

Levine, Caroline. *Forms: Whole, Rhythm, Hierarchy, Network*. Princeton, NJ: Princeton University Press, 2015.

Lewis, Adam. "Imagining Autonomy on Stolen Land: Settler Colonialism, Anarchism, and the Politics of Decolonization?" *Settler Colonial Studies* 7 (2017): 474–95.

Lincoln, Kenneth. *Native American Renaissance*. Berkeley: University of California Press, 1985.

Lorde, Audre. *Sister/Outsider: Essays and Speeches*. Berkeley: Crossing Press, 1984.

Lynd, Staughton, and Andrej Grubačić. *Wobblies and Zapatistas: Conversations on Anarchism, Marxism, and Radical History*. Oakland, CA: PM Press, 2008.

Lyons, Scott. *X-Marks: Native Signatures of Assent*. Minneapolis: University of Minnesota Press, 2010.

———, ed. *The World, the Text, the Indian: Global Dimensions of Native American Literature*. Albany: State University of New York Press, 2017.

MacLean, Cameron. "Raymond Cormier's Defence Tried to Have Case Thrown Out Due to Lack of Evidence." *CBC News*, February 21, 2018. http://www.cbc.ca/news/canada/manitoba/raymond-cormier-trial-judge-instructs-jury-tina-fontaine-1.4544214.

Madsen, Deborah L, ed. *Native Authenticity: Transnational Perspectives on Native American Literary Studies*. Albany: State University of New York Press, 2010.

Maracle, Lee. *Bobbi Lee: Indian Rebel*. Toronto: Women's Press, 1991.

Marks, Alison. *Heaven and Earth*. 2017. Wall text for exhibition *Alison Marks: One Gray Hair, organized and presented at the Frye Art Museum*, Seattle, WA, November 11, 2017, to February 4, 2018.

———. *Space Bear*. 2017. Wall text to exhibition *Alison Marks: One Gray Hair, organized and presented at the Frye Art Museum* (Seattle, WA), November 11, 2017 to February 4, 2018.

Marshall, Peter. *Demanding the Impossible: A History of Anarchism*. Oakland, CA: PM Press, 2010.

Martínez, Elizabeth "Betita." "Where Was the Color in Seattle? Looking for Reasons Why the Great Battle Was So White." *Colorlines*, March 10, 2000. https://www.colorlines.com/articles/where-was-color-seattlelooking-reasons-why-great-battle-was-so-white.

Matsunaga, Kyoko. "Leslie Marmon Silko and Nuclear Dissent in the American Southwest." *Japanese Journal of American Studies* 25 (2014): 67–87.

Maxwell, Barry. "Afterword, Beginning with 'A.'" In Maxwell and Craib, *No Gods, No Masters*, 359–61.

Maxwell, Barry, and Raymond Craib, eds. *No Gods, No Masters, No Peripheries: Global Anarchisms*. Oakland, CA: PM Press, 2015.

May, Katie. "The Cormier Wiretaps: Crown and Defence Interpretations of Wiretap Audio." *Winnipeg Free Press*, February 21, 2018. https://www.winnipegfreepress.com/local/the-cormier-wiretaps----and-the-crown-and-defence-interpretations-474736623.html.

May, Todd. *The Political Philosophy of Poststructuralist Anarchism*. University Park: Penn State University Press, 2005.

McBay, Aric. "DGR and Transphobia." *Aric McBay* (blog), May 14, 2013. http://www.aricmcbay.org/2013/05/14/dgr-and-transphobia/.

McCarthy, Theresa. *In Divided Unity: Haudenosaunee Reclamation at Grand River*. Tucson: University of Arizona Press, 2016.

McGlennan, Molly. *Creative Alliances: The Transnational Designs of Native Women's Poetry*. Norman: University of Oklahoma Press, 2014.

McMahon, Conor. "The *Espada Ancha* in New Mexico: Conservation of a New World Sword." *El Palacio: New Mexico's Magazine of Art, History, and Culture of the Southwest* 111, no. 4 (Winter 2005): 22–25.

McMurtry, Larry. Introduction to Leslie Marmon Silko, *Ceremony*, xxi–xxiii. New York: Penguin Books, 2006.

McNally, David. *Another World Is Possible: Globalization and Anti-Capitalism*. Manitoba: Arbeiter Ring, 2006.

Messer-Kruse, Timothy. *The Haymarket Conspiracy: Transatlantic Anarchist Networks*. Champaign: University of Illinois Press, 2012.https://www.chronicle.com/article/The-Undue-Weight-of-Truth-on/130704.

———. "The 'Undue Weight' of Truth on Wikipedia." *Chronicle of Higher Education*, February 12, 2012.

Mihesuah, Devon Abbott. *Indigenous American Women: Decolonization, Empowerment, and Activism*. Lincoln: University of Nebraska Press, 2003.

Miller, Brenda, and Suzanne Paola. *Tell It Slant: Creating, Refining, and Publishing Creative Nonfiction*. New York: McGraw Hill, 2012.

Million, Dian. *Therapeutic Nations: Healing in an Age of Indigenous Human Rights*. Tucson: University of Arizona Press, 2013.

Milstein, Cindy. *Anarchism and Its Aspirations*. Oakland, CA: AK Press, 2010.

Miranda, Deborah. "'They Were Tough, Those Old Women Before Us': The Power of Gossip in Isabel Meadows's Narratives." *Biography* 39, no. 3 (Summer 2016): 373–401.

Miranda, Deborah. *Bad Indians: A Tribal Memoir*. Berkeley, CA: Heydey Books, 2013.

———. "Dildos, Hummingbirds, and Driving Her Crazy: Searching for American Indian Women's Love Poetry and Erotics." *Frontiers: A Journal of Women's Studies* 23, no 2 (2002): 135–49.

Montgomery, Nick, and carla bergman. *Joyful Militancy: Building Thriving Resistance in Toxic Times*. Oakland, CA: AK Press, 2017.

Morgensen, Scott. "Cutting to the Roots of Colonial Masculinity." In *Indigenous Men and Masculinities*, edited by Kim Anderson and Robert Alexander Innes, 38–61. Manitoba: University of Manitoba Press, 2015.

———. *Spaces between Us: Queer Settler Colonialism and Indigenous Decolonization*. Minneapolis: University of Minnesota Press, 2011.

Morrill, Angela Teresa. "Toward a Native Feminist Reading Methodology." PhD diss., University of California, San Diego, 2016.

Mujeres Creando. "An Interview with Mujeres Creando." In Dark Star Collective, *Quiet Rumours*, 125–28.

Na'puti, Tiara, and Michael Lujan Bevacqua. "Militarization and Resistance from Guåhan: Protecting and Defending Pågat." *American Quarterly* 67, no. 3 (September 2015).

Native Youth Sexual Health Network. "Environmental Health and Reproductive Justice." http://www.nativeyouthsexualhealth.com/environmentalviolenceandreproductivejustice.html.

Nelson, Joshua B. *Progressive Traditions: Identity in Cherokee Literature and Culture*. Norman: University of Oklahoma Press, 2014.

Newman, Saul. *From Bakunin to Lacan: Anti-Authoritarianism and the Dislocation of Power*. Plymouth, UK: Lexington Books, 2007.

Nollman, Jim. "Whaling Report to the Makah Tribal Council." *Interspecies Newsletter*, 1999. https://www.whaleweb.org/intersp/pages/makah.html.

Notes from Everywhere Collective. *We Are Everywhere: The Irresistible Rise of Global Anti-Capitalism*. London: Verso, 2003.

O'Brien, Jean M. *Firsting and Lasting: Writing Indians Out of Existence in New England*. Minneapolis: University of Minnesota Press, 2010.

Obomsawin, Alanis, dir. *Kanehsatake: 270 Years of Resistance*. Montreal: National Film Board of Canada, 1993.

Occupy Boston. "Occupy Boston Declares Solidarity with Indigenous Peoples." OccupyBoston.org, October 10, 2011. http://www.occupyboston.org/2011/10/10/occupy-boston-declares-solidarity-with-indigenous-peoples/.

Occupy Portland. "Working Draft of Occupy Portland Statement of Indigenous Solidarity." *Portland Occupier*, November 25, 2011. http://www.portlandoccupier.org/2011/11/25/working-draft-of-occupy-portland-statement-of-indigenous-solidarity/.

Olsen, Joel. *The Abolition of White Democracy*. Minneapolis: University of Minnesota Press, 2004.

Olson, Alix. "The Promise(s) of Resilience: Governance and Resistance in Complex Times." PhD diss., University of Massachusetts, Amherst, 2018.

Out of the Woods Collective. "Goodbye to the Future." Libcom.org, February 24, 2014. https://libcom.org/blog/goodbye-future-24022014.

Owens, Louis. *Mixedblood Messages: Literature, Film, Family, Place*. Norman: University of Oklahoma Press, 2001.

Park, Mi Sun. ""Reimagining the Nation: Gender and Nationalism in Contemporary U.S. Women's Literature." PhD diss., Texas A&M University, 2007.

Pasternack, Shiri. *Grounded Authority: The Algonquins of Barriere Lake against the State*. Minneapolis: University of Minnesota Press, 2017.

Patten, Melanie. "Elsipogtog First Nation Sees Violence as RCMP Moves To End Protest." *Huffington Post*, October 17, 2013. https://www.huffingtonpost.ca/2013/10/17/elsipogtog-photos-rcmp-protest-violence_n_4114506.html.

Peace, Stevie. "The Power within Us to Create the World Anew: A Discussion with Grace Lee Boggs." In *Uses of a Whirlwind: Movement, Movements, and Contemporary Radical Currents in the United States*, ed ited by Team Colors Collective, 347–61. Oakland, CA: AK Press, 2010.

Perlman, Fredy. *The Continuing Appeal of Nationalism*. Detroit: Black and Red, 1985.

Pollard, Dave. "The Occupy Movement: Don't Tell Us What to Do." *how to save the world* (blog), November 12, 2011. http://howtosavetheworld.ca/2011/11/12/the-occupy-movement-dont-tell-us-what-to-do/.

Porter, Tom (Sakokweniónkwas). *And Grandma Said . . . Iroquois Teachings: As Passed Down Through the Oral Tradition*. New York: Xlibris Press, 2008.

Pratt, Mary Louise. "Arts of the Contact Zone." *Profession* (1991): 33–40.

Price, Wayne. "Anarchist Organisation not Leninist Vanguardism." *Anarchist Library*, May 13, 2009. https://theanarchistlibrary.org/library/wayne-price-anarchist-organisation-not-leninist-vanguardism.

Pulitano, Elvira. *Toward a Native American Critical Theory*. Lincoln: University of Nebraska Press, 2003.

Ramirez, Reyna. *Native Hubs: Culture, Community, and Belonging in Silicon Valley and Beyond*. Durham, NC: Duke University Press, 2012.

Ramnath, Maia. *Decolonizing Anarchism: An Anti-Authoritarian History of India's Liberation Struggle*. Oakland, CA: AK Press, 2011.

———. "No Gods, No Masters, No Brahmins: An Anarchist Inquiry on Caste, Race, and Indigeneity in India." In Maxwell and Craib, *No Gods, No Masters*, 44–79.

Raskin, Johan. *American Scream: Allen Ginsberg's* Howl *and the Making of the Beat Generation*. Berkeley: University of California Press, 2004.

Read, Herbert. *Poetry and Anarchism*. Freeport, NY: Books for Libraries Press, 1938.

Reid, Joshua L. *The Sea Is My Country: The Maritime World of the Makahs*. New Haven, CT: Yale University Press, 2015.

Reid Ross, Alexander. *Against the Fascist Creep*. Oakland, CA: AK Press, 2017.

Reid Ross, Alexander, and Joshua Stephens. "About Schmidt: How a White Nationalist Seduced Anarchists Around the World." *Medium* (blog), October 14, 2015. https://medium.com/@rossstephens/about-schmidt-how-a-white-nationalist-seduced-anarchists-around-the-world-chapter-1-1a6fa255b528.

Rice, David A. "Witchery, Indigenous Resistance, and Urban Space is Leslie Marmon Silko's Ceremony." *Studies in American Indian Literatures* 17, no. 4 (Winter 2005): 114–43.

Rifkin, Mark. *Beyond Settler Time: Temporal Sovereignty and Indigenous Self-Determination*. Durham, NC: Duke University Press, 2017.

———. *Settler Common Sense: Queerness and Everyday Colonialism in the American Renaissance*. Minneapolis: University of Minnesota Press, 2014.

Robbins, Tom. "Here in Geoduck Junction." *Seattle Weekly*, October 9, 2006. http://archive.seattleweekly.com/2000-05-03/news/here-in-geoduck-junction/.

Roger Gilbert, Roger. "Some Parts of a World: Example as Trope in American Poetry." *Western Humanities Review* 48, no. 2 (Summer 1994): 144.

Rogers, Janet. *Totem Poles and Railroad*. Winnipeg: Arbeiter Ring, 2016.

———. "Janet Rogers on 'Totem Poles and Railroads.'" Interview by *CBC News*. *CBC News*, September 11, 2017. http://www.cbc.ca/news/janet-rogers-on-totem-poles-and-railroads-1.4277258.

Rogue, J. "De-essentializing Anarchist Feminism: Lessons from the Transfeminist Movement." In Daring et al., *Queering Anarchism*, 25–32.

Rogue, Jen, and Abbey Volcano. "Insurrection at the Intersection." In Dark Star Collective, *Quiet Rumours*, 43–46.

Rosier, Paul C. *Native American Issues*. Westport, CT: Greenwood Publishing, 2003.

Ross, Luana. "From the 'F' Word to Indigenous/Feminisms." *Wicazo Sa Review* 24, no. 2 (Fall 2009): 39–52.

Ross, John. *¡Zapatistas!: Making Another World Possible, Chronicles of Resistance 2000–2006*. New York: Nation Books, 2006.

Routledge, Paul. "'Our Resistance Will Be as Transnational as Capital': Convergence Space and Strategy in Globalising Resistance." *GeoJournal* 52, no. 1 (2000): 25–33.

Rubin, Gayle. "Thinking Sex: Notes for a Radical Theory of the Politics of Sexuality." In *Pleasure and Danger: Exploring Female Sexuality*, edited by Carole S. Vance, 267–93. London: Pandora, 1992.

———. "The Traffic in Women: Notes on the 'Political Economy' of Sex." In *Toward an Anthropology of Women*, edited by Rayna R. Reiter, 157–210. New York: Monthly Review Press, 1975.

Sakai, J. *Settlers: The Mythology of the White Proletarian from Mayflower to Modern*. Montreal: Kersplebedeb, 2014.

sallydarity. "Gender Sabotage." In Daring et al., *Queering Anarchism*, 47.

Samduzi, Zoé, and William C. Anderson. *As Black As Resistance: Finding the Conditions for Liberation*. Oakland, CA: AK Press, 2018.

Savageau, Cheryl. "The People and the Land." *Women's Review of Books* 27, no. 2 (March 2010): 26–27.

Schneider, Nathan. *Thank You Anarchy: Notes from the Occupy Apocalypse*. Berkeley: University of California Press, 2013.

Scofield, Be. "How Derrick Jensen's Deep Green Resistance Supports Transphobia." *Decolonizing Yoga*, May 14, 2013. http://www.decolonizingyoga.com/how-derrick-jensens-deep-green-resistance-supports-transphobia/.

Serrano, Julia. *Excluded: Making Feminist and Queer Movements More Exclusive*. New York: Seal Press, 2013.

Shannon, Deric, and Jen Rogue. "Refusing to Wait: Anarchism and Intersectionality." *Anarchist Library*, 2009. http://www.anarkismo.net/article/14923.

Shantz, Jeffrey. *Against All Authority: Anarchism and the Literary Imagination*. Charlottesville: Imprint Academic, 2011.

———. "Solidarity and the 6 Nation Struggle for Land." *Northeastern Anarchist* 12 (January 2007).

———. *Spectres of Anarchy: Literature and the Anarchist Imagination*. New York: Algora Publishing, 2015.

Shotwell, Alexis. *Against Purity: Living Ethically in Compromised Times*. Minneapolis: University of Minnesota Press, 2016.

Silko, Leslie Marmon. *Ceremony*. New York: Penguin, 2006.

———. *Storyteller*. Reprint ed. New York: Penguin Books, 2012.

———. *The Turquoise Ledge: A Memoir*. New York: Penguin Books, 2010.

———. *Yellow Woman and a Beauty of the Spirit*. New York: Simon and Schuster, 1997.

———. Leslie Marmon Silko Papers. Yale Collection of American Literature, Beinecke Rare Book and Manuscript Library, Yale University.

———. Per Seyersted Papers Concerning Leslie Marmon Silko. American Literature Collection, Beinecke Rare Book and Manuscript Library, Yale University.

Simpson, Audra. "From White into Red: Captivity Narratives as Alchemies of Race and Citizenship." *American Quarterly* 60, no. 2 (June 2008): 251–57.

———. *Mohawk Interruptus: Political Life Across the Borders of Settler States*. Durham, NC: Duke University Press, 2014.

———. "The State Is a Man: Theresa Spence, Loretta Saunders and the Gender of Settler Sovereignty." *Theory and Event* 19, no. 4 (2016). https://www.muse.jhu.edu/article/633280.

Simpson, Leanne Betasamosake. *As We Have Always Done*. Minneapolis: University of Minnesota Press, 2017.

———. "Elsipogtog Everywhere." 20, 2013. https://www.leannesimpson.ca/writings/2013/10/20/elsipogtog-everywhere.

———. "I Am Not a Nation-State." November 6, 2013. https://www.leannesimpson.ca/writings/i-am-not-a-nation-state.

———. *Islands of Decolonial Love: Stories and Songs*. Winnipeg: Arbeiter Ring, 2013.

Smith, Andrea, and J. Kēhaulani Kauanui. "Native Feminisms Engage American Studies." *American Quarterly* 60, no. 2 (June 2008): 241–49.

Smith, Ernest. "Beat Poets." In *Men and Masculinities: A Social, Cultural, and Historical Encyclopedia*, edited by Michael Kimmel and Amy Aronson, 70–71. Santa Barbara: ABC-CLIO, 2003.

Solnit, Rebecca. "The Occupation of Hope: Letter to a Dead Man." In *This Changes Everything: Occupy Wall Street and the 99% Movement*, edited by Sarah Van Gelder and the staff of *YES!* Magazine, 77–82. Oakland, CA: Berret-Koehler Publishers, 2011.

Solnit, David, and Rebecca Solnit, eds. *The Battle of the Story of the Battle of Seattle*. Oakland, CA: AK Press, 2009.

Somerville, Alice Te Punga, Daniel Heath Justice, and Noelani Arista, eds. "Indigenous Conversations about Biography." Special issue, *Biography* 39, no. 3 (Summer 2016).

Southern Poverty Law Center. "Sexual Assault Against Immigrant Women is a Human Rights Tragedy." April 5, 2011. https://www.splcenter.org/news/2011/04/05/sexual-assault-against-immigrant-women-hidden-human-rights-tragedy.

Specia, Megan. "First, a Symbol of Occupy Wall Street. Then He Waded Into Syria." *New York Times*, July 12, 2017.

Spence, Lester and Mike McGuire. "Occupy and the 99%." In *We Are Many: Reflections on Movement Strategy from Occupation to Liberation*, edited by Kate Khatib and Margaret Killjoy, 53–65. Oakland, CA: AK Press, 2012.

Spinosa, Dani. "Postanarchist Literary Theory and the Experiment: Some Preliminary Notes." *Journal for the Study of Radicalism* 11, no. 1 (Spring 2017): 83–112.

Streeby, Shelley. *Radical Sensations: World Movements, Violence, and Visual Culture*. Durham, NC: Duke University Press, 2013.

Sunseri, Lina. *Being Again of One Mind: Oneida Women and the Struggle for Decolonization*. Vancouver: UBC Press, 2010.

Suzak, Cheryl. "Land Claims, Identity Claims: Mapping Indigenous Feminism in Literary Criticism and in Winona LaDuke's Last Standing Woman." In *Reasoning Together*, edited by Craig S. Womack, Daniel Heath Justice, and Christopher B. Teuton, 169–92. Norman: University of Oklahoma Press.

Tallbear, Kim. *Native American DNA: Tribal Belonging and the False Promise of Genetic Science*. Minneapolis: University of Minnesota Press, 2013.

Tanenbaum, Julia. "To Destroy Domination in All Its Forms: Anarcha-Feminist Theory, Organization and Action 1970–1978." *Perspectives on Anarchist Theory* 29 (May 2016): 13–34.

Te Punga Somerville, Alice. *Once Were Pacific: Māori Connections to Oceania*. Minneapolis: University of Minnesota Press, 2012.

Te Punga Somerville, Alice, and Daniel Heath Justice. "Introduction: Indigenous Conversations about Biography." *Biography* 39, no. 3 (Summer 2016): 239–47.

Teuton, Sean Kicummah. *Red Land, Red Power: Grounding Knowledge in the American Indian Novel*. Durham, NC: Duke University Press, 2008.

Thomas, Ashleigh Rae. "Who is a Settler, According to Indigenous and Black Scholars: Descendants of Slaves Don't Fit into Our Common Definition of Settlers." *VICE Canada*, February 15, 2019. https://www.vice.com/en_us/article/gyajj4/who-is-a-settler-according-to-indigenous-and-black-scholars.

Thomas, Janet. *The Battle in Seattle: The Story Behind and Beyond the WTO Demonstrations*. Golden, CO: Fulcrum Publishing, 2000.

Thrush, Coll. *Indigenous London: Native Travelers at the Heart of Empire*. New Haven, CT: Yale University Press, 2016.

———. *Native Seattle: Histories from the Crossing-Over Place*. Seattle: University of Washington Press, 2008.

Tillett, Rebecca, ed. *Howling for Justice: New Perspectives on Leslie Marmon Silko's* Almanac of the Dead. Tucson: University of Arizona Press, 2014.

Tohe, Laura. "Introduction." In *Sister Nations: Native American Women Writers on Community*, edited by Heid E. Erdrich and Laura Tohe, xiii–xix. Saint Paul: Minnesota Historical Society Press, 2002.

Troian, Martha. "Mi'kmaq Anti-Fracking Protest Brings Women to the Front Lines to Fight for Water." *Indian Country Today*, November 10, 2013. https://indiancountrymedianetwork.com/news/first-nations/mikmaq-anti-fracking-protest-brings-women-to-the-front-lines-to-fight-for-water/.

Tuck, Eve, and C. Ree. "A Glossary of Haunting." In *Handbook of Authoethnography*, edited by Stacey Holman Jones, Tony E. Adams, and Carolyn Ellis, 639–58. Walnut Creek, CA: Left Coast Press, 2013.

Tuck, Eve, and K. Wayne Yang. "Decolonization Is Not a Metaphor." *Decolonization: Indigeneity, Education, and Society* 1, no. 1 (2012): 1–40.

Tuck, Eve, and Rubén A. Gaztambide-Fernández. "Curriculum, Replacement, and Settler Futurity." *Journal of Curriculum Theorizing* 29, no. 1 (2013): 72–89.

Turcato, David. "Nations without Borders: Anarchists and National Identity." In Bantman and Altena, *Reassessing the Transnational Turn*, 25–41. Oakland, CA: PM Press, 2017: 24–42.

United Nations. "'The Right to Enjoy All Human Rights': The UN Declaration on the Rights of Indigenous Peoples and the Potential for Decolonial Cosmopolitanism." In Lyons, *The World, the Text, the Indian*, 257–82.

Van Der Walt, Lucien, and Michael Schmidt. *Black Flame: The Revolutionary Class Politics of Anarchism and Syndicalism*. Oakland, CA: AK Press, 2009.

Van Engen, Dagmar. "Howling Masculinity: Queer Social Change in Allen Ginsburg's Poetry." Gender, Sexuality, and Urban Spaces: Conference 2011, Working Papers Collection 2012, MIT, Cambridge, MA, March 2011. http://web.mit.edu/Gcws/pdf/2012ConfPublication/Papers/Drafts/VanEngen.pdf.

Vidal, John. "Real Battle for Seattle." *Guardian*, December 4, 1999. https://www.theguardian.com/world/1999/dec/05/wto.globalisation.

Vizenor, Gerald. *Manifest Manners: Narratives on Postindian Survivance*. Lincoln: University of Nebraska Press, 1999.

Vogel, Lise. *Marxism and the Oppression of Women: Toward a Unitary Theory*. New Brunswick: Rutgers University Press, 1987.

Walia, Harsha. *Undoing Border Imperialism*. Oakland, CA: AK Press, 2013.

Walker, Richard. "Failed Treaty of Point Elliott [*sic*] Promises Spotlighted in Play." *Indian Country Today*, September 23, 2013. https://indiancountrymedianetwork.com/history/events/failed-treaty-of-point-elliott-promises-spotlighted-in-play/.

Warburton, Theresa. "Coming to Terms: Rethinking Popular Approaches to Anarchism and Feminism." *Perspectives on Anarchist Theory* 29 (May 2016): 66–80.

———. "A Similar Place: Resistance and Existence in 21st Century Black and Native Women's Memoir." *Critical Studies, Cultural Methodologie* 17, no. 1 (2017) : 41–49.

Warrior, Robert. "Native American Scholarship and the Transnational Turn." *Cultural Studies Review* 15, no. 2 (2009): 119–30.

———. *The People and the Word: Reading Native Nonfiction*. Minneapolis: University of Minnesota Press, 2005.

Washuta, Elissa. "Apocalypse Logic." *The Offing*, November 21, 2016. https://theoffingmag.com/insight/apocalypse-logic/.

———. *My Body is a Book of Rules*. Pasadena: Red Hen Press, 2014.

Washuta, Elissa, and Theresa Warburton. Introduction to *Shapes of Native Nonfiction: Collected Essays by Contemporary Authors*, edited by Elissa Washuta and Theresa Warburton, 3–20. Seattle: University of Washington Press, 2019.

Weaver, Jace, Craig S. Womack, and Robert Warrior. *American Indian Literary Nationalism*. Albuquerque: University of New Mexico Press, 2005.

White, Kyle Powys. "White Allies, Let's Be Honest About Decolonization." *YES! Magazine*, April 3, 2018. http://www.yesmagazine.org/issues/decolonize/white-allies-lets-be-honest-about-decolonization-20180403.

White, Roger. "Postcolonial Anarchism: Essays on Race, Repression, and Culture in Communities of Color, 1999–2004." *Anarchist Library*, 2005. https://theanarchistlibrary.org/library/roger-white-post-colonial-anarchism.pdf.

Williams, Kimberly. "Black Lives Matter Gave Me the Confidence to Be Visible in Appalachia," *Slate*, June 27, 2017. https://slate.com/human-interest/2017/06/how-black-lives-matter-gave-a-black-queer-woman-the-confidence-to-be-visible-in-appalachia.html.

Williams, William Carlos. "To Elsie." In *The Collected Poems of Williams Carlos Williams, Volume 1 1909–1939*, edited by A. Walton Litz and Christopher MacGowan, 317. Cambridge, NY: New Directions, 1991.

Wolfe, Patrick. "Settler Colonialism and the Elimination of the Native." *Journal of Genocide Research* 8, no. 4 (Dec 2006): 387–409.

Womack, Craig S. *Red on Red: American Indian Literary Separatism*. Minneapolis: University of Minnesota Press, 1999.

———. "A Single Decade: Book-Length Native Literary Criticism between 1986 and 1997." In *Reasoning Together*, edited by the Native Critics Collective, 3–104. Norman: University of Oklahoma Press, 2008.

Worl, Rico Lanaat', Shaadoo'tlaa, and Donald Heendei Gregoy. *A Basic Guide to Northwest Coast Formline Art*. Juneau: Sealaska Heritage Institute, 2014.

Wright, Dustin. "From Tokyo to Wounded Knee: Two Afterlives of the Sunagawa Struggle." *The Sixties: A Journal of History, Politics, and Culture* 10, no. 2 (October 19, 2017): 133–49.

Zapatista Army of National Liberation. "Sixth Declaration of the Lacandona Jungle." July 2005. https://schoolsforchiapas.org/library/sixth-declaration-lacandona-jungle/.

Zaretsky, Eli. *Capitalism, the Family, and Personal Life*. New York: HarperCollins, 1986.

INDEX